DEC 1 4 2010

P9-ECL-220

Get More and Do More at Dummies.com®

Start with **FREE** Cheat Sheets

Cheat Sheets include

- Checklists
- Charts
- Common Instructions
- And Other Good Stuff!

To access the Cheat Sheet created specifically for this book, go to
www.dummies.com/cheatsheet/newyorkcity

Get Smart at Dummies.com

Dummies.com makes your life easier with 1,000s of answers on everything from removing wallpaper to using the latest version of Windows.

Check out our

- Videos
- Illustrated Articles
- Step-by-Step Instructions

Plus, each month you can win valuable prizes by entering our Dummies.com sweepstakes. *

Want a weekly dose of Dummies?
Sign up for Newsletters on

- Digital Photography
- Microsoft Windows & Office
- Personal Finance & Investing
- Health & Wellness
- Computing, iPods & Cell Phones
- eBay
- Internet
- Food, Home & Garden

Find out "HOW" at Dummies.com

Sweepstakes not currently available in all countries; visit Dummies.com for official rules.

DEC 14 2010

New York City

FOR

DUMMIES®

6TH EDITION

by Myka Carroll

WILEY

Wiley Publishing, Inc.

New York City For Dummies, 6th Edition

Published by
Wiley Publishing, Inc.
111 River St.
Hoboken, NJ 07030-5774
www.wiley.com

Copyright © 2011 by Wiley Publishing, Inc., Indianapolis, Indiana

Published simultaneously in Canada

No part of this publication may be reproduced, stored in a retrieval system, or transmitted in any form or by any means, electronic, mechanical, photocopying, recording, scanning, or otherwise, except as permitted under Sections 107 or 108 of the 1976 United States Copyright Act, without either the prior written permission of the Publisher, or authorization through payment of the appropriate per-copy fee to the Copyright Clearance Center, 222 Rosewood Drive, Danvers, MA 01923, 978-750-8400, fax 978-646-8600. Requests to the Publisher for permission should be addressed to the Permissions Department, Wiley Publishing, Inc., 111 River St., Hoboken NJ 07030, 201-748-6011, fax 201-748-6008, or online at http://www.wiley.com/go/permissions.

Trademarks: Wiley, the Wiley Publishing logo, For Dummies, the Dummies Man logo, A Reference for the Rest of Us!, The Dummies Way, Dummies Daily, The Fun and Easy Way, Dummies.com and related trade dress are trademarks or registered trademarks of John Wiley & Sons, Inc., and/or its affiliates in the United States and other countries, and may not be used without written permission. Frommer's is a trademark or registered trademark of Arthur Frommer. Used under license. All other trademarks are the property of their respective owners. Wiley Publishing, Inc., is not associated with any product or vendor mentioned in this book.

LIMIT OF LIABILITY/DISCLAIMER OF WARRANTY: THE PUBLISHER AND THE AUTHOR MAKE NO REPRESENTATIONS OR WARRANTIES WITH RESPECT TO THE ACCURACY OR COMPLETENESS OF THE CONTENTS OF THIS WORK AND SPECIFICALLY DISCLAIM ALL WARRANTIES, INCLUDING WITHOUT LIMITATION WARRANTIES OF FITNESS FOR A PARTICULAR PURPOSE. NO WARRANTY MAY BE CREATED OR EXTENDED BY SALES OR PROMOTIONAL MATERIALS. THE ADVICE AND STRATEGIES CONTAINED HEREIN MAY NOT BE SUITABLE FOR EVERY SITUATION. THIS WORK IS SOLD WITH THE UNDERSTANDING THAT THE PUBLISHER IS NOT ENGAGED IN RENDERING LEGAL, ACCOUNTING, OR OTHER PROFESSIONAL SERVICES. IF PROFESSIONAL ASSISTANCE IS REQUIRED, THE SERVICES OF A COMPETENT PROFESSIONAL PERSON SHOULD BE SOUGHT. NEITHER THE PUBLISHER NOR THE AUTHOR SHALL BE LIABLE FOR DAMAGES ARISING HEREFROM. THE FACT THAT AN ORGANIZATION OR WEBSITE IS REFERRED TO IN THIS WORK AS A CITATION AND/OR A POTENTIAL SOURCE OF FURTHER INFORMATION DOES NOT MEAN THAT THE AUTHOR OR THE PUBLISHER ENDORSES THE INFORMATION THE ORGANIZATION OR WEB SITE MAY PROVIDE OR RECOMMENDATIONS IT MAY MAKE. FURTHER, READERS SHOULD BE AWARE THAT INTERNET WEB SITES LISTED IN THIS WORK MAY HAVE CHANGED OR DISAPPEARED BETWEEN WHEN THIS WORK WAS WRITTEN AND WHEN IT IS READ.

PLEASE BE ADVISED THAT TRAVEL INFORMATION IS SUBJECT TO CHANGE AT ANY TIME AND THIS IS ESPECIALLY TRUE OF PRICES. WE THEREFORE SUGGEST THAT READERS WRITE OR CALL AHEAD FOR CONFIRMATION WHEN MAKING TRAVEL PLANS. THE AUTHOR AND THE PUBLISHER CANNOT BE HELD RESPONSIBLE FOR THE EXPERIENCES OF READERS WHILE TRAVELING.

For general information on our other products and services, please contact our Customer Care Department within the U.S. at 877-762-2974, outside the U.S. at 317-572-3993, or fax 317-572-4002.

For technical support, please visit www.wiley.com/techsupport.

Wiley also publishes its books in a variety of electronic formats. Some content that appears in print may not be available in electronic books.

ISBN: 978-0-470-61825-7

Manufactured in the United States of America

10 9 8 7 6 5 4 3 2 1

WILEY

About the Author

New York–based **Myka Carroll** edited 70-plus travel guides for Frommer's before jumping to the other side of the desk as a freelance writer. Her favorite New York movie is *Smoke,* her favorite New York band is Sonic Youth, and her favorite New York hero is Shirley Chisholm. She would like to thank her family and dearest friends for their unwavering support, and to give props to the gang at Academy Restaurant, the best diner in the city. She dedicates a knife, a fork, a bottle, and a cork to Benjamin Más, the best sun ever.

Publisher's Acknowledgments

We're proud of this book; please send us your comments through our Dummies online registration form located at www.dummies.com/register/.

Some of the people who helped bring this book to market include the following:

Editorial

Editors: Jonathan Scott, Production Editor; Matthew Brown, Development Editor

Copy Editor: Elizabeth Kuball

Cartographer: Anton Crane

Editorial Assistant: Andrea Kahn

Senior Photo Editor: Richard Fox

Cover Photos: ©Mark & Audrey Gibson / Stock Connection Blue / Alamy Images
Coney Island ©Amanda Ahn / dbimages / Alamy Images

Cartoons: Rich Tennant (www.the5thwave.com)

Composition Services

Project Coordinators: Lynsey Stanford and Katie Crocker

Layout and Graphics: Joyce Haughey, Julie Trippetti

Proofreader: Cara L. Buitron

Indexer: Potomac Indexing, LLC

Publishing and Editorial for Consumer Dummies

Diane Graves Steele, Vice President and Publisher, Consumer Dummies

Kristin Ferguson-Wagstaff, Product Development Director, Consumer Dummies

Kelly Regan, Editorial Director, Travel

Publishing for Technology Dummies

Andy Cummings, Vice President and Publisher, Dummies Technology/General User

Composition Services

Debbie Stailey, Director of Composition Services

Contents at a Glance

Introduction *1*

Part I: Introducing New York City *7*

Chapter 1: Discovering the Best of New York City 9
Chapter 2: Digging Deeper into New York City 22
Chapter 3: Deciding When to Go 29

Part II: Planning Your Trip to New York City *35*

Chapter 4: Managing Your Money 37
Chapter 5: Getting to New York City 46
Chapter 6: Catering to Special Travel Needs or Interests 53
Chapter 7: Taking Care of the Remaining Details 61

Part III: Settling Into New York City *67*

Chapter 8: Arriving and Getting Oriented 69
Chapter 9: Checking In at New York City's Best Hotels 91
Chapter 10: Dining and Snacking in New York City 122

Part IV: Exploring New York City *169*

Chapter 11: New York City's Top Sights 171
Chapter 12: Shopping in New York City 213
Chapter 13: Following an Itinerary: Five Great Options 238

Part V: Living It Up After Dark:
New York City Nightlife *249*

Chapter 14: Applauding the Cultural Scene 251
Chapter 15: Hitting the Clubs and Bars 264

Part VI: The Part of Tens *281*

Chapter 16: The Top Ten Cheap New York City
Experiences 283
Chapter 17: The Top Ten Essential New York City
Eating Experiences 288
Chapter 18: Ten New York City Experiences to Avoid 292
Appendix: Quick Concierge 297

Index *304*

Maps at a Glance

Downtown Orientation 10
Midtown Orientation..12
Uptown Orientation...14
New York Metropolitan Area 70
Manhattan Neighborhoods 78
Downtown Hotels 96
Midtown Hotels...98
Uptown Hotels 100
Downtown Dining 126
Midtown Dining...128
Uptown Dining 130
Downtown Brooklyn..132
Downtown Attractions..174
Midtown Attractions 176
Uptown Attractions 178
Central Park...181
Harlem and Upper Manhattan 183
Downtown Shopping...216
Midtown Shopping 218
Uptown Shopping 220
Williamsburg 222
Downtown Arts and Nightlife...266
Midtown Arts and Nightlife 268
Uptown Arts and Nightlife..270

Table of Contents

Introduction *1*

About This Book 1
Conventions Used in This Book 2
Foolish Assumptions 3
How This Book Is Organized 3
    Part I: Introducing New York City..............................3
    Part II: Planning Your Trip to New York City 4
    Part III: Settling Into New York City...........................4
    Part IV: Exploring New York City................................4
    Part V: Living It Up After Dark:
       New York City Nightlife...4
    Part VI: The Part of Tens...4
    Quick Concierge..4
Icons Used in This Book..5
Where to Go from Here 5

Part 1: Introducing New York City *7*

Chapter 1: Discovering the Best of New York City 9

Best Events 9
Best Hotels...16
Best Restaurants 17
Best Attractions 18
Best Shopping..20
Best Culture and Nightlife...20

Chapter 2: Digging Deeper into New York City 22

Hunting Down a Little History...22
Looking at Local Architecture...25
Recommending Books, Movies, and Podcasts.................26
    New York City on paper...26
    New York City on film 27
    New York City on podcast 28

Chapter 3: Deciding When to Go 29

Revealing the Secrets of the Seasons 29
Marking Your Calendar: Year-Round New York..............30
    January...30
    February...30
    March/April 31
    May 31

June 31
July...32
August 32
September..33
October 33
November 33
December..34

Part II: Planning Your Trip to New York City..... 35

Chapter 4: Managing Your Money..............................37
Planning Your Budget..37
Hotel 38
Transportation 38
Food..38
Sights 39
Shopping 39
Nightlife...39
Typical day-to-day purchases 39
Taxes 40
Tips..40
Cutting Costs, but Not the Fun............................41
Handling Money 42
Using ATMs and carrying cash 43
Charging ahead with credit cards 43
Toting traveler's checks 43
Dealing with a lost or stolen wallet 44

Chapter 5: Getting to New York City............................46
Choosing the Airport.....................................46
Flying to New York..47
Finding out which airlines fly there.........................47
Getting the best deal on your airfare 48
Booking your flight online 49
Driving to New York City 49
Arriving by Other Means....................................50
By train...50
By bus..50
Joining an Escorted Tour 51
Choosing a Package Tour.....................................52

Chapter 6: Catering to Special Travel Needs or Interests 53
Traveling with the Brood: Advice for Families..................53
Finding a family-friendly hotel 54
Getting around 54

Finding baby-sitting services 54
Touring the town 54
Making Age Work for You: Advice for Seniors 55
Accessing New York City: Advice for Travelers
     with Disabilities..55
Travel agencies and organizations...........................56
Hotels 56
Transportation...56
Following the Rainbow: Advice for GLBT Travelers.........58
Tying the Knot: Advice for Travelers in Love 59

Chapter 7: Taking Care of the Remaining Details 61

Renting a Car: Not in New York!..61
Playing It Safe: Travel and Medical Insurance.................62
Staying Healthy When You Travel 63
Staying Connected by Cellphone or E-Mail.......................64
Using a cellphone 64
Accessing the Internet away from home 64
With your own computer...65
Keeping Up with Airline Security Measures 65

Part III: Settling Into New York City 67

Chapter 8: Arriving and Getting Oriented 69

Getting from the Airport to Your Hotel.............................69
From JFK 71
From LaGuardia 72
From Newark 73
From MacArthur Airport (Long Island) 75
Arriving by Train..75
Arriving by Car 76
Figuring Out the Neighborhoods 77
Downtown...77
Uptown..82
Finding Information After You Arrive.................................83
Getting Around New York..83
Traveling by subway 84
Traveling by bus 86
Understanding the MetroCard 87
Traveling by taxi 88
Seeing New York on Foot 90

**Chapter 9: Checking In at New York City's
Best Hotels 91**

Getting to Know Your Options 91
Independent hotels...91

Chain hotels...92
Bed-and-breakfasts and inns 92
Short-term apartment rentals 92
Finding the Best Room at the Best Rate.............92
Asking for the best rate..............................93
Choosing your season carefully..................93
Going uptown or downtown . . . or to Brooklyn?....93
Visiting over a weekend...............................93
Surfing the Web for hotel deals 94
Finding a top-notch room 94
Arriving without a Reservation (Not Recommended).......94
New York City's Best Hotels 95
Runner-Up Hotels...118
Index of Accommodations by Neighborhood 119
Index of Accommodations by Price.....................120

Chapter 10: Dining and Snacking in New York City 122

Getting the Dish on the Local Scene...................122
Sources for scoping out the dining scene 123
Trimming the fat from your budget.......................124
New York's Best Restaurants 125
Dining and Snacking on the Go 154
Breakfast and brunch...............................154
Bagels 155
Pizza 156
Hamburgers and hot dogs 157
New York delicatessens 159
More sandwiches and snacks 159
Sweet treats 160
Index of Establishments by Neighborhood 162
Index of Establishments by Cuisine...................164
Index of Establishments by Price.......................167

Part 1V: Exploring New York City...................... 169

Chapter 11: New York City's Top Sights....................171

New York City's Top Sights 172
Finding More Cool Things to See and Do........................192
Other excellent museums.............................192
For culture and history buffs 195
Notable New York City architecture 198
Beautiful places of worship 199
Especially for kids......................................201
New York City for teens 203
Fun for TV fans..204

Surveying the New York Sports Scene 206
    Yankees and Mets: Major leaguers 206
    Down on the farm in New York: The minors 207
    The city game: Basketball 207
    Back on the ice: NHL action 207
Seeing New York by Guided Tour 207
    Seeing the city by tour bus 208
    Cruising around the island 209
    Broadening your mind with specialty tours 210
    Biking, singing, eating, and all-that-jazz tours 211
    Faring well with free walking tours 211

Chapter 12: Shopping in New York City 213

Surveying the Shopping Scene 213
Knowing the Big Names 214
Shopping in Open-Air Markets 215
Discovering the Best Shopping Neighborhoods 224
    Uptown 224
    Midtown 225
    Downtown 227
    Other shopping areas 231
The Best of New York Shopping A to Z 231
    Beauty 231
    Books 232
    Edibles 233
    Electronics 234
    Gifts 235
    Museum stores 235
    Music 236
    Toys 236

**Chapter 13: Following an Itinerary:
Five Great Options..238**

New York in Three Days...238
    Day one 238
    Day two 240
    Day three...240
New York in Five Days..241
    Day one 241
    Day two 242
    Day three...242
    Day four...243
    Day five..243
New York for Museum Mavens 244
New York for Families with Kids.......................................245
New York for History Buffs 246

Part V: Living It Up After Dark: New York City Nightlife 249

Chapter 14: Applauding the Cultural Scene 251

Getting the Inside Scoop 251
Taking in New York Theater.................252
Figuring out the Broadway basics 252
Getting theater tickets 253
Venues That Set the Standard................257
The Lincoln Center for the Performing Arts 257
Carnegie Hall 259
Brooklyn Academy of Music................259
Other major concert spaces................260
Classical Music................261
Opera...................261
Music Alfresco................262
Dance................263

Chapter 15: Hitting the Clubs and Bars 264

All About the Music 264
All that jazz 264
It's only rock 'n' roll................272
The best of the rest 273
Life is a cabaret................273
New York Comedy Is No Joke................274
Hanging Out in New York's Best Bars 275
For creative cocktails................275
For old-world charm................276
For cultural exchange................276
For dive-bar aficionados 277
For drinks with a view................277
For gay and lesbian nightlife 277
Hitting the Dance Clubs and Getting
Beyond the Velvet Rope................278

Part VI: The Part of Tens 281

Chapter 16: The Top Ten Cheap New York City Experiences 283

Befriend a New Yorker 283
Ride the International Express................283
Party at the Brooklyn Museum 284
Explore the (Free) Art in Queens................284
Be a Culture Vulture 285
Roller-Skate Like It's 1979 285

Tour Little Italy in the Bronx 286
Take the High Line 286
Bike along the Hudson River 286
Wander the Streets on Sunday Morning 287

Chapter 17: The Top Ten Essential New York City Eating Experiences 288

A Slice of Pizza...288
Bagel with a Schmear 288
Chicken and Waffles 289
Chino-Latino 289
Dining in a Diner..289
The Hot Dog..290
The New York Cheesecake 290
The New York Oyster 290
The New York Strip..291
Ice Cream with a View.......................................291

Chapter 18: Ten New York City Experiences to Avoid 292

New Year's Eve in Times Square......................292
Chain Stores and Restaurants 292
Street Scams 293
Weekend Subway Rides 293
SoHo on Saturdays..294
The St. Patrick's Day Parade 294
Electronics Stores 294
Driving in the City 294
Horse-Drawn Carriage Rides............................295
The Feast of San Gennaro 296

Appendix: Quick Concierge 297

Fast Facts 297
Where to Get More Information 302
Tourist-information offices.............................302
Newspapers, magazines, and wireless apps 302

Index... 304

Introduction

*W*hen it comes to a city as famous and infamous as New York is, everybody has an opinion, often based on indelible film images or evocative song lyrics. Growing up in other places, I envisioned New York as a city of artists and warriors, where all the critics loved you and you could dance, if you wanted to, in legwarmers on top of a taxicab. The New York I made my home as an adult is tamer and wealthier but still full of hassles and hustles. It's also a place where the only thing you can count on is change. New Yorkers like the shock of the new — it's where the city gets its fabled energy. We have short attention spans here on the bleeding edge; a restaurant, show, club, or store may be the hottest thing to hit the city for a couple of months, and then another opens or is discovered, and that once-hot place quickly becomes yesterday's news.

On the other hand, New Yorkers don't always appreciate change, because it means we may have lost something we had come to love. New Yorkers respect the old standards — places and things that have become a part of the city's core identity. What would we do without that reassuring sight of the Lady in the harbor? Or the gleaming spire of the Empire State Building? Or the perfect pizza slice? Or a Sunday in Central Park? Or the rumbling of the train beneath our feet? Or the sounds of jazz from a Village club? So, even though New York is ever-changing — since 2001, we've bid adieu to the Twin Towers, the subway token, Yankee and Shea stadiums, and Tavern on the Green — certain essential features remain the same. And we wouldn't have it any other way.

In the pages that follow, I do my best to guide you to what's fresh and new, without leaving out some beloved standards. I tell you where to find the best that New York has to offer, both on and off the beaten path. But really, what I hope to accomplish is to present New York as simply as possible so that you can decide what paths *you* want to follow during your visit.

About This Book

Maybe this is your first trip to New York, or maybe you're a repeat visitor; in either case, I assume that you want to find out what you need to know, plus a little bit more. But I don't want to overload you with information, which is easy to do when you're talking about New York.

This is both a guidebook *and* a reference book. You can read it cover to cover, or you can jump in anywhere to find the information you want about a specific task, such as finding a hotel or working out your budget. Whether you're sitting in your living room trying to make a reservation or standing on the corner of 42nd Street and Fifth Avenue wondering where to eat, *New York City For Dummies,* 6th Edition, is set up so that you can quickly get the facts and recommendations you want.

Please be advised that travel information is subject to change at any time — this is especially true of prices. Therefore, I suggest that you write or call ahead to confirm prices and details when making your travel plans. The author, editors, and publisher cannot be held responsible for readers' experiences while traveling. Your safety is important to us, however, so I encourage you to stay alert and be aware of your surroundings. Keep a close eye on cameras, purses, and wallets, all favorite targets of thieves and pickpockets.

Conventions Used in This Book

In this book, I include lists of hotels, restaurants, and attractions. As I describe each, I often include abbreviations for commonly accepted credit cards. Take a look at the following list for an explanation of each.

AE: American Express

DC: Diners Club

DISC: Discover

MC: MasterCard

V: Visa

I've divided the hotels into two categories: my personal picks of the top accommodations the city has to offer and those that don't quite make my preferred list but still get my hearty seal of approval. Don't be shy about considering these "runner-up" hotels if you're unable to get a room at one of my favorites or if your preferences differ from mine — the amenities offered by the runners-up and the services that each provides make all these accommodations good choices to consider as you determine where to rest your head at night.

I also include some general pricing information to help you as you decide where to unpack your bags or dine on the local cuisine. I've used a system of dollar signs to show a range of costs for one night in a hotel (the price refers to a double-occupancy room) or for a meal at a restaurant (included in the cost of each meal is soup or salad, an entree, dessert, and a nonalcoholic drink). Check out the following table to decipher the dollar signs.

Cost	Hotel	Restaurant
$	$209 or less	$34 or less
$$	$210–$309	$35–$59
$$$	$310–$449	$60–$84
$$$$	$450–$599	$85–$99
$$$$$	$600 or more	$100 or more

For those hotels, restaurants, and attractions that are plotted on a map, a page reference is provided in the listing information. If a hotel, restaurant, or attraction is outside Manhattan, it may not be mapped.

Foolish Assumptions

As I wrote this book, I made some assumptions about you and what your needs may be as a traveler. Here's what I assumed about you:

- ✔ You're an experienced traveler who hasn't had much time to explore New York and who wants expert advice when you finally do get a chance to enjoy the city.
- ✔ You're an inexperienced traveler looking for guidance when determining whether to take a trip to New York and how to plan for it.
- ✔ You're not looking for a book that provides all the information available about New York or one that lists every hotel, restaurant, or attraction available to you. Instead, you want a book focusing on the places that will give you the best or most unique experience in New York.

If you fit into any of these categories, *New York City For Dummies,* 6th Edition, gives you the information you're looking for.

How This Book Is Organized

This book is divided into six parts covering the major aspects of your trip. Each part is further broken down into specific components so that you can go right to the subtopic you want — for example, you don't have to read all about nightlife if you're just looking for a jazz club. Following are brief summaries of the parts.

Part I: Introducing New York City

In this part, I give you my opinion on the very best of New York when it comes to hotels, attractions, events, and restaurants. This part also includes some basic information on culture, history, architecture, and food, along with the differences the seasons make in determining when you may want to visit, and a yearly calendar of major events.

Part II: Planning Your Trip to New York City

This part covers the nitty-gritty of trip planning: how to manage your money and plan your budget for your visit, how to get to New York, whether you should join an escorted tour or choose a package tour, what to do if you have special needs, and other nuts 'n' bolts details.

Part III: Settling Into New York City

This part is all about getting around, from the moment your plane lands or you step off the train or bus. I cover ground transportation into Manhattan, the public-transit system, and sights to see on foot. This part also includes information about many New York neighborhoods and what makes them distinctive. From there, I give an overview of the New York lodging scene and how to find the best room rate; I list my favorite hotels along with a few very good runners-up. Finally, this part includes a chapter on eating in New York; here, I give you an idea of the food scene in New York, along with yummy snacking options such as pizza, bagels, and desserts.

Part IV: Exploring New York City

This part describes what to see and do, from touring famous buildings to attending the taping of a TV show. This part also includes a chapter on shopping the local stores. Here, I point out the best shopping neighborhoods and the city's best stores. To help you fit in all that you want to see while you're here, I also provide some sample itineraries to help you organize your time in the city.

Part V: Living It Up After Dark: New York City Nightlife

This part covers New York's major arts attractions, from Broadway shows to clubs, and gives you an idea of what each activity costs and how to get discount tickets. I also include a chapter on nightclubs, places to have a drink, and other more or less civilized forms of relaxation.

Part VI: The Part of Tens

The Part of Tens gives you a few of my top tens of New York. You can take them seriously, or you can take them for what they are — fun. Either way, I think you'll enjoy them.

Quick Concierge

At the back of this book, I include an appendix — your Quick Concierge — containing lots of handy information you may need when traveling in New York, such as phone numbers and addresses for emergency personnel or area hospitals and pharmacies, lists of local newspapers and magazines, protocol for sending mail or finding taxis, and more. Check out this appendix when searching for answers to lots of questions that may come up as you travel. You can find the Quick Concierge easily because it's printed on yellow paper.

Icons Used in This Book

Keep your eyes peeled for icons, which appear in the margins throughout the book. These little pictures serve as a kind of shorthand or code to alert you to special information. Here are the icons I use in this book and a description of each.

Keep an eye out for the Bargain Alert icon as you seek out money-saving tips and/or great deals.

The Best of the Best icon highlights the best that New York has to offer in all categories — hotels, restaurants, attractions, activities, shopping, and nightlife.

Watch for the Heads Up icon to identify annoying or potentially dangerous situations, such as tourist traps, unsafe neighborhoods, budgetary rip-offs, and other things to be aware of.

Find out useful advice on things to do and ways to schedule your time when you see the Tip icon.

Look to the Kid Friendly icon for attractions, hotels, restaurants, and activities that are particularly hospitable to children or people traveling with kids.

The Worth the Search icon highlights secret little finds or useful resources that are worth the extra bit of effort to get to or find.

Where to Go from Here

New York can seem overwhelming, but it doesn't have to be. It can seem budget busting, but it doesn't have to be. In New York, you can find something for everyone — and that's what makes it so special. This book, and all it offers, helps assuage any fears or apprehensions you may have as it guides you to a fun, stress-free trip to the Big Apple.

Part I
Introducing New York City

"And how shall I book your flight to New York City — First Class, Coach, or You Talkin' to Me?"

In this part . . .

I give you a taste of the best of New York City, with a spot-light on the top restaurants, hotels, attractions, sights, and sounds that make up this ever-changing city. I do my best to guide you to what's new, as well as to the classics. I tell you where to find the most uniquely New York experiences, both on and off the beaten path.

In this part, I also give you a brief history of New York City, as well as overviews of the architecture and cuisine, and I finish up with some books and films that you may enjoy as you get ready to hit the town.

Chapter 1

Discovering the Best of New York City

In This Chapter

▶ Celebrating the most festive parades and seasons
▶ Finding rooms in the best hotels
▶ Enjoying all kinds of cuisine at all kinds of restaurants
▶ Visiting Lady Liberty and other top attractions
▶ Giving the credit card a workout at the top shops
▶ Choosing the spots with the best nightlife

*W*elcome to New York, New York, the city so nice they had to name it — oh, *you* know. No matter when you visit, there's sure to be something of interest going on. In this chapter, I list my choices for the best events, hotels, restaurants, attractions, shopping, culture, and nightlife.

Whether you're looking for a world-class hotel, exotic cuisine to enjoy, or the view from the Empire State Building, I have no doubt you'll soon compile your own "best of" list. But here's a good place to start!

Best Events

Best Parade: West Indian–American Day Carnival and Parade. Held on Eastern Parkway in Brooklyn, this is the biggest parade in New York. The music (calypso, soca, reggae, and Latin), the amazing costumes, and the incredible Caribbean food make this an unforgettable experience. If you're lucky enough to be in town on Labor Day, don't miss it. See Chapter 3.

Best Time of Year to Come to New York: Late spring. Many people adore summer, when free outdoor cultural events abound, and I agree that it's a fun time to visit. But late spring is even better: New Yorkers are ecstatically trading their winter coats for summer dresses and shorts the minute that temperatures are consistently in the 60s, the

Downtown Orientation

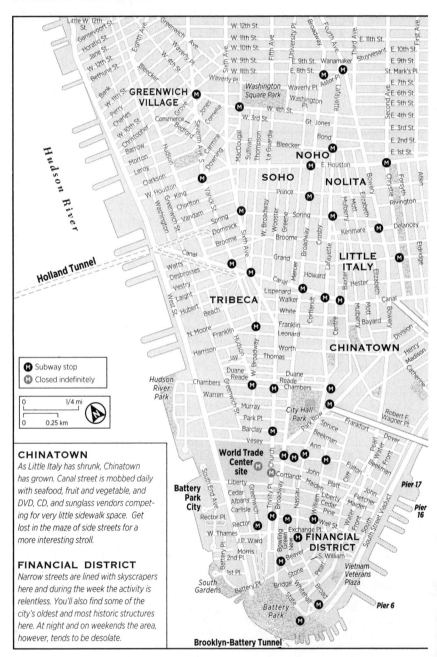

CHINATOWN

As Little Italy has shrunk, Chinatown has grown. Canal street is mobbed daily with seafood, fruit and vegetable, and DVD, CD, and sunglass vendors competing for very little sidewalk space. Get lost in the maze of side streets for a more interesting stroll.

FINANCIAL DISTRICT

Narrow streets are lined with skyscrapers here and during the week the activity is relentless. You'll also find some of the city's oldest and most historic structures here. At night and on weekends the area, however, tends to be desolate.

GREENWICH VILLAGE
The once-famous bohemian enclave where off-beat became the Beats is still a great people-watching neighborhood. You won't find any high-rises here, just quaint, narrow streets and beautifully preserved brownstones and townhouses.

NOHO
This once-tiny stretch of furniture stores, boutiques, and a few restaurants is thriving since the opening of the New Museum. The formerly derelict Bowery is becoming a restaurant row.

EAST VILLAGE
The East Village now is home to some of the city's most interesting restaurants and despite its counter-culture reputation, real estate prices are very "establishment."

NOLITA
Here's another neighborhood that has a cute acronym (North of Little Italy). This is really old Little Italy in architecture, but there is nothing old about the very hip boutiques and cafes that are sprinkled throughout the relatively small enclave.

SOHO
What once was an artist's destination has become a very affluent tourist destination. You'll find just about all the top designer names in retail here housed in historic cast-iron buildings.

LOWER EAST SIDE
This is where so many immigrants, especially Jewish, settled as their first home in America. And there is still some of that old-world feel to the neighborhood, but it has faded as the area has become a hot spot for restaurants, bars, and edgy shops.

TRIBECA
In the 1980s TriBeCa (Triangle Below Canal), with its sprawling lofts and hip restaurants, became one of the most desirable places to live. After September 11, 2001 and its close proximity to the World Trade Center, the area lost a bit of its luster, but that was only temporary. TriBeCa is thriving once again.

LITTLE ITALY
Sadly, this once unique and charming neighborhood, squeezed by the expansion of Chinatown, has shrunk to a mere block or two. And what's left, with very few exceptions, is nothing like what it once was. You can't even get a good plate of pasta here anymore.

Midtown Orientation

MIDTOWN EAST

The heart of corporate Manhattan, Midtown East is also where you'll find such landmarks as Grand Central Station, the Empire State Building, St. Patrick's Cathedral, the Chrysler Building, and the United Nations.

MIDTOWN WEST

This bustling sprawl of an area includes many of the city's best hotels, the Art Deco masterpiece, Rockefeller Center, and a neighborhood called Hell's Kitchen where you'll find some of the city's most ethnically diverse restaurants.

TIMES SQUARE/ THEATER DISTRICT

In the truly American tradition, everything here is big and gaudy and, as a result, the streets here are constantly crammed with people who have come to gawk at the big and the gaudy — meaning the neon wonderland of Times Square.

MURRAY HILL

This is a quiet, mostly residential neighborhood. On its southern fringe is the Indo-Pakistani enclave known as Curry Hill.

GRAMERCY

The heart of this neighborhood is the postcard-perfect little park that's so exclusive you need a key to get into it. You don't need a special key to live in the quaint and very beautiful brownstones that surround the park, but you do need money. Many of the buildings here date back to the 1800s, giving the area a real 19th century feel.

FLATIRON DISTRICT AND UNION SQUARE

Cheaper rents attracted many publishing and media businesses and, as a result, the neighborhood is now bursting with restaurants and clubs. Along with Union Square, and the wildly popular greenmarket, the Flatiron Building embodies the spirit of this vibrant neighborhood.

CHELSEA

With galleries everywhere, Chelsea is now one of the city's arts centers. There is an almost small town feel to this neighborhood, which has also become the center for the city's gay population.

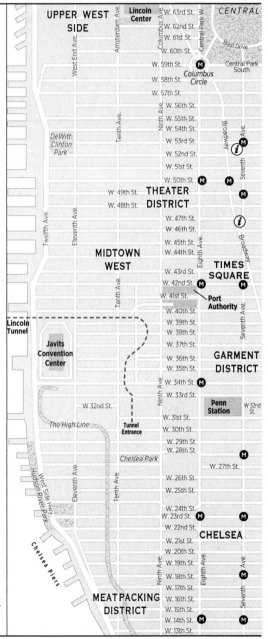

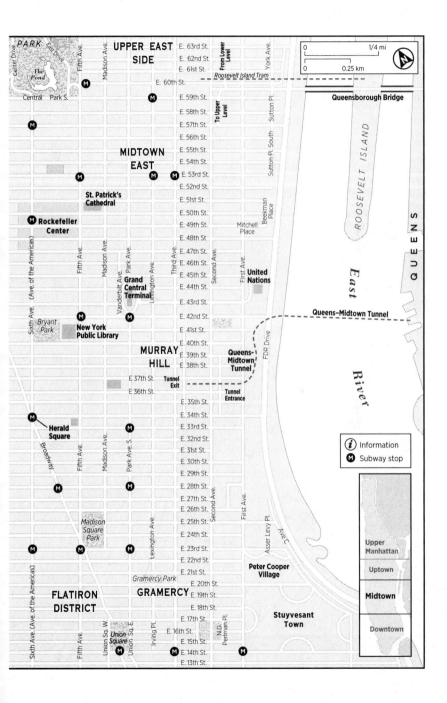

Uptown Orientation

CENTRAL PARK
This 843-acre nature retreat in the heart of Manhattan is one of the great parks of the world. Even if nature is not your thing, from the Central Park Zoo to the Carousel, from playgrounds to skating rinks, there is something for everyone in Central Park.

UPPER WEST SIDE
This mostly residential neighborhood also features landmarks like Lincoln Center, the Museum of Natural History, and the Cathedral of St. John the Divine and is enviable because it is surrounded by two great parks, Central Park and Riverside Park.

UPPER EAST SIDE
Long the address of the rich and famous, the Upper East Side is also the home to the Metropolitan Museum of Art, the Guggenheim, and other fantastic museums along "Museum Mile." You'll also find a thick concentration of restaurants and bars, and, of course, some great and very expensive shopping along tony Madison Avenue.

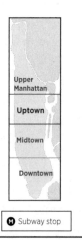

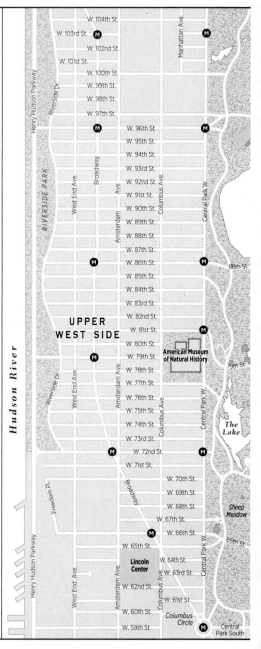

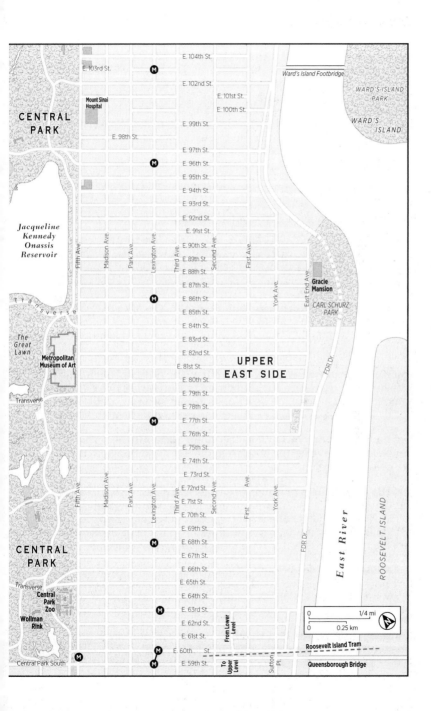

city's in bloom, prices are still reasonable, and there's a lovely sense of anticipation and sociability in the air.

Best Season in New York: The December holidays. Lighted Christmas trees on Park Avenue; the big snowflake at the corner of 57th Street and Fifth Avenue; the trees at Rockefeller Center and Lincoln Center; the Hanukkah menorah at Grand Army Plaza, at Fifth Avenue and 59th Street; the decorations in department store windows, restaurants, and hotels. And even though the crowds, especially around Rockefeller Center, may bring out the Scrooge in you, the atmosphere is almost always festive and like no other time of year.

Best Hotels

For more information on all the hotels listed in this section, refer to Chapter 9.

Best Hotel: The Ritz-Carlton New York, Central Park. The combination of a great location, just across from Central Park; large, well-outfitted rooms; and typically excellent Ritz-Carlton service is as good as it gets.

Best Hotel for Downtown New York Elegance: The Mercer. The Mercer is located in the heart of SoHo. The high-ceilinged, loftlike rooms and suites, some with fireplaces and all with ceiling fans and luxurious bathrooms, are spectacular.

Best Hotel for Downtown New York Edge: The Bowery Hotel. An intimate boutique hotel with cozy public areas, the Bowery Hotel's faded glamour is right at home on New York's former skid row, which is quickly becoming a revitalized dining and culture destination.

Best for Classic Old-World Elegance: Hôtel Plaza Athénée. That European feel pervades the hotel from the old-world design to the first-rate concierge service.

Best Hip Hotel: The Ace Hotel. Musicians and music lovers love the Ace, and with its incredibly well-curated mix of partners (Stumptown Coffee, No. 7 Sub, Other Music, and Opening Ceremony) and the Breslin gastropub, it's transforming this neighborhood north of Madison Square Park into the place to watch for interesting new developments.

Best Moderately Priced Hotel: The Lucerne. This is the best hotel on the Upper West Side. The homey, neighborhood feel of the hotel, its exceptional service, and its nice-sized, well-equipped rooms make this a very attractive midrange option.

Best Budget Hotel: The Pod Hotel. If you don't mind sharing a toilet and shower with other guests, this cheerful hotel offers impeccable comforts — including an in-room sink and your own little flatscreen TV — at budget prices.

Best for Families: Hotel Beacon. Not only is this hotel a great deal — you can get good-sized suites for so much less than you would pay in Midtown — but the Upper West Side, with its parks, the Museum of Natural History, and fun restaurants, is also a great neighborhood for children.

Best Romantic Hotel: Crosby Street Hotel. Maybe it's the location (on an unusually quiet cobblestone street in SoHo), the vibrant original artwork in the lobby, the effortlessly elegant lounges and garden, or the playful mix of colors and fabrics decorating the rooms — or the amazing combination of all these features that makes this hotel so romantic. Whatever it is, the overall aura makes you feel as if you're getting away with something, and who can resist the romance of that?

Best Hotel Bar: Bemelmans Bar. Named after book illustrator Ludwig Bemelmans, who created the *Madeline* books and painted the mural in the bar, the Carlyle's romantic, charming bar features white-glove service and wondrous cocktails.

Best Restaurants

For more information on the restaurants listed in this section, head to Chapter 10.

Best Restaurant: Gramercy Tavern. This New York favorite has been reinvigorated by executive chef Michael Anthony, who creates sophisticated American cuisine that is both refined and deeply satisfying.

Best Special-Occasion Restaurant: Jean Georges. If you want to eat an exceptional meal — one that will make you wonder if you've ever really tasted anything before — you won't go wrong choosing Jean Georges. The room has bona fide New York–style swagger, and the food is consistently superb.

Best French: Daniel. For faultless French cooking, nobody does it better than chef Daniel Boulud, especially here at his signature restaurant.

Best Italian: Lupa. How can you choose just one great Italian restaurant in the city? Impossible . . . but chef Mario Batali continues to deliver high-quality food at great prices in this Roman-style *osteria*.

Best Seafood: Lure. Not only is the seafood superfresh and flavorful, but it's served in a supersexy setting: a subterranean re-creation of a luxury yacht.

Best Steak: Frankie & Johnnie's. Whether you choose the former speakeasy that is the original location in the Theater District or the newer branch in John Barrymore's former town house, your steak, particularly the house sirloin, will remind you why Frankie & Johnnie's has been around since 1926.

Best Jewish Deli: 2nd Avenue Deli. The deli's no longer on Second Avenue, but the pastrami sandwiches and chicken soup are as good as ever. And now you get free chicken cracklins *(gribenes)* with your meal.

Best Burger: Burger Joint. Who woulda thunk that a fancy hotel like Le Parker Meridien would be the home to a place called Burger Joint that serves great burgers at great prices?

Best Breakfast: Good Enough to Eat. They've been lining up on Amsterdam Avenue on weekend mornings for over 20 years to get a taste of chef/owner Carrie Levin's bountiful home-cooked breakfasts.

Best Dessert: Haveli. I've got an incorrigible sweet tooth, so I can find something to love on *any* dessert menu. But the one I most look forward to is Haveli's *gulab jaman,* always served hot and just this side of impossibly sweet. It's a pure sugar rush to heaven.

Best Ice Cream: Brooklyn Ice Cream Factory. A treat from the Ice Cream Factory is the perfect reward after a brisk walk across the Brooklyn Bridge. Rich, homemade ice cream with a view of the Manhattan skyline — that's a tough combination to beat.

Best Bagel: Ess-a-Bagel. Big and fluffy, with a thick schmear of cream cheese — "ess" the best in its class.

Best Times Square Restaurant: Virgil's Real Barbecue. In a restaurant wasteland loaded with bad theme restaurants and overpriced national chains, Virgil's is, in a sense, a barbecue-theme restaurant, but it does an excellent job of smoking meats.

Best Attractions

For more information on the attractions in this section, refer to Chapter 11.

Best Attraction: Statue of Liberty. If you have time to do only one thing on your visit to New York, sail to the Lady in the harbor. No other monument embodies the nation's — and the world's — notion of political freedom and economic potential more than Lady Liberty. It's also the ultimate symbol of New York, the personification of the city's vast diversity and tolerance.

Best Skyscraper: Empire State Building. Like the Statue of Liberty, the Empire State Building, once again the tallest building in New York, is one of the city's definitive icons. The view from the 86th-floor observatory is unforgettable.

Best-Looking Building: Chrysler Building. This award goes to the chrome-topped, gargoyle-laden Art Deco masterpiece. It's my personal beacon on the skyline.

Best Historic Building: Grand Central Terminal. Even if you don't have to catch a train, make sure you visit this Beaux Arts gem that was built in 1913, saved from destruction in the 1960s, and beautifully restored in the 1990s to recapture its initial brilliance.

Best Art Museum: Metropolitan Museum of Art. It's not only the best art museum in New York, but also the best in North America. The number of masterworks housed here is mind-boggling.

Best Museum for Children (Big and Small): American Museum of Natural History. You could spend your entire visit to New York at this 4-square-block museum; there's that much to see. From the famed Dinosaur Hall to the adjoining Rose Center for Earth and Space, the Museum of Natural History houses the world's greatest natural science collection.

Best Park: The High Line. Okay, obviously Central Park is the best of the traditional parks, but the High Line has redefined the idea of what an urban park can be. It's a strip of tranquillity high above the road-river-and-rail bustle of Manhattan.

Best Location in Central Park for a Picnic: The Pool. At 100th Street, the Pool is like being in another world. It's relatively quiet and undiscovered, and with weeping willows, ducks, geese, egrets, and a hawk or two, this watering hole is an oasis of tranquillity.

Best Place to Take the Kids: Central Park. With a lovely carousel, a zoo, two ice-skating rinks, and numerous playgrounds and ball fields, Central Park is a children's wonderland.

Best Street: Broadway. Fifth Avenue has the better reputation, but it's lost some luster in the past few years with the proliferation of chain and theme stores, so my pick is Broadway. Because it stretches from one end of Manhattan to the other, no street captures the city's diversity better than Broadway.

Best Neighborhood to Stroll: Greenwich Village. With its historic streets, hidden cafes, cozy restaurants, and eccentric characters, Greenwich Village is a constant but pleasant barrage on the senses.

Best Bridge: Brooklyn Bridge. New York is a city of bridges connecting the various islands to the mainland and beyond. But none equals the splendor and originality of the Brooklyn Bridge. Walking across it is a must.

Best Free Attraction: Staten Island Ferry. On the Staten Island Ferry you get views of the Statue of Liberty, Ellis Island, lower Manhattan, the Verrazano Narrows Bridge, and the rest of New York Harbor — and the chance to mingle with commuters. Plus, you can't beat the price of this ride.

Best Shopping

For more information on the stores in this section, skip to Chapter 12.

Best Department Store: Saks Fifth Avenue. Not as overwhelming as other department stores, Saks is consistently good. Don't miss the windows at Christmastime!

Best Clothes Store: Barneys. This store is the pinnacle, with prices to match.

Best Market: The Brooklyn Flea. A whisky-soaked brainstorm by a Brooklyn blogger and a Brooklyn speechwriter yielded a festive flea market that has raised the bar for all open-air markets across the city. Fleas seem to be popping up ten-a-penny around town these days, but this is still the one to see.

Best Bookstore: McNally Jackson. In a city of many terrific bookstores, McNally Jackson has distinguished itself with a lovingly curated selection of general-interest literature and a comprehensive roster of special events.

Best Music Store: Other Music. I've been a loyal customer since I was a college-radio DJ, and I still make unexpected discoveries that broaden my horizons at Other Music.

Best Shopping Zone: SoHo, NoHo, and Nolita. All three are within easy walking distance of one another and feature the best, trendiest boutiques.

Best Culture and Nightlife

For more information on the listings in this section, jump to Chapters 14 and 15.

Best Performance Space: Carnegie Hall. You can find few greater performance spaces in the world than this one. Visually and acoustically brilliant, Carnegie Hall regularly attracts an amazing array of talent.

Best Free Cultural Event: Shakespeare in the Park. Imagine Shakespeare performed by stars, under the stars, in Central Park. No wonder it has become a New York institution.

Best Children's Theater: Paper Bag Players. For children ages 4 to 9, this group performs in the winter only and offers tales told in imaginative and original ways.

Best Jazz Club: Village Vanguard. The acoustics and sightlines aren't great, but you can't do better for finding consistent, good-quality jazz.

Best Rock Club: Mercury Lounge. This venue is intimate, but not obscure. The Merc is the best for hard-edge rock 'n' roll.

Best Comedy Club: Gotham Comedy Club. Comfortable and sophisticated, this is where the best come to hone their acts.

Best Pub: Ear Inn. Located in an old hanger-on in chic SoHo, the Ear Inn continues to survive among the lush lounges that surround it.

Best Bar for Cocktails: Pegu Club. Owned by master mixologist Audrey Saunders, Pegu Club's creative cocktails — whether shaken, stirred, or poured — are always perfect.

Chapter 2

Digging Deeper into New York City

In This Chapter

▶ Exploring the history of New York City

▶ Appreciating Manhattan's architecture

▶ Tasting the local cuisine

▶ Absorbing New York City through films, books, and podcasts

*N*o matter how much you know (or don't know) about New York, it may help you to get a little background on the city before you arrive. Here's a quick overview — historical timelines, architectural highlights, culinary tidbits, a recommended reading and film list — that may help you discover a part of what makes New York unique.

Hunting Down a Little History

The area that became New York City was the home to many Native Americans before Giovanni da Verrazano arrived in 1524. Even though Verrazano didn't stay, a bridge was named after him. And it wasn't until 1609, when Henry Hudson, while searching for the Northwest Passage, claimed it for the Dutch East India Company, that New York was recognized as a potential, profitable settlement in the New World.

Hudson (the river is named for him) said of New York, "It is as beautiful a land as one can hope to tread upon." The treading didn't really start until years later, but by 1625, Dutch settlers established a fur trade with the locals and called their colony New Amsterdam. A year later, Peter Minuit of the Dutch West India Company made that famous deal for the island: He bought New Amsterdam from the Lenape Tribe for $24.

New Amsterdam became a British colony in the 1670s, and, during the Revolutionary War, it was occupied by British troops. England controlled New York until 1783, when it withdrew from the city two full years after the end of the American Revolution. Two years after *that*, New York was named the first capital of the United States. The first

New York City timeline: 1524–1792

1524 Giovanni da Verrazano sails into New York Harbor.

1609 Henry Hudson sails up the Hudson River.

1621 The Dutch West India Company begins trading from New York City.

1626 The Dutch pay 60 guilders ($24) to the Lenape Tribe for the island of New Amsterdam.

1664 The Dutch surrender New Amsterdam to the British and the island is renamed after the brother of King Charles II, the Duke of York.

1765 The Sons of Liberty burn the British governor in effigy.

1776 Independence from England is declared.

1789 The first Congress is held at Federal Hall on Wall Street, and George Washington is inaugurated.

1792 The first stock exchange is established on Wall Street.

Congress was held at Federal Hall on Wall Street in 1789, and George Washington was inaugurated president. But New York's tenure as the capital didn't last long. A year later, the government headed south to the newly created District of Columbia.

By 1825, New York City's population swelled to 250,000, and it rose to a half-million by midcentury. The city was a hotbed of Union recruitment during the Civil War; in the 1863 draft riots, Irish immigrants violently protested the draft and lynched 11 African Americans.

With industry booming, the late 19th century was termed the "Gilded Age." New York City was an example of this label in action; millionaires built mansions on Fifth Avenue, while rows of tenements teeming with families (made up of the cheap, mostly immigrant laborers who were employed by the industrial barons) filled the city's districts. In 1880, the city's population boomed to 1.1 million.

More European immigrants poured into the city between 1900 and 1930, arriving at Ellis Island and then fanning out into neighborhoods such as the Lower East Side, Greenwich Village, Little Italy, and Harlem. With the city population at 7 million in 1930 and a Depression raging, New York turned to a feisty mayor named Fiorello La Guardia for help. With the assistance of civic planner Robert Moses, who masterminded a huge public-works program, the city was remade. Moses did some things well, but his highway, bridge, tunnel, and housing projects ran through (and sometimes destroyed) many vibrant neighborhoods.

New York City timeline: 1820–1929

1820 New York City is the nation's largest city with a population of 124,000.

1863 The draft riots rage throughout New York; 125 people die, including 11 African-Americans who are lynched by mobs of Irish immigrants.

1883 The Brooklyn Bridge opens.

1886 The Statue of Liberty is completed.

1892 Ellis Island opens and begins processing over a million immigrants yearly.

1904 The first subway departs from City Hall.

1920 Babe Ruth joins the New York Yankees.

1923 Yankee Stadium opens.

1929 The stock market crashes.

While most of the country prospered after World War II, New York, with those Moses-built highways and a newly forming car culture, endured an exodus to the suburbs. By 1958, the Dodgers had left Brooklyn and the Giants had left the Polo Grounds. This economic slide climaxed in 1975 when the city nearly declared bankruptcy (as the famous *Daily News* headline said, "Ford to City: Drop Dead").

As Wall Street rallied during the 1980s, New York's fortunes also improved. In the 1990s, with Rudolph Giuliani — whom they haven't named anything after (yet) — as the mayor, the city rode a wave of prosperity that left it safer, cleaner, and more populated. The flip side of this boom was that Manhattan became more homogenized. Witness the Disney-fication of Times Square — the ultimate symbol of New York's homogenization — and the yawning gap between the rich and the poor.

The city — and the world — was shocked on September 11, 2001, when terrorists flew planes into the Twin Towers of the World Trade Center. But New York's grit and verve showed itself once more, as the city began to rebound emotionally and financially from that terrible tragedy. The housing bubble helped many New Yorkers live high on the hog (and accelerated the exodus of those who could not afford to keep up), but despite the global financial crisis of late 2008, and a subsequent slowdown in the manic pace of new development in the city, New York has proven to be more resilient than expected, with lower unemployment and crime rates than in many other parts of the country.

New York City timeline: 1931–2010

1931 The Empire State Building opens and is the tallest building in the world.

1939 The New York World's Fair opens in Flushing Meadows, Queens.

1947 The Brooklyn Dodgers sign Jackie Robinson, the first African American to play in the Major Leagues.

1957 Elvis Presley performs live in New York on *The Ed Sullivan Show*.

1969 The gay-rights movement begins with the Stonewall Rebellion in Greenwich Village.

1990 David Dinkins is elected as the first African-American mayor of New York City.

2000 The New York Yankees beat the New York Mets in the first Subway Series in 44 years. New York's population exceeds 8 million.

2001 Terrorists use hijacked planes to crash into the Twin Towers of the World Trade Center, which brings both towers down and kills more than 3,000 people.

2003 Smoking is banned in all restaurants and bars.

2006 Construction begins on the "Freedom Tower" (officially to be known as One World Trade Center); it is expected to be complete in 2013.

2008 Lehman Brothers, the Wall Street financial services firm, collapses and files for bankruptcy, helping to trigger a freeze in credit markets and a global economic crisis.

2009 Baseball fans flock to the new Yankee Stadium, across the street from the original House That Ruth Built. New York Mets fans get a new Citi Field. Debate immediately ensues about which stadium is superior. Mayor Michael Bloomberg uses the economic crisis to justify an amendment to the city's term-limits law, winning a third term in 2009.

Looking at Local Architecture

New York has many impressively ornate buildings, along with a slew of tall, sleek, modern skyscrapers (one of my lesser-known favorites is the Lipstick Building at Third Avenue and 53rd Street). The architectural styles in New York are as diverse as the population. Table 2-1 lists some of New York's more prominent styles, dates, and structures that represent those styles.

Table 2-1	New York Examples of Architectural Styles
Architectural Style	**Building**
Georgian (1700–1776)	St. Paul's Chapel (1766)
Greek Revival (1820–1860)	Federal Hall National Memorial (1842)
Gothic Revival (1830–1860)	Trinity Church (1846)
Early Skyscraper (1880–1920)	Flatiron Building (1902), Woolworth Building (1913)
Beaux Arts (1890–1920)	U.S. Customs House (1907), Grand Central Station (1913), New York Public Library (1911)
Art Deco (1925–1940)	Chrysler Building (1930), Empire State Building (1931), Rockefeller Center (1940)
Art Moderne (1930–1945)	Radio City Music Hall (1932)
Postmodern (1975–1990)	Sony Building (1984)

Recommending Books, Movies, and Podcasts

New York City has inspired writers for hundreds of years, and filmmakers since the invention of the form. You may gain understanding of the city by reading or watching some of the following.

New York City on paper

For the definitive history of New York City from its birth to the end of the 19th century, you won't find a better read than the Pulitzer Prize–winning *Gotham: A History of New York City to 1898*, by Edwin G. Burrows and Mike Wallace (Oxford University Press).

One of master biographer Robert A. Caro's early works, *The Power Broker: Robert Moses and the Fall of New York* (Vintage), focuses on how the vision of master builder Robert Moses transformed New York to what it became in the second half of the 20th century.

In *Great Bridge: The Epic Story of the Building of the Brooklyn Bridge* (Simon & Schuster), David McCullough devotes his estimable talents to the story of the building of the Brooklyn Bridge.

The companion volume to a PBS Series (see *New York: A Documentary Film,* later in this chapter), *New York: An Illustrated History,* by Ric Burns, Lisa Ades, and James Sanders (Knopf), uses lavish photographs and illustrations to show the growth of New York City.

Luc Sante, in his highly regarded *Low Life: Lures and Snares of Old New York* (Farrar, Straus, and Giroux), details New York's 19th- and early-20th-century criminal underbelly.

A personal favorite, *New York Calling,* a collection of essays and photographs edited by Marshall Berman and Brian Berger (Reaktion Books), provides engrossing firsthand accounts of life in the city during the rough years of the 1970s and early 1980s.

The great essayist E. B. White's classic, *Here Is New York* (Little Bookroom), is as relevant today as it was in 1948 when it was written. Another timeless masterpiece is Miroslav Sasek's illustrated children's book from 1960, *This Is New York* (Universe Books).

New York City on film

Few places are as cinematic as New York City. Filmmakers sometimes think of the city as a character itself. These are some of the top New York City movies, worth viewing before you visit.

Possibly the best New York City promotional film is the musical *On The Town,* with Gene Kelly and Frank Sinatra. This film is about three sailors who spend their 24-hour leave exploring Gotham. Shot on location, all the landmarks, circa 1949, are captured in Technicolor.

"I love this dirty town," says Burt Lancaster in the gritty, crackling *Sweet Smell of Success.* In this beautifully photographed black-and-white movie from 1957, Lancaster plays gossip columnist J. J. Hunsecker, and Tony Curtis is the groveling publicist Sidney Falco.

Despite his recent forays to London, Woody Allen is known as a quintessential New York filmmaker. I'm too big a fan to choose just one to recommend; among his best looks at neurotic New York are *Annie Hall* (1977), *Manhattan* (1979), and *Hannah and Her Sisters* (1986).

Another filmmaker identified with New York is Martin Scorsese, who has made many films in which New York plays a central role, including *Mean Streets* (1973), *After Hours* (1984), and *The Age of Innocence* (1993). But the one Scorsese film in which New York is a character, and not a very flattering one, is *Taxi Driver* (1976), about an alienated and psychotic cabbie; it's tough and bloody, with images of precleanup Times Square.

Two of the best recent glimpses of New York life beyond Manhattan are Spike Lee's *Do the Right Thing* (1989) and Wayne Wang's *Smoke* (1995). These Brooklyn-based award-winning films feature characters from a fabric that could have been woven only in New York.

The best history of New York on video is the Ric Burns documentary *New York: A Documentary Film* (1999). The 7-disc, 14-hour film, with a poignant, post-9/11 epilogue, is a must-see for anyone interested in the evolution of this great city.

New York City on podcast

Some great New York City–oriented podcasts are available. The **Bowery Boys** (http://theboweryboys.blogspot.com) is useful for learning more about New York City history; recent episodes covered Ellis Island and the city's marathon. For insight into Brooklyn's arts-and-crafts renaissance, **Hey Brooklyn** (www.heybrooklyn.com) features interviews with local creative types and small-business owners.

Classical music lovers should subscribe to award-winning podcasts of the **New York Philharmonic** (www.nyphil.org). Clubbers headed for **Pacha NYC** can tune into its DJ series (www.pachanyc.com/podcast), while those with eclectic tastes can stream **East Village Radio** (www.eastvillageradio.com) using its EVR Mobile application.

Leonard Lopate is a New York City institution: His show (www.wnyc.org/shows/lopate) features interesting conversations about culture and politics. **Science & the City** (www.nyas.org), presented by the New York Academy of Sciences, broadens your mind with discussions on everything from grizzly bears to chaos theory.

Chapter 3

Deciding When to Go

. . . .

In This Chapter
▶ Choosing the best time to visit New York City
▶ Keeping your cool or dressing warmly
▶ Flipping through the calendar of events

. . . .

*B*ecause New York offers such a wide variety of attractions and sights, people visit the city year-round, regardless of the weather. In addition to giving you the lowdown on New York life during each season, this chapter includes a calendar of events in case you'd like to plan your visit around a particular activity.

Revealing the Secrets of the Seasons

Summer or winter, rain or shine, great stuff is always going on in New York City, so I can't really tell you a "best" time to go. I can, however, give you some of the pros and cons, season by season.

▬ **Winter:** With the exception of the holiday weeks in December, winter is a great time to come to New York if you're searching for bargains. Hotel rates are at their lowest, tickets to top shows are attainable, and reservations at the best restaurants are manageable. But if your idea of a vacation doesn't involve walking around bundled in layers to insulate you from the face-breaking cold, then don't come during a New York winter.

▬ **Spring:** This is the wettest time of year, but, in between the showers, the trees and flowers in the park bloom and the temperatures are more pedestrian-friendly. As a result, the tourists make their way back to the city and hotel rates begin to rise, especially in late spring.

▬ **Summer:** The city is sticky, streets begin to radiate a pungent stench, and tempers can be testy. Why, then, would you come to New York in the summer? Because you've got so many free outdoor events, such as concerts and plays, to choose from. Restaurants are less crowded, museums and other attractions are more manageable, you can picnic in Central Park, and you can walk around in summer dresses or shorts and sandals.

> ✔ **Fall:** With mild temperatures and dry days, fall is New York's best weather season. But it's also the busiest time of year in the city. Everyone is back to school or work; street fairs continue through the early fall; and reservations at restaurants and hotels are tougher to snag. You'll also be hard-pressed to find bargains during this period.

To get an idea of the kind of temperatures and weather you may experience during a particular month in New York, take a look at Table 3-1.

Table 3-1	Average Temperature and Rainfall in New York City											
	Jan	Feb	Mar	Apr	May	June	July	Aug	Sep	Oct	Nov	Dec
Daily (°F/ temperature °C)	38/ 3	40/ 4.5	48/ 9	61/ 16	71/ 21.5	80/ 26.5	85/ 29.5	84/ 29	77/ 25	67/ 19.5	54/ 12	42/ 5.5
Days of rain	11	10	11	11	11	10	11	10	8	8	9	10

Marking Your Calendar: Year-Round New York

Regardless of when you plan to visit, you can find events that draw people by the millions. This section lists the highlights, month by month.

January

New York National Boat Show, Jacob K. Javits Convention Center. Expect to find a leviathan fleet of boats, and marine products from the world's top manufacturers. Call ☎ **212-984-7000,** or visit www.newyorkboat show.com or www.javitscenter.com. Third week in January.

Winter Restaurant Week. Participating fine-dining restaurants offer two- or three-course fixed-price meals. At lunch, the deal is $24.07 (because the city is open 24/7, get it?), while dinner is $35. For a list of restaurants and exact dates, go to www.nycgo.com/restaurantweek.

February

Chinese New Year, Chinatown. The famous dragon parade and fireworks highlight this two-week celebration. Visit the Better Chinatown Society Web site at www.betterchinatown.com. Early February.

Westminster Kennel Club Dog Show, Madison Square Garden. As many as 2,500 dogs and their owners compete for the top prize. For information, call ☎ **212-465-6741,** or visit www.westminsterkennelclub. org. Mid-February.

March/April

St. Patrick's Day Parade, Fifth Avenue between 50th and 86th streets. Make sure to wear green to this parade of 200,000 marchers showing their love of all things Irish. For information, call NYC & Company at ☎ **212-484-1222,** or visit http://nyc-st-patrick-day-parade.org or www.nycgo.com. March 17.

Ringling Brothers and Barnum & Bailey Circus, Madison Square Garden. Don't miss the parade from 12th Avenue and 34th Street to the Garden the morning before the show opens. For information, call ☎ **212-465-6741,** or visit www.ringling.com. Mid-March through early April.

New York International Auto Show, Javits Convention Center. This car show, featuring classics, futuristic models, and everything in between, is the largest in the United States. For information, call ☎ **800-282-3336,** or check www.autoshowny.com. Mid-April.

The Easter Parade, Fifth Avenue from 49th to 57th streets. Silly hats abound; expect to see a variety of animals sporting Easter bonnets. For information, call NYC & Company at ☎ **212-484-1222,** or check www.nycgo.com. Easter Sunday.

May

The Great Saunter. Join hundreds of ramblers for a 32-mile hike around the rim of Manhattan, beginning and ending near the South Street Seaport. Pre-registration is required. For information, visit the Shorewalkers Web site at www.shorewalkers.org. First Saturday in May.

Ninth Avenue International Food Festival, 42nd to 57th streets. The food isn't quite as exciting as it used to be, but this 15-block fair is still worthwhile if you're in town. For information, call the Ninth Avenue Association at ☎ **212-581-7217,** or visit www.ninthavenuefood festival.com. Mid-May.

Fleet Week. A plethora of ships and thousands of crew members visit New York during Fleet Week; activities include flyovers, ship tours, 21-gun salutes, and more. Last week in May.

June

River to River Festival. Free concerts along the river, parks, and public spaces of Battery Park City. Go to www.rivertorivernyc.com for information. June through August.

SummerStage, Central Park at 72nd Street. Free afternoon concerts feature a wide range of contemporary groups and often some big-name performers. For information, call ☎ **212-360-2777,** or visit www.summerstage.org. Concerts run June through August.

The Puerto Rican Day Parade and **LGBT Pride Week and March,** Fifth Avenue. The Puerto Rican Day Parade (www.nationalpuertorican dayparade.org) is in mid-June while the Pride March (www.nyc pride.org) is the last Sunday in June.

Museum Mile Festival, Fifth Avenue from 82nd to 105th streets. Free admission to nine museums along the mile-long stretch of Fifth Avenue, plus live music and street performers, makes this a mile of fun. For information, call ☎ **212-606-2296,** or visit www.museummilefestival.org. Mid-June.

Restaurant Week. Participating restaurants around the city offer two- or three-course lunches for $24.07 and $35 for dinner. (See the entry for "Winter Restaurant Week" under Jan events.) Third week in June.

July

Fourth of July fireworks. Get to as high a vantage point as you can to watch any of the several fireworks shows that light up the skyline. Usually the fireworks are set off from barges in the East River. For information, call ☎ **212-494-4495,** or check www.macys.com/fireworks. July 4.

Midsummer Night's Swing, Josie Robertson Plaza at Lincoln Center. Dance under the summer skies to live bands playing everything from swing to disco. For information, call ☎ **212-875-5456,** or check www.lincolncenter.org. July.

Mostly Mozart, Avery Fisher Hall. An important appointment for classical music fans. For information, call ☎ **212-875-5456,** or check www.lincolncenter.org. July and August.

Lincoln Center Festival, Lincoln Center. Enthusiasts of dance, opera, ballet, and theater enjoy this festival. For information, call ☎ **212-875-5456,** or check www.lincolncenter.org. July and August.

Shakespeare in the Park, Central Park. The Public Theater stages a free play by the Bard each summer at the Delacorte Theater in Central Park. Shows often feature top stars. For information, call ☎ **212-539-8500,** or visit www.publictheater.org. July and August.

August

Harlem Week, Harlem and other public areas around the city, including City Hall, Gracie Mansion, Columbia University, and the Schomburg Center. This weeklong celebration features theater, symposia, art, sport, and the famous Harlem Jazz and Music Festival. For information, call ☎ **212-862-7200,** or visit www.harlemdiscover.com/harlemweek. August.

Lincoln Center Out of Doors, Damrosch Park, Lincoln Center. Treat yourself to free concerts and dance performances. For information, call ☎ **212-875-5456,** or check www.lincolncenter.org. August.

U.S. Open Tennis Championships, Flushing Meadows, Queens. The world's best tennis players gather for the final Grand Slam tournament of the year. Visit www.usopen.org for information. Late August through mid-September.

September

West Indian–American Day Carnival and Parade. This annual Brooklyn event is New York's largest and best street celebration. Come for the extravagant costumes, pulsating rhythms (soca, calypso, reggae), bright colors, folklore, food, and two million hip-shaking revelers. The route usually runs along Eastern Parkway, from Utica Avenue to Grand Army Plaza (at the gateway to Prospect Park). Visit www.wiadca.com for information. Labor Day.

New York Film Festival, sponsored by the Film Society of Lincoln Center. This two-week festival has seen many important premieres over the years. Get your tickets in advance. For information, call ☎ **212-875-5600,** or check www.filmlinc.com. September and October.

October

Greenwich Village Halloween Parade, West Village/Chelsea. Not your average group of trick-or-treaters, this parade — the nation's largest public Halloween parade — features outrageous costumes and people (soon to be outnumbered by boring floats advertising radio stations and the like). Check www.halloween-nyc.com for information. October 31.

Next Wave Festival, Brooklyn Academy of Music. Enjoy experimental dance, theater, and music. For information, call ☎ **718-636-4100,** or visit www.bam.org. October through December.

November

New York City Marathon, ends in Central Park. Join this race, which runs through all five boroughs, or cheer on the thousands of competitors. (Shout their names whenever possible; one marathoner told me that it provides a tremendous boost.) For exact route and information, call ☎ **212-423-2249,** or visit www.nycmarathon.org. First Sunday in November.

Big Apple Circus, Lincoln Center. My 4-year-old still raves about the acrobats, but you don't have to be a kid to enjoy this fabulous spectacle. Call ☎ **800-922-3772,** or visit www.bigapplecircus.org. November through January.

Macy's Thanksgiving Day Parade, Central Park West/Broadway. Watching the balloon inflation the day before (3–10 p.m., along 77th Street and 81st Street, between Central Park West and Columbus Avenue) is even more fun than the parade itself. For information, call NYC & Company at ☎ **212-484-1222,** or check www.macys.com. Thanksgiving Day, the fourth Thursday in November.

December

Rockefeller Center Christmas Tree Lighting, Rockefeller Center. Join thousands of others to watch the lighting of the huge tree, which remains on display through the New Year. For information, call ☎ **212-588-8601,** or visit www.rockefellercenter.com.

New Year's Eve, Times Square. Okay, if freezing your buns off among thousands of intoxicated people from everywhere (except New York) is what you've wanted to do all your life, then this is the place for you. You won't find many New Yorkers here. But arrive early, or you'll get a better view of the ball dropping from the television in your hotel room. For information, call ☎ **212-768-1560,** or check www.timessquarenyc.org. December 31.

Part II
Planning Your Trip to New York City

The 5th Wave   By Rich Tennant

You know, getting us to the front door of the Empire State Building would have been quite sufficient, driver.

In this part . . .

I suggest ways to get the best value out of your travel budget and prepare you for how much things cost in New York City (a lot!). I also discuss your options for getting to New York City, whether you're flying, driving, or taking the train.

I cover planning resources that can be a big help for families, seniors, travelers with disabilities, GLBT travelers — and romantics hoping to tie the knot.

Finally, I go over the important details, from renting a car (which I suggest you *don't* do) to travel insurance to staying in touch.

Chapter 4

Managing Your Money

. . . .

In This Chapter

▶ Deciding how to spend your money
▶ Cutting the costs, but not the fun
▶ Getting, carrying, and keeping your funds

. . . .

*N*ew York has a way of devouring your cash. I walk a mere 5 blocks and somehow wind up $20 lighter on a regular basis. With almost as many ATMs (and their accompanying fees) as there are things to spend money on, the Big Apple can be a budget-buster. But as long as you set realistic goals for your spending, and plan ahead, you don't have to worry about mortgaging the house to finance your trip. In this chapter, I share ways you can get the best value for your dollar without going broke.

Planning Your Budget

New York has a reputation as one of the most expensive cities to live in, not only in the United States but in the world. So dismiss any notions that you can get off entirely on the very cheap here — one way or another, it will cost you. But that reputation is also fairly exaggerated; you can spend a week in the Big Apple for somewhat less than a king's ransom. In fact, you can make your trip to New York wallet-friendly in lots of ways. You just have to do a bit of groundwork. Frommer's lists exact prices in the local currency. The currency conversions quoted in Table 4-1 were correct at press time. However, rates fluctuate, so, before departing, consult a currency exchange website such as www.oanda. com/convert/classic to check up-to-the-minute rates.

Table 4-1	The Value of the US Dollar vs. Other Popular Currencies			
US$	*Can$*	*UK£*	*Euro (€)*	*Aus$*
$1	C$1.03	£0.66	0.79€	A$1.13

Hotel

The biggest challenge in terms of saving money in New York is finding an affordable place to stay. As I discuss in Chapter 9, a decent hotel room in New York can run at least $250 per night, plus a hotel tax of 14.75 percent, plus an additional $3.50 per night. This expense is the biggest drain on your budget, unless you want to share a bathroom or explore a youth hostel. So, look for bargains, but be realistic: A hotel room is going to cost you some dough.

Transportation

First and foremost, pack comfortable walking shoes — walking is the preferred mode of transportation in New York. Next, invest in a MetroCard (the coin of the realm for public transportation). One ride on the subway costs $2.25 (although you can purchase an Unlimited Ride MetroCard — more about that in Chapter 8), and if you transfer to a bus, the transfer is free with MetroCard. The New York subway system is a marvel. At times, it's overcrowded (avoid riding it at rush hour), and in the summer, the stations can be extremely toasty (even though all the trains are air-conditioned), but no other means of transit can get you to your destination within the city cheaper and faster. See Chapter 8 for more information about getting around New York.

Buses, which accept both MetroCards and exact change, are also an inexpensive alternative to the subway and a nice way to see the city. But with many stops and the regular heavy traffic in Manhattan, they can be extremely slow.

Yellow cabs are the city's other great resource. They're usually plentiful — they say approximately 13,000 cabs are on the streets at any given time — and you can usually get a cab without too much hassle (except on rainy days and at the pre-theater hour). Cabs offer relatively affordable rides, particularly if you're in a group of up to three people. They're also the most convenient way to get to parts of town where the subway doesn't go. You pay $2.50 as soon as the cabbie turns on the meter, plus 40¢ per ⅕ mile, or 30¢ per minute when stuck in traffic. You also pay a 50¢ nighttime surcharge and a $1 surcharge Monday through Friday from 4 to 8 p.m.

As signs all over Manhattan say: Don't even *think* about parking here. If you're considering renting a car in New York or using your own car for transportation around town, think again. (You can find more on parking and driving in Chapter 7.)

Food

You can get every conceivable kind of food in New York at just about any price. We all know about those three- and four-star restaurants that may cost more than two nights at a New York hotel, but not as well-known are those hidden gems (and there are plenty) that cost you less than $40 for an excellent meal. If you want to save even more, you can always get pizza, bagels, hot dogs, falafel, and other (surprisingly) good street food to satisfy your hunger pangs. Chapter 10 offers tips on selecting food that fits both your appetite and your budget.

Sights

Entrance fees vary from attraction to attraction. If you're planning on visiting a lot of them, consider buying a CityPass, which gets you reduced admission to six top attractions for $79 (a savings of 45 percent off what you would pay for separate admissions). See Chapter 11 for more information about places and things to see in the city.

Some attractions request a "suggested contribution" for admission, which means that you can pay whatever you want. But be reasonable — if you offer up a couple of dollars to get a family of six into the Metropolitan Museum, you're likely to get a sneer with your tickets. Some museums also offer a free admission night, which, for obvious reasons, is usually the busiest night of the week. See the individual museum listings in Chapter 11 for details.

Shopping

When it comes to shopping, only you know how much you want to spend. You can find bargains in New York on electronics and clothes (especially now that clothes under $110 per item are tax-free purchases in the city). But unless you happen upon a sample sale or another sale, top designer duds are going to cost you. (Of course, you can buy designer knockoffs on the street, but the quality is somewhat less than the real thing, to say the least.) See Chapter 12 for the best places offering the best gear.

Nightlife

Again, how much you spend on nightlife entertainment depends on what you're interested in doing. At the top end are Broadway shows, which average $100 and up for the best seats, and supper clubs where you can see a cabaret act for around $60, not including drinks. If you just want to people-watch at a wine bar or pub around happy hour, you'll be hard-pressed to spend more than $20. See Chapters 14 and 15 to get an idea of your many options.

Typical day-to-day purchases

Table 4-2 gives you an idea of what you can expect to pay for typical purchases in New York.

Table 4-2	What Things Cost in New York City
Item	*Price*
Subway or city bus ride	$2.25
Bottle of water	$1.25
Slice of pizza	$2.25–$3.50
Hot dog from a street vendor	$1–$3
Coffee (a real cuppa joe at a diner)	80¢–$1.50
New York Yankees baseball cap from street vendor	$5–$10
Ticket to top of the Empire State Building	$19
Cover charge at a Village jazz club (excluding 1- or 2-drink minimum)	$20–$30
Boat ride around Manhattan on the Circle Line, adult	$35
Ride on the Staten Island Ferry	Free
Admission to MoMA, adult	$20
Club signature cocktail	$12–$18
Three-course prix-fixe dinner at Daniel	$105

Taxes

Regular sales tax is 8.875 percent — not a small amount, especially if you buy expensive stuff. Remember that advertised prices, from restaurants to hotels to most shops, almost always exclude sales tax. The prices in this book also do not include sales tax.

There is no tax on clothing and footwear items under $110 in New York City.

Hotel taxes add up to 14.75 percent. If you think this seems ridiculous, be glad that you didn't plan your trip a decade or so ago, when the hotel tax was 19.25 percent! (Occasionally, things in New York do get cheaper.) A room charge of $3.50 per night is also added to your bill. Remember to ask whether the price quoted to you includes these fees, both for travel packages and hotel rooms; they can make quite a difference.

Tips

Bottom line: Expect to tip for every service you get in New York. Use the following guidelines when tipping:

✔ **Waiters:** Simply double the tax on your bill and round up to the nearest dollar (which is a tip of about 17 percent). Often, restaurants add the tip (15 percent to 20 percent) to the bill automatically for parties of six or more.

✔ **Bartenders:** If you're just drinking at a bar, 10 percent to 15 percent takes care of it.

✔ **Taxi drivers:** No matter how bumpy the ride, tip 15 percent.

✔ **Everybody else:** Bellhops get $1 or $2 per bag; maids get $1 per day; coat-check people get $1 per garment; and automobile valets get $1.

Cutting Costs, but Not the Fun

You can cut costs in plenty of ways — some little and some big. Note the Bargain Alert icons scattered throughout this book, which offer hints on ways to trim the fat from your budget. While you're planning a trip, keep a few things in mind:

✔ **Travel at off-peak times.** Although New York doesn't have a real off season, the prices at some hotels during nonpeak times are half of what they are during the peak travel seasons. (See Chapter 3 for a discussion of the New York travel seasons.)

✔ **Try a package tour.** For many destinations, you can book airfare, hotel, ground transportation, and even some sightseeing just by making one call to a travel agent or packager, for a price much less than if you put the trip together yourself. (See Chapter 5 for more on package tours.)

✔ **Reserve a room with a refrigerator and coffeemaker.** You don't have to slave over a hot stove to cut a few costs; several hotels have minifridges and coffeemakers. Buying supplies for breakfast will save you money.

✔ **Always ask for discount rates.** Membership in AAA, frequent-flier plans, trade unions, AARP, or other groups may qualify you for savings on car rentals, plane tickets, hotel rooms, and even meals. Ask about everything; you may be pleasantly surprised.

✔ **Ask if your kids can stay in the room with you.** A room with two double beds usually doesn't cost any more than one with a queen-size bed. And many hotels won't charge you the additional-person rate if the additional person is pint-size and related to you. Even if you have to pay $20 or $30 extra for a rollaway bed, you'll save hundreds by not taking two rooms.

✔ **Try expensive restaurants at lunch rather than at dinner.** Lunch tabs are usually a fraction of what dinner costs at most restaurants, and the menu often offers many of the same specialties, in smaller portions. Many of New York's best restaurants participate in

Restaurant Week in January and June — $24 and some change nets you a two- or three-course lunch — and some restaurants extend this fixed-price bargain throughout the summer or even year-round.

✔ **Don't use the hotel phone.** Some hotels in the moderate-to-expensive range now offer free local calls from rooms, but don't count on it. Instead, bring your cellphone and use it. (See Chapter 7 for more info.)

✔ **Stay away from the minibar.** I know it's tempting, but if you want a snack, pick one up at the closest deli. Open that minibar and crack open that can of peanuts and then a beer, and before long you've spent $20 on a snack.

✔ **Use the buses and subways.** Taxis get expensive quickly, especially in gridlock traffic. (See Chapter 8 for hints on navigating the public-transit system.)

✔ **Buy a daily or weekly MetroCard pass.** (See Chapter 8 for more info about the MetroCard and its budget-saving powers.)

✔ **Walk a lot.** A good pair of walking shoes can save lots of money in taxis and other transportation. Plus, you get to know your surroundings more fully because you explore at a slower pace.

✔ **Seek out small, local restaurants.** Often, not only is the food less expensive, but it's also better than some of what you get at the big-name tourist traps. (Turn to Chapter 10 for suggestions.)

✔ **Visit museums that have a "suggested donation," or go on the nights that are free.** (See Chapter 11 to find out which days and nights are free at my favorite museums.)

✔ **Buy your Broadway and Off-Broadway tickets at TKTS.** You can get same-day performances for some of Broadway's best shows at the TKTS booth in Times Square or downtown at the South Street Seaport. (See Chapter 14 for more info.)

✔ **Buy your drinks at happy hour.** Many bars have happy hours, usually between the hours of 4 and 8 p.m. or thereabouts, when you can save considerably on the price of a drink.

Handling Money

New York is one of the safest cities in the country, but that doesn't mean you should go around carrying wads of cash (although you should always make sure you have at least $20 in taxi fare on hand). In this section, I tell you the best ways to access money in New York.

You're the best judge of how much cash you feel comfortable carrying or what alternative form of currency is your favorite. You're probably going to be moving around more and incurring more expenses than you generally do (unless you happen to eat out every meal when you're at home), and you may let your mind slip into vacation gear and not be as vigilant about your safety as when you're in work mode. But, those factors aside, the only type of payment that isn't quite as easy to use when you're away from home is your personal checkbook — some places don't accept out-of-town checks.

Using ATMs and carrying cash

The easiest and best way to get cash away from home is from an ATM, sometimes referred to as a *cash machine* or *cashpoint*. The **Cirrus** (☎ **800-627-8372;** www.mastercard.com) and **PLUS** (☎ **800-847-2911;** www.visa.com) networks span the globe; look at the back of your bank card to see which network you're on, and then call or check online for ATM locations at your destination. Be sure to find out your daily withdrawal limit before you depart. Also, keep in mind that many banks impose a fee every time your card is used at a different bank's ATM, and that fee can be higher for international transactions (up to $5 or more) than for domestic ones. On top of this, the bank from which you withdraw cash may charge its own fee. To compare banks' ATM fees within the U.S., use www.bankrate.com. For international withdrawal fees, ask your bank.

If your own bank doesn't have branches in New York, call to find out if it's affiliated with a bank in the city. Doing so may save you the extra charge of $2 or more for using a nonaffiliated ATM.

ATMs are everywhere in New York, including in banks, supermarkets, pharmacies, and delis. You can get cash at any hour of the day or night, but you pay a higher surcharge at the non-bank-affiliated ATMs. Some clubs (where there's no reentry after you leave) have up to a $5 surcharge, so make sure you have enough cash on you when you go in.

Charging ahead with credit cards

Credit cards are a safe way to carry money; they also provide a convenient record of all your expenses, and they generally offer relatively good exchange rates. You can also withdraw cash advances at banks or ATMs, if you know your PIN. If you've forgotten yours, or didn't even know you had one, call the number on the back of your credit card and ask the bank to send it to you. It usually takes five to seven business days.

Some credit cards let you get cash advances at ATMs. However, interest rates for cash advances are often significantly higher than rates for credit card purchases. More important, you start paying interest on the advance the moment you receive the cash.

Toting traveler's checks

These days, traveler's checks are less necessary because most cities have 24-hour ATMs that allow you to withdraw small amounts of cash as needed. However, keep in mind that you'll likely be charged an ATM withdrawal fee if the bank is not your own, so if you're withdrawing money every day, you may be better off with traveler's checks — provided you don't mind showing identification every time you want to cash one.

You can get traveler's checks at almost any bank. **American Express** offers denominations of $20, $50, $100, $500, and (for cardholders only) $1,000. You'll pay a service charge ranging from 1 percent to 4 percent. You can also get American Express traveler's checks over the phone by calling ☎ **800-807-6233** (or ☎ **800-221-7282,** which accepts collect calls, offers service in several foreign languages, and exempts Amex gold and platinum cardholders from the 1 percent fee).

Visa (☎ **800-732-1322**) and **MasterCard** (☎ **800-223-9920**) also offer traveler's checks.

If you choose to carry traveler's checks, be sure to keep a record of their serial numbers separate from your checks in case they're stolen or lost. You'll get a refund faster if you know the numbers.

Dealing with a lost or stolen wallet

As my brother discovered during his first trip to New York to visit me, losing your wallet can put a serious damper on your trip. The good Samaritan who found the wallet mailed it to my brother's home two weeks later with everything inside — except his cash, of course. That was a best-case scenario, so you should take some precautionary steps as soon as you discover your wallet has been lost or stolen.

Contact all your credit-card companies, and file a report at the nearest police precinct. Your credit-card company or insurer may require a police-report number. Most credit-card companies have an emergency toll-free number to call, if your card is lost or stolen; they may be able to wire you a cash advance or deliver an emergency credit card in a day or two. Call the following emergency numbers in the United States:

- **American Express:** ☎ **800-221-7282** (for cardholders and traveler's check holders)
- **MasterCard:** ☎ **800-307-7309** or 636-722-7111
- **Visa:** ☎ **800-847-2911** or 410-581-9994

For other credit cards, call toll-free directory assistance at ☎ **800-555-1212.**

If you need emergency cash over the weekend when all banks and American Express offices are closed, you can have money wired to you via **Western Union** (☎ **800-325-6000;** www.westernunion.com).

Identity theft and fraud are potential complications of losing your wallet, especially if you've lost your driver's license along with your cash and credit cards. Notify the major credit-reporting bureaus immediately; placing a fraud alert on your records may protect you against liability for criminal activity. The three major U.S. credit-reporting agencies are **Equifax** (☎ **800-766-0008;** www.equifax.com), **Experian** (☎ **888-397-3742;** www.experian.com), and **TransUnion** (☎ **800-680-7289;** www.transunion.com). Finally, if you've lost all forms of photo ID, call your airline and explain the situation; you may be allowed to board the plane if you have a copy of your passport or birth certificate and a copy of the police report you've filed.

Chapter 5

Getting to New York City

In This Chapter
▶ Taking a plane, train, or automobile
▶ Choosing between a package and escorted tour
▶ Finding the best package or tour for your needs

*Y*ou can get to New York in a variety of ways, depending on where
you're starting from. Choosing the best mode of transit for your
needs and preference depends on distance, convenience, and cost. Are
you willing to arrange your own transportation? Or would you prefer to
have someone else make all the arrangements (such as a travel agent or
tour company)? When you arrive, do you want to explore the city by
yourself? Or do you want the company of a group? In this chapter, I give
you the pros and cons of each option.

Choosing the Airport

Three major airports serve New York City: **LaGuardia, JFK** (also known
as Kennedy or John F. Kennedy), and **Newark Liberty.** The city is easily
accessible from all three (see Chapter 8 for details on transportation
between each airport and the city), although choosing to arrive at one
or another may affect the price of your ticket. If you're looking for the
best price, be flexible and accept a flight to any of these three airports.
However, if saving money isn't your first priority, you may want to consider these differences:

   ✔ **LaGuardia Airport,** in northern Queens, is the closest to Manhattan
   (therefore, the cab rides are cheaper and get you to and from the airport faster). It's also the smallest of the three. Although the number
   of flights allowed to arrive here has increased in recent years, the
   choices are more limited than at the other two airports. This is
   primarily a domestic — not an international — airport. Also, the
   increased number of flights has led to an increase in delays.

   ✔ **John F. Kennedy International Airport (JFK),** in southern Queens,
   is the official international airport for New York City. Its international status makes it the largest and busiest airport in the metro
   area in terms of the volume of arrivals and departures (although

Newark rivals it). Also, of the three major airports, it's the farthest from the center of Manhattan.

✔ **Newark International Airport** is in New Jersey, but it's closer to Manhattan than JFK is. It's especially convenient if you're staying on the West Side or downtown. However, in my experience, delays (and weather-related cancellations) are even more frequent here than at LaGuardia and Kennedy.

 Two other airports in outlying areas service New York City: Westchester Airport in White Plains, New York (25 miles north of the city), and MacArthur Airport in Islip, Long Island (50 miles east of the city). MacArthur is a major hub for budget carrier Southwest. However, the inconvenience and high cost of getting into the city from these out-of-the-way airports far outweigh the money you save by using them.

Flying to New York

If you're in the Northeast or mid-Atlantic, flying may be only one of your options for getting here (see the later sections on arriving by car, train, and bus). If, however, you're coming from farther away, then flying is your best bet. You have a lot of options when it comes to airlines, number of flights, and price range (from no-frills to first-class).

Finding out which airlines fly there

Almost every major domestic carrier serves a New York–area airport; most serve two or all three. The major ones include

✔ **American** (☎ 800-433-7300; www.aa.com)

✔ **Continental** (☎ 800-525-0280; www.continental.com)

✔ **Delta** (☎ 800-221-1212; www.delta.com)

✔ **JetBlue** (☎ 800-538-2583; www.jetblue.com)

✔ **Southwest** (☎ 800-435-9792; www.southwest.com)

✔ **United** (☎ 800-241-6522; www.united.com)

✔ **US Airways** (☎ 800-428-4322; www.usairways.com)

In addition to the domestic airlines, many international carriers serve JFK and Newark Liberty. Among the ones who offer the most frequent service are

✔ **Aer Lingus** (☎ 800-474-7424 or 01-886-8888; www.aerlingus.ie)

✔ **Air Canada** (☎ 888-247-2262; www.aircanada.ca)

✔ **Air New Zealand** (☎ 0800-737-767; www.airnewzealand.co.nz)

✔ **British Airways** (☎ 0845-77-333-77; www.britishairways.com)

✔ **Qantas** (☎ **800-227-4500** or 612-9691-3636; www.qantas.com.au)

 ✔ **Virgin Atlantic** (☎ **0870-380-2007;** www.virgin-atlantic.com)

Southwest Airlines (☎ **800-435-9792;** www.southwest.com) frequently offers cheap fares to New York from destinations across the country, connecting through Chicago's Midway Airport or Baltimore.

Getting the best deal on your airfare

Competition among the U.S. airlines is unlike that of any other industry. Every airline offers virtually the same product (basically, a coach seat is a coach seat is a . . .), yet prices can vary by hundreds of dollars.

Business travelers who need the flexibility to buy their tickets at the last minute and change their itineraries at a moment's notice — and who want to get home before the weekend — pay (or at least their companies pay) the premium rate, known as the *full fare.* But if you can book your ticket far in advance, stay over Saturday night, and travel midweek (Tues, Wed, or Thurs), you can qualify for the least expensive price — usually a fraction of the full fare. On most flights, even the shortest hops within the United States, the full fare can be $1,000 or more, but a 7- or 14-day advance-purchase ticket may cost less than half of that amount. Obviously, planning ahead pays.

Watch airline Web sites for **promotional specials** or **fare wars,** when airlines lower prices on their most popular routes. These sales are becoming more difficult to predict, but they tend to take place in seasons of low travel volume — January through March in New York. You almost never see a sale around the peak vacation months of July and August, or around Thanksgiving or Christmas, when many people fly, regardless of the fare they have to pay.

Also keep an eye on price fluctuations and deals at Web sites such as **airfarewatchdog** (www.airfarewatchdog.com).

Frequent-flier membership doesn't cost a cent, but it does entitle you to better seats; faster response to phone inquiries; and prompter service if your luggage is lost or stolen, if your flight is canceled or delayed, or if you want to change your seat. And you don't have to fly to earn points; **frequent-flier credit cards** can earn you thousands of miles for doing your everyday shopping. With more than 70 mileage awards programs on the market, consumers have never had more options. Investigate the program details of your favorite airlines before you sink points into any one. Consider which airlines have hubs in the airport nearest you and, of those carriers, which have the most advantageous alliances, given your most common routes. To play the frequent-flier game to your best advantage, consult Randy Petersen's **Inside Flyer** (www.insideflyer.com). Petersen and friends review all the programs in detail and post regular updates on changes in policies and trends.

Booking your flight online

Search the Internet for cheap fares. The most popular online travel agencies are **Travelocity** (www.travelocity.com), **Expedia** (www.expedia.com), and **Orbitz** (www.orbitz.com). In the U.K., go to **TravelSupermarket** (☎ 0845-345-5708; www.travelsupermarket.com), a flight search engine that offers flight comparisons for the budget airlines whose seats often end up in bucket-shop sales. Other Web sites for booking airline tickets online include **Cheapflights** (www.cheapflights.com), **SmarterTravel.com, Priceline** (www.priceline.com), and **Opodo** (www.opodo.co.uk). Meta search sites (which find and then direct you to airline and hotel Web sites for booking) include **SideStep** (www.sidestep.com) and **Kayak** (www.kayak.com) — the latter includes fares for budget carriers like JetBlue and Spirit, as well as for the major airlines. A great source for last-minute flights and getaways is **lastminute.com**. In addition, most **airlines** offer online-only fares that even their phone agents know nothing about.

Driving to New York City

If you're visiting from the Northeast or mid-Atlantic, certainly consider driving your car; but just as certainly, park it after you get here.

Some long-term outdoor lots charge less than $35 a day for parking. You can find them along the West Side Highway and in the 50s west of Eighth Avenue. Also, ask if your hotel has an arrangement with a nearby parking lot for a discount on its daily rate. Most do, but you may not have in-and-out privileges.

You also can park near a commuter train station in New York, New Jersey, or Connecticut and take the commuter rail into the city. You still have to find parking near the station, but it's somewhat cheaper than parking in Manhattan. For information about PATH train stations in New Jersey, contact the Port Authority of New York & New Jersey (☎ 800-234-7284; www.panynj.gov). The Metropolitan Transportation Authority (MTA) New York City Transit (www.mta.info) operates not only the city's subways and buses but also the Long Island Rail Road (☎ 718-217-5477), which serves Long Island, and the Metro-North Railroad (☎ 212-532-4900), which serves upstate New York and Connecticut.

Plan your arrival to avoid rush hours. Traffic jams can be dreadful at the points of connection between the island of Manhattan and the surrounding metropolitan area (where all the airports are located). At rush hour, tunnels and bridges clog up. And don't think that you can get around the traffic by "reverse commuting" — coming into the city when everybody is leaving — because it doesn't work that way. Even if most of the traffic is outbound at around 5 p.m., a significant number of people commute back to Manhattan and the number of inbound lanes is reduced to help the traffic that's leaving get out more quickly.

Try to arrive well outside the peak hours of 8 to 10 a.m. and 4:30 to 7 p.m. The weekend rush is the worst. In summer, outbound traffic starts as early as 2 p.m. on Fridays, and inbound traffic on Sunday evenings is absolutely nightmarish.

Arriving by Other Means

If you don't want to fly or drive, many modes of land-based transportation service New York City.

By train

New York is well served by **Amtrak** (☎ **800-872-7245;** www.amtrak. com). The most convenient route to New York City is the Northeast Corridor line, which runs between Washington, D.C., and Boston. If you're coming from anywhere on this line, in my opinion taking the train is a lot smarter and *far* more enjoyable than flying. The ride is likely to be shorter and less stressful: You don't have to commute to and from the airport, you don't need to be there two hours in advance to check in and struggle through security, and there's no waiting on the other end to collect your luggage. The train is also more comfortable — no dry airplane air, more freedom to stroll along the aisle, and more room to work or sleep; some trains have a quiet car where chatter isn't allowed (shhh!). Be sure to book in advance.

The train isn't necessarily cheaper. Prices on Amtrak remain high, but there are specials and package tours worth looking into. Call or check the Web site for information about special rates.

Amtrak trains arrive at Penn Station, on the West Side, a hub for land transportation in the heart of the city. The average round-trip fare to New York on regular trains is around $126 from Boston (a 4½-hour journey), $168 and up from Chicago (a 16- to 18-hour trip, usually overnight), and $142 from Washington, D.C. (about 3½ hours). Note that these are coach fares, which means (except from Chicago) that seats are unreserved and not guaranteed — if all the seats are full, you have to stand. You can reserve a seat in the pricier business-class and first-class wagons if you don't want to risk standing.

Amtrak's **Acela** (www.amtrak.com) express train cuts down on travel time, though you pay for it. For example, the New York–Boston run costs about $220 round-trip. Travel on Acela between Washington, D.C., and New York takes about 2 hours and 45 minutes; between Boston and New York about 3 hours. Check the schedules, however; the additional cost may not be worth shaving 15 or 20 minutes off your trip.

By bus

The bus can be a reasonable option for getting to New York City if you're coming from as far north as Boston, as far south as Washington, D.C., and as far west as the middle of Pennsylvania. Offering express bus service from several northeastern and mid-Atlantic cities, **Peter Pan Bus Lines** (☎ 800-343-9999; www.peterpanbus.com) features wide-body coaches equipped with viewing screens (which show movies during the trip), climate control, and overhead storage compartments. Buses arrive at the Port Authority Bus Terminal at 42nd Street and Eighth Avenue, connecting to subways, city buses, and taxis.

For other regional bus companies (there are more than 20) that offer runs to New York City, check with the Port Authority (☎ 212-564-8484; www.panynj.gov).

The bus is probably the cheapest way to reach New York from most cities in the Northeast (with discount fares available for seniors, students, and children, and occasional bargain-basement special sales). Travel time from Washington, D.C., to New York City is between three and four hours; from Philadelphia, usually less than two hours.

Joining an Escorted Tour

You may be one of the many people who love escorted tours. The tour company takes care of all the details and tells you what to expect at each leg of your journey. You know your costs upfront and don't get many surprises. Escorted tours can take you to the maximum number of sights in the minimum amount of time with the least amount of hassle.

If you decide to go with an escorted tour, I strongly recommend purchasing travel insurance, especially if the tour operator asks you to pay upfront. But don't buy insurance from the tour operator! If the tour operator doesn't fulfill its obligation to provide you with the vacation you paid for, don't think that it will fulfill its insurance obligations either. Get travel insurance through an independent agency. (I tell you more about the ins and outs of travel insurance in Chapter 7.)

Depending on your recreational passions, I recommend one of the following tour companies:

- ✔ **Globus** (☎ 866-755-8581; www.globusandcosmos.com) sometimes runs first-class independent tours of New York (often as part of a larger, multicity itinerary). A "host" is available to answer questions but doesn't take you around the city, except on a designated day. The package includes everything — hotel, local transportation, and even tips. Check the Web site for the most up-to-date tour offerings.

- ✔ **Maupintour** (☎ 800-255-4266 or 913-843-1211; www.maupintour.com) specializes in lavish "grand tours." These escorted tours often feature Broadway shows and an excursion to the Hudson Valley. The cost of a tour may run about $2,000 per person, depending on the options you select, plus airfare.

For more information on escorted general-interest tours, including questions to ask before booking your trip, see www.frommers.com/planning.

Choosing a Package Tour

For lots of destinations (including New York City, with its expensive hotel rooms), package tours can be a smart way to go. In many cases, a package tour that includes airfare, hotel, and ground transportation costs less than the hotel alone when you book yourself. That's because packages are sold in bulk to tour operators, who resell them to the public. It's kind of like buying your vacation at a buy-in-bulk store — except the tour operator is the one who buys the 1,000-count box of garbage bags and resells them 10 at a time at a cost that undercuts the local supermarket.

Package tours can vary in terms of what's provided. Some offer a better class of hotels than others; others provide the same hotels for lower prices. Some book flights on scheduled airlines; others sell charters. In some packages, your choice of accommodations and travel days may be limited. Some let you choose between escorted and independent vacations; others allow you to add on excursions or escorted day trips (also at discounted prices) without booking an entirely escorted tour.

Here are two options to consider:

- ✔ **New York City Vacation Packages** (☎ **888-692-8701;** www.nycvp.com) offers a wide variety of packages year-round, some of them at unbeatable prices. Call, check the Web site, or e-mail info@nycvp.com for information.

- ✔ **NYC & Company** (☎ **800-692-4843** or 800-692-8474; www.nycgo.com), the city's visitor's bureau, offers special packages, usually during the slower first months of the year.

For more information on package tours and for tips on booking your trip, see www.frommers.com/planning.

Chapter 6

Catering to Special Travel Needs or Interests

In This Chapter
▶ Bringing the kids to New York City
▶ Using your seniority
▶ Planning an accessible stay
▶ Finding the gay-friendliest places
▶ Getting hitched

*N*ew York may seem intimidating, but if you can get over your initial awe, you may find that things are easier for people with special needs here than in other cities. New York offers so many things to see and do that anybody can find something suitable, and specialized services are available for just about everything and everyone.

Traveling with the Brood: Advice for Families

With all due respect to Disney World, New York is the true kid capital of the United States. (And a focus group of three — my nieces and nephew, who live in the House of The Mouse — support me on this.) As long as you come prepared, you can have a safe, enjoyable, enriching experience that the kids will long remember.

You can find good family-oriented New York vacation advice on the Internet at sites such as **Family Travel Forum** (www.familytravel forum.com), a comprehensive site that offers customized trip planning; **Family Travel Network** (www.familytravelnetwork.com), an award-winning site that offers travel features, deals, and tips; and **Family Travel Files** (www.thefamilytravelfiles.com), which offers an online magazine and a directory of off-the-beaten-path tours and tour operators for families.

Research all the places your family plans to visit; see Chapter 8 for descriptions of New York's neighborhoods.

Caregivers and children should go over safety issues before leaving (see the Quick Concierge); be sure to create a plan so that children know what to do if they get lost.

Finding a family-friendly hotel

Finding a hotel that caters to children may be your biggest concern. But you're in luck: Some New York hotels market special services just for families, including children's amenities and programs. Be sure to ask about these services when you call for a reservation.

To keep costs reasonable, look for a hotel that lets children stay in your room for free. You may also want to consider getting a room with a kitchenette; eating some meals in your room (or preparing and taking food with you) can help defray food costs. In Chapter 9, look for the Kid Friendly icon next to hotels that offer family-friendly options.

Getting around

If you and your children don't want to tangle with public transportation from the airport or around the city, you can always take taxis. But if your children are patient enough, you can get almost anywhere on the bus or subway. Make sure to review the safety tips I give in Chapter 8 and in the Quick Concierge before hitting the road. (By the way, children under 3'8" tall ride New York's subways for free.)

Finding baby-sitting services

Many hotels have baby-sitting services or can provide lists of reliable sitters. If your hotel can't make a recommendation, try the **Baby Sitters Guild** (☎ 212-682-0227; www.babysittersguild.com), where the sitters are licensed, insured, and bonded, and will take your children on an outing.

Touring the town

To help you plan outings with your children, look for the Kid Friendly icon throughout this book, which points out places of particular interest to children. You find this icon next to such sights as the Bronx Zoo, Central Park Zoo, and Central Park. For more information about planning activities for children, pick up a copy of the excellent *Frommer's New York City with Kids* (Wiley).

Time Out New York, a magazine that comes out every Wednesday (and is available online at www.timeoutny.com), is a great source for finding out about child-friendly activities and events. Look for the "Kids" listings. In addition, you can pick up *Time Out New York Kids,* which helps to steer you in the right direction for fun with your kids.

For teenagers, some neighborhoods may be more interesting than others. Downtown neighborhoods (such as Chelsea, the East Village, the

West Village, SoHo, NoHo, and Nolita) have younger crowds, coffee shops, and funky clothing stores. (For more-detailed descriptions of these neighborhoods, see Chapter 8.)

Making Age Work for You: Advice for Seniors

Mention the fact that you're a senior citizen when you make your travel reservations. Although none of the major U.S. airlines offers senior discount and coupon-book programs anymore, many hotels still offer senior discounts. In most cities, New York included, people 60 and older qualify for reduced admission to theaters, museums, and other attractions, as well as discounted fares on public transportation.

Members of **AARP** (☎ **888-687-2277** or 202-434-2277; www.aarp.org) get discounts on hotels, airfares, and car rentals. AARP offers members a range of benefits, including *AARP The Magazine* and a monthly newsletter. Anyone over 50 years of age can join.

Many reliable agencies and organizations target the 50-plus market. **Elderhostel** (☎ **877-426-8056;** www.elderhostel.org) arranges study programs for those 55 and older (and a spouse or companion of any age) in the United States and in more than 80 countries around the world. Recent offerings for New York City include "Five Days, Five Boroughs" and "Great Art Centers in New York."

Recommended publications offering travel resources and discounts for seniors include the quarterly magazine ***Travel 50 & Beyond*** (www.travel50andbeyond.com); ***Travel Unlimited: Uncommon Adventures for the Mature Traveler*** (Avalon); ***101 Tips for Mature Travelers,*** available from Grand Circle Travel (☎ **800-221-2610** or 617-350-7500; www.gct.com); and ***Unbelievably Good Deals and Great Adventures That You Absolutely Can't Get Unless You're Over 50,*** by Joann Rattner Heilman (McGraw-Hill).

 Seniors get a 50 percent discount on bus and subway fares in New York (see the following section for more info). Be sure to carry identification with proof of age.

Accessing New York City: Advice for Travelers with Disabilities

Most disabilities shouldn't stop anyone from traveling because more options and resources exist than ever before. In general, New York is progressive in its efforts to make the city accessible for the disabled. Equal access is now mandated by law, but implementation has been gradual and is not complete.

Travel agencies and organizations

Many travel agencies offer customized tours and itineraries for travelers with disabilities. Among them are **Flying Wheels Travel** (☎ 507-451-5005; www.flyingwheelstravel.com), **Access-Able Travel Source** (☎ 303-232-2979; www.access-able.com), and **Accessible Journeys** (☎ 800-846-4537 or 610-521-0339; www.disabilitytravel.com). **Big Apple Greeter** (☎ 212-669-2896 or 212-669-8273 TTY; www.bigapple greeter.org) offers tours for travelers with disabilities free of charge. Advance reservations are necessary.

Organizations that offer assistance to disabled travelers include **MossRehab** (www.mossresourcenet.org), the **American Foundation for the Blind** (AFB; ☎ 800-232-5463; www.afb.org), the **New York Society for the Deaf** (☎ 212-777-3900 TTY; www.nysd.org), and **Society for Accessible Travel and Hospitality** (SATH; ☎ 212-447-7284; www.sath.org). SATH offers a wealth of travel resources for people with all types of disabilities and recommends access guides, travel agents, tour operators, companion services, and more. Annual membership costs $49 for adults and $29 for seniors and students. **AirAmbulanceCard.com** is partnered with SATH and allows you to preselect top-notch hospitals in case of an emergency.

Hospital Audiences, Inc. (☎ 212-575-7676 or 212-575-7673 TTY; www.hospitalaudiences.org), has various programs including "Describe!," which allows theatergoers who are blind or visually impaired to enjoy theater with audio-describers giving a summary of the action onstage. The Web site provides accessibility information to performance and art venues and about programs that are signed for the hearing impaired.

For more information targeted to travelers with disabilities, check out the magazine *Emerging Horizons* (www.emerginghorizons.com) and *Open World Magazine,* published online by SATH.

Hotels

In the past year or so, the Department of Justice has sued a number of New York hotels, forcing them to become ADA compliant. Many hotels offer features that accommodate wheelchairs, like roll-in showers, lower sinks, and extra space for maneuverability. Simply ask for one of these accessible rooms when you make your reservation.

Transportation

Taxis are required by law to take people with disabilities, wheelchairs, and guide dogs. For getting into the city from one of the airports, the **Gray Line Shuttle** (☎ 800-451-0455 or 212-315-3006; www.grayline.com) has minibuses with lifts. The vans go only to Midtown hotels, and you must make a reservation to get a ride.

All buses in Manhattan, and 95 percent of New York City buses in the other boroughs, are equipped with wheelchair lifts and seating areas where the bus seats fold up to make extra room. The buses also "kneel," lowering their front ends so that the first step is more accessible. Wheelchair passengers don't have to request these bus services in advance; just show up at the bus stop. The driver can help put a wheelchair on the ramp and secure the chair inside the bus.

Subway access for travelers with disabilities is limited, but the Metropolitan Transportation Authority (MTA) New York City Transit is increasing accessibility. You can certainly experience the thrill of a New York subway ride by boarding and getting off at the accessible stations, but the bus is a much more flexible option. Also, out-of-service subway elevators are not unheard of — a problem the MTA really needs to address more effectively.

The following are a few major wheelchair-accessible stations and lines in Manhattan:

- ✔ Brooklyn Bridge/City Hall (4, 5, 6)
- ✔ West 4th Street (A, B, C, D, E, F, M)
- ✔ 14th Street/Union Square (L, N, Q, R 4, 5, 6)
- ✔ 34th Street/Herald Square (B, D, F, M, N, Q, R)
- ✔ 42nd Street/Port Authority Bus Terminal (A, C, E)
- ✔ Grand Central/42nd Street (4, 5, 6)
- ✔ 50th Street (southbound only, C, E)
- ✔ 51st Street (6)
- ✔ Lexington/63rd Street (F)
- ✔ 66th Street/Lincoln Center (1, 2)
- ✔ 125th Street (4, 5, 6)
- ✔ 175th Street (A)
- ✔ Roosevelt Island (F)

Accessible stations are marked with an icon on the free subway map distributed in the subway. You also can get the *MTA Guide to Accessible Transit* at www.mta.info/mta/ada (large-print, Braille, and audiotape versions are available by calling ☎ 718-330-3322).

Seniors and people with disabilities get a 50 percent discount with the MTA. Getting a discount MetroCard takes a little planning, however. You need to get an application by writing to the Customer Service Center, MTA, 3 Stone St., New York, NY 10004. Or you can download the application from the MTA Web site (www.mta.info/nyct/fare/rfindex.htm), or call ☎ 718-243-4999.

Following the Rainbow: Advice for GLBT Travelers

New York ranks with San Francisco as one of the most gay-friendly cities in the United States. Greenwich Village and Chelsea have large gay populations, and the Village and Chelsea offer abundant nightlife.

Many agencies offer tours and travel itineraries specifically for GLBT travelers.

- **Above and Beyond Tours** (☎ **800-397-2681** or 760-325-0702; www.abovebeyondtours.com) plans group packages, as well as individual itineraries.

- **Now, Voyager** (☎ **800-255-6951;** www.nowvoyager.com) is a well-known San Francisco–based gay-owned and -operated travel service.

- **International Gay & Lesbian Travel Association** (IGLTA; ☎ **800-448-8550** or 954-776-2626; www.iglta.org) provides information about gay-friendly hoteliers, tour operators, and airline representatives.

The following are a few of the major gay organizations in the city:

- The **Lesbian, Gay, Bisexual & Transgender Community Center,** 208 W. 13th St. (between Seventh and Eighth avenues; ☎ **212-620-7310;** www.gaycenter.org), is a fabulous source of information, and also offers hundreds of events and activities each month, from readings, films, and dances to advice and medical referrals. Call or visit the Center's excellent Web site to get information about the programs it sponsors. The Center also offers a list of gay-friendly accommodations and a calendar of local cultural events.

- The **Organization of Lesbian and Gay Architects and Designers** (☎ **212-475-7652**) created a free map of lesbian and gay historical landmarks; the Greenwich Village Society transformed it into a Google map, available at www.gvshp.org/lesbianandgayhistory.htm.

- **Gay Men's Health Crisis** (GMHC), 119 W. 24th St. (☎ **212-807-6655;** www.gmhc.org), has an AIDS hot line, serves anyone with HIV, and offers a wide variety of programs.

For the most up-to-date information about events and entertainment, try any of the city's gay-friendly publications. The weekly *Time Out New York* (www.timeoutny.com) includes a comprehensive gay and lesbian section. *Next Magazine* (www.nextmagazine.com), a free publication available in restaurants, clubs, and bars, lists events around town. *Gay City News* (www.gaycitynews.com) appears every Thursday. *GO Magazine* is a free glossy monthly that focuses on articles and listings of interest to lesbians (www.gomag.com).

The following travel guides are available online and at most travel bookstores:

- ✔ *Out Traveler* (www.outtraveler.com) offers free online articles about 14 cities, including New York.

- ✔ The *Damron* guides (www.damron.com) produce annual books for gay men and lesbians.

Tying the Knot: Advice for Travelers in Love

With its iconic backdrops, bright energy, and luxurious hotel and dining options for celebrations, New York has become a favored destination for proposals and elopements. If you're ready to pop the question, here are some highly recommended spots to consider:

- ✔ Empire State Building (p. 184)

- ✔ Brooklyn Bridge (p. 173)

- ✔ The Cloisters (p. 182)

- ✔ Central Park, including Belvedere Castle or the Boathouse (p. 180)

- ✔ Coney Island

- ✔ Yankee Stadium (p. 191)

- ✔ Grand Central Terminal's Whispering Gallery, at the end of the Oyster Bar ramps (p. 185)

- ✔ A romantic restaurant — where, upon request, an engagement ring can be hidden in a dessert — such as Daniel (p. 138)

If you want to get hitched during your trip, the city makes it relatively easy. In a bid to compete with Las Vegas for wedding business, the New York City Clerk's office recently unveiled a renovated **Marriage Bureau,** 141 Worth St. (☎ **311** in New York City, or 212-639-9675; http://city clerk.nyc.gov), where you can apply for a marriage license that costs $35 and is valid for 60 days. You can begin the license application online, but you must complete it in person within 21 days. No blood test is required, but you need official identification (such as a passport or driver's license); after receiving your marriage license, you must wait 24 hours to perform the ceremony.

When you've satisfied the initial legal requirements, you have two options for a quick ceremony:

- ✔ The Marriage Bureau has two chapels (complete with photo-ready City Hall backdrop) and a store for any last-minute items you may need (such as flowers and inexpensive rings). You can choose to be married, in one of 170 languages, Monday through Friday between 8:30 a.m. and 3:45 p.m.

✔ If you'd rather elope at one of the city's great sights — including Central Park, the Brooklyn Bridge, the Empire State Building — or just in the comfort and privacy of your own hotel room, I highly recommend enlisting the services of **Weddings of New York** (☎ **718-312-8424;** www.weddingsofnewyork.com). Mary Beaty and her partners will perform a customized civil ceremony as bare bones or elaborate as you want; they also can expertly guide you through the process in advance of your trip.

Note: Although the State of New York legally recognizes same-sex marriages performed in other jurisdictions, at press time, same-sex marriages cannot be performed in the state. However, the officiants of Weddings of New York do perform commitment ceremonies for same-sex couples.

Chapter 7

Taking Care of the Remaining Details

In This Chapter

▶ Renting a car . . . not!

▶ Insuring your good time

▶ Staying healthy and connected

▶ Finding the latest security tips

etails, details, details. Who wants to spoil the fun of planning some big-city sightseeing and shopping by worrying about travel insurance? But paying attention to these less-interesting details *now* can spare you many last-minute hassles. Go over the points in this chapter so that you can enjoy a worry-free trip.

Renting a Car: Not in New York!

It's one of the first questions that come to mind when organizing a trip: "Do I need to rent a car?" In New York, the answer is clear: No! You just don't need one; New York is a great walking city, and you can take fast and cheap public transportation almost anywhere. Need I mention that car-rental rates and gas are expensive; parking is a nightmare; and driving the city streets is — more often than not — a high-speed, high-stakes game of dodge-'em that's *not* for the weak of heart?

If I haven't managed to dissuade you — perhaps New York is a jumping-off point for exploring nearby cities such as Boston or Philadelphia or areas such as Long Island or the Hudson Valley — all the major car-rental companies are found around town. But be aware that rates are higher for cars rented in the city; consider taking a train (Amtrak, Metro North, or Long Island Railroad) to avoid the inevitably horrible traffic congestion exiting New York, and pick up a car at your destination, where the rental rate is likely less expensive. Companies to try include **Alamo** (☎ 877-222-9075; www.alamo.com), **Budget** (☎ 800-527-0700; www.budget.com), and **Enterprise** (☎ 800-261-7331; www.enterprise.com). Members of the car-sharing network **Zipcar** (☎ 866-494-7227; www.zipcar.com) will also find a good number of cars in New York.

Playing It Safe: Travel and Medical Insurance

The types of insurance that travelers are most likely to need are trip-cancellation insurance and medical insurance. The cost of travel insurance varies widely, depending on the cost and length of your trip, your age and health, and the type of trip you're taking. You can get estimates from various providers through **InsureMyTrip.com**. Enter your trip cost and dates, your age, and other information, for prices from more than a dozen companies.

U.K. citizens who make more than one trip abroad per year may find that an annual travel-insurance policy works out cheaper. Check **Moneysupermarket** (www.moneysupermarket.com), which compares prices across a range of providers for single- and multitrip policies.

Most big travel agents offer their own insurance and will probably try to sell you their package when you book a holiday. **Britain's Consumers' Association** recommends that you insist on seeing the policy and reading the fine print before buying travel insurance. **The Association of British Insurers** (☎ 020-7600-3333; www.abi.org.uk) gives advice by phone and publishes *Holiday Insurance,* a free guide to policy provisions and prices. You might also shop around for better deals: Try **Columbus Direct** (☎ 0870-033-9988; www.columbusdirect.net).

Here's my advice on trip-cancellation and medical insurance:

- ✔ **Trip-cancellation insurance** helps you get your money back if you have to back out of a trip, if you have to go home early, or if your travel supplier goes bankrupt. Trip-cancellation insurance traditionally covers such events as sickness, natural disasters, and State Department advisories. A recent development in trip-cancellation insurance is the availability of **expanded hurricane coverage** and the **"any-reason"** cancellation coverage — which costs more but covers cancellations made for any reason. You won't get back 100 percent of your prepaid trip cost, but you'll be refunded a substantial portion. **TravelSafe** (☎ 888-885-7233; www.travelsafe.com) offers both types of coverage. Other companies to try are **Access America** (☎ 800-284-8300; www.accessamerica.com); **Travel Guard International** (☎ 800-826-4919; www.travelguard.com); **Travel Insured International** (☎ 800-243-3174; www.travel insured.com), or **Travelex Insurance Services** (☎ 800-228-9792; www.travelex-insurance.com).

- ✔ For domestic travel, buying **medical insurance** for your trip doesn't make sense for most travelers. Most existing health policies cover you if you get sick away from home — but check before you go.

- ✔ International visitors to the United States should note that unlike many European countries, the U.S. does not usually offer free or low-cost medical care to its citizens or visitors. Doctors and hospitals are expensive and, in most cases, will require advance payment or proof of coverage before they render their services. Good policies will cover the costs of an accident, repatriation, or death. Packages such as **Europ Assistance's Worldwide Healthcare Plan** are sold by European automobile clubs and travel agencies at attractive rates. **Worldwide Assistance Services, Inc.** (www. worldwideassistance.com), is the agent for Europ Assistance in the U.S. Though lack of health insurance may prevent you from being admitted to a hospital in non-emergencies, don't worry about being left on a street corner to die: The American way is to fix you now and bill you later.

✔ If you're ever hospitalized more than 150 miles from home, **MedjetAssist** (☎ 800-527-7478; www.medjetassistance.com) will pick you up and fly you to the hospital of your choice in a medically equipped and staffed aircraft 24 hours a day, 7 days a week. Annual memberships are $250 individual, $385 family; you can also purchase short-term memberships.

✔ Canadians should check with their provincial health-plan offices or call **Health Canada** (☎ 866-225-0709; www.hc-sc.gc.ca) to find out the extent of their coverage and what documentation and receipts they must take home if they're treated in the U.S.

✔ Travelers from the U.K. should carry their European Health Insurance Card (EHIC), which replaced the E111 form as proof of entitlement to free/reduced-cost medical treatment abroad (☎ 0845-606-0707; www.ehic.org.uk). Note, however, that the EHIC covers only "necessary medical treatment"; for repatriation costs, lost money, baggage, or trip cancellation, you should buy travel insurance from a reputable company. For recommendations, visit www.travelinsuranceweb.com, a site where you can purchase insurance for your trip-specific needs.

Staying Healthy When You Travel

Getting sick can ruin your vacation, so I *strongly* advise against it. (Of course, last time I checked, the germs weren't listening to me.) New York won't make you sick more than any other city, and New York City tap water is some of the nation's finest. Beyond that, follow the basic advice below for keeping your health in tiptop shape.

For information on purchasing additional medical insurance for your trip, see the previous section.

Talk to your doctor before leaving on a trip if you have a serious and/or chronic illness. For conditions such as epilepsy, diabetes, or heart problems, wear a **MedicAlert identification tag** (☎ 888-633-4298; www.medicalert.org), which alerts doctors to your condition and gives them access to your records through MedicAlert's 24-hour hot line. The U.S. **Centers for Disease Control and Prevention** (☎ 800-311-3435; www.cdc.gov) provides up-to-date information on health hazards by region or country and offers tips on food safety. **Travel Health Online** (www.tripprep.com), sponsored by a consortium of travel-medicine practitioners, may also offer helpful advice on travel health.

If you need medical attention in New York, turn to the Quick Concierge section, for doctors at urgent-care clinics and hospital locations around town.

Staying Connected by Cellphone or E-Mail

Staying in touch with the folks at home (or with each other) is a snap. Access to the Internet from your phone or laptop, or at hotel or public terminals, makes communicating while traveling so simple that you may prefer to unplug.

Using a cellphone

If you don't have a cellphone and you need one during your stay in New York, **rent** a phone from **Mobal** (☎ 888-888-9162; www.mobal.com) or from a rental-car location, but it'll be a hefty $1 a minute or more for airtime.

If you're not from the U.S., you'll be surprised at the lackluster reach of our **Global System for Mobiles (GSM) wireless network,** which is used by much of the rest of the world. Your phone will work in New York and most major U.S. cities. And you may or may not be able to send SMS (text messaging) home.

If you have Web access while traveling, consider a broadband-based telephone service — **Voice over Internet Protocol** (VoIP) — such as Skype (www.skype.com) or Vonage (www.vonage.com), which allows you to make free international calls from your laptop or in a cybercafe. Neither requires the people you're calling to also have that service (though there are fees if they don't). Check the Web sites for details.

Accessing the Internet away from home

Travelers have any number of ways to check their e-mail and access the Internet. Of course, using your own laptop or smartphone gives you the most flexibility. But even if you don't have a computer, you can still access your e-mail and even your office computer.

Without your computer

Here are some of the places you can check your e-mail in New York:

- **Times Square Information Center,** Seventh Avenue between 46th and 47th streets (☎ 212-768-1560; www.timessquarenyc.org; Open: Mon–Fri 9 a.m.–7 p.m., Sat–Sun 8 a.m.–8 p.m.).

✔ **CyberCafe,** in Times Square at 250 W. 49th St. (between Broadway and Eighth Avenue; ☎ **212-333-4109;** www.cyber-cafe.com; Open: Mon–Fri 8 a.m.–11 p.m., Sat–Sun 11 a.m.–11 p.m.).

✔ **FedEx Office** (www.fedex.com), at numerous locations, including 21 Astor Place (between Broadway and Lafayette Street; ☎ **212-228-9511**), 239 Seventh Ave. (at 24th Street; ☎ **212-929-0623**), 60 W. 40th St. (between Fifth and Sixth avenues; ☎ **212-921-1060**), and 221 W. 72nd St. (at Broadway; ☎ **212-362-5288**).

✔ **New York Public Library** — the branch libraries around town offer free Internet access; check the Web site (www.nypl.org) for locations and hours.

Most **budget hotels** have at least one computer you can use to access the Internet. More hotels offer free Internet access in their business centers, but it's not something they all do, so watch out for exorbitant rates.

Most major airports have **Internet kiosks** scattered throughout their gates. These kiosks, which you may also see in shopping malls and tourist-information offices, give you basic Internet access for a high per-minute fee. Avoid them whenever possible.

To retrieve your e-mail, ask your **Internet service provider** (ISP) if it has a Web-based interface tied to your existing e-mail account. If your ISP doesn't have such an interface, you can use the free **mail2web** service (www.mail2web.com) to view and reply to your home e-mail. If you need to access files on your office computer, look into a service called **GoToMyPC** (www.gotomypc.com). The service provides a Web-based interface for you to access and manipulate a distant PC from anywhere, provided your "target" PC is on and has an always-on connection to the Internet.

With your own computer

More and more hotels, cafes, and retailers are Wi-Fi hotspots from which you can get high-speed connection without cable wires, networking hardware, or a phone line. Starbucks and Barnes & Noble stores offer complimentary Wi-Fi nationwide. **Bryant Park,** between 40th and 42nd streets and Fifth and Sixth avenues (www.bryantpark.org/amenities/wireless.php), is a Wi-Fi hotspot, as are the **New York Public Library** and its branch libraries around town (www.nypl.org).

To locate other hotspots that provide **free wireless networks** in cities around the world, go to **JiWire** (www.jiwire.com), where you can also download the free Wi-Fi Finder mobile application.

Keeping Up with Airline Security Measures

With the federalization of airport security, procedures at U.S. airports are more stable and consistent than ever. Generally, you won't be delayed if you arrive at the airport **one hour** before a domestic flight; if you show up late, tell an airline employee so that he might usher you to the front of the line.

Don't leave home without a **current, government-issued photo ID,** such as a driver's license or passport. Keep your ID at the ready to show at check-in, at the security checkpoint, and sometimes even at the gate. (Children under 18 don't need government-issued photo IDs for domestic flights.)

Passengers can beat the ticket-counter lines by using airport **electronic kiosks** or **online check-in** from your home computer. Online check-in involves logging on to your airline's Web site, accessing your reservation, and printing out your boarding pass. If you're using a kiosk at the airport, bring the credit card you used to book the ticket or your frequent-flier card. Print out your boarding pass from the kiosk and simply proceed to the security checkpoint with your pass and a photo ID. **Curbside check-in** is also a good way to avoid lines, although a few airlines still ban curbside check-in; call before you go.

Speed up security by **not wearing metal objects** such as big belt buckles. If you've got metallic body parts, a note from your doctor can prevent a long chat with the security screeners. Keep in mind that only **ticketed passengers** are allowed past security, except for folks escorting disabled passengers or children.

Federalization has stabilized **what you can carry on** and **what you can't.** Travelers in the U.S. are allowed one carry-on bag, plus a "personal item" (such as a purse, briefcase, or laptop bag). You can stuff all sorts of things into a laptop bag — as long as it has a laptop in it, it's still considered a personal item. In any of your carry-on items, check on the restrictions on liquids and gels, if you're carrying your personal toiletries. The Transportation Security Administration (TSA) has issued a list of restricted items; check its Web site (www.tsa.gov) for what you can and can't bring onboard.

Airport screeners may decide that your checked luggage needs to be searched by hand. You can purchase luggage locks that allow screeners to open and relock a checked bag, if hand-searching is deemed necessary. Look for Travel Sentry–certified locks at luggage or travel shops and Brookstone stores (you can buy them online at www.brookstone.com). For more information on the locks, visit www.travelsentry.org.

Part III

Settling Into New York City

In this part . . .

1 help you get oriented in New York City with information about getting around and where you can find additional help in the city after you're here. I also give you the lowdown on where to stay and where to eat.

Chapter 8

Arriving and Getting Oriented

In This Chapter

▶ Getting in by train, plane, or automobile
▶ Figuring out the neighborhoods
▶ Finding info after you arrive
▶ Getting around New York City
▶ Walking (or, when you get tired of walking, taking a taxi)

*W*hether you're landing at one of the three major area airports, alighting from Amtrak, or taking the family car to New York City, this chapter helps you get to where you're going.

Getting from the Airport to Your Hotel

The New York airports are located away from the center of things — LaGuardia and Kennedy are in the borough of Queens, and Newark airport is across the Hudson River in New Jersey. From any of these airports, taking a taxi is the easiest and most hassle-free option, but it's also the most expensive. Another possibility is to use a car service or van service (see the following sections for information). At the cheaper end, you can take a bus or a train.

If you take a cab, make sure that a uniformed, official taxi dispatcher hails your cab. Always stand in the official taxi line and take a licensed New Jersey taxi or New York City yellow cab. If someone approaches you offering a cab ride, just keep walking toward the cab line; illegal drivers, who may take you on an unwelcome ride, abound at all three main airports. Remember that taxis are required by law to take no more than four people, and you should tip 15 percent of the fare regardless of whether the driver helps you with your bags.

New York Metropolitan Area

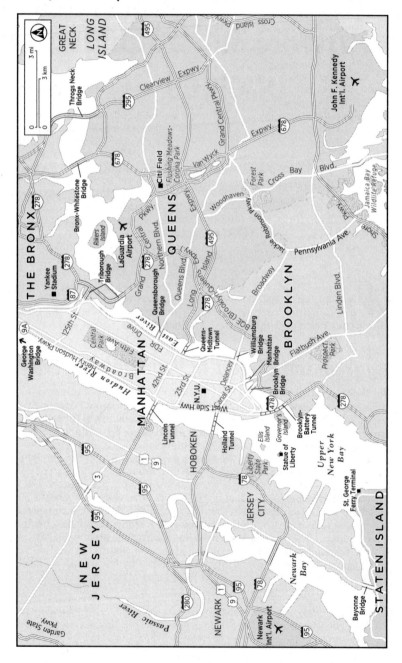

From JFK

John F. Kennedy International (JFK) is New York's largest airport. Its several terminals are located along a great loop. Each terminal has a taxi stand, bus stops, and car-service pickup points. After collecting your luggage, follow the ground transportation signs or the signs for the closest exit to the transportation of your choice.

A cab from JFK to Manhattan takes about 45 minutes, depending on the traffic (which can be fierce), and costs a flat rate of $45 plus tolls and tip. The toll is $5.50 cash/$4.57 EZ-Pass for the Queens Midtown Tunnel or the Triborough Bridge (officially known as the Robert F. Kennedy Bridge); the Queensborough Bridge is free, as are the Williamsburg and Manhattan bridges, but they can get very crowded. Still, if your destination is downtown and the Williamsburg and Manhattan bridges are free of construction, they should be your best bets to get into the city quickly. Your cabdriver should know the fastest way into town considering the traffic situation. You have to pay a 50¢ surcharge between 8 p.m. and 6 a.m., and a $1 surcharge Monday through Friday from 4 to 8 p.m.

A private car service (sometimes known as a "limo" in New York–ese) is another option. In fact, a ride in a private car can cost a little less than a cab ride. Also, the driver meets you just outside the baggage-claim area, so you don't have to wait in line for a cab. Here are some of the car companies that service JFK; call ahead for a reservation.

- **Allstate:** ☎ **800-453-4099** or 212-333-3333; www.allstate limo.com

- **Carmel:** ☎ **866-666-6666** or 212-666-6666; www.carmellimo.com

- **Dial 7:** ☎ **800-777-8888** or 212-777-7777; www.dial7.com

Another possibility is to take a shared transportation service (a "minivan" in New York lingo). Follow the ground transportation signs upon your arrival and sign up at one of the desks. Options include the following:

- **New York Airport Service** (☎ **718-875-8200;** www.nyairport service.com) offers regular bus service to and from Manhattan. The buses stop outside each terminal at JFK; follow the directions to ground transportation and wait by the sign. When boarding the bus at the airport, purchase your ticket on the bus or from the dispatcher at the sign. Buses leave every 30 minutes.

- The bus makes four stops in Manhattan: across from Grand Central Terminal (the southeast corner of 42nd Street and Park Avenue), Bryant Park, the Port Authority Bus Terminal (42nd Street and Eighth Avenue), and Penn Station (1 Penn Plaza between 31st and 33rd streets, just off Seventh Avenue). The price is $15 one-way or $27 round-trip; children 11 and under ride free, but watch out for the limit of one free child per full-fare adult. Discounted rates are available for students and seniors, but only if tickets are purchased from the ticket counters in Manhattan. Add $5 for the Midtown Hotel Shuttle, which serves hotels between 31st and 60th streets. When you leave New York, you can take the bus service from any of these four stops, but you need to call 24 hours in advance to reserve a hotel pickup.

✔ **SuperShuttle** (☎ **800-258-3826** or 212-258-3826; `www.super shuttle.com`) has vans on call 24 hours a day to all destinations in Manhattan. The price is $17 to or from the airport if you're staying at a hotel; if you're staying at a residential address, the price is $23 to or from the airport for the first passenger in your party and $10 for each additional passenger; children 2 and under ride free. You can reserve in advance for your pickup to head back to the airport.

Last *and* least is public transportation. Going from JFK to Manhattan by public transportation is *really* cheap but *really* time-consuming. This option is best reserved for those traveling light and with more time than money. **AirTrain JFK** operates relatively efficiently, and you can't beat the price — only $7.25 if you take a subway to the AirTrain, $13 if you take Long Island Rail Road. From Midtown Manhattan, the ride can take anywhere from 40 minutes to an hour, depending on your connections. Subway lines that connect with the AirTrain are the A, E, J, and Z; the E, J, and Z to Jamaica Station and Sutphin Boulevard–Archer Avenue Station, and the A to Howard Beach/JFK Airport Station. The Metropolitan Transportation Authority (MTA) is contemplating adding connections to the AirTrain in lower Manhattan sometime in the next decade, but there's not much they can do now to speed up the trip.

From LaGuardia

Smaller than JFK, LaGuardia receives fewer flights than its two New York–area counterparts — but, paradoxically, it experiences more flight delays, according to the Federal Aviation Administration. Just step outside the terminal at the baggage-claim level for ground transportation.

The metered fare for a taxi ride from LaGuardia to Midtown runs about $30 plus tolls and tip. The toll is $5.50 ($4.50 with EZ-Pass) for the Queens Midtown Tunnel or Triborough (Robert F. Kennedy) Bridge; the Queensborough Bridge is free, as are the Williamsburg and Manhattan bridges. Allow 30 minutes or more for this trip, depending on traffic.

A private car service is also an option (see "From JFK," earlier in this chapter). Call ahead to one of these reliable car companies for a reservation:

✔ **Allstate:** ☎ **800-453-4099** or 212-333-3333; `www.allstate limo.com`

✔ **Carmel:** ☎ **866-666-6666** or 212-666-6666; `www.carmellimo.com`

✔ **Dial 7:** ☎ **800-777-8888** or 212-777-7777; `www.dial7.com`

New York Airport Service (☎ 718-875-8200; www.nyairportservice.
com) also serves LaGuardia. It offers the same service to and from
LaGuardia as for JFK (see "From JFK," earlier in this chapter). Buses
leave every 30 minutes, and the cost is $12 one-way or $21 round-trip
(free for children 11 and under; discounted rates for students and
seniors available only from the service's ticket counters in Manhattan).
Add $6 for the Midtown Hotel Shuttle service.

Shared transportation services are a good option from LaGuardia as
well. Follow the ground transportation signs upon your arrival and sign
up at one of the desks.

SuperShuttle (☎ 800-258-3826 or 212-258-3826; www.supershuttle.
com) has vans on call 24 hours a day to all destinations in Manhattan.
The price is $13 to and from the airport if you're going to a hotel; if
you're staying at a private residence, the price is $15 to or from the air-
port for the first passenger in your party and $10 for each additional
passenger. Children 2 and under ride free. You can reserve in advance
for pickup to go back to the airport.

For public transportation, the **M60 bus** gets you from the airport to a
choice of subway stops: first the Astoria Boulevard stop in Queens on
the N or Q subway line, and then into Manhattan at one of the subway
stops on 125th Street (A, B, C, D, 2, 3, 4, 5, or 6 subway line), and finally
to Cathedral Parkway/110th Street and 116th Street/Columbia University
on the 1 subway line. Another possibility: The **Q48** and **Q33** buses bring
you to a stop of the 7 train in Queens, which eventually takes you to
Times Square. Curbside bus signs and stops are clearly marked. If you're
using the bus-and-subway system's MetroCard, you're allowed free
transfers to approved connecting buses and subways within two hours
of initial card use. In both cases, you face a complicated, two-hour odys-
sey that you shouldn't attempt unless you're really looking to save
money. Check the MTA's Web site at www.mta.info/nyct/service/
airport.htm for LaGuardia Airport bus schedules.

From Newark

Although it's in New Jersey, Newark Liberty International is closer to
Manhattan than JFK is, especially if your final destination is downtown
or the West Side of Manhattan. The AirTrain to Newark airport connects
Newark's three terminals with the long-term parking lots and with the
Rail Link (the railroad station of Newark airport). From there, you can
catch a train directly into New York's Penn Station ($17 via New Jersey
Transit). See the end of this section for details.

The price of a cab from Newark to Manhattan is the metered fare (often
$40–$50) plus a $15 surcharge, to which you add toll and tip. You pay an
$8 inbound-only toll (entering Manhattan) for either the Holland Tunnel
or the Lincoln Tunnel, and you should tip 15 percent. You'll most likely
take a New Jersey cab on the way in and a New York cab on the way

back to the airport. The trip takes about 40 minutes each way, assuming traffic is moving.

You can take a private bus as well. **Newark Liberty Airport Express** (☎ **877-863-9275** or 908-354-3330; www.coachusa.com/olympia) offers regular service between Newark and destinations in Manhattan for $15 each way or $25 round-trip (children 11 and under ride free; seniors and travelers with disabilities pay $7.50 one-way or $15 round-trip). Buses run every 15 minutes, and the ride takes 30 minutes or longer, depending on traffic. From the Grand Central Station stop (at 120 E. 41st St., between Park and Lexington avenues), you can transfer to Olympia Trails' **Midtown Shuttle,** which takes you to any destination between 30th and 65th streets for an additional $5; you can purchase the ticket at the airport. Other stops in Manhattan are Bryant Park (Fifth Avenue and 42nd Street) and the Port Authority Bus Terminal (gates 316 and 317 at the Airport Bus Center, on 42nd Street between Eighth and Ninth avenues).

In the airport, follow the ground transportation signs and stop at the Coach USA/Olympia counter, or go directly to the bus stop outside that corresponds to your destination; you can buy your ticket at the counter or from the driver. If you're traveling from Manhattan, you can find a dispatcher on duty at the bus stop at 34th Street and Eighth Avenue and at a counter in the Airport Bus Center; at the 41st Street stop, you can buy your ticket from the Western Union office or from the driver.

Another possibility is to take a minivan. Follow the signs for ground transportation upon your arrival and sign up at this desk. **SuperShuttle** (☎ **800-258-3826** or 212-258-3826; www.supershuttle.com) has vans on call 24 hours a day to all destinations in Manhattan. The price is $17 to or from the airport, if you're going to a hotel; if you're staying at a private residence, the price is $23 from the airport for the first passenger in your party and $10 for any additional passengers; children 2 and under ride free. You can reserve in advance for pickup to go back to the airport.

You also can take public transportation:

✔ To get to the **AirTrain** (☎ **800-772-2222** or 973-762-5100; www.airtrainnewark.com) from your terminal, take the airport monorail (monorail stations are located in each terminal) to the Rail Link station served by Amtrak and New Jersey Transit, where you can catch a direct train to New York's Penn Station (a 30-minute ride). Trains run every 20 minutes on weekdays and every half-hour on weekends; service is less frequent in the evening after 9 p.m. A one-way trip on New Jersey Transit is $17 for adults and $12 for children and seniors. (It's $30 for adults on Amtrak — no reason to pay nearly twice as much if you don't have to do so.) Purchase tickets from the automated vending machines in the station; if you purchase a ticket from the conductor on the train, add $5 to the price.

✔ An even cheaper option is to catch a **New Jersey Transit train** to Newark's Penn Station (a 5-minute ride; $8.25 adults, $6.75 children and seniors), where you can hop a **PATH train** to Manhattan. The PATH train works quite well and costs only $1.75. From Newark, the train makes four stops in New Jersey and five stops in Manhattan, which are Christopher Street (in Greenwich Village on Hudson Street), 9th Street, 14th Street, 23rd Street, and 33rd Street, all along Sixth Avenue. Allow about 40 minutes for the trip between Newark's Penn Station and 33rd Street.

✔ Note that the PATH train to Manhattan is *very* crowded with commuters during morning rush hour and from Manhattan during the evening rush hour. If you're toting luggage, paying the extra $3 to take the train directly to New York's Penn Station is far easier.

From MacArthur Airport (Long Island)

Although I don't recommend flying into MacArthur Airport in Islip, Long Island, 50 miles east of Manhattan, Southwest flies there. So if you get an unusually cheap airfare, or if you have reasons to stop first on Long Island before heading into the city, you may decide it's worth it to fly into MacArthur instead of LaGuardia. Be aware that taxi service into the city is not available from there, but you can reserve a private car, which costs about $125 for a 1½-hour trip (though that may negate the benefit of a really low fare). Call **Colonial Transportation** (☎ 631-589-3500; www.colonialtransportation.com) for reservations.

Another option is to take the **shuttle,** also run by Colonial Transportation (a white van marked express service) from outside the terminal to the Ronkonkoma train station. From there you can take the Long Island Rail Road (www.mta.info/lirr) into New York's Penn Station. A shuttle comes every 20 minutes and costs $5; the train ride costs about $12, depending on the time of day. The trip takes about 1 hour and 45 minutes.

Finally, you can use the **Hampton Jitney** (☎ 631-283-4600; www.hamptonjitney.com). Take a local cab to the Jitney's bus stop in Ronkonkoma for about $15, and then catch the bus (a 1½-hour ride) into Manhattan for $27.

Arriving by Train

As I mention in Chapter 5, Amtrak offers regular service to New York from many cities. Amtrak trains arrive at Penn Station (between Seventh and Eighth avenues and 31st and 33rd streets), a large, noisy space with fast-food outlets galore and cramped waiting areas.

From the station, you can take a cab to wherever you're headed; signs guide you to the taxi stand on Penn Plaza Drive, a passageway situated between Penn Station (close to Eighth Avenue) and the Long Island Rail Road Terminal (LIRR; close to Seventh Avenue).

Another option is public transportation; the station is well connected with the A, C, E, 1, 2, and 3 trains and several buses. However, this isn't the best alternative, especially if you're unfamiliar with the city and you have a lot of luggage. Elevators are sparse in subway stations, so count on lugging your bags up and down multiple flights of stairs.

Arriving by Car

I don't recommend having a car in New York for the reasons I outline in Chapter 7. If you decide to arrive by car, you'll immediately understand why I try to dissuade you. I've driven highways and byways all over the United States, and I still find the drive into New York City to be the most consistently confusing and teeth-gnashing trip in the country.

You know you're approaching New York when the traffic and signs multiply beyond all expectations. Open your eyes and sharpen your senses; if you're unfamiliar with the tangle of highways, thoroughfares, and parkways, then getting into Manhattan can be a nerve-racking experience. Remember that you won't find signs for Manhattan; signs give the names of specific tunnels, bridges, and streets instead.

If you arrive from the west or south, the **New Jersey Turnpike** is your jumping-off point to Manhattan. Take exit 14C for the **Holland Tunnel** (which lets you out around Canal Street in Manhattan), exit 16E for the **Lincoln Tunnel** (which deposits you in far-west Midtown at 42nd Street), or exit 18, the turnpike's end, for the **George Washington Bridge** (which lets you out at 181st Street, far uptown). The inbound-only toll (toward Manhattan) is $8; you pay no outbound toll (you're free to leave, so to speak).

From the north, take the **Deegan Expressway** (I-87); from the northeast, take the **New England Thruway** (I-95) to the Bruckner Expressway. To get to the East Side of Manhattan, follow the signs to the Triborough/RFK Bridge ($5.50 toll in both directions, $4.55 with EZ-Pass), but then be careful to follow the signs to **FDR Drive** and avoid going on to Queens — unless that's your destination. FDR Drive runs along the East River all the way to the southern tip of Manhattan and has exits at different points. If you want to get to the West Side of Manhattan, exit I-87 at the Sawmill River Parkway and follow it to the Henry Hudson Parkway, pass the Henry Hudson Bridge (a $3 toll, $2.10 with EZ-Pass), and you find yourself on the **West Side Highway,** which runs along the Hudson River and has exits at different streets.

When approaching a toll plaza, stay in the lanes marked cash and *not* EZ-pass (unless, of course, you *have* an EZ-Pass). EZ-Pass is a toll payment system where a scanner identifies your car by an electronic tag mounted on your windshield and deducts the toll from a prepaid account. No attendants staff the EZ-Pass booths, so you can't pay cash in those lanes.

If you're coming from the Northeast, many of the contiguous states have an EZ-Pass program (www.e-zpassny.com), and your tag will work in New York City.

The **Cross Bronx Expressway** runs east–west and connects to the George Washington Bridge; you can use it to get to whichever side of the island you want, but its traffic jams are infamous (especially on days when the Yankees play at home).

After you're on the West Side Highway or FDR Drive, take the exit closest to your destination — all exits have street names — and calm down: You've made it to New York!

Figuring Out the Neighborhoods

Getting to know New York and all its neighborhoods is easy (see map p. 78). Most of the city's famous sights are on the island of Manhattan, bounded by the Hudson River to the west and the East River — guess where? — to the east. With the exception of a few of the downtown streets, the main avenues run north–south and the streets run east–west.

Downtown

"Downtown" is both a place and a state of mind; physically, everything below 14th Street is considered downtown. Chelsea, the Flatiron District, and Gramercy Park are not, strictly speaking, downtown, but I include them in this section because they're in that nebulous zone that's neither downtown nor Midtown.

Lower Manhattan and the Financial District

Lower Manhattan is where the city was born, and, as a result, the area is home to some of the most important historic landmarks, including Trinity Church, South Street Seaport, and the Brooklyn Bridge.

Much of the area is considered the **Financial District.** Until September 11, 2001, the Financial District was anchored by the **World Trade Center,** with the World Financial Center complex and Battery Park City to the west, and **Wall Street** running crosstown a little south and to the east. A construction site now occupies where the Twin Towers and five other buildings stood. It will be several years before designs for the new center are fully realized. (For more information about visiting the World Trade Center site, see Chapter 11.)

City Hall remains the northern border of the district, abutting Chambers Street. Most of the streets of this neighborhood are narrow concrete canyons, with Broadway serving as the main uptown–downtown artery. Just about all the major subway lines congregate here before they either end or head to Brooklyn.

Manhattan Neighborhoods

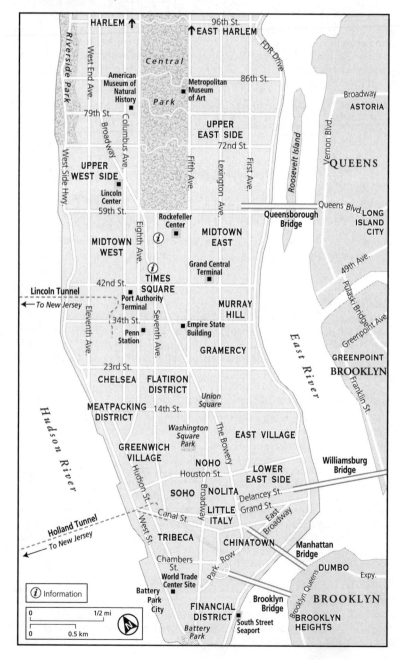

In the decade since the September 11, 2001 attacks, lower Manhattan has revitalized itself and now has much to offer. The local community has united to promote the area. Check out www.lowermanhattan.info and www.downtownny.com for useful information on new developments and exciting events that you can find downtown. Both are updated daily.

TriBeCa, Chinatown, Little Italy, and the Lower East Side

TriBeCa, the acronym for the **Tri**angle **Be**low **Ca**nal (Street), is the city's priciest neighborhood. It's an area of residential lofts (housing the likes of Jay-Z and Beyoncé), as well as the home of some highly fashionable restaurants. Trendy doesn't translate into big crowds, though; the neighborhood, especially at night, tends to be quiet. Canal Street runs straight across the island, going through the heart of **Chinatown,** which lies to the east of TriBeCa. Chinatown is a sprawling neighborhood that bursts with shops selling Asian wares, cheap souvenirs, bootleg DVDs, and counterfeit watches, bags, and sunglasses (more about these in Chapter 12). The streets are lined with Asian restaurants of every variety, and the sometimes very ripe aroma of fish from the countless seafood stalls fills the air.

North of Chinatown and centered on Mott and Mulberry streets is **Little Italy** — or what's left of it anyway: The neighborhood, squeezed by the encroachment of Chinatown, has been reduced to not much more than a tourist trap, with just a few remaining cafes, stores, and mediocre restaurants. To the east and north of Little Italy is the **Lower East Side,** a historic area that was a Jewish ghetto in the 19th century. The neighborhood is now a bubbling mix of hipster-cool (indie music clubs, adventurous new restaurants) and old-world remnants from its historic past. The farther east you go, the sketchier the neighborhood can get.

Orchard Street is where you can find great bargain hunting in many old-world fabric and clothing stores that thrive between club-clothes boutiques and trendy lounges. Keep in mind that the old-world shops close early on Friday afternoon and remain closed all day on Saturday (the Jewish Sabbath). The exponentially expanding hipster set can be found in the blocks between Allen and Clinton streets south of Houston and north of Delancey, with more new shops, bars, and restaurants popping up in the blocks to the east every day. The **Lower East Side Business Improvement District** operates a neighborhood visitor center at 54 Orchard St. (between Hester and Grand streets; ☎ 866-224-0206 or 212-226-9010; www.lowereastsideny.com); it's open daily from 10 a.m. to 4 p.m. (sometimes later). If you're interested in art, stop in for a gallery guide (which they can also send you in advance).

Greenwich Village, the East Village, SoHo, and NoHo

SoHo (which stands for **so**uth of **Ho**uston Street — pronounced *how*-ston, not *hyoo*-ston) is famous for its cast-iron architecture and, for some time, its thriving art scene. The art scene, however, has vacated; artists can no longer afford the astronomical rents. Still, SoHo's cachet is long-established, and you can find numerous chic boutiques and some interesting restaurants here. The eastern part of SoHo, rebaptized **Nolita** (**no**rth of **Lit**tle Italy), is where innovative fashion and accessory designers have opened small shops. The neighborhood has merged north into **NoHo** (**no**rth of **Ho**uston), a small, fashionable area just east of Broadway and north of Houston Street.

Greenwich Village, also called simply "the Village," is a center of art, dining, shopping, music, and gay life. The neighborhood is roughly bordered by Houston Street to the south and 14th Street to the north. Known for its architecture, the Village has the shortest street in the city (Weehawken, just 1 block long) and the narrowest house (on Bedford Street, where poet Edna St. Vincent Millay once lived). It's an area that never sleeps, yet it still manages to give off a sense of quiet and beauty. Within the Village itself is the **West Village,** west of Seventh Avenue, which is the historic center of New York's gay community and is centered on Sheridan Square and Christopher Street. It has a residential feel, with tree-lined streets and comfortable neighborhood cafes. East of Broadway, the Village becomes the **East Village,** which draws a younger, edgier crowd. Still a little less polished despite rising rents, the East Village clings proudly to the last remnants of its former seediness. Some excellent restaurants and boutiques can be found in the East Village. The area between the East Village and the West Village (that is, between Broadway and Seventh Avenue) is simply referred to as the Village. In the middle sit New York University and Washington Square Park, landmarked by the park's famous arch.

Chelsea, the Flatiron District, and Gramercy Park

Chelsea, which extends from 14th Street to 26th Street and from the Hudson River to Fifth Avenue, remains one of the city's largest gay communities. The neighborhood lays claim to lots of art galleries, cafes, restaurants, and a congregation of high-end, velvet-rope-guarded nightclubs. East of Chelsea is the **Gramercy Park** area — a quiet, elegant, moneyed neighborhood known for its jewel of a park and handsome architecture. In between are **Union Square** and the **Flatiron District,** a lively hub of New York life that is still home to publishing and Web 2.0 companies. This area, bordered by the historic Flatiron Building to the north (at Broadway and Fifth Avenue at 23rd Street) and Union Square to the south, is where members of the fashion industry — models, advertising people, photographers, and so on — meet and eat.

Midtown

Midtown is roughly defined by 26th Street to the south and 59th Street to the north. This is concrete canyon territory, where skyscrapers block out most of the sun and sky. During the day, Midtown is a hectic center of commerce, seething with people on their way to or from work, while at night, the restaurant scene is lively and generally very expensive. This is the city's biggest hotel neighborhood, with choices running the gamut from cheap to chic.

Within Midtown to the southeast lies **Murray Hill,** just east of Fifth Avenue and below 42nd Street. It's a mixture of business and residential property, where a 40-story slab may rub up against a 5-story apartment building. The Murray Hill area is safe and quiet — for New York. The Empire State Building is the major sightseeing stop here. Above 42nd Street is **Midtown East,** which is more commercial and includes a number of famous shops that line 59th Street between Fifth and Lexington avenues. The main attractions in this area are the United Nations, Grand Central Terminal, St. Patrick's Cathedral, Rockefeller Center, and the Chrysler Building. The stretch of **Fifth Avenue** from Saks at 49th Street extending to the Plaza Hotel at 59th is home to the city's most high-profile, haute shopping, including Tiffany & Co. and Bergdorf Goodman. Here you can find the city's finest collection of grand hotels, mostly along Lexington Avenue and near the park at the top of Fifth.

To the southwest lies the **Fashion** or **Garment District** (roughly between 26th and 42nd streets west of Fifth Avenue), with its array of fabric shops and wholesale fashion stores. At the heart of it, at the intersection of 34th Street, Broadway, and Sixth Avenue (also called the Avenue of the Americas), is **Herald Square,** a bustling (read: choked-with-crowds) shopping area. Herald Square is the home of Macy's, and with ongoing development, more national chain stores are appearing all the time. Other than that, it's a pretty grim commercial area that lacks any real charisma; frankly, I tend to avoid it. Just south of Herald Square around Broadway, the Ace Hotel (p. 97) anchors an area newly known as **NoMad** (**no**rth of **Mad**ison Square Park); time will tell if developers are able to turn it into the hot neighborhood of the moment.

Farther north, on the west side, is **Times Square,** a once legendary place full of peep shows and sex shops until a business partnership completed an ambitious (and completely transformational) improvement campaign. Times Square is now a family-oriented area with renovated theaters, pedestrian plazas, and the famous neon, which is bigger, brighter, and louder than ever (including the largest TV screen in the world, the Sony JumboTron). Crowds are sometimes impenetrable, so be prepared for a major jostling. Just up Broadway is the **Theater District.** The area churns with activity, and the scale is grand, so it's not the kind of place to step out for a casual stroll under the trees (there aren't any, anyway). Famed Restaurant Row is close by on 46th Street. A number of hotels are centered on Times Square, so if you don't mind the crowds and generally higher prices, and you want to be as close as possible to the pulse of the city, this is where you want to be.

Just west of the Theater District is **Hell's Kitchen,** probably the most picturesquely named neighborhood in New York City. Once a rough-and-tumble immigrant community and the home turf of Irish gangs, Hell's Kitchen has seen some gentrification. In an amusing example of New York's constant effort to reinvent itself, real-estate developers have attempted to rename the area "Clinton" or "Theater District West," but, thankfully, the natives have resisted. Ninth Avenue has blossomed into one of the city's finest dining avenues; just stroll along and choose from a world of great, inexpensive dining options, from American diner to Mediterranean to traditional Thai.

Uptown

Most of the northern part of the island of Manhattan is composed of three major neighborhoods, each with its own distinctive character.

The Upper West Side

Located to the west of Central Park, the **Upper West Side** is bordered by Columbus Circle, the Time Warner Center, and Lincoln Center to the south, and Columbia University and the Cathedral of St. John the Divine to the north. The area is home to some beautiful, historic residential buildings, such as the Dakota, where John Lennon lived and died, and the Ansonia, once the home of Babe Ruth. Other streets are lined with brownstones, town houses, and apartment buildings. In the past decade, the area has grown tremendously with a proliferation of superstores, movie theaters, and some very good new restaurants. Also in this neighborhood, you find the American Museum of Natural History. Though it's a bit away from the action of Midtown and downtown, the Upper West Side is a good option for reasonably priced hotels.

The Upper East Side

To the east of Central Park and stretching to the East River, the **Upper East Side**'s main draw is Museum Mile, a stretch of Fifth Avenue that includes the Metropolitan Museum of Art, the Guggenheim, the Museum of the City of New York, the International Center of Photography, the Frick Museum, and the Jewish Museum, all within a walkable stretch. Madison Avenue from 60th Street well into the 80s is the moneyed crowd's main shopping strip. The neighborhood has an upper-crust, old-money feel and, west of Lexington Avenue, is generally pretty quiet after sundown. East of Lexington along Third, Second, and First avenues, you encounter a number of lively (though somewhat bland) restaurants and bars.

Harlem

Harlem stretches from about 96th Street east of Fifth Avenue and 110th Street west of Fifth Avenue to 155th Street. **Spanish Harlem** (El Barrio) runs between East 100th and East 125th streets. Harlem real estate has shot up the past few years; restaurants, new apartments, and clubs now line the streets, and historic brownstones have been restored. Exploring the area has become safer, and that's a very good thing considering there's so much to see here, such as the Morris-Jumel Mansion, the Schomburg Center, the Studio Museum, and the Apollo Theater. North of Harlem, you find **Washington Heights** and Fort Tryon Park, home to the Cloisters annex of the Metropolitan Museum of Art.

Finding Information After You Arrive

The following places can help you get your bearings after you arrive in New York:

- ✔ **NYC & Company** has a sleek **Information Center,** 810 Seventh Ave. (between 52nd and 53rd streets; ☎ 212-484-1200; www.nycgo. com; Open: Mon–Fri 8:30 a.m.–6 p.m., Sat–Sun 9 a.m.–5 p.m.), where you can find useful interactive stations offering information in ten languages, pick up coupons for theaters and attractions, and buy tickets for New York's top sights, as well as the CityPass (see Chapter 11).

- ✔ The **Grand Central Partnership,** Grand Central Terminal, East 42nd Street and Vanderbilt Avenue (www.grandcentralpartnership. org; Open: Mon–Fri 8:30 a.m.–6:30 p.m., Sat–Sun 9 a.m.–6 p.m.), offers an information window inside Grand Central on the main concourse and a cart outside.

- ✔ The **34th Street Partnership,** Penn Station, Seventh Avenue between 31st and 33rd streets (☎ 212-719-3434; www.34thstreet.org; Open: Mon–Fri 8:30 a.m.–5:30 p.m., Sat–Sun 9 a.m.–6 p.m.), has a window inside Penn Station and an information cart at the Empire State Building at Fifth Avenue and 32nd Street. You find carts at Greeley Square (32nd Street at Broadway and Sixth Avenue) in the summer and at Madison Square Garden (above Penn Station at Seventh Avenue and 32nd Street) in above-freezing weather. The carts open a little later and close a little earlier than the indoor window does.

- ✔ The **Times Square Visitor Center,** Seventh Avenue between 46th and 47th streets (☎ 212-484-1200; www.timessquarenyc.org; Open: Mon–Fri 9 a.m.–7 p.m., Sat–Sun 8 a.m.–8 p.m.), features a helpful info desk offering loads of citywide information. You can buy tickets for Gray Line bus tours and Circle Line boat tours. An MTA desk is staffed to sell MetroCards, provide public-transit maps, and answer your questions about the transit system; a Broadway Ticket Center providing show information and selling full-price show tickets; ATMs and currency-exchange machines; and computer terminals with free Internet access.

Getting Around New York

You may not be used to riding a subway, taking a bus, hailing a taxi, or, yes, walking where you want to go, but that's what most New Yorkers do. You'll find yourself doing the same. The guidelines and tips in this section will have you navigating the island of Manhattan like a native in no time. Remember taxis, subways, and most buses run 24 hours a day.

Traveling by subway

Besides walking, riding the subway is my preferred mode of transport. And nearly five million people seem to agree with me each day, because they ride it, too. The subway is quick, inexpensive, and relatively safe and efficient, as well as being a thoroughly New York experience.

The subway runs 24 hours a day, 7 days a week. The rush-hour crushes are roughly from 8 to 9:30 a.m. and from 5 to 6:30 p.m. on weekdays; the trains are relatively uncrowded the rest of the time.

The subway fare is $2.25 (half-price for seniors and those with disabilities), and children under 44 inches tall ride free (up to 3 per adult).

For more information, visit www.mta.info/nyct.

Finding the entrance and getting onboard

You can easily locate a subway entrance along the sidewalk by looking for a set of stairs that heads underground. Most stops also have signs above them that list the lines that run through those stations.

Some subway entrances close at night. Each stairway has a globe on top of it that's supposed to tell you whether the entrance is open (green for open, red for closed), but the globes aren't always accurate; look down the stairs to find out whether the entrance is open — a locked gate at the bottom of the staircase is a big clue!

The way to gain entry to the subway is with the **MetroCard,** a magnetically encoded card that debits the fare when swiped through the turnstile (or the fare box on any city bus). After you're in the system, you can transfer freely to any subway line that you can reach without exiting your station. MetroCards also allow you **free transfers** between the bus and subway within a two-hour period.

You can purchase a MetroCard from staffed token booths (which is what they're still called, even though the token itself has been phased out), where you can pay only with cash. At the ATM-style vending machines located in just about every subway station, you can pay with cash, credit cards, and debit cards. See the "Understanding the MetroCard" section, later in this chapter, for details.

All the maps in this book show subway stops. You can usually find a subway map inside each subway car, on the platform, and on the wall in the subway station. You also can get a detailed subway map from the token booth.

Getting where you want to go

If you need directions in the subway, trying to get information from the token-booth attendant (if one is even present) can be frustrating. The acoustics are horrible, the people behind you are impatient, and it's difficult to make yourself understood. Instead, pick out a friendly or knowledgeable face; you'd be surprised how willing we New Yorkers are to help out.

The orientation of the subway system is mainly north–south (or uptown–downtown); you can find only a few points at which the lines go straight east–west. To travel up and down the West Side (and also to the Bronx and Brooklyn), take the 1, 2, or 3, line; the A, C, or E line; or the B, D, or F line.

The N, Q, and R lines first cut diagonally across town from east to west and then snake under Seventh Avenue before shooting out to Queens and Brooklyn.

The crosstown S line, the Shuttle, runs between Times Square and Grand Central Terminal. The 7 line also goes from Times Square to Grand Central (with a stop at Fifth Avenue). Farther downtown, across 14th Street, the L line works its own crosstown magic.

Lines have assigned colors on subway maps and trains — red for the 1, 2, and 3 trains; green for the 4, 5, and 6 trains; and so on — but nobody ever refers to them by color. Always refer to them by number or letter when asking questions. Within Manhattan, the distinction between different numbered trains that share the same line is usually that some are express and others are local.

Express trains often skip about three stops for each one that they make; express stops are indicated on subway maps with a white (rather than a solid) circle. Local stops usually come about 9 blocks apart.

Directions are almost always indicated using uptown (northbound) and downtown (southbound), so be sure to know what direction you want to head in. The outsides of some subway entrances are marked uptown only or downtown only; read carefully, because it's easy to head in the wrong direction. After you're on the platform, check the signs overhead to make sure that the train you're waiting for is traveling in the right direction. If you do make a mistake and get on the wrong train, it's a good idea to wait for an express station, like 14th Street or 42nd Street, so you can get off and change for the other direction without paying again.

Staying safe

To keep yourself safe in the subway, heed this advice:

- ✔ At night, use the off-hours waiting areas, which are usually close to the exits to the street. They're clearly marked with signs overhead.

- ✔ Don't tempt thieves by displaying money or valuables (including iPods, cellphones, and laptops) on the subway.

✔ Don't try to stop a subway door that's closing. You can end up with a bruised hand or foot — or something more serious. Just wait for the next train.

✔ Always stand a few feet back from the tracks on the subway platform. People have survived a fall, but believe me when I say that you do *not* want to try your luck.

✔ Avoid subways late at night, and splurge on a cab after about 10 or 11 p.m. — it's money well spent to avoid a long wait on a deserted platform. Or take the bus.

Traveling by bus

The New York City bus system reaches far and wide, traveling to just about all points of the city on a north–south *and* an east–west grid. You even get a tour of the city as you ride (the M5 down Fifth Avenue from Central Park to Greenwich Village is a personal fave). Remember that, because traffic can be horrific during the day, buses are much slower going than the subway. Also, avoid buses during rush hour if you have luggage or lots of shopping bags in hand.

To check out the bus routes, grab one of the free city bus maps available by the front door of every bus and in the booths at subway stations. If you want to scan the routes before you get to town, you can access full bus maps via the Internet at www.mta.info/maps.

Bus stops are located every couple of blocks along each route. The stop is either a small, glass-walled shelter or a simple sign on a post (blue with a bus icon) stating the bus numbers. Each bus has a sign above the windshield that flashes its route and end destination. Schedules for buses are posted at most bus stops and are relatively reliable. The buses run every 5 to 20 minutes or so, depending on the time of day.

Some buses are labeled "limited" and make only a few major stops along the line; they're particularly useful when you want to go a long distance. These express buses are designated only by an orange "limited" sign placed on the dashboard to the right of the driver. Limited bus stops also display the orange sign.

Local bus fare is $2.25 ($5.50 for express buses) — half-price for seniors and riders with disabilities, free for lap-sitting infants and children under 44 inches (up to 3 per adult). A seven-day express bus pass costs $45. The fare is payable with a **MetroCard** or **exact change.** Bus drivers don't make change, and fare boxes don't accept dollar bills or pennies. You can't purchase MetroCards on the bus, so you have to have them before you board.

If you pay with a MetroCard, you can transfer to another bus or to the subway for free within two hours. If you pay cash, you must request a **free transfer** slip that allows you to change to an intersecting bus route only (legal transfer points are listed on the transfer paper) within one hour of issue. Transfer slips can't be used to enter the subway.

All buses in Manhattan, and 95 percent of New York City buses in the other boroughs, are equipped with wheelchair lifts and special areas where the seats in the back fold up to make room for securing wheelchairs onboard. The buses also "kneel," scrunching down when they stop so that the first step isn't quite so high up.

 The Alliance for Downtown New York's **Downtown Connection** offers a free bus service that provides access to important downtown destinations, including Battery Park City, the World Financial Center, and South Street Seaport. The service, which operates from 10 a.m. to 7:30 p.m. seven days a week, brings lower Manhattan residents, workers, and visitors closer to downtown businesses, events, shopping, and attractions.

The Downtown Connection's 5-mile route runs in two directions: from Chambers Street on the West Side to Beekman Street on the East Side. The service makes stops at dozens of locations and is able to transport about 30 passengers per bus (20 seated, 10 standing). Six buses run on weekdays; four buses run on the weekend.

The climate-controlled buses are ADA wheelchair accessible and run on ultra-low-sulfur fuel. Each vehicle is also equipped with diesel-particulate filters and electronically controlled fuel-injected engines. For more information on the Downtown Connection, call the **Downtown Alliance** at ☎ **212-566-6700,** or visit www.downtownny.com.

Understanding the MetroCard

The MetroCard fare card is a high-tech system that encodes a certain number of rides on a magnetic strip on the back of a thin plastic card. MetroCards are accepted on buses and subways alike and have a lot of advantages over the old tokens: They don't weigh a ton, you can slip the card in your wallet or pocket, you can buy and recharge it in an automatic vending machine, and last but not least, you get one free transfer between bus and subway (or vice versa) for each ride as long as you make the transfer within two hours of your initial boarding.

Two types of MetroCards are available for purchase:

- ✔ **Pay-Per-Ride,** the regular card described above, can be used for up to four people by swiping up to four times (bring the whole family). You can put any amount from $4.50 (2 rides) to $80 on your card. Every time you put at least $8 on your Pay-Per-Ride MetroCard, it's automatically credited with an additional 15 percent. (The minimum amount to avoid any leftover balance is $45, which gets you 23 rides.) You can refill your card at any subway station at any time until its expiration date, which is usually about a year from the date of purchase.

✔ **Unlimited-Ride** can't be used for more than one person at a time or more frequently than 18-minute intervals. These cards are available in four values: the **Daily Fun Pass,** which allows you a day's worth of unlimited subway and bus rides for $8.25; the **7-Day MetroCard,** for $27; the **14-Day MetroCard,** for $52; and the **30-Day MetroCard,** for $89. Seven- and 30-day Unlimited-Ride MetroCards can be purchased at any subway station or MetroCard merchant.

✔ Fun Passes can't be purchased at token booths. Buy them at a MetroCard vending machine, from a MetroCard merchant, or at the MTA desk at the Times Square Information Center.

✔ Unlimited-Ride MetroCards go into effect *the first time you use them* — so if you buy a card on Monday and don't use it until Wednesday, Wednesday is when the clock starts ticking. A Fun Pass is good from the first time you use it until 3 a.m. the next day, while 7- and 30-day MetroCards run out at midnight on the last day. These unlimited MetroCards can't be refilled; throw them out after they've been used up and buy a new one.

In addition to being sold in the subway, MetroCards are sold at many hotels and in thousands of shops all over town. If a shop offers the card, it has a sign in its window saying so.

The MetroCard has one corner snipped off and a small hole on one side. To use your MetroCard in the subway, swipe the card forward through the reader, with the cut-off corner on top and at the back (and between your fingers) and the little hole leading the way. To use your MetroCard on the bus, insert the card downward into the machine with the snipped-off corner up and to the left, the little hole on the bottom and the side with the magnetic strip facing you. The machine "eats" the card momentarily and then spits it back out and beeps — also displaying how much money is left on your card.

Seniors and people with disabilities get a 50 percent discount from the MTA. You can apply for the discount by going to 3 Stone St. (between Broadway and Broad Street), weekdays between 9 a.m. and 5 p.m. Or you can download the application at www.mta.info, complete it, and mail it in before your visit. You can recharge your discounted MetroCard at the vending machines and ticket booths in subway stations.

Traveling by taxi

There are times when I have to break down, open my wallet, and get into a taxi. Like when I'm late, it's not rush hour, and I need to be somewhere fast. Or when I'm not near public transportation, if I'm with a group of three or four, or if it's just too late at night and I want to be home safe and fast.

Taking a cab costs you $2.50 for the initial charge, plus 40¢ per ⅕ mile or 40¢ per 120 seconds waiting charge, plus a 50¢ night surcharge

(8 p.m.–6 a.m.) or a $1 surcharge between 4 and 8 p.m. The average fare in Manhattan is $7.

 When you're waiting on the street for an available taxi, look at the **medallion light** on the top of oncoming cabs. If the light is out, the taxi is in use. When the center part (the number) is lit, the taxi is available — this is when you raise your hand to flag the cab. (Observe flagging etiquette and put a respectful distance between you and any fellow flaggers; don't steal someone else's cab.) If all the lights are on, the driver is off duty. A taxi can't take more than four people, so expect to split up if your group is larger. If it's raining or it's rush hour and everyone is looking for a cab, either be prepared to battle it out among the seasoned (read: "ruthless") New York cab riders, or just head for the nearest subway station.

Follow these suggestions to make your ride as smooth as possible:

- ✔ **Plant yourself in the backseat and *then* indicate your destination.** Once you're in the cab, a driver can't refuse to take you anyplace in the five boroughs (and unscrupulous drivers sometimes will do that, for destinations they fear are unsafe, such as Harlem, or too out of their way, such as Brooklyn or Queens). When announcing your destination to the driver, speak clearly. Remember that English is probably not your driver's first language.

- ✔ **Try to know the cross-street of your destination ("Third Avenue and 41st Street").** Many drivers don't know the city as well as they ought to (especially outside central Manhattan), and if you give a specific street address (like "1500 Broadway"), the driver may not immediately know the exact location, and his confusion may end up costing you more money.

- ✔ **If your driver is driving too fast for you, ask him nicely to slow down.** You can also ask him to stop talking on his cellphone, even if it's hands-free. You have the right to a safe (as well as a smoke-free and noise-free) trip.

- ✔ **When you get to your destination, have your money or credit card ready.** You can track the charge on the meter; remember to add the 50¢ night surcharge or the $1 surcharge for rides between 4 and 8 p.m.). You want to disembark rapidly to avoid traffic jams.

- ✔ **Have small bills with you; drivers generally don't accept bills larger than $20.** You can also pay with a credit or debit card — all taxicabs are required by law to accept them (and you should report the driver if he claims his card machine is broken).

- ✔ **Tip 15 percent.** That said, it is within your rights to decline to tip for poor service.

- ✔ **Ask for a receipt.** The receipt has the taxi medallion number on it, which is a useful detail if you forget something in the car. If you leave anything behind in the cab, or if you want to register a complaint, call the New York City Taxi & Limousine Commission Consumer Hotline (☎ 311 in New York City or 212-692-8294) and reference the medallion number to help identify your driver.

✔ **Check that you have all your belongings before leaving.** Taxi drivers are usually very honest, but the same is not necessarily true of the customers who use the cab immediately after you.

✔ **Disembark from the curbside door to avoid the stream of traffic dodging around your stopped vehicle on the other side.**

✔ **Wear a seat belt.** Accidents do happen.

Seeing New York on Foot

Walking is one of the preferred modes of transportation in New York. It lets you take in the wonder that is New York, and it's free.

When walking in New York, however, don't do as we New Yorkers do. We zigzag across the streets, rush against the lights, dodge taxis and buses, and tempt fate on an almost daily basis. So, be smart and exercise some caution. Always be careful when crossing the street, even when you have the light; drivers sometimes get distracted. And cross only at crosswalks. Keep your eyes open for distracted walkers who sometimes resemble NFL blockers. And if you're gawking at some amazing edifice, do it standing still. Otherwise, you may find yourself flattened by one of those blockers. Walk as if you're driving, staying to the right.

Unfortunately, many bicyclists seem to think that the traffic laws don't apply to them; they often blithely fly through red lights and dash the wrong way on one-way streets, so be on your guard. Be extra cautious in bike-messenger-heavy areas such as Fifth Avenue in the Flatiron District; I've been nearly sideswiped here many times.

Walking is sometimes faster than taking the bus or a taxi. Traffic can move through Midtown at a snail's pace — especially during rush hour — and pedestrians typically outdistance cars and buses by blocks.

Be sure to bring comfortable shoes! Not only are you on your feet seeing the city all day, but you're probably on your feet indoors, too — you can rack up a lot of mileage inside the Metropolitan Museum of Art, for example.

Chapter 9

Checking In at New York City's Best Hotels

. . . .

In This Chapter

▶ Choosing the right hotel for you

▶ Finding the best room rate

▶ Arriving without a reservation

▶ Deciding among New York's best hotels

▶ Choosing a backup if your favorite isn't available

. . . .

*W*ith the feverish pace of hotel development pushing the number of rooms to 90,000, the sleeping options in New York are staggering. Do you want to spend most of your travel budget on a luxurious hotel? Do you want to stay close to the neon and noise of Times Square? Do you want a room with a view of Central Park? Will you settle for a room barely bigger than your linen closet back home? These are some of the questions you need to ask yourself before you book a room.

Getting to Know Your Options

In some cities and regions, chain hotels may be the most prevalent option, but that's not the case in New York City. In this section, I briefly discuss nationally known chains as well as one-of-a-kind hostelries and bed-and-breakfasts you can find only in New York.

Independent hotels

Many of the hotels I list in this chapter fall in the class of "independent" hotels (versus chains) because I feel such hotels give you more of a taste of the city. Don't be misled, though; in New York, independent hotels include everything from huge hotels run by large corporations — or by the master builder, Donald Trump — to small boutique hotels that are family-owned and run the gamut from very expensive to inexpensive.

Chain hotels

Just a few of the hotels I list are major national chains. Far from the kind of cookie-cutter sameness you may find elsewhere, the chains I choose, usually moderate in price, hold up well in comparison to similarly located independent hotels. (See the Quick Concierge for the toll-free numbers and Web sites of New York's major chain hotels.)

Bed-and-breakfasts and inns

New York is not the Berkshires, where there are B&Bs galore. Still, the city has some nice B&Bs and inns (frequently in historic brownstones in residential neighborhoods) that offer quaint alternatives to the big, cold behemoth of a hotel the city is more famous for. If you'd like to check out B&B options, try **City Sonnet** (☎ 212-614-3034; www.citysonnet.com), **Manhattan Lodgings** (☎ 212-677-7616; www.manhattanlodgings. com), or **Metro-Home** (☎ 646-274-1505; www.metro-home.com).

Short-term apartment rentals

If you want to look into renting a furnished apartment or subletting someone's place as an alternative to staying in a hotel, which can be a money-saving option if you're traveling with your family or staying more than several days, try **Manhattan Getaways** (☎ 212-956-2010; www. manhattangetaways.com), **New York Habitat** (☎ 212-255-8018; www. nyhabitat.com), or **NYC Residence** (☎ 212-226-2700; www.nyc residence.com).

Finding the Best Room at the Best Rate

In all but the smallest accommodations, the rate you pay for a room depends on many factors — chief among them being how you make your reservation. The most competitive rates are likely found on the Internet.

The **rack rate** is the maximum rate a hotel charges for a room. It's the rate you get if you walk in off the street and ask for a room for the night.

Hotels are happy to charge you the rack rate, but you can almost always do better. The best way to avoid paying the rack rate is surprisingly simple: Just ask for a cheaper or discounted rate. You may be pleasantly surprised.

 As you proceed with the selection process, don't forget that the basic rate a hotel charges you isn't what you end up paying. The hotel tax in New York City is 14.75 percent, and don't forget the room charge of $3.50 per night. When you reserve a room, make sure to find out whether the price you're being quoted includes taxes. (The prices listed in this chapter do not include taxes.)

You don't have to just take the room and rate that a hotel offers you. With a little know-how, you can get the room you want at a price you can afford.

In the following sections, I offer some tried-and-true tips to help you locate the best room for the best available price.

Asking for the best rate

Sometimes the easiest approach is a straightforward one. A hotel typically won't extend its discount room rates unless you ask for them. Call the hotel's direct local number and find out if the hotel is offering specials or discounted packages. When you reserve a room, mention your membership in AAA, AARP, frequent-flier programs, and any other corporate rewards programs you belong to. These memberships may shave a few dollars off your room rate.

Choosing your season carefully

Room rates can vary dramatically — by hundreds of dollars in some cases — depending on what time of year you visit. The dead of winter (Jan–Mar) is best for bargains in New York; summer is pricier but not stratospheric. Fall is the busiest and most expensive season, running from September right up through the end-of-the-year holidays; expect to pay top dollar for everything, especially at Christmastime. See Chapter 3 for more information on the best time to visit the city.

Going uptown or downtown . . . or to Brooklyn?

A New York subway can whisk you anywhere in minutes, so you don't have to stay in Midtown or the Upper East Side, where some of the most expensive hotels are. You get better value for your money by staying *outside* the Theater District, in neighborhoods such as Greenwich Village, Chelsea, Murray Hill, or the Upper West Side.

A Manhattan-based hotel may be the only kind you're considering; that's understandable, especially if you have only a few days in New York. However, believe it or not (and this Brooklynite is still in shock), hotels are popping up in downtown Brooklyn at a fierce rate. The Downtown Brooklyn Partnership — a nonprofit organization overseeing Brooklyn's booming development — counts 12 hotels, with more than 2,000 rooms combined, set to open. The hotels include major chains such as Aloft, Hilton Garden Inn, Holiday Inn, Homewood Suites, and Sheraton. If you have friends or family in Brooklyn, a hotel there may be a great option for you. But if not, keep it in mind as a possible alternative, if you can't find a room in your price range in Manhattan; downtown Brooklyn is also just a quick subway (or cab) ride away.

Visiting over a weekend

If your trip includes a weekend, you may be able to save big. Business hotels tend to empty out on weekends, and rooms that go for a pretty penny Monday through Thursday can drop prices dramatically — as low as $200 or less — after the execs have headed home. These deals are especially prevalent in the Financial District, but they're often available in tourist-friendly Midtown, too. Check the hotel's Web site for attractive weekend rates, or ask when you call to reserve.

Surfing the Web for hotel deals

Hotels often offer Internet-only deals that can save you 10 percent to 20 percent over what you'd pay if you booked over the telephone. Also, hotels often advertise all their available deals on their Web sites. What's more, some of the discount reservations agencies (including those listed in this section) have sites that allow you to book online.

Consider joining the **Playbill Online Theater Club** (www.playbill club.com), a free service that offers some excellent members-only rates at select city hotels, in addition to discounts on theater tickets. **American Automobile Association** (AAA) members can often score the best discounts by booking at www.aaa.com.

Travel search sites, such as **Orbitz** (www.orbitz.com), **Expedia** (www.expedia.com), **Hotwire** (www.hotwire.com), **Priceline** (www.price line.com), and **Travelocity** (www.travelocity.com), offer other discount options. If you have special needs — say, a quiet room — call the hotel and make your needs known after you've booked online.

Always **get a confirmation number** and **make a printout** of any online booking transaction.

Finding a top-notch room

After you make your reservation, asking a few more pointed questions can go a long way toward making sure you get the best room in the house. Always ask for a corner room; they are usually larger and quieter and have more windows and light than standard rooms, and they don't always cost more. Inquire, too, about the location of the restaurants and bars in the hotel — all potential sources of annoying noise.

If you aren't happy with your room when you arrive, talk to the front desk. If they have an unoccupied room, they should be happy to accommodate you, within reason.

Arriving without a Reservation (Not Recommended)

Your lodging options are limited if you arrive without a reservation. Even with the economic downturn, hotel occupancy rates in the city have hovered around 80 percent for the past couple of years. However, making a few phone calls can get you a room most of the time.

As with airline travel, services that call themselves consolidators or wholesalers purchase lots of rooms at a big discount and then pass some of the savings on to you. The hotel stays full, the consolidator makes money, and you may save a lot (or only a little) in the deal.

If you arrive in New York without a reservation and have trouble booking directly with the hotels, the first place to try is **Quikbook** (☎ 800-789-9887; www.quikbook.com), which is particularly good for New York City hotels. Your other options are **Turbotrip.com** (☎ 800-473-7829; www.turbotrip.com), which provides comprehensive lodging and travel information for destinations throughout the United States and worldwide, or **Hotel Discount** (☎ 800-715-7666; www.hoteldiscount.com), a good source for last-minute reservations.

New York City's Best Hotels

Hotel rates in New York are the most expensive in the United States. In 2007, the average price of a hotel room soared close to the $300 mark, and the recession has since brought it down only to around $260. And not only are you paying more for your room, but you're getting less than you would in other cities. Here's a breakdown of what sort of space and amenities you can expect at each price level.

- ✔ **$ ($209 or less):** These hotels are relative bargains, but services are sparse. Your room will probably be small, you may have to share a bathroom, and don't expect room service, fitness equipment, cable channels, or bellhops.

- ✔ **$$ ($210–$309):** Expect these rooms to be a little larger and of better quality and comfort than those in the first category. You may have access to a fitness center and business facilities, and the hotel may throw in a complimentary continental breakfast and/or free Internet access.

- ✔ **$$$ ($310–$449):** Typically, you get room service, probably a refrigerator and perhaps a kitchen or kitchenette, cable TV and/or DVD, free access to a health club, wireless Internet, complimentary breakfast or beverages (and possibly afternoon wine and cheese), and an on-site restaurant.

- ✔ **$$$$ ($450–$599):** On top of the amenities listed for the preceding category, you can expect plenty of space, fine furnishings, a variety of dining and drinking options in the hotel, and excellent service. Because these hotels often cater to businesspeople, they sometimes offer special amenities like complimentary car service to the Financial District.

- ✔ **$$$$$ ($600 or more):** In this range, you get more than a place to stay: You get an experience. These hotels have style, elegance, and a reputation for impeccable service.

Downtown Hotels

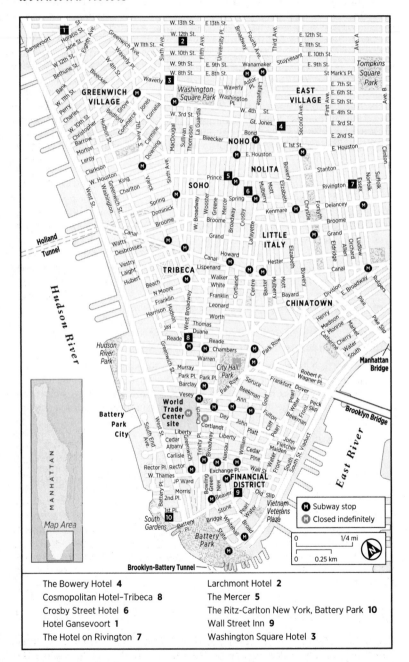

The Bowery Hotel **4**
Cosmopolitan Hotel–Tribeca **8**
Crosby Street Hotel **6**
Hotel Gansevoort **1**
The Hotel on Rivington **7**

Larchmont Hotel **2**
The Mercer **5**
The Ritz-Carlton New York, Battery Park **10**
Wall Street Inn **9**
Washington Square Hotel **3**

The Ace Hotel
$$$ Herald Square/NoMad

At the Ace Hotel chain's largest property (with 260 rooms spread across 12 floors), the crunked-up, low-lit lobby is the hub of a carefully crafted, rocked-out experience. If you forgot your guitar picks or strings, they're for sale at the reception desk, along with flowers and scented candles; the taxidermied birds, however, are for show only. There are six room types, ranging from bunk bedrooms to loft suites, all with a mix of vintage and reproduction furniture, original artwork on the walls, flatscreen TVs, elegantly appointed bathrooms, and minibars disguised as touring cases. Some rooms also have turntables (with albums provided by Other Music, a local independent record store; see p. 236), fully stocked Smeg refrigerators, and guitars, so request what you need when you make your reservation. The Ace is known for its high-style collaborations; the property also has on-site branches of Stumptown Coffee, Opening Ceremony, and Project No. 8; a sandwich shop off-shoot of No. 7 Greene (see p. 159); an event space, Liberty Hall; and The Breslin, the hotel's acclaimed gastropub. The clientele is a diverse mix of the young and the young-at-heart, and families are welcome (all ages enjoy the lobby's vintage photo booth). Stay here if you like a scene, of-the-moment amenities, and lots of black.

See map p. 98. 20 W. 29th St. (between Broadway and Fifth Avenue). ☎ **212-679-2222.** *Fax: 212-679-1947.* www.acehotel.com. *Subway: N or R to 28th Street. Parking: $55. Rack rates: $209–$599 double. Pets allowed. Children stay free in parent's room. AE, DISC, MC, V.*

Affinia Dumont
$$$ Midtown East

A bit away from the center of Midtown, but still within easy walking distance of Herald Square, the Empire State Building, Madison Square Garden, and Grand Central, this may be New York's only fitness-suite hotel. When you book a room, you can request an Experience Kit with no extra charge, to be used if you have time only to work out in your room. The hotel also has a complete fitness spa with weights, cardio equipment, and massage and skin treatments. But even if you don't want to break a sweat, each hotel room features attractive amenities that include a full kitchen, at least one 27-inch television, a large desk with an ergonomic chair, the Affinia Bed with a custom-designed mattress, a six-selection Dream Pillow menu, and a stocked minibar.

See map p. 98. 150 E. 34th St. (between Second and Third avenues, 3 blocks east of the Empire State Building). ☎ **212-481-7600.** *Fax: 212-889-8856.* www.affinia.com. *Subway: 6 to 33rd Street. Valet parking: $45. Rack rates: $280–$899 suite. AE, DC, DISC, MC, V.*

The Algonquin
$$$ Midtown West

The atmosphere in this 1902 landmark building is so steeped in writers' lore that you feel guilty turning on the television instead of reading the

Midtown Hotels

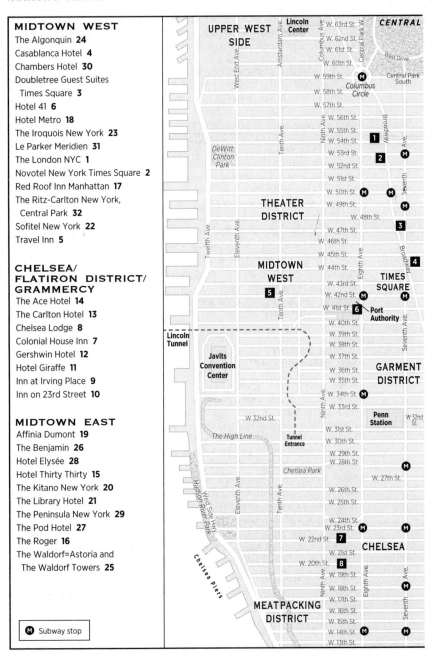

MIDTOWN WEST
The Algonquin **24**
Casablanca Hotel **4**
Chambers Hotel **30**
Doubletree Guest Suites
Times Square **3**
Hotel 41 **6**
Hotel Metro **18**
The Iroquois New York **23**
Le Parker Meridien **31**
The London NYC **1**
Novotel New York Times Square **2**
Red Roof Inn Manhattan **17**
The Ritz-Carlton New York,
Central Park **32**
Sofitel New York **22**
Travel Inn **5**

**CHELSEA/
FLATIRON DISTRICT/
GRAMMERCY**
The Ace Hotel **14**
The Carlton Hotel **13**
Chelsea Lodge **8**
Colonial House Inn **7**
Gershwin Hotel **12**
Hotel Giraffe **11**
Inn at Irving Place **9**
Inn on 23rd Street **10**

MIDTOWN EAST
Affinia Dumont **19**
The Benjamin **26**
Hotel Elysée **28**
Hotel Thirty Thirty **15**
The Kitano New York **20**
The Library Hotel **21**
The Peninsula New York **29**
The Pod Hotel **27**
The Roger **16**
The Waldorf=Astoria and
The Waldorf Towers **25**

Ⓜ Subway stop

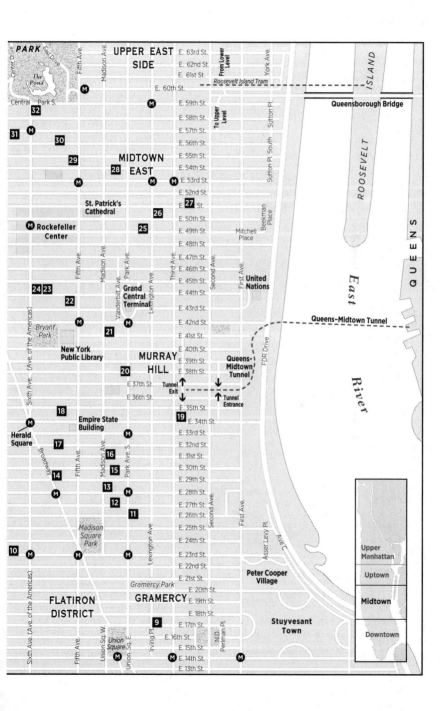

Uptown Hotels

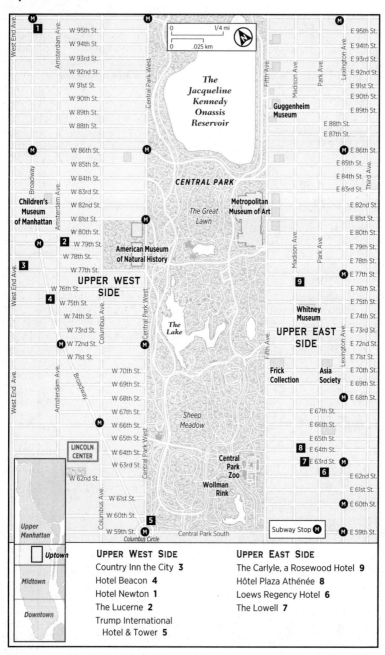

UPPER WEST SIDE
Country Inn the City **3**
Hotel Beacon **4**
Hotel Newton **1**
The Lucerne **2**
Trump International
   Hotel & Tower **5**

UPPER EAST SIDE
The Carlyle, a Rosewood Hotel **9**
Hôtel Plaza Athénée **8**
Loews Regency Hotel **6**
The Lowell **7**

latest issue of *The New Yorker* provided in each of the guest rooms. Rooms can be cramped, but they have been renovated recently and are equipped with possibly the most comfortable, inviting beds in the city, as well as 21st-century technology such as free Wi-Fi, flatscreen televisions, Kindles upon request, and MP3 docks. In the plush lobby, you can sit in cushy chairs, sip exquisite (and expensive) cocktails, have a snack, make friends with Matilda the Algonquin cat, or just read or play on your laptop. Meals are served in the celebrated Round Table Room, while the fabulous **Oak Room** is one of the city's top cabarets. The publike Blue Bar is home to a rotating collection of Al Hirschfeld drawings that's well worth a browse.

See map p. 98. 59 W. 44th St. (between Fifth and Sixth avenues, 1 block from Times Square). ☎ 888-304-2047 or 212-840-6800. Fax: 212-944-1618. www.algonquin hotel.com. Subway: B, D, F, or M to 42nd Street. Parking: $30. Rack rates: $329–$699 double. AE, DC, DISC, MC, V.

The Benjamin
$$$$ **Midtown East**

From the Jazz Age design of the exterior and lobby, you would never know that the Benjamin is barely more than a decade old. But after you check into your spacious room and notice the high-tech amenities, such as a combo printer/fax/copier, high-speed Internet access, and an ergonomic chair at an executive desk with movable workstation, you know you're in the 21st century. Many of the amenities are geared toward business travelers, but there are luxurious touches anyone can appreciate. All rooms are airy, but the deluxe studio and one-bedroom suites are extra large. The hotel even offers a few one-bedroom suites with terraces. Lexington Avenue can get very busy most weeknights and mornings, so if you're a light sleeper, book a room off Lexington. Or call the "sleep concierge," who consults with you and recommends the right choice from a pillow menu to help you sleep (white-noise machines are also available). Bathrooms feature Frette robes and shower water pressure that's strong enough to make you think you've just experienced a deep-tissue massage.

See map p. 98. 125 E. 50th St. (at Lexington Avenue; close to Rockefeller Center, St. Patrick's Cathedral, and Saks Fifth Avenue). ☎ 866-222-2365 or 212-715-2500. Fax: 212-715-2525. www.thebenjamin.com. Subway: 6 to 51st Street; E or V to Lexington Avenue. Parking: $45. Rack rates: $360–$569 double. AE, DC, DISC, MC, V.

The Bowery Hotel
$$$ **East Village**

For most of the past 50 years the Bowery was best known for its bums and the punk club CBGB. The recent boom times haven't entirely swept away its grit, though, and the Bowery Hotel winks at that history while providing the classiest accommodations this former skid row has seen in more than a century. The luxurious, faded era is evoked in the reception area and in the remarkably inviting lobby bar, which is open only to hotel guests and, therefore, maintains an intimate, subdued feel, aided by the lodgelike décor: mosaic tile flooring and Persian rugs, dark woods, vintage velvet couches and chairs, and a fantastic fireplace. The hotel has 14 floors but only 135 rooms, all of which have floor-to-ceiling windows that help even the smallest accommodations (250 sq. ft.) seem light and airy. The corner suites have the best views in the hotel; there are seven suites with private terraces (including one with a hot tub). The basement fitness room is nothing special, but **Gemma,** the hotel's Italian restaurant, provides an excellent setting for a meal (and 24-hour room service if you'd rather dine in). The overall effect is a cozy oasis on a legendary underdog strip, where you're somehow in the middle of everything and still on the edge at the same time.

See map p. 96. 335 Bowery (between Great Jones and Bond streets). ☎ *212-505-9100. Fax: 212-505-9700.* www.theboweryhotel.com. *Subway: 6 to Bleecker Street. Valet parking: $45. Rack rates: $320–$650 double. Children stay free in parent's room. AE, DC, DISC, MC, V.*

The Carlton Hotel
$$$ Flatiron District

This 1904 Beaux Arts hotel was getting worn around the edges when it was rescued by architect David Rockwell and magnificently refurbished. The highlight of that $60-million renovation is the grand, sweeping lobby complete with a curving marble staircase and a cathedral-like high ceiling. The Carlton has recaptured the glory of the past and blended it with contemporary furnishings in the lobby along with a two-story waterfall. Rooms are generously sized and retain the Beaux Arts motif with the addition of modern amenities such as Frette linens, free Wi-Fi, and iPod docking stations. The marble bathrooms offer plenty of counter space and Molton Brown toiletries; some rooms have bathtubs, while others just have showers. Off the lobby is the acclaimed bi-level restaurant **Country.**

See map p. 98. 88 Madison Ave. (between 28th and 29th streets, a few blocks south of the Empire State Building). ☎ *800-601-8500 or 212-532-4100.* www.carlton hotelny.com. *Subway: 6 to 28th Street. Parking: $40. Rack rates: $239–$469 double. Pets under 25 lbs. allowed with $50-per-night fee. AE, DC, DISC, MC, V.*

The Carlyle, A Rosewood Hotel
$$$$$ Upper East Side

This 34-story grande dame towers over Madison Avenue, epitomizing the old-world, moneyed neighborhood where it stands. Service is white-glove (literally) and doormen wear bowler hats; the many celebrities or dignitaries, some with faces obscured by silk scarves, sip tea in the hotel's cozy Gallery. Guest rooms range from singles to seven-room suites, some with terraces and full dining rooms. All have marble bathrooms with whirlpool tubs and every amenity you'd expect from a hotel of this caliber; even your pet is served Fiji water. Many suites have breathtaking views of either downtown or the West Side and Central Park. The Carlyle is also the home of **Bemelmans Bar,** the gorgeously redesigned **Café Carlyle** for great cabaret, and the elegant **Carlyle Restaurant.**

See map p. 100. 35 E. 76th St. (at Madison Avenue, 1 block north of the Whitney Museum). ☎ **800-227-5737** *or 212-744-1600. Fax: 212-717-4682.* www.thecarlyle. com. *Subway: 6 to 77th Street, then walk 1 block west on 76th Street to Madison Avenue. Parking: $50. Rack rates: $700–$1,050 double. Pets allowed with $50-per-night fee. AE, DC, MC, V.*

Casablanca Hotel
$$$ Midtown West

Picture the exotic, romantic setting of the movie *Casablanca* — ceiling fans, mosaic tiles, and North African–themed art — and then picture that setting in the heart of neon-blinding, cacophonous Times Square. The combination seems unlikely, but who wouldn't want a desert oasis in the middle of all that mayhem? And that's what the Casablanca Hotel really is: a calming refuge where you can escape from the noise and crowds. The soundproofed rooms may not be the biggest around, but they're well-outfitted with the aforementioned ceiling fans, DVD players, complimentary Wi-Fi, and beautifully tiled bathrooms where, if you want, you can open the window and let sounds outside remind you where you really are. Because of its location, moderate prices, size (only 48 rooms), and accolades, the Casablanca is in high demand, so book early.

See map p. 98. 147 W. 43rd St. (just east of Broadway, in the heart of Times Square). ☎ **888-922-7225** *or 212-869-1212. Fax: 212-391-7585.* www.casablancahotel. com. *Subway: N, R, 1, 2, or 3 to 42nd Street/Times Square. Parking: $25 next door. Rack rates: $299–$499 double. Rates include continental breakfast and evening wine and cheese in Rick's Café. AE, DC, MC, V.*

Chambers Hotel
$$$ Midtown West

From the moment you enter the lobby — with its soothing brown, gray, and purple hues and inviting lounge spaces — this understated boutique hotel feels like an oasis of calm in the Midtown hustle. With only 77 rooms and suites, it's a more intimately scaled alternative to the larger hotels that are typical of the neighborhood. Rooms have a lofty feel with industrial touches (such as pulley-style lights and concrete ceilings) softened by rich fabrics. Business travelers may be fine with the smaller, interior rooms, but if lots of light is important to you, ask for a room with southern exposure (ending in 03). The hotel is attached to an uptown branch of **Momofuku Milk Bar** (see Chapter 10), as well as **Má Pêche,** the latest restaurant by chef David Chang.

See map p. 98. 15 W. 56th St. (between Fifth and Sixth avenues). ☎ **866-204-5656** *or 212-974-5656. Fax: 212-974-5657.* www.chambershotel.com. *Subway: F to 57th Street. Valet parking: $35. Rack rates: $275–$550 double, from $825 suite. Children 17 and under stay free in parent's room. Pets allowed. AE, DC, DISC, MC, V.*

Chelsea Lodge
$ Chelsea

Not only is this small hotel in a Chelsea brownstone a charmer, but it's also a great value for those on a budget. Though the rooms are small, they're furnished in an appealing, old-fashioned Americana style and everything is in top-notch condition. Rooms on the first floor have high ceilings and give the appearance of being bigger. Beds are full-size and each room has its own sink and in-room shower stall; toilets are shared. I like the location in the heart of trendy, yet residential Chelsea, and, coupled with the stylishness of the rooms, you'd be hard-pressed to do better for the money. It's best for couples rather than shares. *Tip:* If you have a little more room in your budget, suites are available a few doors down; the $229 price reflects the upgrade in amenities (including queen-size beds, private bathrooms, and free Wi-Fi).

See map p. 98. 318 W. 20th St. (between Eighth and Ninth avenues). ☎ **800-373-1116** *or 212-243-4499. Fax: 212-243-7852.* www.chelsealodge.com. *Subway: 1 to 18th Street; C or E to 23rd Street. Parking: About $20 nearby. Rack rate: $119 single, $129 double. AE, DC, DISC, MC, V.*

Cosmopolitan Hotel–Tribeca
$ TriBeCa

If you're looking for an affordable hotel and you don't want to share a bathroom, go to this decent TriBeCa choice. The modern IKEA-ish furniture includes a work desk and an armoire; other amenities include free Wi-Fi, ceiling fans and air-conditioning, and satellite TV. Beds are comfy, and sheets and towels are of good quality. Rooms are small but utilize the limited space, and the place is pristine. The location is safe, hip, and subway-convenient. Don't expect much in the way of services; if you want food, call in for delivery, and plan to get your coffee from the store around the corner. But this is a fine choice for the money (though, like the rest of New York, it's more expensive than it used to be).

See map p. 96. 95 W. Broadway (at Chambers Street). ☎ **888-895-9400** *or 212-566-1900. Fax: 212-566-6909.* www.cosmohotel.com. *Subway: 1, 2, or 3 to Chambers Street. Parking: $20, 1 block away. Rack rates: $169–$240 double. AE, DC, MC, V.*

Crosby Street Hotel
$$$$ SoHo

On a quiet cobblestone street just a block from the circus of SoHo shopping, the Crosby Street Hotel opened in late 2009 and immediately raised the bar for the luxury boutique hotel experience in New York. From the moment you enter the hotel, which is filled with original art, you know you're in a truly unique space. The hotel has 86 comfortably sized rooms and suites, all individually decorated with a playful mixture of bright colors and patterns that is at once stimulating and comforting. The rooms feature floor-to-ceiling double-glazed windows and bathrooms with double pedestal sinks, Miller Harris toiletries, and bidets; suites add tubs and sofa beds. In addition to a gym, a sculpture garden, and the **Crosby Bar** (serving all meals and traditional afternoon tea), the hotel's 99-seat cinema hosts the Sunday Night Film Club (open to the public; advance reservations recommended). The refined hotel is a hit with fashion-, film-, and entertainment-industry types (the proximity to Balthazar, an enduring celebrity haunt, can't hurt), but it's also an unpretentious, family-friendly place.

See map p. 96. 79 Crosby St. (between Prince and Spring streets). ☎ **888-559-5508** *or 212-226-6400. Fax: 212-226-0055.* www.crosbystreethotel.com. *Subway: N or R to Prince Street. Valet parking: $55. Rack rates: $495–$650 double, from $795 suites. Children stay free in parent's room with existing bedding or crib. Dogs under 25 pounds accepted. AE, DC, MC, V.*

Doubletree Guest Suites Times Square
$$$ Midtown West

In the heart of ear-splitting, eye-blinding Times Square, this 45-story Doubletree is a wonderland for children. From the fresh-baked chocolate-chip cookies you get upon arrival, the spacious suites big enough for two preschoolers to play hide-and-seek, and the all-day children's room-service menu, to the proximity to the gargantuan Toys "R" Us, American Girl Place, Build-a-Bear Workshop, and other kid-friendly Times Square offerings, this Doubletree is hard to beat for families. Bathrooms have two entrances, so the kids don't have to traipse through the parent's room, and every suite has two televisions with on-demand video games.

See map p. 98. 1568 Broadway (at 47th Street and Seventh Avenue). ☎ **800-222-8733** *or 212-719-1600. Fax: 212-921-5212.* www.doubletree.com. *Subway: N or R to 49th Street. Parking: $35. Rack rates: $285–$1,999 suite. Children 11 and under stay free in parent's suite. AE, DC, DISC, MC, V.*

Gershwin Hotel
$$ Flatiron District

This creative-minded, Warhol-esque hotel caters to up-and-coming artistic types — and well-established names with an eye for value — with its bold modern-art collection and wild style. The standard rooms are clean and bright, with Picasso-style wall murals and Philippe Starck–ish takes on motel furnishings. Superior rooms are better and well worth the extra money; all have either a queen-size bed, two twins, or two doubles, plus a private bathroom with cute, colorful tile. If you're bringing the brood, the Family & Friends rooms are the best option. Budget travelers willing to bunk should consider the Auberge rooms ($40). The hotel is more service oriented than you usually see at this price level (laundry service and babysitting are even available), and the staff is very professional.

See map p. 98. 7 E. 27th St. (between Fifth and Madison avenues). ☎ **212-545-8000.** *Fax: 212-684-5546.* www.gershwinhotel.com. *Subway: N, R, or 6 to 28th Street. Parking: $25, 3 blocks away. Rack rates: $135–$355 double. AE, MC, V.*

Hotel Beacon
$$ Upper West Side

Okay, so you're not in Times Square or in trendy SoHo, but when you're at the Hotel Beacon, you're on the Upper West Side, and, for families, you won't find a better location — or value. Close to Central Park and Riverside Park, the Museum of Natural History and Lincoln Center, and major subway lines, it's not like the Beacon is in a desolate spot. Rooms here are generously sized and feature a kitchenette, a roomy closet, and a marble bathroom. Nearly all standard rooms feature two double beds, and they're big enough to sleep a family on a budget. The large one- and two-bedroom suites are decent deals; each has two closets and a pullout sofa in the well-furnished living room. The two-bedrooms have a second bathroom, making them well outfitted enough to house a small army. There's no room service, but a wealth of good budget dining options deliver, and excellent markets, such as Fairway, are nearby, making the Beacon even more of a home away from home.

See map p. 100. 2130 Broadway (at 75th Street). ☎ **800-572-4969** *or 212-787-1100. Fax: 212-724-0839.* www.beaconhotel.com. *Subway: 1, 2 or 3 to 72nd Street. Parking: $29. Rack rates: $235–$325 double, $295–$550 1-bedroom suite, from $650 2-bedroom suite. AE, DISC, MC, V.*

Hotel Elysée
$$$ Midtown East

This romantic gem in the heart of Midtown is dwarfed by the glass towers on either side of it — but the fact that it's so inconspicuous is part of the Elysée's romantic appeal. Built in 1926, the hotel has a storied past as the preferred address for artists and writers. The hotel still retains a sexy, discreet feel and is run expertly by HK Hotels (the Casablanca, the Gansevoort, and the Library). The renovated rooms have many quirky features; some have fireplaces, others have kitchens or solariums, and all are decorated in French-country furnishings. Good-sized bathrooms are done in Italian marble and well outfitted. On the second floor is the Club Room, where a free continental breakfast is offered daily, along with complimentary wine and cheese on weekday evenings. The hotel also provides daily passes to a nearby branch of the New York Sports Club.

See map p. 98. 60 E. 54th St. (between Park and Madison avenues, a few blocks north of Rockefeller Center). ☎ **800-535-9733** *or 212-753-1066. Fax: 212-980-9278.* www.elyseehotel.com. *Subway: E or M to Fifth Avenue. Valet parking: $30. Rack rates: $305–$610 double. AE, DC, MC, V.*

Hotel Gansevoort
$$$$ Meatpacking District

Built from the ground up by hotelier Henry Kallan (of the Casablanca, Hotel Elysée, Hotel Giraffe, and the Library), the Gansevoort became the first major hotel in the transformed Meatpacking District. This sleek, 14-floor, zinc-colored tower, with its clubby lobby and the indoor/outdoor rooftop bar and pool, is still an anchor of the district. Despite its trendiness, the Gansevoort offers excellent, personable service. Rooms are good-sized with comfortable furnishings in soft tones and amenities such as Nintendo Wii and free wireless Internet. Some have small balconies and bay windows with seating nooks. Suites have Hudson River views. The generously sized bathrooms are done up in ceramic, stainless steel, and marble, and impeccably appointed. You find original art by New York artists on display in all the guest rooms and throughout the hotel. Cellphone rentals and complimentary bikes are also on offer.

See map p. 96. 18 Ninth Ave. (at 13th Street). ☎ **212-206-6700.** *Fax: 212-255-5858.* www.hotelgansevoort.com. *Subway: A, C, or E to 14th Street. Parking: $45. Rack rates: From $525 double, from $895 suite. Pets allowed. AE, DC, MC, V.*

Hotel Giraffe
$$$$ Flatiron District

This hotel, in the fashionable Madison Park area, has a cozy, intimate, feel. Guest rooms evoke an urban European character with high ceilings, velveteen upholstered chairs, and original black-and-white photographs from the '20s and '30s. All the rooms are good sized with high ceilings, and deluxe rooms and suites feature French doors that lead to small balconies with large windows and remote-controlled blackout shades. Bathrooms are spacious with plenty of marble counter space and glass-paneled doors. But the services — characteristic of the HK Hotels group — are what separate this place from many others: complimentary continental breakfast each morning; wine and cheese in the evenings; and coffee, cookies, and tea all day; plus free passes to the New York Sports Club. The lovely rooftop garden is the perfect place for a glass of wine in the evening or morning coffee during warm weather.

See map p. 98. 365 Park Ave. S. (at 26th Street). ☎ **877-296-0009** *or 212-685-7700. Fax: 212-685-7771.* www.hotelgiraffe.com. *Subway: 6 to 28th Street. Parking: $28. Rack rates: $279–$609 double. Rates include continental breakfast and evening wine and cheese. AE, DC, MC, V.*

Hotel Metro
$$$ Midtown West

With its Art Deco style, decent-size rooms, and plenty of free amenities, the Metro, just a block from the Empire State Building, is one of Manhattan's better values. The rooms are outfitted with modern furnishings in earth tones, and include iPod docking stations and laptop-size safes. Though on the small side, the marble bathrooms are lovely and have shower stalls big enough for two. The two-room family suite has a second bedroom in lieu of a sitting area; small families on tighter budgets can opt for a roomy double/double. The comfy, fire-lit library/lounge area off the lobby — where complimentary buffet breakfast is laid out and the coffeepot's on all day — is a popular hangout. The well-furnished rooftop terrace boasts a breathtaking view of the Empire State Building and makes a great place to order up room service.

See map p. 98. 45 W. 35th St. (between Fifth and Sixth avenues, 1 block north of the Empire State Building). ☎ **800-356-3870** *or 212-947-2500. Fax: 212-279-1310.* www. hotelmetronyc.com. *Subway: B, D, F, M, N, or R to 34th Street. Parking: $20 nearby. Rack rates: $295–$475 double. Rates include continental breakfast. AE, DC, DISC, MC, V.*

Hotel Newton
$$ Upper West Side

On the burgeoning northern extreme of the Upper West Side, the Newton is a budget hotel that seems a notch above in almost every category. The lobby is small but tasteful, and the rooms are generally large, with good, firm beds; a work desk; and a sizable bathroom; plus, roomy closets in most. Some rooms are big enough for families, with two doubles or two queen-size beds. The suites feature two queen-size beds in the bedroom, sofas in the sitting rooms, plus such niceties as microwaves, minifridges, and irons, making them well worth the few extra dollars. This AAA-approved, smoke-free hotel is impeccably kept. The 96th Street express subway stop is a block away, providing convenient access to the rest of the city, and the Key West Cafe next door is a favorite for huge, cheap breakfasts.

See map p. 100. 2528 Broadway (between 94th and 95th streets). ☎ **800-643-5553** *or 212-678-6500. Fax: 212-678-6758.* www.thehotelnewton.com. *Subway: 1, 2, or 3 to 96th Street. Parking: $25 nearby. Rack rates: $180–$350 double. Children 14 and under stay free in parent's room. AE, DC, DISC, MC, V.*

The Hotel on Rivington
$$$$ Lower East Side

The contrast of a 21-story glass tower luxury hotel in the midst of 19th- and early-20th-century Lower East Side low-rise tenement buildings is striking, but an accurate representation of what that neighborhood has become. You may not be close to the center of Manhattan if you stay at the Hotel on Rivington, but you are in an almost painfully trendy location. From the floor-to-ceiling windows of some rooms, furnished with modern amenities such as flatscreen televisions, huge Japanese soaking tubs in the bathrooms, and Tempur-Pedic mattresses on the beds, you have incredible city views. (If the view matters, ask for a high floor and be prepared to pay extra for it; the best view you get from other lower-floor rooms is the back of a neighboring building.) A majority of the rooms have private terraces, the option of in-room spa services, and heated, tiled floors in the large bathrooms. Room service is provided by the hotel's restaurant, **LEVANTeast at THOR.**

See map p. 96. 107 Rivington St. (between Ludlow and Essex streets). ☎ **800-915-1537** *or 212-475-2600. Fax: 212-475-5959.* www.hotelonrivington.com. *Subway: F to Delancey Street. Parking: $30. Rack rates: $295–$750 double. Pets allowed. AE, DC, MC, V.*

Hôtel Plaza Athénée
$$$$$ Upper East Side

If money is no object and you don't want to stray too far from Madison Avenue shopping, this elegant, sophisticated hideaway is for you. Antique furniture, hand-painted murals, and the Italian marble floor that adorns the exquisite lobby give the Hotel Plaza Athénée a distinctly European feel. Service here is as good as it gets, with personalized check-in and an attentive staff. The rooms (some newly added) come in a variety of sizes, but all are high-ceilinged and spacious with entrance foyers that give them a residential feel. The suites have closet space the size of some New York apartments. The marble bathrooms are outfitted with thick robes made exclusively for the hotel. The lush lounge, appropriately called **Bar Seine,** is a welcome spot for a predinner cocktail.

See map p. 100. 37 E. 64th St. (between Madison and Park avenues). ☎ **800-447-8800** *or 212-734-9100. Fax: 212-772-0958.* `www.plaza-athenee.com`. *Subway: F to Lexington Avenue. Parking: $48. Rack rates: $875–$1,190 double. AE, DC, MC, V.*

Hotel Thirty Thirty
$$ Midtown East

Thirty Thirty is a solid option for those looking for style and value. The design-conscious tone is set in the loftlike, industrial-modern lobby. Rooms are mostly on the smallish side, but they do the trick for those who intend to spend their days out on the town rather than holed up here. Configurations include standard and superior rooms, with a queen-size bed or two twins; deluxe executive rooms, intended for families or business travelers; and single rooms, meant for single occupancy and the least expensive rooms here. Nice features include cushioned headboards, firm mattresses, built-in wardrobes, and spacious, nicely tiled bathrooms. A few larger units have kitchenettes, great if you're staying in town for a while, as you can appreciate the extra room and the fridge. There's no room service, but delivery is available from nearby restaurants.

See map p. 98. 30 E. 30th St. (between Madison and Park avenues). ☎ **800-804-4480** *or 212-689-1900. Fax: 212-689-0023.* `www.thirtythirty-nyc.com`. *Subway: 6 to 28th Street. Parking: $35, 1 block away. Rack rates: $249–$499 double. Pets allowed. AE, DC, DISC, MC, V.*

The Kitano New York
$$$$ Midtown East

This elegant, Japanese-owned Murray Hill gem offers a unique mix of East and West sensibilities. The marble and mahogany lobby, with its Y-shaped staircase and Botero bronze *Dog,* is one of the most attractive in New York. If you're a very lucky (and wealthy) individual, you get the opportunity to stay in one of three one-bedroom town-house suites, each with sunken living rooms, bay windows, and original, eclectic art. Or, for those whose sensibilities are Eastern-oriented, the hotel offers a Tatami suite, with tatami mats, rice-paper screens, and a Japanese Tea Ceremony room. Most rooms are not quite that luxurious or unique, but all include tasteful mahogany furniture, soundproof windows, and green tea upon arrival. Marble bathrooms are large and have heated towel racks and removable shower heads. At the mezzanine-level bar lounge, Wednesday through Saturday evenings feature live jazz.

See map p. 98. 66 Park Ave. (at 38th Street, near Grand Central Station and the New York Public Library). ☎ **800-548-2666** *or 212-885-7000. Fax: 212-885-7100.* www. kitano.com. *Subway: S, 4, 5, 6, or 7 to Grand Central. Parking: $40. Rack rates: $415–$670 double. AE, DC, DISC, MC, V.*

Larchmont Hotel
$ **Greenwich Village**

On a tree-lined block in a residential part of Greenwich Village, you find this wonderful European-style hotel. Maybe that's why it has a loyal European following. Each bright guest room is tastefully outfitted with a writing desk, a minilibrary of books, an alarm clock, a sink, and a few extras that you normally have to pay a lot more for, such as cotton bathrobes, slippers, and ceiling fans. Every floor has two shared bathrooms (with hair dryers) and a small, simple kitchen. This hotel is a great choice if you're on a budget and don't mind sharing a bathroom. (The $249 Family Room has a private bathroom.) And if you're looking for a downtown base that's close to some of the city's best shopping, dining, and sightseeing (and with your choice of subway lines just a walk away), you can't do much better than the Larchmont.

See map p. 96. 27 W. 11th St. (between Fifth and Sixth avenues). ☎ **212-989-9333.** *Fax: 212-989-9496.* www.larchmonthotel.com. *Subway: A, C, E, F, or M to West 4th Street (use the 8th Street exit); F to 14th Street. Parking: $18 nearby. Rack rates: $109–$165 double. Rates include continental breakfast. Children 12 and under stay free in parent's room. AE, MC, V.*

Le Parker Meridien
$$$$ **Midtown West**

With its central location, incredible amenities (such as the 17,000-square-foot fitness center with a rooftop pool), and three excellent restaurants, Le Parker Meridien just about has it all. The gorgeous, bustling lobby also serves as a public space, and elevators with televisions that show *Tom & Jerry* cartoons and Charlie Chaplin shorts are a wonder for the kids. The spacious hotel rooms, decorated in a Room & Board style, have a fun feel to them with hidden drawers and swirling television platforms, inventively exploiting an economical use of space. The slate-and-limestone bathrooms are large but come with only a shower. **Norma's** serves one of the best breakfasts in the city, and the burgers at **Burger Joint** are the finest in the city (see Chapter 10). A stay at Le Parker Meridien is definitely a New York experience in itself.

See map p. 98. 119 W. 56th St. (between Sixth and Seventh avenues, 1 block from Carnegie Hall). ☎ **800-543-4300** *or 212-245-5000. Fax: 212-307-1776.* www.parker meridien.com. *Subway: F, N, Q, or R to 57th Street. Parking: $45. Rack rates: $279–$669 double. Pets allowed. AE, DC, DISC, MC, V.*

The Library Hotel
$$$ Midtown East

I'm usually suspicious of theme hotels, but because I'm a degreed librarian, this one is an exception. Each of the ten guest-room floors is dedicated to one of the ten major categories of the Dewey Decimal System. In the Geography and Travel room, for example, are books such as *Barcelona* by Robert Hughes and *Bella Tuscany* by Frances Mayes. You may not have the chance to read any of them, but there is something comforting about having them by the bed. Or maybe it's just the comfy rooms, which come in three categories: petite (really small), deluxe, and junior suite; they feature mahogany built-ins, generous desks, and immaculate marble bathrooms. The public spaces feature a reading room where wine and cheese and a complimentary breakfast are served daily, and a writer's den with a fireplace, a flatscreen TV, and a rooftop terrace.

See map p. 98. 299 Madison Ave. (at 41st Street, near the New York Public Library). ☎ **877-793-7323** *or 212-983-4500. Fax: 212-499-9099.* www.libraryhotel.com. *Subway: S, 4, 5, 6, or 7 to 42nd Street/Grand Central. Parking: $30 nearby. Rack rates: $279–$529 double. Rates include continental breakfast, all-day snacks, and weekday wine and cheese. AE, DC, MC, V.*

The London NYC
$$$$ Midtown West

At the all-suites London NYC, rooms generally begin at 500 square feet, and the overall atmosphere is one of discreet luxury. The suites are furnished in muted blue, gray, and cream tones and come with custom furniture, wonderfully roomy bathrooms (some with soaking tubs), and separate dressing areas. The spaciousness of the suites and smart design features, such as coffee tables that convert into dining tables and the ability to project from your laptop to the sitting room TV, make this a great choice for families and business travelers alike. The two-bedroom duplex penthouse has spectacular views of the city, Central Park, and the Hudson River, but even if it's beyond your budget, you can still request a room with a view: The hotel guarantees views from floor 39 up. Chef Gordon Ramsay oversees the hotel's two restaurants, **Gordon Ramsay at the London** (serving fine French cuisine) and the more informal **Maze;** traditional afternoon tea is served in the **London Bar.** Add to the accommodations one of the nicer hotel gyms in town, the hotel's proximity to Fifth Avenue shopping, Lincoln Center and Broadway, and attractions such as MoMA, and you've found an excellent Midtown base.

See map p. 98. 151 W. 54th St. (between Broadway and Eighth Avenue). ☎ **866-690-2029** *or 212-698-8128. Fax: 212-468-8747.* www.thelondonnyc.com. *Subway: B, D, or E to Seventh Avenue. Valet parking $55. Rack rates: $349–$789 double, from $899 luxury suites. Each additional person age 2 and older $50. Pets under 25 pounds allowed with $125 cleaning fee. AE, DISC, MC, V.*

Country in the city

If you're looking for an alternative to the quintessential huge New York hotel, or if you want a taste of urban hominess where you may actually meet your innkeeper, you have a number of options to consider.

On the pricey side, but worth the expense (if authentic 19th-century Victorian romance is what you're seeking), is the fabulous **Inn at Irving Place,** 56 Irving Place (between 17th and 18th streets; ☎ 800-685-1447 or 212-533-4600; www.innatirving.com; see map p. 98). Rates range from $445 to $645. All 12 rooms in this 170-year-old town house are named after late-19th-century or early-20th-century New Yorkers, many inspired by the works of Edith Wharton and Henry James. Complimentary breakfast is served in Lady Mendl's Tea Salon, where, if the weather is nippy, you can find a comforting fire roaring.

Breakfast prepared by culinary students at the New School is one of the highlights of the **Inn on 23rd,** 131 W. 23rd St. (between Sixth and Seventh avenues; ☎ 877-387-2323 or 212-463-0330; www.innon23rd.com; see map p. 98). Each of the 16 rooms, ranging in price from $249 to $389, was distinctly decorated by the personable owner, Annette Fisherman, with items collected from her travels.

The first home of the Gay Men's Health Crisis, an 1850 brownstone in the heart of Chelsea, is now the charming **Colonial House Inn,** 318 W. 22nd St. (between Eighth and Ninth avenues; ☎ 800-689-3779 or 212-243-9669; www.colonialhouseinn.com; see map p. 98). This 20-room, four-story walk-up caters to a largely GLBT clientele, but everybody is welcome, and straight couples are a common sight. Some rooms have shared bathrooms; deluxe rooms have private bathrooms, and some have working fireplaces. The inn has a roof deck with a clothing-optional area. Breakfast is included in the rates, which range from $130 to $150 for a shared bathroom, or $180 to $300 for superior rooms with private bathrooms.

On the popular yet still residential Upper West Side is the aptly named **Country Inn the City,** 270 W. 77th St. (between Broadway and West End Avenue; ☎ 212-580-4183; www.countryinnthecity.com; see map p. 100). This 1891 town house has four spacious but quaintly decorated rooms, all with full kitchens. Rates range from $210 to $375 and include breakfast items stocked in your refrigerator. But you're largely on your own here: You won't find a resident innkeeper, and a maid only services your room every few days. Still, if you're the independent sort, the inn's charm makes it an excellent choice.

The Lowell
$$$$$ Upper East Side

The Lowell's style of luxury is best described as sophisticated opulence. It has the feel of a residential dwelling; the lobby is small and clubby with first-rate European, old-world service. The rooms are the real treasures here, each different from the other and all very good sizes. About two-thirds are suites with kitchenettes or fully equipped kitchens; some have private terraces and most have working fireplaces. In the rooms you also find nice big, cushy armchairs, lots of leather, interesting artwork, and porcelain figurines scattered about. Bathrooms are Italian marble and out-fitted with Bulgari amenities. The **Pembroke Room** offers breakfast, including a hearty English breakfast and afternoon tea, while the **Post House** is best known for its steaks. On a quiet, tree-lined street 1 block from Central Park and right in the middle of Madison Avenue shopping, the Lowell has a location that's ideal for those who want (and can afford) an urban retreat away from the Midtown madness.

See map p. 100. 28 E. 63rd St. (between Madison and Park avenues). ☎ *800-221-4444 or 212-838-1400. Fax: 212-319-4230.* www.lowellhotel.com. *Subway: F to Lexington Avenue. Parking: $45. Rack rates: $575–$750 double. AE, DC, MC, V.*

The Lucerne
$$$ Upper West Side

A luxury boutique hotel in a magnificent 1903 landmark building, the Lucerne captures the feel of the Upper West Side, and you won't do better in this neighborhood. Service is impeccable, especially for a moderately priced hotel. The rooms are comfortable and big enough for king-size, queen-size, or two double beds with attractive bathrooms with marble counters. Some rooms have views of the Hudson River. The suites are extra-special and include kitchenettes, stocked minifridges, microwaves, sitting rooms with sofas, and extra televisions. The ground-floor Mediterranean restaurant, **Nice Matin,** offers room service. Or you may want to order takeout from nearby Zabar's or H&H Bagels.

See map p. 100. 201 W. 79th St. (at Amsterdam Avenue, 1 block from the American Museum of Natural History). ☎ *800-492-8122 or 212-875-1000. Fax: 212-721-1179.* www.thelucernehotel.com. *Subway: 1 to 79th Street. Parking: $25 nearby. Rack rates: $280–$450 double. Children 15 and under stay free in parent's room. AE, DC, DISC, MC, V.*

The Mercer
$$$$$ SoHo

Still the best of the downtown, celebrity-crawling, hip hotels, the Mercer is where even those who represent the antithesis of hip can feel at home. The hotel is at the corner of Mercer and Prince streets, the epicenter of SoHo, but once you get inside, there is a pronounced calm — from the postmodern library lounge and the relaxed staff, to the huge, soundproof, loftlike guest rooms; the hotel is a perfect complement to the scene outside your big window. The Mercer is one of the few New York hotels with ceiling fans, and even if you don't need to use them, they look very nice whirring above your extremely comfortable bed. Each of the tile-and-marble bathrooms has a steel cart for storage and an oversize shower stall or oversize two-person tub (state your preference when booking).

See map p. 96. 147 Mercer St. (at Prince Street). ☎ **888-918-6060** *or 212-966-6060. Fax: 212-965-3838.* www.mercerhotel.com. *Subway: N or R to Prince Street. Parking: $55. Rack rates: $595–$895 double. Pets allowed with $100 fee. AE, DC, DISC, MC, V.*

The Peninsula New York
$$$$$ **Midtown East**

Housed in a beauty of a Beaux Arts building, the Peninsula is the perfect combination of old-world charm and modern technology. Rooms are huge, with plenty of closet and storage space, but best of all is the bedside control panel that allows you to regulate lighting, television, stereo, air-conditioning, and the do-not-disturb sign on your door. Even though you really don't have to leave the comfort of your bed, eventually you will need to go to the bathroom, and, when you do, you won't be disappointed. Each huge marble bathroom has a spacious soaking tub with yet another control panel, for a television (in most rooms) so you can watch while taking your bubble bath. (Now *that's* happy excess.) The hotel also features one of the best and biggest New York hotel health clubs and spas, the rooftop **Salon de Ning** bar, and the Peninsula Kids' Academy program. All this wonderfulness doesn't come cheap, but if a splurge is what you want, you won't do much better than the Peninsula.

See map p. 98. 700 Fifth Ave. (at 55th Street). ☎ *800-262-9467 or 212-956-2888. Fax: 212-903-3949. www.peninsula.com. Subway: E or M to Fifth Avenue. Valet parking: $60. Rack rates: $775–$1,125 double. Children 11 and under stay free in parent's room. Pets allowed. AE, DC, DISC, MC, V.*

The Pod Hotel
$ **Midtown East**

The Pod was an immediate hit when it opened in 2007, and it maintains a 90 percent occupancy rate thanks to a thoughtful but fun design and modest prices. The hotel draws a large European clientele, as well as twenty- and thirty-something creative types seeking a step up from a hostel. The mod lobby, with communal tables and an outdoor cafe (open in warm months), is designed for socializing and interaction. The rooms are, well, pods, but the mass-transit-inspired design touches cleverly maximize the small spaces so that they include not only a bed but also a desk, a small flatscreen TV, and an MP3 docking station. Double and Queen pods have private bathrooms, while Bunk and Single pods include stainless steel sinks and displays above the door that indicate when the shared bathrooms (kept immaculately clean) are unoccupied. There are now also larger pods that sleep up to four travelers; these have good closet space and large flatscreen TVs (if you'd like a hanging bubble chair, ask for Townhouse Suite 3A). There's no hotel restaurant, but next door is the scenester-y East Side Social Club, and there are several other dining options on this relatively quiet block. (I highly recommend Amma, an Indian restaurant just a few doors down, at no. 246.)

See map p. 98. 230 E. 51st St. (between Second and Third avenues). ☎ *800-742-5945 toll-free in the U.S., 800-874-0074 toll-free in Canada, or 212-355-0300. Fax: 212-755-5029. www.thepodhotel.com. Subway: 6 to 51st Street; E or M to 53rd Street. Parking: $35. Rack rates: $149–$309. Children stay free in parent's room. AE, MC, V.*

Red Roof Inn Manhattan
$ **Midtown West**

Manhattan's first and only Red Roof Inn offers some relief from Midtown's high-priced hotel scene. Both the recently renovated rooms and bathrooms are more spacious than you may find at most hotels in this price category. The high-ceilinged lobby also has an elegant feel — unusual for a budget hotel. What's more, the amenities are as good as those at more expensive competitors, and furnishings are comfortable. Located near the Empire State Building and Herald Square, the hotel is in Manhattan's Koreatown. (The air is permeated by the smell of Korean barbecue.) Complimentary continental breakfast adds to the good value.

See map p. 98. 6 W. 32nd St. (between Broadway and Fifth Avenue, 2 blocks south of the Empire State Building). ☎ *800-567-7720 or 212-643-7100. Fax: 212-643-7101.* www.redroof.com. *Subway: B, D, F, M, N, or R to 34th Street. Parking: $26. Rack rates: $199–$269 double. Rates include continental breakfast. Children 12 and under stay free in parent's room. AE, DC, DISC, MC, V.*

The Ritz-Carlton New York, Battery Park
$$$$ **Financial District**

You can't get farther downtown than this hotel, at the extreme southern end of Manhattan. And if you don't mind being away from most of the action, no options are better than this one. Not only do you get typically excellent Ritz service, but you also get amazing views of New York Harbor from most of the recently updated guest rooms. You can even use one of the hotel telescopes for close-ups of Lady Liberty. This modern, Art Deco-influenced high-rise is different in style from the English countryside look of most Ritz-Carlton hotels, but that's where the differences end. Here, you find the full slate of comforts and services typical of Ritz-Carlton, from Frette-dressed feather beds to the chain's signature Bath Butler, who will draw a scented bath for you in your own deep soaking tub. Standard rooms are all very large and have huge bathrooms, while suites are bigger than most city apartments.

See map p. 96. 2 West St. (across the street from Battery Park). ☎ *800-241-3333 or 212-344-0800. Fax: 212-344-3801.* www.ritzcarlton.com. *Subway: 4 or 5 to Bowling Green. Valet parking: $50. Rack rates: $325–$675 double. Pets under 25 pounds allowed with $125 fee. AE, DC, DISC, MC, V.*

The Ritz-Carlton New York, Central Park
$$$$$ **Midtown West**

Not only does this Ritz own one of the best locations in the city, on Central Park South overlooking Central Park, but despite the incredible luxuriousness, it also manages to maintain a homey unintimidating elegance. Spacious rooms are decorated in traditional, English countryside style; those with park views are equipped with telescopes and birding books. Suites are huge, and the oversize marble bathrooms feature a choice of bathrobes — terry or sateen — and Etro bath amenities. For families who can afford the very steep prices, the hotel is extremely kid-friendly. Suites have sofa beds, and cribs, and rollaway beds can be brought in. Adults can enjoy **BLT Market** restaurant (by chef Laurent Tourondel, also responsible for BLT Fish and BLT Steak, both reviewed in Chapter 10) and the Switzerland-based **La Prairie Spa.**

See map p. 98. 50 Central Park S. (at Sixth Avenue, across the street from Central Park). ☎ *212-308-9100. Fax: 212-207-8831.* www.ritzcarlton.com. *Subway: B, N, Q, or R to 57th Street. Parking: $50. Rack rates: $695–$1,620 double. Pets under 60 pounds allowed. AE, DC, DISC, MC, V.*

The Roger
$$$ Midtown East

This Murray Hill hotel, also known as the Hotel Roger Williams, was renovated and reborn with a bold, colorful new look and style. The welcoming lobby has an odd assortment of mod yet comfortable seating. The rooms come in a number of varieties — some small, some generous, some with huge landscaped terraces, others with views of the nearby Empire State Building — all with solid amenities such as colorful quilts, flatscreen televisions, complimentary wireless Internet, and good-size marble bathrooms with Aveda products. The Roger is one of the top choices in what is a quiet yet convenient Midtown location. A floating granite staircase leads from the lobby to a mezzanine lounge, where you can breakfast in the morning and drink cocktails by candlelight at night.

See map p. 98. 131 Madison Ave. (at 31st Street). ☎ **888-448-7788** *or 212-448-7000. Fax: 212-448-7007.* www.hotelrogerwilliams.com. *Subway: 6 to 28th Street. Rack rates: $275–$540 double. AE, DC, DISC, MC, V.*

Sofitel New York
$$$ Midtown West

The block of 44th Street between Fifth and Sixth avenues is known as "Hotel Row," and the soaring Sofitel is the best of the bunch. Thanks to the hotel's entrance and the warm, inviting lobby with check-in tucked off to the side, it feels as if you're entering a grande dame hotel and not one that is only a decade old. The décor melds modern amenities with European old-world elegance. The spacious, ultracomfortable rooms are adorned with art from New York and Paris. The lighting is soft and romantic, and walls and windows are soundproof. Suites are equipped with king-size beds, two televisions, and pocket doors separating the bedroom from the sitting room. Bathrooms in all rooms are fantastic, with separate showers and soaking tubs. A stylish French restaurant, **Gaby,** bakes delicious croissants for breakfast.

See map p. 98. 45 W. 44th St. (between Fifth and Sixth avenues, 1 block east of Times Square). ☎ **212-354-8844.** *Fax: 212-354-2480.* www.sofitel.com. *Subway: B, D, F, or M to 42nd Street. Parking: $45. Rack rates: $345–$636 double. Pets allowed. AE, DC, MC, V.*

Travel Inn
$$ Midtown West

Though it's a bit too close to the busy, exhaust-choked Lincoln Tunnel, the Travel Inn makes up for its location with extras such as a huge outdoor pool and sun deck, a sunny and up-to-date fitness room, and free indoor parking (with in-and-out privileges!). The interior is clean and reminiscent of a chain motel, but for these prices, you get good-size rooms that are comfortably furnished, with extra-firm beds and work desks; even the smallest double is sizable and has a roomy bathroom, while double/doubles make great affordable shares for families. Bathrooms are basic yet clean and fresh-looking. This spot is close to Times Square, many Off-Broadway theaters, and the inexpensive dining options of nearby Hell's Kitchen.

See map p. 98. 515 W. 42nd St. (just west of Tenth Avenue). ☎ **800-869-4630** *or 212-695-7171. Fax: 212-967-5025.* www.thetravelinnhotel.com. *Subway: A, C, or E to 42nd Street/Port Authority. Free self-parking. Rack rates: $250–$400 double. Children 15 and under stay free in parent's room. AE, DC, DISC, MC, V.*

Trump International Hotel & Tower
$$$$$ Upper West Side

From the outside, it's just your typical tall, not-very-attractive Trump monolith, but spend a night here, and you'll forgive the Donald's hokey grandiose taste in design. Experience services like your own Trump Attaché, a personal concierge who provides comprehensive services; take advantage of the 6,000-square-foot health club with a lap pool and full-service spa; or order room service from the hotel's signature restaurant, the exquisite **Jean-Georges** (or arrange for a chef to prepare a meal in your room's fully equipped kitchen). Enjoy the hotel's impeccable service and first-class facilities from a lovely yet surprisingly understated high-ceilinged room with floor-to-ceiling windows, some of which offer incredible views of Central Park. You also get sumptuous bathrobes, telescopes for taking in the view, and marble bathrooms with Jacuzzi tubs.

See map p. 100. 1 Central Park W. (at 60th Street, across from Central Park). ☎ **888-448-7867** *or 212-299-1000. Fax: 212-299-1150.* www.trumpintl.com. *Subway: A, B, C, D, or 1 to 59th Street/Columbus Circle. Parking: $45. Rack rates: $495–$875 double. Pets allowed. AE, DC, DISC, MC, V.*

The Waldorf-Astoria and The Waldorf Towers
$$$$ Midtown East

This 1-square-block Art Deco masterpiece is a New York City landmark and the epitome of old-school elegance. The lobby is so big and grand, it's reminiscent of Grand Central Terminal, down to its own signature clock. With over 1,000 rooms, the pace can be hectic, but after you're in your room — all airy with high ceilings, traditional décor, comfortable linens and beds, and spacious marble bathrooms — you quickly chill out. If you crave more luxury, book a room on the Astoria level, which features huge suites, deluxe bathroom amenities, access to the Astoria Lounge for breakfast or afternoon hors d'oeuvres, and free entry to the hotel's fitness club (others pay a fee); for even more opulence, try a suite in the Waldorf Towers. One of three bars in the hotel, **Sir Harry's Bar** (off the lobby) is the main gathering spot for a pre- or post-dinner cocktail, but even better is **Bull & Bear** with its signature round mahogany bar, classic original cocktail creations, and celebrated steaks.

See map p. 98. Astoria: 301 Park Ave. (between 49th and 50th streets); Towers: 100 E. 50th St. (at Park Avenue). ☎ **800-925-3673**, *212-355-3000 (Astoria), or 212-355-3100 (Towers). Fax: 212-872-7272 (Astoria) or 212-872-4799 (Towers).* http://waldorf newyork.com. *Subway: 6 to 51st Street. Parking: $45. Rack rates: Astoria, $259–$629 double; Towers, $419–$829 double. Children 17 and under stay free in parent's room. AE, DC, DISC, MC, V.*

Wall Street Inn
$$ Financial District

This seven-story hotel is ideal for those Wall Street businesspeople who want a lower Manhattan location without corporate blandness. It's also a good choice for visitors not working on Wall Street. The lovely Early American interiors boast a pleasing freshness. The hotel is warm, comforting, and serene, and the friendly, professional staff offers the kind of personalized service you won't get from a chain. Rooms aren't huge, but the bedding is top quality and all the conveniences (including soundproofed windows and Wi-Fi) are at hand. Room service is provided by **Smörgås Chef** (see Chapter 10). If you don't mind the weekend quiet of Wall Street, you can find amazing deals after the execs go home.

See map p. 96. 9 S. William St. (at Broad Street). ☎ **877-747-1500** *or 212-747-1500. Fax: 212-747-1900.* www.thewallstreetinn.com. *Subway: 2 or 3 to Wall Street; 4 or 5 to Bowling Green. Parking: $35–$40 nearby. Rack rates: $179–$349 double. Rates include continental breakfast. AE, DC, DISC, MC, V.*

Runner-Up Hotels

Hotel 41
$$ Midtown West   A heartbeat away from the crossroads of the world, Hotel 41 is an affordable boutique alternative to the gleaming Times Square high-rises. *See map p. 98. 206 W. 41st St. (between Seventh and Eighth avenues).* ☎ **212-703-8600**. *Fax: 212-302-0895.* www.hotel41nyc.com.

Hotel Le Jolie
$$ Brooklyn   This hotel is your best bet if you want to base yourself in Williamsburg, which gentrified rapidly from an affordable pocket for artists into a trust-funded hipster heaven. The nearby L subway stop on Bedford Avenue connects you to Manhattan within a few minutes. *See map p. 222. 235 Meeker Ave.* ☎ **866-526-4097** *or 718-625-2100. Fax: 718-625-7100.* www.hotellejolie.com.

The Iroquois New York

$$$ **Midtown West** Just a few steps from Times Square and the famed Hotel Row, this 1923 building houses one of the best small luxury hotels of the world. *See map p. 98. 49 West 44th St. (between Fifth and Sixth avenues).* ☎ *800-332-7220 or 212-840-3080. Fax: 212-398-1754.* www.iroquoisny.com.

Loews Regency Hotel

$$$$ **Midtown East** For years the Regency has been a haven for celebrities and those who aspire to celebrity status, but even if you aren't on the cover of a magazine, a stay at the Regency may make you feel as though you are. *See map p. 100. 540 Park Ave. (at 61st Street, 1 block east of Barneys, 1 block west of Bloomingdale's).* ☎ *800-233-2356 or 212-759-4100. Fax: 212-826-5674.* www.loewshotels.com.

New York Marriott at the Brooklyn Bridge

$$$ **Brooklyn** This 665-room tower has long been the prime choice for accommodations in downtown Brooklyn. The closest subway stop is Jay Street, on the A, C, and F lines; it's a good pick if you want to explore Brooklyn Heights and Cobble Hill, DUMBO, or Fort Greene (home to the Brooklyn Academy of Music and the Brooklyn Flea). *See map p. 132. 333 Adams St.* ☎ *888-436-3759 or 718-246-7000. Fax: 718-246-0563.* www.marriott.com.

Novotel New York Times Square

$$ **Midtown West** This 480-room hotel features excellent bargains and spectacular views of Times Square and the Hudson River. The glass-enclosed Cafe Nicole in the seventh-floor lobby is one of the best spots to watch both the dropping of the ball on New Year's Eve and the Macy's Thanksgiving Day Parade. *See map p. 98. 226 W. 52nd St. (at Broadway).* ☎ *212-315-0100. Fax: 212-765-5365.* www.novotel.com.

Washington Square Hotel

$$ **Greenwich Village** Tiny, well-outfitted rooms with private bathrooms in a great location at moderate prices (that include breakfast) make this a solid value option downtown. *See map p. 96. 103 Waverly Place (between Fifth and Sixth avenues, off Washington Square, the center of the Village).* ☎ *800-222-0418 or 212-777-9515. Fax: 212-979-8373.* www.wshotel.com.

Index of Accommodations by Neighborhood

Upper West Side
Country Inn the City ($$)
Hotel Beacon ($$)
Hotel Newton ($$)
The Lucerne ($$$)
Trump International Hotel & Tower ($$$$$)

Upper East Side
The Carlyle, A Rosewood Hotel ($$$$$)
Hôtel Plaza Athénée ($$$$$)
The Lowell ($$$$$)

Midtown East
Affinia Dumont ($$$)
The Benjamin ($$$$)
Hotel Elysée ($$$)
Hotel Thirty Thirty ($$)
The Kitano New York ($$$$)
The Library Hotel ($$$)
Loews Regency Hotel ($$$$)
The Peninsula New York ($$$$$)
The Pod Hotel ($)
The Roger ($$$)
The Waldorf=Astoria and The Waldorf Towers ($$$$)

Midtown West
The Algonquin ($$$)
Casablanca Hotel ($$$)
Chambers Hotel ($$$)
Doubletree Guest Suites Times Square ($$$)
Hotel 41 ($$)
Hotel Metro ($$$)
The Iroquois New York ($$$)
Le Parker Meridien ($$$$)
The London NYC ($$$$)
Novotel New York Times Square ($$)
Red Roof Inn Manhattan ($)
The Ritz-Carlton New York, Central Park ($$$$$)
Sofitel New York ($$$)
Travel Inn ($$)

Chelsea/Flatiron District/Gramercy Park/Herald Square/NoMad
The Ace Hotel ($$$)
The Carlton Hotel ($$$)
Chelsea Lodge ($)
Colonial House Inn ($)
Gershwin Hotel ($$)
Hotel Giraffe ($$$$)
Inn at Irving Place ($$$$)
Inn on 23rd ($$$)

Greenwich Village/Meatpacking District/SoHo
Crosby Street Hotel ($$$$)
Hotel Gansevoort ($$$$)
Larchmont Hotel ($)
The Mercer ($$$$$)
Washington Square Hotel ($$)

TriBeCa/Financial District/Lower East Side/East Village
The Bowery Hotel ($$$)
Cosmopolitan Hotel–Tribeca ($)
The Hotel on Rivington ($$$$)
The Ritz-Carlton New York, Battery Park ($$$$)
Wall Street Inn ($$)

Brooklyn
Hotel Le Jolie ($$)
New York Marriott at the Brooklyn Bridge ($$$)

Index of Accommodations by Price

$$$$$
The Carlyle, A Rosewood Hotel (Upper East Side)
Hôtel Plaza Athénée (Upper East Side)
The Lowell (Upper East Side)
The Mercer (SoHo)
The Peninsula New York (Midtown East)
The Ritz-Carlton New York, Central Park (Midtown West)
Trump International Hotel & Tower (Upper West Side)

$$$$
The Benjamin (Midtown East)
Crosby Street Hotel (SoHo)
Hotel Gansevoort (Meatpacking District)
Hotel Giraffe (Flatiron District)
The Hotel on Rivington (Lower East Side)

Inn at Irving Place (Gramercy Park)
The Kitano New York (Midtown East)
Le Parker Meridien (Midtown West)
Loews Regency Hotel (Midtown East)
The London NYC (Midtown West)
The Ritz-Carlton New York, Battery
Park (Financial District)
The Waldorf=Astoria and The Waldorf
Towers (Midtown East)

$$$

The Ace Hotel (Herald Square/NoMad)
Affinia Dumont (Midtown East)
The Algonquin (Midtown West)
The Bowery Hotel (East Village)
The Carlton Hotel (Flatiron District)
Casablanca Hotel (Midtown West)
Chambers Hotel (Midtown West)
Doubletree Guest Suites Times Square
(Midtown West)
Hotel Elysée (Midtown East)
Hotel Metro (Midtown West)
Inn on 23rd (Chelsea)
The Iroquois New York (Midtown
West)
The Library Hotel (Midtown East)
The Lucerne (Upper West Side)
New York Marriott at the Brooklyn
Bridge (Brooklyn)

The Roger (Midtown East)
Sofitel New York (Midtown West)

$$

Country Inn the City (Upper West Side)
Gershwin Hotel (Flatiron District)
Hotel Beacon (Upper West Side)
Hotel 41 (Midtown West)
Hotel Le Jolie (Brooklyn)
Hotel Newton (Upper West Side)
Hotel Thirty Thirty (Midtown East)
Novotel New York Times Square
(Midtown West)
Travel Inn (Midtown West)
Wall Street Inn (Financial District)
Washington Square Hotel (Greenwich
Village)

$

Chelsea Lodge (Chelsea)
Colonial House Inn (Chelsea)
Cosmopolitan Hotel–Tribeca (TriBeCa)
Larchmont Hotel (Greenwich Village)
The Pod Hotel (Midtown East)
Red Roof Inn Manhattan (Midtown
West)

Chapter 10

Dining and Snacking in New York City

In This Chapter

- Landing a reservation at a hot restaurant
- Finding out about your dining options
- Getting the most out of your food budget
- Discovering the top New York City restaurants

You can't do better than New York for dining possibilities — the city is bursting with restaurants of every type and category. You could eat out every night of the year and still have a mountain of restaurants to climb before you'd been to them all. Chefs are as famous as rock stars, and when a new restaurant opens, the pomp and circumstance sometimes equals the opening of a Broadway show. What I'm trying to say is that eating out in New York is a *very* big deal — something many New Yorkers take seriously.

The variety of restaurants in New York is staggering — from American to multiethnic, from a simple diner to an elegant four-star palace. All that variety can be intimidating, but it shouldn't be. You know what you like; now you just need to know where to find it.

Getting the Dish on the Local Scene

Unless the restaurant you're interested in doesn't accept reservations, it always pays to make a reservation, especially if your party is bigger than two. You've got nothing to lose by calling ahead. If you're booking dinner on a weekend night, it's a good idea to call at least a few days in advance. And if you're really set on visiting one very special restaurant, let's say Gramercy Tavern, call well in advance, preferably before you even arrive in the city. You can make reservations for many of New York's great restaurants online at **Open Table** (www.opentable.com).

If you can't get a reservation for the dates you want, try for an early dinner, between 5 and 6 p.m., or a later one, after 9 p.m. That's all you may be offered anyway, so you may have to take what you can get.

Most top places start taking reservations 30 days in advance, so if you want to eat at a hot restaurant at a popular hour — Saturday at 8 p.m., say, at Daniel — start dialing 30 days prior at 9 a.m. If you're booking a holiday dinner, call earlier. Many of the top restaurants require you to leave a credit card number when making a reservation, and if you don't show up, they penalize you with a service charge.

Smoking is banned in all the city's restaurants, with the exception of some outdoor spaces.

Sources for scoping out the dining scene

The best online restaurant sources are

- ✔ *New York* **magazine** (www.nymag.com/restaurants): The online arm of weekly *New York* magazine keeps a tally of restaurant openings and closings and offers an extensive searchable database, with links to menus.

- ✔ *The New York Times* (www.nytimes.com): The "Dining & Wine" features in the Styles section include the paper's very influential restaurant reviews and blogs by critic Sam Sifton and award-winning cookbook author Mark Bittman.

- ✔ *The Village Voice* (www.villagevoice.com): Especially good for the cheap-eats reviews ("Counter Culture") by Robert Sietsema.

The best online source for the serious foodie is **Chowhound** (www.chowhound.com), a national Web site with message boards in local areas, including New York, where you can make an inquiry about a certain restaurant, type of food, or location, and, within a few hours, you may have five or more very informative responses.

The *Zagat Survey* (www.zagat.com), a guide that made a name for itself by rating restaurants based on extensive diner surveys, maintains a searchable database. It charges a fee to access more complete online details, which, with all the other better online options available, doesn't seem worth it just for restaurant information. If you're really interested in what your fellow diners have to say, you're better off just buying the book (or browse the free member reviews and judge for yourself).

If you don't feel the need for a book, stop at any newsstand for a copy of the slick weekly *Time Out New York;* the "Eat Out" section includes listings for *TONY*'s 100 Favorite Restaurants in every issue, as well as coverage of new openings and dining trends. Weekly *New York* magazine also maintains restaurant listings in the "Agenda" section at the back of the magazine.

Fixed-price deals at top restaurants

New York's popular **Restaurant Week,** held every January and June, pioneered the idea of offering *prix-fixe* (fixed-price) bargain meals to attract new customers to the city's best restaurants. In 2010, the price was $24.07 (24/7, get it?) for lunch, $35 for dinner. The idea was wildly successful, and a number of restaurants have extended the offer throughout the year. Restaurant Week has its detractors, however; some kitchens seem to be asleep at the wheel, perhaps turned off by what is perceived as a less-discerning clientele, and offering meals that are not representative of their usual high (and higher-priced) quality. When choosing a restaurant, consider the Restaurant Week menu on offer (it's sometimes available on the restaurant's Web site); the places that maintain fixed-price menus year-round tend to remain on their game even during hectic Restaurant Week. Also, make your choices quickly and snap up your reservations; the top tables are taken *fast.* Check www.nycgo.com or www.opentable.com for participating restaurants and reservation information.

Trimming the fat from your budget

Prices in New York are high, but you can eat well without spending a fortune if you follow a few simple rules — and you never need to sacrifice quality. The best and most famous restaurants are expensive, but you don't need to pay through the nose if you keep these tips in mind:

- ✔ **Go for the prix-fixe menu at top restaurants.** Usually, the best deals are at lunch, when many of the best restaurants in New York offer a three-course meal for considerably less than you would pay a la carte or at dinnertime.

- ✔ **Watch your drinks tab.** Restaurants get you with the drinks, especially the wine. That's where they make their money. I wouldn't dream of suggesting that you deny yourself the pleasure of an aperitif or a properly paired wine with your meal, but if money is an object, go for quality over quantity.

- ✔ **Skip the national fast-food chains.** It may be fast, but it's not as cheap as advertised, and with so many good, inexpensive local restaurants, you really have no excuse for eating at a national fast-food chain while in New York. See "Dining and Snacking on the Go," later in this chapter, for suggestions.

- ✔ **Seek out food markets.** The city's greenmarkets — especially the one at Union Square, on Mondays, Wednesdays, Fridays, and Saturdays year-round — provide a wealth of locally grown foods at great prices. The New Amsterdam Market (www.newamsterdam market.org) is another draw for locavores; check the Web site for opening times and locations. The Brooklyn Flea (www.brooklyn flea.com; p. 222 is also known for its carefully selected food purveyors, so definitely plan to eat there while you browse the wares.

> ✔ **Order takeout.** Thousands of takeout places all over Manhattan deliver to hotel rooms for free, and they offer food more varied and far less expensive than room service. (Don't forget to tip the delivery person.)
>
> ✔ **Avoid eating in Times Square and Rockefeller Center.** Not only are food prices jacked up in these major tourist attractions, but the food is usually not very good. Try to plan your meals and snacks for before or after you visit the big tourist sights, or in adjacent neighborhoods, rather than in the busiest hubs of visitor activity.

For the listings in this chapter, I offer two price indicators for each restaurant: a number of dollar signs, which gives you an idea of what a complete meal costs, and the price range of the entrees on the menu.

One dollar sign ($) means inexpensive, and the maximum five dollar signs ($$$$$) means extravagant. The symbols reflect what one person can expect to pay for an appetizer, entree, dessert, one drink, tax, and tip. Here's a more complete key to the dollar-sign ratings that I use in this chapter:

Dollar Sign(s)	*Price Range*
$	$34 or less
$$	$35–$59
$$$	$60–$84
$$$$	$85–$99
$$$$$	$100 or more

The dollar signs give you a rough idea of how much a meal will cost, but don't use them as the only factor in your decision; restaurants may offer prix-fixe meals or other deals that aren't reflected in their price rankings.

As you peruse the listings, check the corresponding maps to pinpoint a restaurant's location. The indexes at the end of this chapter can help you select a restaurant by location, cuisine, or price.

New York's Best Restaurants

Antique Garage
$$ SoHo MEDITERRANEAN

It is exactly what it says it is: a former auto garage that now sells antiques — and Mediterranean food. Truth to tell, I'm recommending this place at least as much for the atmosphere as for the food. The décor is fantastically alluring — mirrors, candelabras and lamps, velvet chairs, and paintings hanging from brick walls — and live jazz nearly every evening and during the weekend brunch hours (noon to 5 p.m.) enlivens the

Downtown Dining

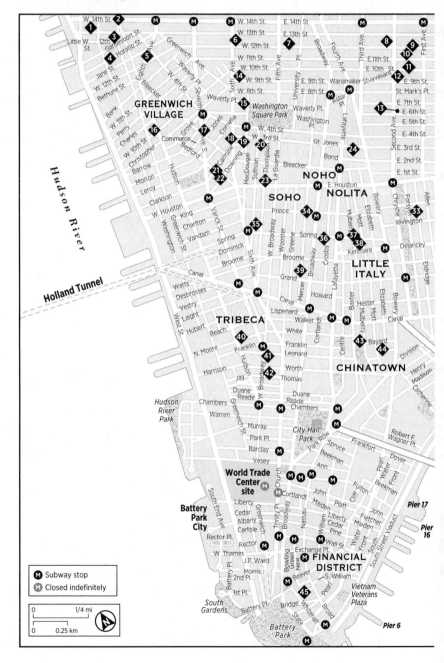

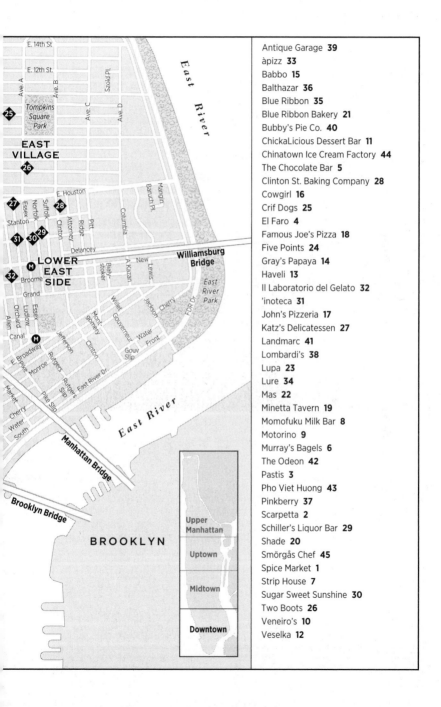

Antique Garage **39**
àpizz **33**
Babbo **15**
Balthazar **36**
Blue Ribbon **35**
Blue Ribbon Bakery **21**
Bubby's Pie Co. **40**
ChickaLicious Dessert Bar **11**
Chinatown Ice Cream Factory **44**
The Chocolate Bar **5**
Clinton St. Baking Company **28**
Cowgirl **16**
Crif Dogs **25**
El Faro **4**
Famous Joe's Pizza **18**
Five Points **24**
Gray's Papaya **14**
Haveli **13**
Il Laboratorio del Gelato **32**
'inoteca **31**
John's Pizzeria **17**
Katz's Delicatessen **27**
Landmarc **41**
Lombardi's **38**
Lupa **23**
Lure **34**
Mas **22**
Minetta Tavern **19**
Momofuku Milk Bar **8**
Motorino **9**
Murray's Bagels **6**
The Odeon **42**
Pastis **3**
Pho Viet Huong **43**
Pinkberry **37**
Scarpetta **2**
Schiller's Liquor Bar **29**
Shade **20**
Smörgås Chef **45**
Spice Market **1**
Strip House **7**
Sugar Sweet Sunshine **30**
Two Boots **26**
Veniero's **10**
Veselka **12**

Midtown Dining

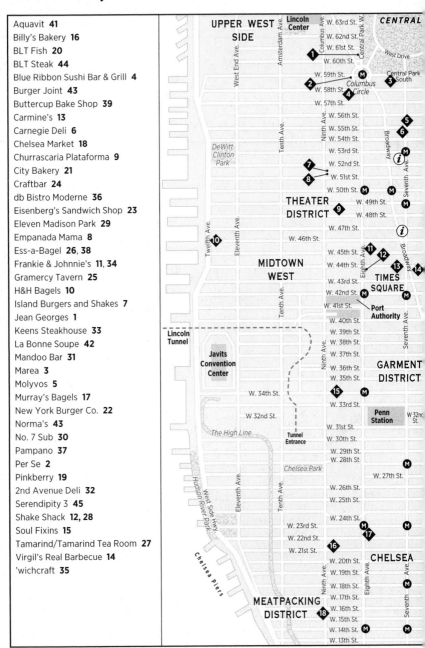

Aquavit **41**
Billy's Bakery **16**
BLT Fish **20**
BLT Steak **44**
Blue Ribbon Sushi Bar & Grill **4**
Burger Joint **43**
Buttercup Bake Shop **39**
Carmine's **13**
Carnegie Deli **6**
Chelsea Market **18**
Churrascaria Plataforma **9**
City Bakery **21**
Craftbar **24**
db Bistro Moderne **36**
Eisenberg's Sandwich Shop **23**
Eleven Madison Park **29**
Empanada Mama **8**
Ess-a-Bagel **26**, **38**
Frankie & Johnnie's **11**, **34**
Gramercy Tavern **25**
H&H Bagels **10**
Island Burgers and Shakes **7**
Jean Georges **1**
Keens Steakhouse **33**
La Bonne Soupe **42**
Mandoo Bar **31**
Marea **3**
Molyvos **5**
Murray's Bagels **17**
New York Burger Co. **22**
Norma's **43**
No. 7 Sub **30**
Pampano **37**
Per Se **2**
Pinkberry **19**
2nd Avenue Deli **32**
Serendipity 3 **45**
Shake Shack **12**, **28**
Soul Fixins **15**
Tamarind/Tamarind Tea Room **27**
Virgil's Real Barbecue **14**
'wichcraft **35**

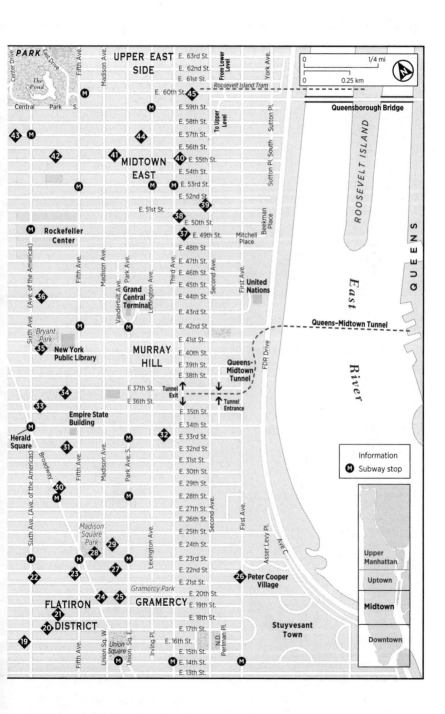

Uptown Dining

Absolute Bagels **1**
Alice's Tea Cup **16, 21, 22**
Artie's Delicatessen **8**
Beard Papa **13**
Big Nick's Burger Joint **12**
Buttercup Bake Shop **18**
Café Sabarsky **25**
Calle Ocho **10**
Carmine's **4**
'Cesca **15**
Daniel **20**
Flor de Mayo **3, 9**
Good Enough to Eat **7**
Gray's Papaya **17**
H&H Bagels **11**
Mermaid Inn **5**
Noche Mexicana **2**
Ouest **6**
Paola's **26**
Papaya King **23**
Pinkberry **19**
Shake Shack **14, 24**

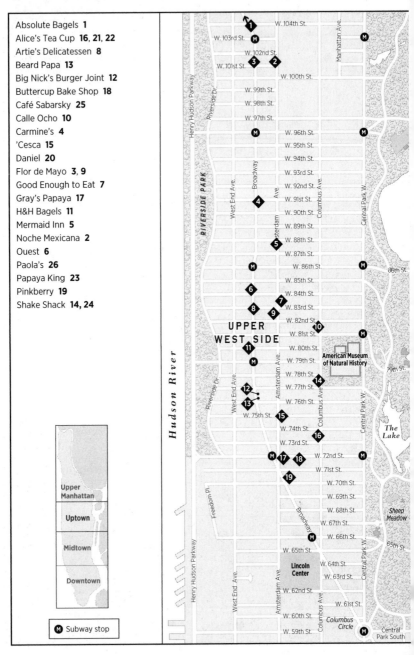

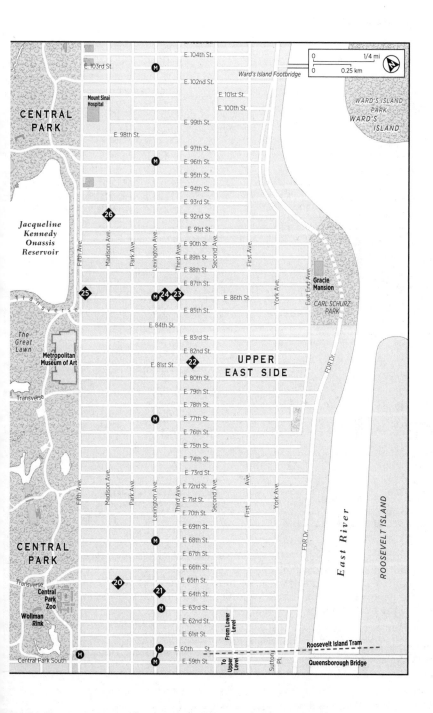

Downtown Brooklyn

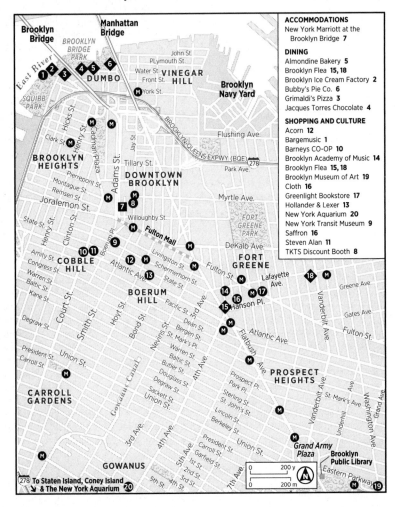

ACCOMMODATIONS
New York Marriott at the
  Brooklyn Bridge **7**

DINING
Almondine Bakery **5**
Brooklyn Flea **15, 18**
Brooklyn Ice Cream Factory **2**
Bubby's Pie Co. **6**
Grimaldi's Pizza **3**
Jacques Torres Chocolate **4**

SHOPPING AND CULTURE
Acorn **12**
Bargemusic **1**
Barneys CO-OP **10**
Brooklyn Academy of Music **14**
Brooklyn Flea **15, 18**
Brooklyn Museum of Art **19**
Cloth **16**
Greenlight Bookstore **17**
Hollander & Lexer **13**
New York Aquarium **20**
New York Transit Museum **9**
Saffron **16**
Steven Alan **11**
TKTS Discount Booth **8**

buzzing social scene. It's an unpretentious place for mezes such as hummus and Circassian chicken (shredded breast meat in a garlicky sauce), panini, and salads. In warm-weather months, it's the perfect spot to have a feta cheese omelet and Bellini for brunch while enjoying some of the best people-watching in SoHo.

See map p. 126. 41 Mercer St. (near Grand Street). ☎ **212-219-1019.** www.antique garagesoho.com. *Reservations recommended. Subway: A, C, E, N, or R to Canal Street. Main courses: $16–$18 lunch, $20–$28 dinner. AE, DC, DISC, MC, V. Open: Daily noon to midnight.*

àpizz

$$$ **Lower East Side** **ITALIAN**

The neon red sign outside is just the flicker of the warmth you find inside this romantic, rustic brick-walled oasis. I always wondered what the word *canoodle* really meant, and if you bring your lover to àpizz, that's exactly what you do . . . whenever you can pry the forks from one another's hands. *Primi* include salads and Margherita (tomato) and *bianco* ("white," or ricotta) brick-oven pizzas, all excellent starts and not overly filling. For *secondi*, I highly recommend the *razza*, baked skate fish in white-wine sauce — for this skate fan, it's one of the best in town. You can't go wrong with any of the house-made desserts (including apple-pecan crumble and cheesecake). It can get rather warm in here, but whether that's due to the oven dominating the room or the heat between you and your date is for you to determine.

See map p. 126. 217 Eldridge St. (between Stanton and Rivington streets). ☎ *212-253-9199. www.apizz.com. Reservations strongly recommended. Subway: F to Second Avenue. Main courses: $22–$34. AE, MC, V. Open: Daily 6–11 p.m.*

Aquavit

$$$$$ **Midtown East** **SCANDINAVIAN**

This sleek restaurant is in the bottom of a glass tower on East 55th Street, and designed in Scandinavian style with modernist furniture. In the front of the restaurant is an informal and less-expensive cafe; past a long bar is the dining room. After a long association with respected chef and co-owner Marcus Samuelsson, the kitchen is now in the hands of Marcus Jernmark, and everything here remains first-rate. The menu is more focused than it has been in recent years, with an emphasis on modern Scandinavian flavors. The smoked fish — really all the fish — is prepared perfectly. The herring sampler is the stuff of daydreams: three types of herring, which you should enjoy with a glass of Aquavit, distilled liquor not unlike vodka, flavored with fruit and spices. The foie-gras ganache and the hot-smoked salmon have been recent winners. The Sunday prix-fixe brunch is a smorgasbord ($48). The bistro serves Swedish favorites including meatballs and gravlax.

See map p. 128. 65 E. 55th St. (between Park and Madison avenues). ☎ *212-307-7311. www.aquavit.org. Reservations recommended. Subway: E or M to Fifth Avenue. Bistro: Main courses $14–$29; 3-course prix-fixe meal $24 at lunch, $35 at dinner. Main dining room: Prix-fixe meal $35 at lunch, $78 at dinner; tasting menus $42 at lunch, $105 at dinner; supplement for paired wines $65 at dinner. AE, DC, MC, V. Open: Daily 5:30–10:30 p.m., Mon–Fri noon to 2:30 p.m., Sun noon to 2:30 p.m. Bistro closed all day Saturday and at Sunday brunch. Jackets preferred.*

BLT Fish

$$$$ **Flatiron District** **SEAFOOD**

BLT (Bistro Laurent Tourondel) Fish is one of several restaurants in chef/owner Tourondel's Manhattan mini-empire (see the following review of

BLT Steak). This, his seafood branch, is actually two restaurants with two distinct kitchens. The downstairs is a casual, moderately priced faux seafood shack with a raw bar, fried fare, and the much-in-demand lobster roll. Upstairs — you can walk the steps or take a glass elevator — is the elegant (with prices to match) dining room. Here you can sit under a skylight or near the open kitchen and watch an army of servers move from the kitchen through the room with huge platters topped with whole fish, which are dressed up beautifully and ready for consumption. The crispy, Cantonese-style red snapper is filleted table-side. But you have to crack the hard shell of the sea-salt-crusted New Zealand pink snapper to get to the tender, juicy flesh underneath. Expect great seafood, but don't expect quiet conversation.

See map p. 128. 21 W. 17th St. (between Fifth and Sixth avenues). ☎ **212-691-8888.** www.bltfish.com. *Reservations recommended. Subway: L, N, Q, R, 4, 5, or 6 to 14th Street/Union Square. Main courses: $31–$44. Open: BLT Fish Mon–Wed 5–10 p.m., Thurs 5–11 p.m., Fri–Sat 5–11:30 p.m.; BLT Fish Shack Mon–Wed 11:45 a.m.–2:30 p.m. and 5–10 p.m., Thurs 11:45 a.m.–2:30 p.m. and 5–11 p.m., Fri 11:45 a.m.–2:30 p.m. and 5–11:30 p.m., Sat 5–11:30 p.m., Sun 5–10 p.m.*

BLT Steak
$$$$$ Midtown East STEAKHOUSE

Steakhouses are often stereotyped as bastions of male bonding, testosterone-fueled with red meat and hearty drinks. But BLT Steak breaks that mold in a big way; the crowd is more eclectic, and there are plenty of slinky women chomping on thick cuts of beef. (Tourondel's reinvention of the steakhouse is broadly appealing: BLT Steak now has outposts in ten other cities, including San Juan, Puerto Rico.) The beef is served in cast-iron pots and finished in steak butter with a choice of sauces — béarnaise, red wine, horseradish, and blue cheese, to name a few. I tend to go for the hangar steak, but the New York strip and the short ribs braised in red wine are also good bets. Save room for the complimentary popovers and an appetizer like the incredible tuna *tartare* or a side of onion rings. This is not a restaurant for intimate conversation; even the music is muffled by the cacophonous din of the diners.

See map p. 128. 106 E. 57th St. (between Park and Lexington avenues). ☎ **212-752-7470.** www.bltsteak.com. *Reservations highly recommended. Subway: N, R, 4, 5, or 6 to 59th Street. Main courses: $26–$92. AE, DC, MC, V. Open: Mon–Thurs 11:45 a.m.–2:30 p.m. and 5:30–11 p.m., Fri 11:45 a.m.–2:30 p.m. and 5:30–11:30 p.m., Sat 5:30–11:30 p.m.*

Blue Ribbon
$$$ SoHo AMERICAN

Brothers Bruce and Eric Bromberg opened this American-style brasserie nearly two decades ago to such success that they now have eight restaurants in their New York mini-empire. The Jersey-bred, French-trained chefs built on two key features: late hours for night owls and a wide-roaming menu with room for everything from burgers, fried chicken, and catfish to escargots, pirogies, and paella. I can tick off many favorites here:

the mixed greens and smoked trout salads; the onion soup — in my opinion the only one in the city really worth eating; the red trout with almonds; the chocolate bruno dessert. . . . In case you're wondering if there's anything the brothers Bromberg don't serve, the answer is no: **Blue Ribbon Sushi,** one of the city's top sushi bars, is just down the street at no. 119 (☎ 212-343-0404); **Blue Ribbon Sushi Bar & Grill** is uptown at 308 W. 58th St. (at Columbus Circle; ☎ 212-397-0404); and they also offer their delicious version of bar food at **Brooklyn Bowl** (p. 273).

See map p. 126. 97 Sullivan St. (between Spring and Prince streets). ☎ *212-274-0404.* www.blueribbonrestaurants.com. *Reservations accepted only for groups of 5–8. Subway: C or E to Spring Street. Main courses: $15–$34. AE, DC, DISC, MC, V. Open: Daily 4 p.m.–4 a.m.*

Bubby's Pie Co.
$$ TriBeCa AMERICAN

Brave the lines to get in, squeeze into one of the close tables, try to block out the noise, and as soon as you begin to eat Bubby's comfort food, you immediately forget all that discomfort. Whether it's the slow-cooked pulled-pork barbecue; the magnificent meatloaf; or the buttermilk-fried half-chicken, with sides such as sautéed spinach, macaroni and cheese, or onion straws, Bubby's dishes define comfort. Save room for the desserts, especially the homemade pies; one taste of the apple pie immediately brings on a flood of happy childhood flashbacks. Breakfast is big here and lasts well into the middle of the day. Weekend brunch is a big thing in trendy TriBeCa, and the waits can get very lengthy. Celebrities need comfort, too, and you may spot one or two at Bubby's seeking anonymity and down-home chow. There is a second location, in Brooklyn at 1 Main St. in DUMBO (☎ 718-222-0666; see map p. 132); note that it isn't open 24/7 and accepts cash only.

See map p. 126. 120 Hudson St. (at North Moore Street). ☎ *212-219-0666.* www.bubbys.com. *Reservations recommended for dinner (not accepted for brunch). Subway: 1 to Franklin Street; A, C, or E to Canal Street. Main courses: $8–$18 breakfast, brunch, and lunch; $15–$23 dinner. AE, DC, DISC, MC, V. Open: 24 hours, except Mon midnight through Tues 8 a.m.*

Calle Ocho
$$$ Upper West Side LATIN

The Upper West Side was long considered a culinary wasteland, so Calle Ocho's arrival — and with it, a big, boisterous space, adventurous pan-Latin food, and killer mojitos — was greeted with an enthusiasm that has yet to abate. The entrees, such as *lechón* (stewed pork), paella, and Cuban skirt steak, may take a back seat to appetizers including Puerto Rican rum-glazed shrimp and Costa Rican soft tacos, as well as a variety of ceviche, washed down with mojitos, sangria, or *caipirinhas,* a potent traditional Brazilian cocktail. (The wine list isn't extensive — cocktails are what you want here.) Come to party; the space can get noisy, and it's not really the spot for intimate conversations. Sunday brunch is also popular here.

See map p. 130. 446 Columbus Ave. (between 81st and 82nd streets). ☎ *212-873-5025.* www.calleochonyc.com. *Reservations recommended. Subway: B or C to 81st Street. Main courses: $21–$28. AE, DC, DISC, MC, V. Open: Mon–Thurs 6–11 p.m., Fri 6 p.m. to midnight, Sat noon to 3 p.m. and 5 p.m. to midnight, Sun noon to 3:30 p.m. and 5–10 p.m.*

Carmine's
$$ Upper West Side   ITALIAN

This fun, family-style Upper West Side institution will not let you go home hungry. Portions are huge, and though big can often mean bad, it doesn't at Carmine's. Remarkably, this place turns out better pasta and entrees than many 20-table Italian restaurants in the city. I've never had pasta here that wasn't al dente, and the marinara sauce is as good as any I've had in Manhattan. For starters, the daily salads are always fresh, and the mountainous platter of fried calamari perfectly tender. Rigatoni with sausage and broccoli is a pasta standout; the best meat entrees include veal parmigiana, broiled porterhouse steak, and the chicken *scarpariello* (chicken pan-broiled with a lemon-rosemary sauce). The tiramisu is pie-size, thick and creamy, and bathed in Kahlúa and Marsala. Order half of what you think you can eat. Bring the kids and plan to enjoy a raucous meal. Unless you come early, expect to wait. Carmine's also has a usually jam-packed outlet in Times Square at 200 W. 44th St. (☎ **212-221-3800**).

See map p. 128. 2450 Broadway (between 90th and 91st streets). ☎ **212-362-2200.** www.carminesnyc.com. *Reservations strongly recommended before 6 p.m.; accepted for 6 or more after 6 p.m. Subway: 1, 2, or 3 to 96th Street. Family-style main courses: $25–$42. AE, DC, DISC, MC, V. Open: Sun–Thurs 11:30 a.m.–11 p.m., Fri–Sat 11:30 a.m. to midnight.*

'Cesca
$$$$ Upper West Side   ITALIAN

The Italian food at 'Cesca is not quite as innovative as it once was, but it's still special. With a wood-burning oven used to roast everything from oysters to peppers, this place is as rustic as it gets. Imagine yourself in an Italian farmhouse where you're served slow-cooked meats, like pork shank with the fat cooked off and the meat falling from the bone, or a slow-roasted duck. Try to save room for the delectable desserts, like rosemary panna cotta. Service is friendly and informal, and the restaurant is spacious and comfortable, with a large bar area with long tables where you snack on marinated olives, *fritto misto,* or spicy Parmesan and prosciutto fritters while sipping unusual Italian wines. 'Cesca is one of the most popular restaurants on the Upper West Side, so call well ahead for reservations.

See map p. 130. 164 W. 75th St. (at Amsterdam Avenue). ☎ **212-787-6300.** www.cescanyc.com. *Reservations recommended. Subway: 1, 2, or 3 to 72nd Street. Main courses: $23–$38; 3-course pre-theater menu: $31. AE, DC, MC, V. Open: Mon–Thurs 5–11 p.m., Fri–Sat 5–11:30 p.m., Sun noon to 3 p.m. and 5–10 p.m.*

Bright lights, big names

"The best?" you scoff as you browse the restaurants listed in this section. "How can these be the best when [insert famous restaurant name here] isn't reviewed?" I've reviewed a cross-section of restaurants intended to highlight the variety of experiences across the city for every budget, but there's no way to possibly cover them all here. However, there are some specific reasons certain restaurants that you may want to try aren't included. Here are a few:

✔ **Babbo,** 110 Waverly Place (☎ **212-777-0303;** www.babbonyc.com): Of all the restaurants in the Batali empire, Lupa (p. 144) continues to provide the best value for the money. But if you can get a reservation at Babbo, it's a worthwhile, more amped-up experience.

✔ **Minetta Tavern,** 113 MacDougal St. (between West 3rd and Bleecker streets; ☎ **212-475-3850;** www.minettatavernny.com): At press time, it's still too hot, in spite of the fact that restaurateur Keith McNally has already moved on to open another place (Pulino's). Try your luck when you read this to see if the hype has finally died down and the focus is on the food and service instead of the celebrity scene. In the meantime, note that several of his other gems — Pastis, Schiller's Liquor Bar, and Balthazar — have all had mentions throughout this guide, which tells you how inescapable a force McNally is on the New York restaurant scene.

✔ **Per Se,** 10 Columbus Circle (at 60th Street; ☎ **212-823-9935;** www.perseny.com): I have yet to have a spare $275 to spend on a single meal, no matter how phenomenal. If you do, by all means knock yourself out; chef Thomas Keller is known for the French Laundry restaurant in California, and Per Se is a similarly superlative experience.

✔ **Tavern on the Green, the Rainbow Room, Chanterelle,** or **Cafe des Artistes:** They're all closed. New York's dining scene is known for its volatility, even in the best of times, and the recession was a restaurant killer in 2009, taking down many long-standing, well-respected places. If you have your heart set on a specific dining experience, call not only to make a reservation but also to confirm that it's still standing.

Charles' Country Pan-Fried Chicken
$ Harlem   SOUL FOOD

Having been born and largely raised in the South, I'm not about to waste your time or embarrass myself by recommending a soul-food joint that I wouldn't take my folks to. So, you can trust that Charles' is bona fide. You don't come here for a fancy setting; you come for soul food at its simplest and freshest. And you'd better come hungry. The all-you-can-eat buffet features Charles Gabriel's signature crunchy, moist pan-fried chicken; ribs in a tangy sauce with meat falling off the bone; smoky stewed oxtails in a thick brown onion gravy; macaroni and cheese; collard greens with bits of smoked turkey; black-eyed peas; and cornbread warm and not overly sweet. Mmm.

2839 Frederick Douglass Blvd. (a.k.a. Eighth Ave., at 151st Street). ☎ *212-281-1800. Reservations not accepted. Subway: B, C, or D to 155th Street. All-you-can-eat buffet: $11 lunch, $14 dinner. AE, MC, V. Open: Mon–Thurs 11 a.m.–11 p.m., Fri–Sat 11 a.m.–1 a.m., Sun 11 a.m.–8 p.m.*

Churrascaria Plataforma
$$$ Midtown West   BRAZILIAN

Brazilians do many things with style, and one of them is the *rodizio,* or steak-house. If a seemingly endless procession of grilled meats is your idea of a dream meal, then Churrascaria Plataforma is for you. Even if it's not, you can find something to appreciate here; I am probably the last person to try all-you-can-eat anything (as I rarely eat my money's worth), but the meats are truly delicious, and they keep the caipirinhas coming, too. Just graze the buffet-style salad bar and don't fill up on the tempting breads. Keep your eyes on the prize: the steady line of cuts of beef, pork, chicken, lamb, even fish delivered to your table until you cry uncle. (The beef cuts are particularly tasty.) Go with a group so you can lean on one another as you stagger out.

See map p. 128. 316 W. 49th St. (between Eighth and Ninth avenues). ☎ *212-245-0505.* www.churrascariaplataforma.com. *Reservations recommended. Subway: C, E, or 1 to 50th Street. Main courses: $36 prix-fixe lunch; $57 prix-fixe dinner; children 6–10 $20; children 5 and under free. AE, DC, MC, V. Open: Sun–Mon noon to 11 p.m., Tues–Sat noon to midnight.*

Craftbar
$$$ Flatiron District   AMERICAN

You may know award-winning chef Tom Colicchio as the head judge on *Top Chef,* but he built his reputation as a co-founder of Gramercy Tavern and the architect of his own Craft restaurant mini-empire. Craftbar is the more informal sister in the chain, and it applies Colicchio's philosophy of celebrating simply prepared ingredients to a laid-back setting. The joy of eating here is in rediscovering the true flavor of your dish; in the salt cod croquettes, for example, the flaky deliciousness of the fish really comes through. There are also surprising combinations, such as a hint of citrus in the orecchiette with fennel sausage that cuts the pork's saltiness and greasiness. Not everything is a winner (I've had a disappointing pan-fried skate wing, for example), but the menu changes with the seasons, and the chatty atmosphere and the friendly service makes it pleasurable to try.

See map p. 128. 900 Broadway (at East 20th Street). ☎ *212-461-4300. Reservations recommended. Subway: R or 6 to 23rd Street. Main courses: $17–$24. AE, DC, MC, V. Open: Mon–Wed noon to 10 p.m., Thurs noon to 10:30 p.m., Fri noon to 11 p.m., Sat 10 a.m.–4 p.m. and 5–11 p.m., Sun 10 a.m.–4 p.m.*

Daniel
$$$$$ Upper East Side   FRENCH

Many reasons explain why Daniel (Daniel Boulud's signature restaurant) is a *New York Times* four-star winner: the luxurious décor, the comfortable seating, the impeccable, white-gloved service — but the best reason is Boulud's faultless classic country French cooking. The menu is heavy with game dishes in elegant but unfussy preparations, plus Daniel signatures like black sea bass in a crisp potato shell, with tender leeks and a light Syrah sauce. Excellent starters include foie gras terrine with fennel confit, and hazelnut-crusted sea scallops. Sublime entrees include bonito-and-sesame-crusted black cod, and lamb loin with polenta. The wine list is terrific and, divided between seasonal fruits and chocolates, the desserts are uniformly excellent. *Tip:* You can dine in the lounge and sample the same food without the formality (jacket-and-tie for men is not enforced in the lounge).

See map p. 130. 60 E. 65th St. (between Madison and Park avenues). ☎ 212-288-0033. www.danielnyc.com. Reservations required. Subway: 6 to 68th Street. Main courses: $34–$38 in bar and lounge; 3-course fixed-price dinner: $105 (wine pairings $60 extra); tasting menus: $185–$205 (wine pairings $105–$130 extra). AE, DC, MC, V. Open: Mon–Sat 5:45–11 p.m. (lounge until 11:30 p.m.). Jacket and tie required for men in main dining room.

db Bistro Moderne
$$$$ Midtown West   FRENCH/AMERICAN

Compared to Daniel Boulud's signature and formal restaurant Daniel (see preceding listing), db Bistro Moderne is as casual as a burger joint. But casual means the models who dine here wear Armani T-shirts while digging into burgers that cost $32. Okay, so it's not your typical coffee-shop burger: Boulud's famous creation is made with minced sirloin, foie gras, preserved black truffle, and braised short ribs on a Parmesan onion roll. Casual may mean many things, but here it does not mean cheap. Despite the silly burger excess, the food is, like at all Boulud's ventures, outstanding — especially bistro favorites such as rabbit, coq au vin, and sole.

See map p. 128. 55 W. 44th St. (between Fifth and Sixth avenues). ☎ 212-391-2400. www.danielnyc/dbbistro. Reservations required. Subway: B, D, F, or Q to 42nd Street. Main courses: $28–$36; 3-course pre-theater menu: $45. AE, DC, MC, V. Open: Mon 7–10 a.m., noon to 2:30 p.m., and 5–10 p.m.; Tues–Thurs 7–10 a.m., noon to 2:30 p.m., and 5–11 p.m.; Fri 7–10 a.m., noon to 2:30 p.m., and 5–11:30 p.m.; Sat 8 a.m.–2:30 p.m. and 5–11:30 p.m.; Sun 8 a.m.–2:30 p.m.

Dressler
$$$ Brooklyn   AMERICAN

Williamsburg's dining scene has flourished in the past decade, as some of the city's most promising chefs have chosen the hipster haven as a proving ground for artful new cooking. Dressler is one of the most sophisticated neighborhood restaurants in the city, and it's well worth a cab ride over the East River to taste what's happening here. You find yourself in a gorgeously appointed room — deep reds, elaborate chandeliers, and intricate metal work (see if you can spot the playful hiding monster figures) by Brooklyn artisans — with a diverse crowd. Expect to see lots of couples; despite the noise level, it's one of the most romantic restaurants in the city. The food is as alluring as the décor; this is one of the few places in the city where I have struggled mightily with choosing just one main course, and I can assure you that it's next to impossible to go wrong with anything on the menu. The cocktails are also divine (I make mine the "La Bicyclette").

See map p. 222. 149 Broadway (between Bedford and Driggs avenues). ☎ **718-384-6343.** www.dresslernyc.com. *Reservations recommended. Subway: J, M, or Z to Marcy Avenue; L to Bedford Avenue. Main courses: $24–$30; 5-course tasting menu: $60 (wine pairings $35 extra). AE, MC, V. Open: Mon–Thurs 6–11 p.m., Fri–Sat 6 p.m. to midnight, Sun 11 a.m.–10:30 p.m.*

Eleven Madison Park
$$$$$ Flatiron District FRENCH

Part of chef Danny Meyer's restaurant group (which also includes Gramercy Tavern, reviewed later in this chapter), Eleven Madison Park has finally established a strong identity of its own, thanks in large part to a reinvigoration by executive chef Daniel Humm. The main dining room is spectacular, with sky-high ceilings, huge windows, and fresh flowers everywhere. The colorful, creative food presentation is a worthy rival for your attention, however; clearly a lot of thought goes into stoking your appetite. Recent knockouts include the Vermont Farm suckling pig and the lavender-honey-glazed Muscovy duck. The service here is a notable balance of formal and friendly.

See map p. 128. 11 Madison Ave (at 24th Street). ☎ **212-889-0905.** www.eleven madisonpark.com. *Reservations strongly recommended. Subway: 6 to 23rd Street. 2-course lunch menu: $28; 3-course lunch menu: $42; 6-course gourmand lunch menu: $78 (wine pairings an additional $55); 3-course dinner menu: $95; 11-course gourmand dinner menu: $175 (wine pairings $125 extra). AE, DC, DISC, MC, V. Open: Mon–Fri noon to 2 p.m. and 5:30–10 p.m., Sat 5:30–10 p.m.*

El Faro
$$ Greenwich Village LATIN

The oldest Spanish restaurant in New York, El Faro celebrated its 80th birthday in 2007. But with one visit, you feel like a regular and longtime friend of the Lurgis family, who has owned the restaurant since 1959. Maybe you get to sit in what was writer James Baldwin's favorite corner table (the restaurant is mentioned in his biography), or one of the tables off the bar, possibly the one that a resident ghost is rumored to occasionally inhabit. The menu here features Spanish dishes that are now so familiar here, such as *paella a la Valenciana,* shrimp *al ajillo,* and *mariscada* (mixed seafood) with green sauce. Of course, all this is complemented with El Faro's particularly potent signature sangria, also known as "truth serum."

See map p. 126. 823 Greenwich St. (at Horatio Street). ☎ **212-929-8210.** *Reservations not accepted. Subway: A, C, or E to 14th Street. Main courses: $16–$30. AE, MC, V. Open: Tues–Sun noon to midnight.*

Flor de Mayo
$ Upper West Side CHINO-LATINO

Cuban/Chinese cuisine is a New York phenomenon that started in the late 1950s when Cubans of Chinese heritage immigrated to New York after the revolution. Most of the immigrants took up residence on the Upper West Side, and Cuban/Chinese restaurants flourished. Many have disappeared, but the best one, Flor de Mayo, remains and has morphed into a Chinese/Peruvian joint. The kitchen does fine with both sides of the massive menu (lean toward the Latin side), but the best dish is the *la brasa* half-chicken lunch special — beautifully spiced and slow-roasted until it's fork tender and falling off the bone, served with a giant pile of fried rice, bounteous with roast pork, shrimp, and veggies. Service and atmosphere are reminiscent of Chinatown: efficient and lightning quick.

See map p. 130. 2651 Broadway (between 100th and 101st streets). ☎ **212-663-5520** *or 212-595-2525. Reservations not accepted. Subway: 1 to 103rd Street. Main courses: $9–$17; lunch specials (Mon–Sat to 4:30 p.m.): $6–$8. AE, MC, V ($15 minimum). Open: Daily noon to midnight.*

Frankie & Johnnie's
$$$$ Midtown West STEAKHOUSE

When a restaurant starts opening branches, red flags immediately go up. Does that mean the restaurant has become a chain and quality has eroded to chain-food status? In the case of Frankie & Johnnie's, the legendary theater district speakeasy-turned-steakhouse, which opened this outlet in the two-story town house once owned by actor John Barrymore, those fears were allayed after one bite of their signature sirloin. Not only are Frankie & Johnnie's steaks vastly underrated in the competitive world of New York steakhouses, but the other nonsteak options are superb. The crab cake appetizer has an overwhelmingly high crab-to-cake ratio. Service is old-school steakhouse, and there's a special perk at this particular location: If you're staying in Midtown, the restaurant provides complimentary stretch-limo service to and from the restaurant. Also at 269 W. 45th St (at Eighth Avenue; ☎ **212-997-9494**).

See map p. 128. 32 W. 37th St. (between Fifth and Sixth avenues). ☎ **212-947-8940.** www.frankieandjohnnies.com. *Reservations recommended. Subway: B, C, D, F, M, N, Q, or R to 34th Street/Herald Square; A, C, E, N, Q, R, S, 1, 2, 3, or 7 to 42nd Street. Main courses: $23–$52. Open: Mon–Thurs noon to 3 p.m. and 4–10:30 p.m., Fri noon to 3 p.m. and 4–11 p.m., Sat 4–11 p.m.*

Gramercy Tavern
$$$$$ Flatiron District AMERICAN

Gramercy Tavern has been a New York favorite for special occasions for more than 15 years, but it has seen a recent resurgence thanks to executive chef Michael Anthony. If you can't score a reservation for the dining room, try your luck for a meal at the more casual bar. In either case, you are rewarded with truly delicious, sophisticated American cuisine served by a crisply professional but friendly and accommodating staff. Menus change seasonally; I recently had a refreshing carrot-and-calamari salad in lemon vinaigrette, followed by seared scallops with pickle and peas. Mains such as the black bass with walnuts and thinly shredded squash, and the papardelle with tender lamb ragu and scallion, are so satisfying that you wish you could re-create them at home. The entire experience is effortlessly artful. If you have room in a limited budget for only one special dinner while you're in New York, make this one it.

See map p. 128. 42 E. 20th St. (between Broadway and Park Avenue). ☎ **212-477-0777.** www.gramercytavern.com. *Reservations strongly recommended. Subway: N, R, or 6 to 23rd Street. Main courses: $12–$25 lunch; 5-course lunch tasting menu: $55; 2-course dinner menu: $82; 6-course dinner tasting menu: $110 (vegetable tasting menu $88). AE, DC, DISC, MC, V. Open: Mon–Thurs noon to 2 p.m. and 5:30–10 p.m., Fri noon to 2 p.m. and 5:30–11 p.m., Sat 5:30–11 p.m., Sun 5:30–10 p.m.*

Haveli
$$ East Village   INDIAN

New York is blessed with a number of great Indian restaurants, but I'm fondest of Haveli for its low-key atmosphere and consistently satisfying food. The dark, bi-level interior is more subdued and upscale than the cheaper joints on "Curry Row" (nearby on Sixth Street), and a meal here is an excellent value, given the high quality for reasonable prices. I like to start with the *palaka* soup, even in summertime, and I usually opt for the puri rather than nan bread, even though both are equally tasty. You can't go wrong with a single main dish; even the traditional *murga tikka muslam* (otherwise known as chicken tikka masala), *rogan josh,* and mushroom *saag* are revelations. Don't leave without having the *gulab jaman* for dessert; you never know how heavenly fried cheese balls in syrup can be until you have them here.

See map p. 126. 100 Second Ave. (at Sixth Street). ☎ **212-982-0533.** www.haveli nyc.com. *Reservations recommended. Subway: F to Second Avenue; 6 to Astor Place. Main courses: $9–$26. AE, DC, DISC, MC, V. Open: Daily noon to midnight.*

'inoteca
$$ Lower East Side   ITALIAN

The Lower East Side was once the home to many kosher wine factories, but you find only Italian wines at cozy 'inoteca. The impressive list is over 600 bottles long, but even better are the exquisitely prepared small plates that complement the wines. The panini are notable for their freshness and their delicacy, with the *coppa* (a spicy cured ham), hot peppers, and *rucola* (arugula) being the standout. The *tramezzini* (crustless sandwiches) are nothing like the crustless sandwiches served at high tea; here you can have yours stuffed with tuna and chickpeas or with *mortadella* and pickled red peppers. The "Fritto" section of the menu includes a wonderful mozzarella *in carrozza* (breaded mozzarella stuffed with a juicy anchovy sauce and lightly fried). Whatever you order, don't rush — 'inoteca is a place to go slowly. Savor both the wine and the food, not to mention the scene.

See map p. 126. 98 Rivington St. (at Ludlow Street). ☎ **212-614-0473.** www.inoteca
nyc.com. *Reservations accepted for parties of 6 or more. Subway: F, J, M, or Z to
Delancey Street. Main courses: $11–$18 panini and piatti. AE, MC, V. Open: Daily
noon to 3 a.m., Sat–Sun brunch 10 a.m.–4 p.m.*

Jean Georges
$$$$$ **Midtown West**   **FRENCH**

You're in the hands of a true master at Jean Georges, one of the world's
finest culinary experiences. The restaurant is housed in Trump
International Tower, and the main dining room overlooks the Columbus
Circle steel globe, so a certain New York swagger is built in to the atmosphere, but the food is truly the star of the show. Every one of your senses
will be engaged by the beautifully presented, incredibly fragrant, and
intoxicatingly flavorful dishes. If I sound rhapsodic, it's because I am —
when I'm lucky enough to eat here. Every morsel elevates your idea of
what the word *delicious* means. I still crave the nutty mushroom risotto,
lightened by notes of citrus zest, as well as a smoky cod I recently had. By
no means should you let the dinner prices hold you back; chef
Vongerichten practically performs a service to the community by offering
a $29 two-course lunch menu. My only complaint: The somewhat distant
and uneven service here does not quite match the quality of the cooking,
which is surprising at a restaurant of this caliber.

See map p. 128. 1 Central Park West (between 60th and 61st streets). ☎ **212-299-
3900.** *Reservations required. Subway: A, B, C, D, or 1 to 59th Street. Lunch 2-course
menu: $29 ($15 each additional course); dinner tasting menus: $148 and $168;
3-course prix-fixe menu: $98. AE, DC, DISC, MC, V. Open: Mon–Sat noon to 2:30 p.m.
and 5:30–11 p.m. Jacket required at dinner.*

Keens Steakhouse
$$$$$ **Midtown West**   **STEAKHOUSE**

One of the oldest steakhouses in New York, Keens, established in 1885,
not only serves the basics of a steakhouse — aged prime porterhouse for
two or three, T-bone, and filet mignon with the requisite sides such as
creamed spinach and hash browns — but it also serves chops: lamb
chops, prime rib, short ribs, and, most notably, mutton chops. The mutton
chop, with its two flaps of long, thick, rich subtly gamey meat on either
side of the bone, has made Keens the original that it is. It's no gussied-up
remake of old New York — it's the real thing. Its authenticity shows in
everything from the thousands of ceramic pipes on the ceiling (regular
diners, including celebrities like Babe Ruth, George M. Cohan, and Albert
Einstein, were given their own personal pipes) to the series of wood-
paneled rooms (some with fireplaces), leather banquettes, a clubby bar
with a three-page menu of single malts, and even the framed playbill
Lincoln was reading at Ford's Theatre that infamous evening in 1865.

See map p. 128. 72 W. 36th St. (at Sixth Avenue). ☎ **212-947-3636.** www.keens
steakhouse.com. *Reservations recommended. Subway: B, D, F, M, N, Q, or R to*

34th Street/Herald Square. Main courses: $24–$54. AE, DC, DISC, MC, V. Open: Mon–Fri 11:45 a.m.–10:30 p.m., Sat 5–10:30 p.m., Sun 5–9 p.m.

Landmarc
$$$ TriBeCa   MEDITERRANEAN

This cozy, intimate TriBeCa restaurant is too good to be considered just a neighborhood joint. Chef/owner Marc Murphy has put his own distinctive spin on this Italian/French rendition of a bistro. Here you find excellent smoked mozzarella and ricotta fritters alongside escargots bordelaise. You have to decide whether you imagine yourself in a Tuscan trattoria or a Provençal bistro. Or you can mix and match cuisines. Try the pasta special of the day accompanied by mussels with a choice of sauce — Provençal, Dijonnaise, or the comforting blend of shallots, parsley, and white wine. Steaks and chops are cooked over an open fire, and the steaks are also offered with a variety of sauces. In addition to the excellent food, what keeps the neighbors pouring into Landmarc are the remarkably affordable wines, sold by the bottle or half-bottle.

See map p. 126. 179 W. Broadway (between Leonard and Worth streets). ☎ 212-343-3883. www.landmarc-restaurant.com. Reservations accepted for parties of 6 or more. Subway: 1 to Franklin Street. Main courses: $16–$34. AE, DC, DISC, MC, V. Open: Mon–Fri noon to 2 a.m., Sat–Sun 9 a.m.–2 a.m.

Lupa
$$ Greenwich Village   ITALIAN

More than a decade into its existence, this Roman-style *osteria* has remained a hot ticket. Lupa is blessed with an impeccable pedigree: Among its owners is Mario Batali, the Food Network "Iron Chef" who has built a mini-empire in the Manhattan restaurant world. It offers high-quality food at good value; you can eat very well here without maxing out your credit card. The food is consistently tasty, but don't expect big portions. The menu is thoughtful and creative, focusing on lusty Roman fare like ricotta gnocchi with sausage and fennel, or saltimbocca. Wines, too, have been carefully chosen, and you can order a bottle from the extensive list or sample one of several varieties that come in a carafe. Here, perhaps more than at any other Batali enterprise, the service hits just the right notes: Servers are both warm and supremely knowledgeable. Make a reservation, or go early to snag one of the tables set aside for walk-ins.

See map p. 126. 170 Thompson St. (between Houston and Bleecker streets). ☎ 212-982-5089. www.luparestaurant.com. Reservations recommended. Subway: A, B, C, D, E, F, or M to West 4th St. Main courses: $11–$17 primi, $18–$23 secondi. AE, MC, V. Open: Daily noon to midnight.

Lure
$$$ SoHo   SEAFOOD

The closest you may ever get to boarding a luxury yacht is dining at this subterranean seafood/sushi restaurant, all highly polished woods, navy-blue fabrics, white leather, and porthole windows. The interiors were damaged in a fire several years ago, but you'd never know it — the restoration was seamless. What has changed is that it now has more extensive sushi offerings than before. If you're going to do surf and turf, you may as well do it here; there are several options (chicken, steak, even a cheeseburger) for those who got roped into coming with a seafood-loving dining partner. My one gripe is the separate charge for sides such as rice and hand-cut fries, a practice that started with city steakhouses and seems to have spread to nearly every high-end restaurant in town. The service is top-notch, and the atmosphere is grown-up but fun. Happy hour is weekdays from 5 to 7 p.m. (ahoy the Dark and Stormy!) and features a special bar snack menu.

See map p. 126. 142 Mercer St. (at Prince Street). ☎ **212-431-7676.** www.lure fishbar.com. *Reservations recommended. Subway: B, D, F, or M to Broadway-Lafayette; N or R to Prince Street. Main courses: $15–$43. AE, MC, V. Open: Mon–Thurs 11:30 a.m.–11 p.m., Fri–Sat 11:30 a.m. to midnight, Sun 11:30 a.m.–10 p.m.*

Mandoo Bar
$ Midtown West KOREAN

When you think of Korean food, you probably think of table-side barbecue. Not so at Mandoo Bar, where the specialty is *mandoo,* or dumplings. In the heart of New York's Koreatown, Mandoo features freshly rolled dumplings stuffed with a variety of ingredients. The many options include *mool* mandoo (the basic white dumpling filled with pork and vegetables), kimchee mandoo (steamed dumplings with potent kimchee, Korean spiced cabbage, tofu, pork, and vegetables), and *goon* mandoo (a pan-fried dumpling filled with pork and vegetables). Can't choose? Sample them all with a combo! Soups are also special here; try the beef noodle in a spicy, sinus-clearing broth. The seats are nothing more than wooden benches here, so Mandoo Bar is better suited for quick eats rather than a lingering meal. This makes it perfect for nearby Empire State Building touring and/or shopping in Herald Square after lunch.

See map p. 128. 2 W. 32nd St. (just west of Fifth Avenue). ☎ **212-279-3075.** *Reservations not accepted. Subway: B, D, F, M, N, Q, or R to 34th Street/Herald Square. Main courses: $8–$20. AE, MC, V. Open: Daily 11 a.m.–11 p.m.*

Marea
$$$$ Midtown West ITALIAN/SEAFOOD

Chef Michael White has established himself in New York as a master of refined Italian cuisine, and Marea is his note-perfect exploration of Italian-style seafood. In his modern but intimately lit dining room, you barely notice the bustle of Central Park South outside the wall of windows. The plates include such treats as a delectable skate wing carefully seared to highlight the delicate flavor and texture of the fish, and a satisfying garganelli pasta in sausage ragu. There's also an artful array of raw fish and shellfish appetizers; I can vouch for the *sgombro* of mackerel, rhubarb, and duck prosciutto. The service strikes a rare balance of understated but friendly. If you love Italian cuisine *and* seafood in equal measures, this is your one essential dining experience in the city.

See map p. 128. 240 Central Park S. (between Broadway and Seventh Avenue). ☎ *212-582-5100. Reservations required. Subway: A, B, C, D, or 1 to 59th Street. Main courses: Lunch 2-course menu $42 ($21 each additional course); dinner main courses $24–$49, 4-course prix-fixe menu $89. AE, DC, DISC, MC, V. Open: Mon–Thurs noon to 2:30 p.m. and 5:30–10 p.m., Fri noon to 2:30 p.m. and 5:30–11:30 p.m., Sat 5:30–11:30 p.m., Sun 5–10 p.m.*

Mas
$$$$ Greenwich Village FRENCH

An atmosphere of urban sophistication permeates Mas; a glass-enclosed wine cellar is visible from the small dining room, the restaurant stays open late, and you find hipsters as well as suits eating here. The combination of urban and rural, along with the creative menu, makes Mas so special. The dishes are innovative, and the ingredients are fresh — many of them are supplied from upstate New York farms. The menu changes with the seasons; recent entrees have included sea scallops roasted in a tomato-saffron broth, and roasted striped bass with sautéed ramps. Service is low-key but attentive, and seating, though somewhat cramped, is not so bad that it dims the romantic aura.

See map p. 126. 39 Downing St. (between Bedford and Varick streets). ☎ *212-255-1790. www.masfarmhouse.com. Reservations strongly recommended. Subway: 1 to Houston Street; A, B, C, D, E, F, or M to West 4th Street. Main courses: $29–$36; 3-course tasting menu: $68; 6-course tasting menu: $95. AE, DC, MC, V. Open: Daily 6–11:30 p.m.*

Mermaid Inn
$$ Upper West Side SEAFOOD

After the opening of its first location in the East Village in 2003, the Mermaid Inn became quite popular, resulting in a perhaps inevitable backlash from people who wondered what the big deal is. Its success is in finding a sweet spot: unpretentious, fresh seafood served in a seaside-inn setting. Danny Abrams took his formula to the Upper West Side in 2007, and the place is kept busy by a well-heeled local crowd. The two locations have different chefs, and menu items change based on what's available, but recent winners have included a juicy fried skate (served with slightly too-salty fries) and rich, garlicky spaghetti topped with tangy salad, mussels, and clams. The only dessert served is a complimentary pot of chocolate pudding with cream. The beer list is interesting; trust your waiter to suggest a perfect accompaniment.

See map p. 130. 568 Amsterdam Ave. (between 87th and 88th streets). ☎ *212-799-7400. www.themermaidnyc.com. Reservations recommended. Subway: B, C, 1, or 2 to 86th Street. Main courses: $17–$26. AE, DC, DISC, MC, V. Open: Mon–Thurs 5:30–11 p.m., Fri–Sat 5–11 p.m., Sun 10 a.m.–3 p.m. and 5–11 p.m.*

Molyvos
$$$$ **Midtown West** **GREEK**

Molyvos serves some of the best unpretentious traditional Greek food you can find in the city, albeit at upscale prices. But if you like Greek food, Molyvos is worth the splurge. Start with the cold *mezedes* (appetizers), *tzatziki* (yogurt-based sauce), *melitzanosalata* (eggplant salad), and *tara-mosalata* (caviar mousse), and *dolmades,* grape leaves filled with rice, raisins, and pine nuts. Move on to hot *mezedes,* such as *spanakopita* (spinach pie), or an appetizer of grilled octopus. Traditional entrees include *stifado* (a short ribs stew), lamb *yuvetsi* (lamb shanks baked in a clay pot with orzo, cheese, and tomatoes), and a whole fish roasted in Molyvos's wood-burning grill. Many Greek wines and, even better, dozens of ouzos are available. The baklava is the perfect end to your meal.

See map p. 128. 871 Seventh Ave. (between 55th and 56th streets). ☎ **212-582-7500.** *www.molyvos.com. Reservations recommended. Subway: N or R to 57th Street; B, D, or E to Seventh Avenue. Main courses: $16–$32 lunch, $22–$38 dinner. AE, DC, DISC, MC, V. Open: Mon–Thurs noon to 11:30 p.m., Fri–Sat noon to midnight, Sun noon to 11 p.m.*

Noche Mexicana
$ **Upper West Side** **MEXICAN**

This tiny Mexican restaurant serves some of the best tamales in New York. Wrapped in cornhusks, as a good tamale should be, they come in two varieties: in a red mole sauce with shredded chicken, or in a green tomatillo sauce with shredded pork. Each order contains three tamales and costs $6, making it a cheap and almost perfect lunch. The burritos are authentic and meals unto themselves. The *tinga* burrito, shredded chicken in a tomato-and-onion chipotle sauce, is a favorite. Each is stuffed with rice, beans, and guacamole. Don't get fancy here; stick with the tamales, burritos, and soft tacos, the best being the taco *al pastor,* a taco stuffed with pork marinated with pineapple and onions. And try the jamaica (pronounced ha-*my*-kah), a refreshing hibiscus flower drink that's surprisingly hard to come by in the city's Mexican restaurants.

See map p. 130. 852 Amsterdam Ave. (between 101st and 102nd streets). ☎ **212-662-6900.** *www.noche-mexicana.com. Reservations not accepted. Subway: 1 to 103rd Street. Main courses: $9–$10 burritos; $2.50–$3 tacos; $6 tamales; $11–$13 Mexican dishes. AE, DISC, MC, V. Open: Sun–Thurs 10 a.m.–11 p.m., Fri–Sat 10 a.m. to midnight.*

The Odeon
$$ **TriBeCa** **AMERICAN**

Since 1980 the Odeon has been a symbol of the TriBeCa sensibility. In fact, the restaurant can claim credit for the neighborhood's cachet: It was the first to lure artists, actors, writers, and models to the area below Canal Street to drink, schmooze, and enjoy the hearty, no-frills American brasserie grub like the excellent beet, fig, and shaved-fennel salad; roasted free-range chicken; steak frites; and crispy pan-roasted cod. Though the restaurant isn't the celebrity magnet it once was, the food, the drink, and that inviting, open, deco-ish room has withstood the test of time and now claims well-deserved New York establishment status.

See map p. 126. 145 W. Broadway (at Thomas Street). ☎ *212-233-0507.* www. theodeonresaurant.com. *Reservations recommended. Subway: 1, 2, or 3 to Chambers Street. Main courses: $13–$34; fixed-price lunch: $20. AE, DC, DISC, MC, V. Open: Mon–Wed 11:30 a.m.–1 a.m., Thurs–Fri 11:30 a.m.–2 a.m., Sat 10 a.m.–2 a.m., Sun 10 a.m. to midnight.*

Ouest
$$$$ Upper West Side   AMERICAN

When chef/restaurateur Tom Valenti opened Ouest a decade ago, it signaled a welcome renaissance in the Upper West Side dining scene. And Ouest is still one of the neighborhood's shining stars. With plush red banquettes and an intimate balcony area, Ouest is both cozy and clubby. Service is personable but also efficiently professional. But what draws the crowds is Valenti's mastery in the kitchen, especially with meats such as his melt-in-your-mouth braised beef short ribs. The quality suffers not one iota when you switch to seafood. The poached cod is perfectly prepared with truffle custard and asparagus, while the baby calamari in a spicy tomato sopressata sauce is delicious. The desserts, including chocolate cake and a variety of sorbets, are excellent.

See map p. 130. 2315 Broadway (at 84th Street). ☎ *212-580-8700.* www.ouestny. com. *Reservations required. Subway: 1 to 86th Street. Main courses: $24–$42; 3-course prix fixe (Mon–Fri only): $34. AE, DC, DISC, MC, V. Open: Mon–Tues 5–9:30 p.m., Wed–Thurs 5–10:30 p.m., Fri–Sat 5–11 p.m., Sun 11 a.m.–2 p.m. and 5–9:30 p.m.*

Pampano
$$$$ Midtown East   MEXICAN/SEAFOOD

In my mind, good Mexican food shouldn't be expensive; it should be simple, cheap, and available near a beach. Pampano, however, and the things it does with Mexican ingredients, especially seafood, tempts me to reconsider. Set in a lovely, lush town house, seating here is remarkably comfortable. But even if you were seated on a hard bench, the ceviche here would taste spectacular. For a rare and very special treat, try a lobster taco — you won't find anything like it at your local *taquería*. Of the entrees, the *churrasco* (grilled beef), has received raves. Save room for *chocoflan* (exactly what it sounds like — chocolate flan) for dessert and maybe a cleansing shot of one of the restaurant's many excellent tequilas.

See map p. 128. 209 E. 49th St. (at Third Avenue). ☎ *212-751-4545.* www.modern mexican.com/pampano. *Reservations recommended. Subway: E or M to Lexington Avenue/53rd Street; 6 to 51st Street. Main courses: $23–$33. AE, MC, V. Open: Mon–Wed 11:30 a.m.–2:30 p.m. and 5–10 p.m., Thurs–Sat 11:30 a.m.–2:30 p.m. and 5–10:30 p.m., Sun 5–9:30 p.m.*

Paola's
$$$ Upper East Side   ITALIAN

Italian restaurants are plentiful on the Upper East Side, but strength is not always in numbers, and many are mediocre at best. Paola's is anything but mediocre, and having survived in the neighborhood for over two decades is testament to the restaurant's quality and charms. It continues to thrive in a new location in the Hotel Wales, where it attracts loyal regulars. The food is as delicious as ever. Pastas are usually homemade; the papardelle, with a rich duck meat ragu, is a standout, while the hand-rolled *trofie* with pesto is a Paola's specialty. Try something roasted in the wood-burning oven such as the naturally raised Cornish hens served with roasted potatoes. The poached, port-soaked figs are the decadent way to finish.

See map p. 130. 1295 Madison Ave. (at 92nd Street). ☎ **212-794-1890.** *www. paolasrestaurant.com. Reservations recommended. Subway: 4 or 5 to 86th Street; 6 to 96th Street. Main courses: $20–$22 primi, $22–$40 secondi. AE, MC, V. Open: Tues–Fri and Sun 12:30–10 p.m., Sat 12:30–11 p.m.*

Peter Luger Steakhouse
$$$$$ Brooklyn   STEAKHOUSE

You want one of the best steaks in New York? You gotta cross the Williamsburg Bridge into Brooklyn to find it. It's definitely worth the search. And you don't need a jacket and tie. In fact, you can come to Peter Luger's any way you want — just come hungry and bring cash (no credit cards accepted here). This century-old institution is porterhouse heaven. The first-rate cuts — the only ones this 123-year-old institution serves — are dry-aged on the premises and come off the grill dripping with fat and butter, crusty on the outside and pink within. If you really want to be foolish, you can order sole or lamb chops, but why bother? The $8.95 Peter Luger burger, however, served only at lunch, is a little-known treasure. As sides go, the German fried potatoes are crisp and delicious, and the creamed spinach is everything it should be.

See map p. 222. 178 Broadway (at Driggs Avenue), Williamsburg. ☎ **718-387-7400.** *www.peterluger.com. Reservations required. Subway: J, M, or Z to Marcy Avenue (or take a cab). Main courses: $9–$20 lunch, $32–$40 dinner. No credit cards (Peter Luger Card accounts only). Open: Mon–Thurs 11:45 a.m.–9:45 p.m., Fri–Sat 11:45 a.m.–10:45 p.m., Sun 12:45–9:45 p.m.*

Pho Viet Huong
$ Chinatown   VIETNAMESE

Chinatown has its own enclave of Vietnamese restaurants, and the best among them is Pho Viet Huong. The menu is vast and needs intense perusing, but your waiter will help you pare it down. The Vietnamese know soup, and *pho* (a beef-based soup) is the most famous, but the hot-and-sour *canh* soup, with either shrimp or fish, is also the real deal. The small portion is more than enough for two to share, while the large is plenty for a family. The odd pairing of barbecued beef wrapped in grape leaves is another of the restaurant's specialties and should not be missed. The *bun*, various meats and vegetables served over rice vermicelli, are simple, hearty, and inexpensive. New York has experienced a *banh mi* (Vietnamese sandwich) renaissance, and you find them here: French bread filled with ham, chicken, eggs, lamb, and even pâté. All the above is best washed down with an icy cold Saigon beer.

See map p. 126. 73 Mulberry St. (between Bayard and Canal streets). ☎ **212-233-8988.** *Subway: N, Q, R, or 6 to Canal Street. Main courses: $11–$18; soups: $6–$15. AE, MC, V. Open: Daily 10:30 a.m.–10 p.m.*

Scarpetta
$$$$ Meatpacking District ITALIAN

The town-house exterior of Scarpetta is so unassuming on this stretch of busy 14th Street that it would be easy to pass by completely unaware of the terrific cooking happening behind its doors. In a modern, airy space under a glass roof, impressive care is shown to every ingredient by chef Scott Conant and knowledgably served by an amiable staff. The *primi* are fantastic; the braised short ribs of beef are a dream that still keep me warm at night. Conant is known for his signature spaghetti dish (richly delicious, with perfectly cooked house-made noodles), but at $24, you may be inclined to simply download the recipe from the restaurant's Web site and make it for yourself at home. With the bar set so high by the *primi* and pastas, it's surprising that the main dishes fall short; the black cod was far superior to a bland halibut at my last visit, but I can't recommend the *piatti* with the same level of enthusiasm. Still, what Scarpetta gets right, it gets oh so right, and that includes the olive-oil cake.

See map p. 126. 355 W. 14th St. (near Ninth Avenue). ☎ **212-691-0555.** *www.scarpettanyc.com. Reservations recommended. Subway: A, C, E, or L to West 14th Street. Main courses: Primi $14–$22; piatti $23–$36. AE, DC, DISC, MC, V. Open: Mon–Thurs 5:30–11 p.m., Fri–Sat 5:30 p.m. to midnight, Sun 5:30–10:30 p.m.*

Smörgås Chef
$$ Financial District SCANDINAVIAN

If you're unfamiliar with Scandinavian cuisine, Smörgås Chef provides a graceful introduction (and one less pricey than Aquavit). Located on a cobblestone pedestrian street, the restaurant is part of a special row for outdoor warm-weather dining in the Financial District. Get comfortable at a window or sidewalk table and enjoy *smorbrod* (open-faced sandwiches such as Norwegian smoked salmon); Swedish meatballs with lingonberries; duck breast in a cloudberry reduction, served with spaetzle; or a herring sampler. The crowd is as you might expect at the heart of Wall Street, but the side-alley feel of the street makes this a relaxed spot for lunch when you're exploring the Financial District. Check the Web site for promotions; they occasionally offer free bottles of wine. You can find two additional locations, in Midtown at 58 Park Ave. (between 37th and 38th streets; ☎ **212-847-9745**), and downtown at 283 W. 12th St. (between Seventh and Eighth avenues; ☎ **212-243-7073**).

See map p. 126. 53 Stone St. (between Whitehall and Broad streets). ☎ **212-422-3500.** *www.smorgaschef.com. Subway: 2 or 3 to Wall Street; 4 or 5 to Bowling Green. Main courses: $11–$17 lunch, $16–$26 dinner; sandwiches and burgers: $10–$13. AE, MC, V. Open: Mon–Fri 10:30 a.m.–4:30 p.m. and 5–11:30 p.m., Sat–Sun 10:30 a.m.–11:30 p.m.*

Soul Fixins
$ Midtown West   SOUL FOOD

Common New York wisdom holds that if you want soul food, you head uptown to Harlem. But you don't need to hike that far: From a storefront in a nondescript part of Midtown, Soul Fixins has been satisfying cravings for fried chicken, meatloaf, mac 'n' cheese, candied yams, collard greens, and sweet-potato pie for years. The menu is a bit pricey, and the sides are sometimes better than the entrees, but it's one of the only places in town where I even bother with the collard greens (and I'm a snob when it comes to greens), let alone seek them out, which I do here. If you're near Penn Station and Madison Square Garden, and you can score a seat here, at least have some sides as a snack and enjoy the hospitality.

See map p. 128. 225 W. 28th St. (between Seventh and Eighth avenues). ☎ **212-736-1345.** *www.soulfixins.com. Subway: 1 to 28th Street; C or E to 23rd Street. Main courses: $9–$12; sides: $2.95–$3.50. AE, DISC, MC, V. Open: Daily 11 a.m.–10 p.m.*

Spice Market
$$$ Meatpacking District   ASIAN

Of all the acclaimed restaurants in celebrity chef Jean-Georges Vongrichten's empire, Spice Market is unquestionably the most fun. A wide-ranging menu inspired by Asian street food plus creative cocktails (try the Pattaya) plus attentive but nonintrusive service plus a subtropical Eastern-themed interior add up to a perfect party, whether you're on a date or out with a group of friends. Good luck with trying to settle on one main dish. Do yourself a favor and opt for the $48 (5-course) or $62 (6-course) tasting menu, the best way to sample an array of flavors as intended by the chef. (The $24 bento box, served from noon to 4 p.m., is a lunchtime alternative.) I can't get enough of the black-pepper shrimp with sun-dried pineapple or the spiced chicken samosas. Mains include crispy salt-and-pepper skate with Thai basil and lime; frankly, the entrees are perhaps the weakest part of the menu. For dessert, the fudgy Ovaltine kulfi is popular, but for me, it's the green apple cobbler all the way.

See map p. 126. 403 W. 13th St. (at Ninth Avenue). ☎ **212-675-2322.** *www.jean-georges.com. Reservations recommended. Subway: A, C, or E to 14th Street. Main courses: $16–$36. AE, DC, DISC, MC, V. Open: Sun–Wed noon to midnight, Thurs–Sat noon to 1 a.m.*

Family-friendly restaurants

Although it's always smart to call ahead to make sure a restaurant has kids' menus and highchairs, you can count on the following restaurants to be especially accommodating. And don't forget pizzerias — **John's Pizzeria** and **Lombardi's** especially.

Choose from some of these other great options for the whole family.

- ✔ **Blue Ribbon** (see the "Breakfast and brunch" section, later in this chapter): You don't have to forego a sophisticated dining experience to keep your kids happy at Blue Ribbon Bakery, where they're sure to find something satisfying on the menu (save Blue Ribbon Sushi for the adventurous little eaters).

- ✔ **Bubby's Pie Co.** (see listing in this chapter): Even the pickiest kid can find something on this menu.

- ✔ **Carmine's** (see listing in this chapter): This rollicking, family-style Italian restaurant was created with kids in mind. You won't have to worry about them making too much noise here.

- ✔ **Cowgirl,** 519 Hudson St. (at West 10th Street; ☎ **212-633-1133**; www.cowgirl nyc.com; see map p. 126): This Western-themed restaurant is not as cheesy as it may seem on first appearance. Kids big and small enjoy the corn dogs, burgers, and barbecue sandwiches, served up by a slyly sassy staff.

- ✔ **Good Enough to Eat** (see the "Breakfast and brunch" section, later in this chapter): Kids love the comfort food, like macaroni and cheese, pizza, and great desserts.

- ✔ **Serendipity 3** (see the "Ice cream" section, later in this chapter): Kids love this whimsical restaurant and ice-cream shop, which serves up a huge menu of American favorites, followed by colossal ice-cream treats.

- ✔ **Virgil's Real Barbecue** (see listing in this chapter): This raucous Times Square barbecue joint is possibly one of the loudest restaurants in New York, so the kids will fit right in.

Strip House
$$$$ Greenwich Village STEAKHOUSE

For enormous portions of perfectly charred and seasoned red meat in a burlesquelike setting (complete with seminude, old-time stripper photos, which adorn the red-velvet walls, roomy banquettes, and a steady flow of lounge music), visit the appropriately named Strip House. As soon as one of those steaks lands on your table, the seminudes quickly take a back seat to the enjoyable task in front of you: devouring that meat. You do fine with the signature strip steak or the filet mignon for two, carved at your table. The sides here are innovative variations on the standards: creamed spinach with black truffles, french fries with herbs and garlic, and, best of all, the crisp goose-fat potatoes. Desserts are monumental — especially the multilayered chocolate cake — so have your waiter bring extra forks for sharing. With the exception of those few previously mentioned ban-quettes, seating is tight, so don't expect intimacy.

See map p. 126. 13 E. 12th St. (between University Place and Fifth Avenue). ☎ **212-328-0000.** www.striphouse.com. *Reservations recommended. Subway: L, N, Q, R, 4, 5, or 6 to 14th Street/Union Square. Main courses: $29–$49. AE, DC, DISC, MC, V. Open: Mon–Sat 5–11:15 p.m., Sun 5–10 p.m.*

Tamarind
$$$ Flatiron District   INDIAN

Inexpensive Indian restaurants abound in Manhattan, so much so that it's often not worth splurging on a more upscale restaurant when you can get the same quality food at a cheaper price. In Tamarind's case, innovative and flavorful variations on the old standards served flawlessly in a sleek, gallery-like setting make the splurge definitely worth it. Adjacent to the bar is a glassed-in cubicle where you can watch the chefs work the tandoor ovens. The breads and the assorted crisps and noodles with sweet-and-sour chut-neys make great starters, especially when accompanied by an Indian beer. But save room for entrees such as the *Jhinga Angarey* (jumbo prawns mari-nated in yogurt and chilies). If you venture from the tandoor, try the lamb *pasanda* (apricot-filled grilled lamb in a cashew and saffron sauce) or Tamarind swordfish marinated in tamarind chutney and fenugreek leaves. For dessert, try the *rasmalai,* saffron- and cardamom-flavored cheese balls soaked in sweet milk. I also recommend the **Tea Room,** next door to the main restaurant and serving delicious sandwiches and pastry-and-tea pair-ings. The $15 "Tea for One" (a sandwich, pot of tea, and assorted pastries) menu makes a peaceful midday break from sightseeing.

See map p. 128. 41–43 E. 22nd St. (between Broadway and Park Avenue). ☎ **212-674-7400.** www.tamarinde22.com. *Reservations recommended. Subway: N or R to 23rd Street; 6 to 23rd Street. Main courses: $16–$31. AE, DC, MC, V. Open: Sun–Thurs 11:30 a.m.–3 p.m. and 5:30–11:30 p.m., Fri–Sat 11:30 a.m.–3 p.m. and 5:30 p.m. to midnight.*

Virgil's Real Barbecue
$$$ Midtown West   BARBECUE/SOUTHERN

The pickings are slim in Times Square for decent, value-priced food, so besides Carmine's (see review earlier in this chapter), my suggestion for the best bet in the area is Virgil's. The "theme" is Southern barbecue, and the restaurant, sprawling with dining on two levels, is made to look and feel like a Southern roadhouse with good ol' boy decorations on the walls and blues on the soundtrack. But forget the theme stuff and enjoy the surprisingly authentic smoked meats, especially the spice-rubbed ribs, which are slow-cooked and meaty. For starters, the corn dogs with pob-lano mustard are something New Yorkers rarely have the pleasure of experiencing, and the barbecue nachos — tortilla chips slathered with melted cheese and pulled pork — are a meal in themselves. Desserts are what you would expect from a restaurant emulating a Southern theme: big and sweet. Try the homemade ice-cream sandwich made with the "cookie of the day." Virgil's is a great place to bring the kids; they can make as much noise as they want here and no one will notice.

See map p. 128. 152 W. 44th St. (between Sixth and Seventh avenues). ☎ *212-921-9494.* www.virgilsbbq.com. *Reservations recommended. Subway: N, R, 1, 2, 3, or 7 to 42nd Street/Times Square. Main courses: $19–$34; sandwiches: $11–$16. AE, DC, DISC, MC, V. Open: Mon 11 a.m.–11 p.m., Tues–Fri 11:30 a.m. to midnight, Sat 9 a.m. to midnight.*

Dining and Snacking on the Go

New York is a city where everyone is constantly on the move. The pace feels like you have just 15 minutes before your curtain goes up, the game begins, or the tour starts. More often than not, you don't have time to sit down to a leisurely dinner. We're well aware of the rush here in New York, which is why you can find so many quick and tasty eats.

Breakfast and brunch

I'm a committed breakfast eater; even if my day doesn't start until noon, I have to have oatmeal or French toast before anything else. I also love the weekend brunch ritual of meeting up with friends for a leisurely late-morning or early-afternoon meal. Food-industry killjoys will tell you that brunch is for suckers, a way for restaurants to charge jacked-up prices for whipping up eggs and repackaging the week's leftovers, but I don't care — the food is somewhat secondary to the social aspect in New York. Luckily, there are many places in the city that treat both breakfast *and* brunch seriously. Here are a few to consider:

✔ **Alice's Tea Cup,** 102 W. 73rd St. (☎ 212-799-3006; www.alices teacup.com; see map p. 130): The scones here are fantastic; the croque-monsieur and salad also make a delicious brunch. Be fore-warned: The décor is a little . . . cutesy; there's a reason it's popular for baby showers. If you have small children along, ask for them to be sprinkled in fairy dust. The city has two more locations, at 156 E. 64th St. (☎ 212-486-9200) and 220 E. 81st St. (☎ 212-734-4832). Open daily from 8 a.m. to 8 p.m.

✔ **Blue Ribbon Bakery,** 35 Downing St. (at Bedford Street; ☎ 212-337-0404; www.blueribbonrestaurants.com; see map p. 126): The breads are delicious (cooked downstairs in a 150-year-old brick oven) and the brunch is known as one of the best in the city. The waiters are good-looking, too. Open for brunch on weekends from 11:30 a.m. to 4 p.m.

✔ **Café Sabarsky,** 1048 Fifth Ave. (at East 86th Street; ☎ 212-288-0665; www.cafesabarsky.com; see map p. 130): Few places in New York will transport you to Europe faster than this atmospheric Viennese-style cafe across from Central Park. I don't know what they do to the eggs here, but they're fantastic. Predictably enough, so's the Viennese coffee. There is often a line to get in; come early on a weekday to avoid the crowds. Open Monday through Sunday from 9 a.m.

✔ **Clinton St. Baking Company,** 4 Clinton St. (at Houston Street; ☎ 646-602-6263; www.clintonstreetbaking.com; see map p. 126): The blueberry pancakes with maple butter and the buttermilk biscuit egg sandwich are worth braving the morning lines for. Or wait until the lines subside and have them for lunch and dinner — they're served all day. Open weekdays at 8 a.m. and weekends at 9 a.m.

✔ **Five Points,** 31 Great Jones St. (between Bowery and Lafayette Street; ☎ 212-253-5700; www.fivepointsrestaurant.com; see map p. 126): Lemon-ricotta pancakes, eggs rancheros, and smoked-salmon eggs Benedict are among the tough choices you have to make here. Open for brunch weekends from 11 a.m. to 3 p.m.

✔ **Good Enough to Eat,** 483 Amsterdam Ave. (at 83rd Street; ☎ 212-496-0163; www.goodenoughtoeat.com; see map p. 130): As much as I like breakfast, I won't wait a long time for it, and the wait for breakfast at this Upper West Side institution on the weekends is often ridiculous. So go during the week when you can gorge on pumpkin French toast or a Wall Street omelet with baked honey-mustard glazed ham with Vermont sharp cheddar. Open weekdays at 8 a.m., weekends at 9 a.m.

✔ **Norma's,** at Le Parker Meridien hotel, 118 W. 57th St. (between Sixth and Seventh avenues; ☎ 212-708-7460; see map p. 128): Norma's is a glorious ode to comfort food. It's pricey but worth it for classics done with style and creativity. Even though they put that silly $1,000 caviar-filled omelet back on the menu. Open weekdays at 7 a.m., weekends at 7:30 a.m.

✔ **Schiller's Liquor Bar,** 131 Rivington St. (☎ 212-260-4555; www.schillersny.com; see map p. 126): From Keith McNally, the owner of Balthazar and Pastis, this is a see-and-be-seen kind of brunch spot, but the food is as good as the people-watching. Open weekdays from 11 a.m., weekends from 10 a.m.

✔ **Veselka,** 144 Second Ave. (at Ninth Street; ☎ 212-228-9682; www.veselka.com; see map p. 126): The Greek diner may be nearly extinct in Manhattan, but this Ukrainian diner lives on. And we're all grateful, because New York would not be the same without Veselka's buckwheat pancakes and cheese blintzes. Open 24 hours.

Bagels

We take our bagels seriously in New York, and I'm as noisily opinionated as everyone else. I like mine moist, plump, and with a generous schmear of cream cheese. Here is a list of places to find some of New York's finest bagels, which, of course, are the world's best:

✔ **Absolute Bagels,** 2788 Broadway (between 107th and 108th streets; ☎ 212-932-2052; see map p. 130): Their bagels, hot out of the oven, are fluffy and melt in your mouth.

✔ **Ess-A-Bagel,** 359 First Ave. (at 21st Street; ☎ 212-260-2252; www. ess-a-bagel.com; see map p. 128) and 831 Third Ave. (between 50th and 51st streets; ☎ 212-980-1010; see map p. 128): These are big, chewy bagels, served with a generous amount of cream cheese — just the way I like 'em, and I don't pretend to understand anyone who doesn't agree with me.

✔ **H&H Bagels,** 2239 Broadway (at 80th Street; ☎ 212-595-8003; www.hhbagels.com; see map p. 130) and 639 W. 46th St. (at 12th Avenue; ☎ 212-765-7200; see map p. 128): The bagels here have a loyal following, and I can admit they're stiff competition for Ess-a-Bagel — if only because their selection includes blueberry bagels.

✔ **Murray's Bagels,** 500 Sixth Ave. (between 12th and 13th streets; ☎ 212-462-2830; www.murraysbagels.com; see map p. 126): There's nothing like a soft, warm bagel to begin your day, and Murray's does them beautifully.

Pizza

Hear this, Chicago: Your deep-dish pizza has nothing on the delectable thin-crusted New York variety. And even though the quality of pizza in the city has noticeably declined, this is still where you can find the best pizza anywhere west of Italy.

So when pizza is what you seek, search out the real deal and don't be tempted by the sad, soggy imitations that seem to litter every block. You can find the best pizza in the city at

✔ **Grimaldi's Pizza,** 19 Old Fulton St. (between Front and Water streets; ☎ 718-858-4300; www.grimaldis.com; see map p. 132): At the foot of the Brooklyn Bridge in Brooklyn, the pizza made by the Grimaldis, who have made pizzas in New York for a century, is cooked in a coal oven and features a crisp, thin crust; homemade mozzarella; and a rich, flavorful sauce. If you need incentive to walk across the Brooklyn Bridge, Grimaldi's is it.

✔ **John's Pizzeria,** 278 Bleecker St. (near Seventh Avenue; ☎ 212-243-1680; www.johnsbrickovenpizza.com; see map p. 126): Thin-crusted and out of a coal oven with the proper ratio of tomato sauce to cheese, the pizza at John's is worthy of its loyal following. The original Bleecker Street location is old-world romantic.

✔ **Lombardi's,** 32 Spring St. (between Mulberry and Mott streets; ☎ 212-941-7994; see map p. 126): Claiming to be New York's oldest pizzeria (circa 1905), Lombardi's still uses a generations-old Neapolitan family recipe. The coal oven kicks out perfectly cooked pies, some topped with ingredients such as pancetta, homemade sausage, and fresh-shucked clams. A garden in the back makes Lombardi's more inviting during warm weather.

✔ **Motorino,** 349 East 12th St. (between First and Second avenues; ☎ 212-777-2644; www.motorinopizza.com; see map p. 126): Mathieu Palombino has been crowned the new pizza king of the city thanks to his Neapolitan pies. Naysayers dismiss it because it's not classic New York–style pizza, but that doesn't mean it isn't seriously good — so good, in fact, that they might even convince you that Brussels sprouts are a perfect topping. The original Motorino location is in Brooklyn at 319 Graham Ave. (between Ainslie and Devoe streets; ☎ 718-599-8899), in Williamsburg.

The preceding pizzerias are the places to go for a pie. You have to look a bit harder for a good slice. If a slice is all you want, a couple of top choices include

✔ **Famous Joe's Pizza,** 7 Carmine St. (at Sixth Avenue; ☎ 212-366-1182; www.famousjoespizza.com; see map p. 126)

✔ **Patsy's Pizzeria,** 2287 First Ave. (between 117th and 118th streets; ☎ 212-534-9783), the legendary former celebrity haunt in East Harlem

✔ **Two Boots,** 42 Avenue A (between Third and Fourth streets; ☎ 212-254-1919; www.twoboots.com; see map p. 126), and five other Manhattan locations including Grand Central Terminal and Rockefeller Center

Hamburgers and hot dogs

While most of the country in the 1960s and 1970s was being inundated with Golden Arches every few miles, New York proudly held out. But then in the 1980s, the arches came, and now, just like everywhere else in the world, they're here to stay. But that doesn't mean that you should settle for what's familiar when you can find so many better, and even cheaper, options that aren't fast-food chains. Check out any of New York's best burger joints:

✔ **Big Nick's Burger Joint,** 2175 Broadway (at 77th Street; ☎ 212-362-9238; see map p. 130): Be careful you don't get singed as you enter Big Nick's, where the griddle is perilously close to the entrance and the burgers are always frying. Trying to decide whether you want your burger with buffalo meat, turkey, or ground beef is one problem; the other is what you want on it, because at Big Nick's, the options are dizzying.

✔ **Burger Joint,** in the Le Parker Meridien hotel, 118 W. 57th St. (between Sixth and Seventh avenues; ☎ 212-245-5000; see map p. 128): This clever addition to the Le Parker Meridien hotel is hidden off the lobby by a red curtain, but word is out about the perfect $6.90 hamburgers sold at this joint, where it's just burgers, fries, and beer.

✔ **Island Burgers and Shakes,** 766 Ninth Ave. (between 51st and 52nd streets; ☎ 212-307-7934; see map p. 128): Not only are the burgers great (and served in a dizzying number of varieties), but so are the grilled chicken sandwiches and the shakes. You may not even miss the fact that they don't serve fries.

✔ **New York Burger Co.,** 303 Park Ave. S. (between 23rd and 24th streets; ☎ 212-254-2727; www.newyorkburgerco.com) and 678 Sixth Ave. (between 21st and 22nd streets; ☎ 212-229-1404; see map p. 128): You won't feel guilty as you devour the burgers at this "healthy" fast-food alternative. The beef is all-natural Coleman beef, free of added hormones or antibiotics and served on a freshly baked brioche bun. The burgers have plenty of flavor and are offered with a variety of toppings and sides.

✔ **P. J. Clarke's,** 915 Third Ave. (at 55th Street; ☎ 212-317-1616; www.pjclarkes.com): P. J. Clarke's has been a New York institution for more than a century, and its hamburger, like the restaurant's old wood walls, the broken cigarette machine and pay phone, and the hidden dining nook for two, has been blessedly preserved. Nothing more than a slab of chopped meat cooked to order on a bun for the curious price of $9.15, the hamburger is a masterpiece of simplicity. "The Cadillac" version adds bacon and cheese.

✔ **Shake Shack,** at Madison Avenue and 23rd Street (☎ 212-889-6600; www.shakeshacknyc.com; see map p. 128): Literally a shack at the southeastern edge of Madison Square Park, this joint attracts long lines in the warm months. Are the burgers and shakes and cheese fries worth it? Yes — to a point. Prepare to spare at least a half-hour, or try your luck at one of the other three locations around town, or at Citi Field if you're catching a Mets game.

Have a craving for a New York City hot dog? Skip the cart and head to the Upper West Side **Gray's Papaya,** 2090 Broadway (at 72nd Street; ☎ 212-799-0243; see map p. 126), for one of the cheapest meals on the planet, the "Recession Special": $4.50 for two beef dogs with unlimited toppings and a fruit drink. And the good thing is that at Gray's, there's always a recession.

If you're on the Upper East Side and have a hot-dog fix, head to **Papaya King,** 179 E. 86th St. (at Third Avenue; ☎ 212-369-0648; www.papaya king.com; see map p. 130), the poor man's Gray's Papaya.

Just as pizza and burgers have received the gourmet treatment in recent years, the humble hot dog has been elevated to a delicacy by **Crif Dogs,** 113 St. Mark's Place (between First Avenue and Avenue A; ☎ 212-614-2728; see map p. 126). If the idea of a bacon-wrapped hot dog slathered in avocados and sour cream doesn't make your stomach lurch, then you are in the right place. If you like Asian flavors, then the kimchi- and curry-dressed concoctions by **Asiadog** (www.asiadognyc.com) are a must; at press time, they can be found primarily at the Brooklyn Flea.

New York delicatessens

The city's delis are all about pastrami and attitude. And New York has plenty of both. Some of the best delis include the following:

- ✔ **Artie's Delicatessen,** 2290 Broadway (at 83rd Street; ☎ 212-579-5959; www.arties.com; see map p. 130): This kid on the deli block — it's only been open for a decade or so — can hold its own on the playground with the big boys, thank you very much, especially in the Reuben department. My corned-beef-loving mom would approve.

- ✔ **Carnegie Deli,** 854 Seventh Ave. (at 55th Street; ☎ 800-334-5606 or 212-757-2245; www.carnegiedeli.com; see map p. 128): Even big eaters may be challenged by mammoth sandwiches with names like "Fifty Ways to Love Your Liver" — chopped liver, hard-boiled egg, lettuce, tomato, and onion.

- ✔ **Katz's Delicatessen,** 205 E. Houston St. (at Ludlow Street; ☎ 212-254-2246; www.katzdeli.com; see map p. 126): The tour buses line up outside Katz's for good reason: This old-world deli is one of the city's best. But be prepared to wait or try to hit it in the off hours.

- ✔ **2nd Avenue Deli,** 162 E. 33rd St. (between Lexington and Third avenues; ☎ 212-689-9000; www.2ndavedeli.com; see map p. 128): This much-beloved deli broke New Yorkers' hearts when it closed its Second Avenue location in 2005. It reopened farther uptown, and you could hear the collective sigh of relief. The sandwiches are great, and the soups are even greater. And unlike Artie's, Carnegie, and Katz's, it's kosher.

More sandwiches and snacks

For other quick meals besides burgers, hot dogs, and pizza, here's a sampling of New York's best places to grab and go:

- ✔ **Eisenberg's Sandwich Shop,** 174 Fifth Ave. (between 21st and 22nd streets; ☎ 212-675-5096; see map p. 128): Time seems to have slowed to a crawl in this old-school luncheonette, where you can wash down one of the greasy BLTs with a lime rickey.

- ✔ **Empanada Mama,** 763 Ninth Ave. (near 51st Street; ☎ 212-698-9008; see map p. 128): This local chain offers more than 40 varieties of *empanadas* (Latin American pastries). Stick to the classics, such as the Colombian-style ground-beef corn-flour *empanada.*

- ✔ **No. 7 Sub,** 1188 Broadway (between 28th and 29th streets; ☎ 212-532-1680; www.no7sub.com; see map p. 128): Brooklyn restaurant No. 7 Greene has collaborated with the Ace Hotel to redefine the sub sandwich shop, with outstanding results. Why waste time trying to understand how the unexpected flavor combinations (lamb meatloaf and strawberry pico de gallo?) are so good — they just are. Even if you're not a vegetarian, don't pass up the fried-tofu sub.

✔ **Shade,** 241 Sullivan St. (at West Third St.; ☎ 212-982-6275; see map p. 126): New Yorkers haven't discovered the perfection of the crepe (and why would they when there's pizza by the slice, right?), but one of my favorite treats is a salmon-and-roasted-zucchini crepe from this little takeaway window. Get yours and stroll over to Washington Square Park on a sunny afternoon.

✔ **'wichcraft,** 11 W. 40th St. (at Sixth Avenue; ☎ 212-780-0577; www. wichcraftnyc.com; see map p. 128): *Top Chef* Tom Colicchio has elevated the humble sandwich into fine dining, using fresh, local ingredients. Finish with an "ice cream'wich." This Bryant Park branch is just one of 12 locations in Manhattan.

Sweet treats

You now know more about my eating habits than my mother or my doctor, but in case it's still unclear: I am a sugar addict. I cannot pass a day without a sweet fix. Be it ice cream, cake, or cookies, I'm like Veruca Salt in the movie *Willy Wonka & the Chocolate Factory.* You know, "I want the world . . . I want the whole world," as long as the major ingredient is sugar. Fortunately, I live in New York, and there's a den of dessert sin on nearly every block. Follow me, if you will, to some of New York's best.

Ice cream

For some of the best ice cream in New York, you have to travel across the Brooklyn Bridge to the **Brooklyn Ice Cream Factory,** 1 Water St. (near Old Fulton Street; ☎ 718-246-3963; see map p. 132), where everything is freshly made, including the hot fudge for your sundae. For original flavors such as Green Tea, Red Bean, and Almond Cookie — perfect complements to a spicy Asian meal in Chinatown — head to the **Chinatown Ice Cream Factory,** 65 Bayard St. (between Mott and Elizabeth streets; ☎ 212-608-4170; www.chinatownicecream factory.com; see map p. 126). Jon Snyder, owner of the curiously named **Il Laboratorio del Gelato,** 95 Orchard St. (between Broome and Delancey streets; ☎ 212-343-9922; www.laboratoriodelgelato. com; see map p. 126), uses only the freshest ingredients to create sweet magic in his laboratory.

People in Los Angeles lost their minds over **Pinkberry,** which has opened nearly a dozen branches around New York to a more muted reception. I know, it's not real ice cream, but the fro-yo craze hasn't been so hyped since TCBY ruled the world and parachute pants were un-ironically in style. Judge for yourself in Nolita at 41 Spring St. (☎ 212-274-8883; www.pinkberry.com; see map p. 126), near Union Square at 563 Sixth Ave. (☎ 212-414-8429; see map p. 128), or on the Upper West Side at 2041 Broadway (☎ 212-580-3410; see map p. 130).

Serendipity 3, 225 E. 60th St. (between Second and Third avenues; ☎ 212-838-3531; www.serendipity3.com; see map p. 128), serves regular meals, but why bother when you can go right to the restaurant's signature dish: the Frrrozen Hot Chocolate, a slushy version of everybody's cold-weather favorite.

Mmmm . . . hot chocolate

I eat ice cream even in the dead of winter, but some people, inexplicably, feel that it's meant only for hot weather. The winter alternative to ice cream is hot chocolate, and at some bakeries and candy stores, the hot chocolate is so good that you realize that Swiss Miss is as authentic a substitute as Spam is for Kobe steak.

One of the most sinfully rich cups in town can be found at **City Bakery,** 3 W. 18th St. (between Fifth and Sixth avenues; ☎ 212-366-1414; www.thecitybakery.com; see map p. 128). Stick to the shot size — trust me, you feel full for hours after drinking it. City Bakery sells its thick hot chocolate year-round (in the summer, it's cold hot chocolate), and, in February, it hosts a **Hot Chocolate Festival** (www.hot-chocolate-festival.com), featuring a new flavor every day of the month, as well as special events.

At **Jacques Torres Chocolate,** 60 Water St. in Brooklyn (☎ 718-875-9772; www.mrchocolate.com; see map p. 132), the lines on winter weekends begin forming at 9 a.m. Customers wait for hot chocolate perfected by the former pastry chef of the restaurant Le Cirque. You can choose from many varieties, but the most popular is the hot chocolate with allspice, cinnamon, sweet ancho chili peppers, and hot chipotle peppers.

The Chocolate Bar, 48 Eighth Ave. (between Jane and Horatio streets; ☎ 212-366-1541; www.chocolatebarnyc.com; see map p. 126), features not only hot chocolate, but chocolate tea, and, if you can't live without the stuff in the middle of August, iced chocolate as well. Both Jacques Torres and the Chocolate Bar also make sinfully delicious chocolates to accompany your chocolate beverage. And if that doesn't get you through the day, nothing will.

Baked goods

New York has no shortage of bakeries; in fact, cupcakes seem to have replaced hot dogs as the street food of choice. The baked goods at the **Buttercup Bake Shop,** 973 Second Ave. (between 51st and 52nd streets; ☎ 212-350-4144; www.buttercupbakeshop.com; see map p. 128), and 141 W. 72nd St. (between Amsterdam and Columbus avenues; ☎ 212-787-3800; see map p. 130), live up to the store's mouthwatering name; the vanilla cupcakes put you in a sugar coma, and the peanut-butter bars are pretty good, too. Even better is another cupcake haven, **Sugar Sweet Sunshine,** 126 Rivington St. (☎ 212-995-1960; www.sugarsweetsunshine.com; see map p. 126), opened by a Buttercup Bake Shop alum. I'm a stickler about red-velvet cake, and for my money, the best is served at **Billy's Bakery,** 184 Ninth Ave. (☎ **212-647-9956;** www.billys bakerynyc.com; see map p. 128); the cupcakes are as delicious as they look, too, less cloyingly sweet than at some other city bakeries. In Brooklyn, **Almondine Bakery,** 85 Water St. (between Main and Washington streets; ☎ **718-797-5026;** see map p. 132), in DUMBO, serves some of the city's best cupcakes, cookies, éclairs, and other goodies; the almond croissants are exquisite.

If your taste in desserts is on the adventurous side, **Momofuku Milk Bar,** 207 Second Ave. (at 13th Street; ☎ **212-254-3500;** www.momofuku.com/ milkbar; see map p. 126), may have just the thing for you. The crack pie, compost cookie, and cereal milk–flavored soft-serve ice cream have lovers and haters, with few moderate opinions in between; give them a try to see where you fall. There's a second location in the Chambers Hotel (p. 103) in Midtown.

If you'd like to sit down while you share a sweet thing with your sweet one, head to **Veneiro's,** 342 E. 11th St. (☎ **212-674-7070;** www.venieros pastry.com; see map p. 126), a traditional Italian bakery. Yes, take the cannoli. Equally delicious is **ChikaLicious Dessert Bar,** 203 E. Tenth St. (between First and Second avenues; ☎ **212-995-9511;** www.chika licious.com; see map p. 126), a more formal three-course dessert experience.

Finally, if you haven't had a Japanese cream puff, stop into **Beard Papa,** on the Upper West Side at 2167 Broadway (☎ **212-799-3770;** see map p. 130). They're best when they're fresh and warm, but be careful — the cream will explode into your mouth (and on your shirt).

Index of Establishments by Neighborhood

Harlem
Charles' Country Pan-Fried Chicken ($)
Patsy's Pizzeria ($)

Upper West Side
Absolute Bagels ($)
Alice's Tea Cup ($)
Artie's Delicatessen ($$)
Beard Papa ($)
Big Nick's Burger Joint ($)
Buttercup Bake Shop ($)
Calle Ocho ($$$)
Carmine's ($$)
'Cesca ($$$$)
Flor de Mayo ($)
Good Enough to Eat ($)
Gray's Papaya ($)
H&H Bagels ($)
Mermaid Inn ($$)
Noche Mexicana ($)
Ouest ($$$$)
Pinkberry ($)
Shake Shack ($)

Upper East Side
Café Sabarsky ($$)
Daniel ($$$$$)
John's Pizzeria ($)
Paola's ($$$)
Papaya King ($)
Serendipity 3 ($$)
Shake Shack ($)

Midtown East
Aquavit ($$$$$)
BLT Steak ($$$$$)
Buttercup Bake Shop ($)
Ess-A-Bagel ($)
Pampano ($$$$)
P. J. Clarke's ($)
'wichcraft ($)

Midtown West/Theater District
Burger Joint ($)
Carmine's ($$)
Carnegie Deli ($$)
Churrascaria Plataforma ($$$)
db Bistro Moderne ($$$$)
Empanada Mama ($)
Frankie & Johnnie's ($$$$)
H&H Bagels ($)
Island Burgers and Shakes ($)
Jean Georges ($$$$$)
John's Pizzeria ($)
Keens Steakhouse ($$$$$)
Mandoo Bar ($)
Marea ($$$$)
Molyvos ($$$$)
Momofuku Milk Bar ($)
Norma's ($$)
Shake Shack ($)
Soul Fixins ($)
Virgil's Real Barbecue ($$$)

Meatpacking District/Chelsea
Billy's Bakery ($)
New York Burger Co. ($)
Scarpetta ($$$$)
Spice Market ($$$)

Flatiron District/Gramercy
BLT Fish ($$$$)
City Bakery ($)
Craftbar ($$$)
Eisenberg's Sandwich Shop ($)
Eleven Madison Park ($$$$$)
Ess-A-Bagel ($)
Gramercy Tavern ($$$$$)
New York Burger Co. ($)
No. 7 Sub ($)
2nd Avenue Deli ($)

Shake Shack ($)
Tamarind ($$$)

Greenwich Village
The Chocolate Bar ($)
Cowgirl ($)
El Faro ($$)
Famous Joe's Pizza ($)
John's Pizzeria ($)
Lupa ($$)
Mas ($$$$)
Murray's Bagels ($)
Shade ($)
Strip House ($$$$)

East Village
ChikaLicious Dessert Bar ($)
Crif Dogs ($)
Five Points ($$)
Haveli ($$)
Momofuku Milk Bar ($)
Motorino ($$)
Veneiro's ($)
Veselka ($)

SoHo/Nolita
Antique Garage ($$)
Blue Ribbon ($$$)
Lombardi's ($)
Lure ($$$)
Pinkberry ($)

Lower East Side
àpizz ($$$)
Clinton St. Baking Company ($)
Il Laboratorio del Gelato ($)
'inoteca ($$)
Katz's Delicatessen ($)
Schiller's Liquor Bar ($$)
Sugar Sweet Sunshine ($)
Two Boots ($)

TriBeCa
Bubby's Pie Co. ($$)
Landmarc ($$$)
The Odeon ($$)

Chinatown
Chinatown Ice Cream Factory ($)
Pho Viet Huong ($)

Financial District
Smörgås Chef ($$)

Brooklyn
Almondine Bakery ($)
Asiadog ($)

Brooklyn Ice Cream Factory ($)
Bubby's Pie Co. ($$)
Dressler ($$$)
Grimaldi's Pizza ($)
Jacques Torres Chocolate ($)
Motorino ($$)
Peter Luger Steakhouse ($$$$$)

Index of Establishments by Cuisine

American
Blue Ribbon (SoHo, $$$)
Bubby's Pie Co. (TriBeCa, Brooklyn, $$)
Cowgirl (Greenwich Village, $)
Craftbar (Flatiron District, $$$)
db Bistro Moderne (Midtown West, $$$$)
Dressler (Brooklyn, $$$)
Good Enough to Eat (Upper West Side, $)
Gramercy Tavern (Flatiron District, $$$$$)
The Odeon (TriBeCa, $$)
Ouest (Upper West Side, $$$$)

Asian
Spice Market (Meatpacking District, $$$)

Austrian
Café Sabarsky (Upper East Side, $$)

Bakeries and hot chocolate
Almondine Bakery (Brooklyn, $)
Beard Papa (Upper West Side, $)
Billy's Bakery (Chelsea, $)
Buttercup Bake Shop (Midtown East, Upper West Side, $)
ChikaLicious Dessert Bar (East Village, $)
The Chocolate Bar (Greenwich Village, $)

City Bakery (Flatiron District, $)
Jacques Torres Chocolate (Brooklyn, $)
Momofuku Milk Bar (East Village, Midtown West, $)
Sugar Sweet Sunshine (Lower East Side, $)
Veneiro's (East Village, $)

Barbecue
Virgil's Real Barbecue (Midtown West, $$$)

Brazilian
Churrascaria Plataforma (Midtown West, $$$)

Breakfast, brunch, and bagels
Absolute Bagels (Upper West Side, $)
Alice's Tea Cup (Upper West Side, $)
Blue Ribbon Bakery (SoHo, $$$)
Bubby's Pie Co. (TriBeCa, Brooklyn, $$)
Café Sabarsky (Upper East Side, $$)
Clinton St. Baking Company (Lower East Side, $)
Ess-A-Bagel (Flatiron District, Midtown East, $)
Five Points (East Village, $$)
Good Enough to Eat (Upper West Side, $)
H&H Bagels (Midtown West, Upper West Side, $)

Murray's Bagels (Greenwich Village, $)
Norma's (Midtown West, $$)
Schiller's Liquor Bar (Lower East
Side, $$)
Veselka (East Village, $)

Burgers

Big Nick's Burger Joint (Upper West
Side, $)
Burger Joint (Midtown West, $)
Island Burgers and Shakes (Midtown
West, $)
New York Burger Co. (Chelsea, Flatiron
District, $)
P. J. Clarke's (Midtown East, $)
Shake Shack (Flatiron District,
Midtown West, Upper East Side, Upper
West Side, $)

Chinese

Flor de Mayo (Upper West Side, $)

French

Daniel (Upper East Side, $$$$$)
db Bistro Moderne (Midtown
West, $$$$)
Eleven Madison Park (Flatiron
District, $$$$$)
Jean Georges (Midtown West, $$$$$)
Mas (Greenwich Village, $$$$)

Greek

Molyvos (Midtown West, $$$$)

Hot dogs

Asiadog (Brooklyn, $)
Crif Dogs (East Village, $)
Gray's Papaya (Upper West Side, $)
Papaya King (Upper East Side, $)

Ice cream

Brooklyn Ice Cream Factory
(Brooklyn, $)
Chinatown Ice Cream Factory
(Chinatown, $)
Il Laboratorio del Gelato (Lower East
Side, $)

Pinkberry (Nolita, Upper West Side, $)
Serendipity 3 (Upper East Side, $$)

Indian

Haveli (East Village, $$)
Tamarind (Flatiron District, $$$)

Italian

àpizz (Lower East Side, $$$)
Carmine's (Upper West Side, Midtown
West, $$)
'Cesca (Upper West Side, $$$$)
'inoteca (Lower East Side, $$)
Lupa (Greenwich Village, $$)
Marea (Midtown West, $$$$)
Paola's (Upper East Side, $$$)
Scarpetta (Meatpacking District, $$$$)

Jewish deli

Artie's Delicatessen (Upper West
Side, $$)
Carnegie Deli (Midtown West, $$)
Katz's Delicatessen (Lower East
Side, $)
2nd Avenue Deli (Gramercy, $)

Korean

Mandoo Bar (Midtown West, $)

Latin

Calle Ocho (Upper West Side, $$$)
El Faro (Greenwich Village, $$)
Flor de Mayo (Upper West Side, $)

Mediterranean

Antique Garage (SoHo, $$)
Landmarc (TriBeCa, $$$)

Mexican

Noche Mexicana (Upper West Side, $)
Pampano (Midtown East, $$$$)

Pizza

Famous Joe's Pizza (Greenwich
Village, $)
Grimaldi's Pizza (Brooklyn, $)

John's Pizzeria (Greenwich Village, Midtown West, Upper East Side, $)
Lombardi's (SoHo, $)
Motorino (Brooklyn, East Village, $$)
Patsy's Pizzeria (Harlem, $)
Two Boots (Lower East Side, $)

Sandwiches and snacks
Eisenberg's Sandwich Shop (Flatiron District, $)
Empanada Mama (Midtown West, $)
No. 7 Sub (Flatiron District, $)
Shade (Greenwich Village, $)
'wichcraft (Midtown East, $)

Scandinavian
Aquavit (Midtown East, $$$$$)
Smörgås Chef (Financial District, $$)

Seafood
BLT Fish (Flatiron District, $$$$)
Lure (SoHo, $$$)
Marea (Midtown West, $$$$)
Mermaid Inn (Upper West Side, $$)
Pampano (Midtown East, $$$$)

Soul food
Charles' Country Pan-Fried Chicken (Harlem, $)
Soul Fixins (Midtown West, $)

Southern
Virgil's Real Barbecue (Midtown West, $$$)

Steakhouse
BLT Steak (Midtown East, $$$$$)
Frankie & Johnnie's (Midtown West, $$$$)
Keens Steakhouse (Midtown West, $$$$$)
Peter Luger Steakhouse (Brooklyn, $$$$$)
Strip House (Greenwich Village, $$$$)

Vietnamese
Pho Viet Huong (Chinatown, $)

Index of Establishments by Price

$$$$$
Aquavit (Midtown East, Scandinavian)
BLT Steak (Midtown East, Steakhouse)
Daniel (Upper East Side, French)
Eleven Madison Park (Flatiron District, French)
Gramercy Tavern (Flatiron District, American)
Jean Georges (Midtown West, French)
Keens Steakhouse (Midtown West, Steakhouse)
Peter Luger Steakhouse (Brooklyn, Steakhouse)

$$$$
BLT Fish (Flatiron District, Seafood)
'Cesca (Upper West Side, Italian)
db Bistro Moderne (Midtown West; American, French)

Frankie & Johnnie's (Midtown West, Steakhouse)
Marea (Midtown West; Italian, Seafood)
Mas (Greenwich Village, French)
Molyvos (Midtown West, Greek)
Ouest (Upper West Side, American)
Pampano (Midtown East; Mexican, Seafood)
Scarpetta (Meatpacking District, Italian)
Strip House (Greenwich Village, Steakhouse)

$$$
àpizz (Lower East Side, Italian)
Blue Ribbon Bakery (SoHo, Breakfast/brunch/bagels)
Calle Ocho (Upper West Side, Latin)

Churrascaria Plataforma (Midtown West, Brazilian)
Craftbar (Flatiron District, American)
Dressler (Brooklyn, American)
Landmarc (TriBeCa, Mediterranean)
Lure (SoHo, Seafood)
Paola's (Upper East Side, Italian)
Spice Market (Meatpacking District, Asian)
Tamarind (Flatiron District, Indian)
Virgil's Real Barbecue (Midtown West; Barbecue, Southern)

$$

Antique Garage (SoHo, Mediterranean)
Artie's Delicatessen (Upper West Side, Jewish deli)
Bubby's Pie Co. (TriBeCa, Brooklyn; American, Breakfast/brunch/bagels)
Café Sabarsky (Upper East Side; Austrian, Breakfast/brunch/bagels)
Carmine's (Midtown West, Upper West Side)
Carnegie Deli (Midtown West, Jewish deli)
El Faro (Greenwich Village, Latin)
Five Points (East Village, Breakfast/brunch/bagels)
Haveli (East Village, Indian)
'inoteca (Lower East Side, Italian)
Lupa (Greenwich Village, Italian)
Mermaid Inn (Upper West Side, Seafood)
Motorino (Brooklyn, East Village; Pizza)
Norma's (Midtown West, Breakfast/brunch/bagels)
The Odeon (TriBeCa, American)
Schiller's Liquor Bar (Lower East Side, Breakfast/brunch/bagels)
Serendipity 3 (Upper East Side, Ice cream)
Smörgås Chef (Financial District, Scandinavian)

$

Absolute Bagels (Upper West Side, Breakfast/brunch/bagels)
Alice's Tea Cup (Upper West Side, Breakfast/brunch/bagels)

Almondine Bakery (Brooklyn, Bakeries/hot chocolate)
Asiadog (Brooklyn, Hot dogs)
Beard Papa (Upper West Side, Bakeries/hot chocolate)
Big Nick's Burger Joint (Upper West Side, Burgers)
Billy's Bakery (Chelsea, Bakeries/hot chocolate)
Brooklyn Ice Cream Factory (Brooklyn, Ice cream)
Burger Joint (Midtown West, Burgers)
Buttercup Bake Shop (Midtown East, Upper West Side; Bakeries/hot chocolate)
Charles' Country Pan-Fried Chicken (Harlem, Soul food)
ChikaLicious Dessert Bar (East Village, Bakeries/hot chocolate)
Chinatown Ice Cream Factory (Chinatown, Ice cream)
The Chocolate Bar (Greenwich Village, Bakeries/hot chocolate)
City Bakery (Flatiron District, Bakeries/hot chocolate)
Clinton St. Baking Company (Lower East Side, Breakfast/brunch/bagels)
Cowgirl (Greenwich Village, American)
Crif Dogs (East Village, Hot dogs)
Eisenberg's Sandwich Shop (Flatiron District, Sandwiches/snacks)
Empanada Mama (Midtown West, Sandwiches/snacks)
Ess-A-Bagel (Flatiron District, Midtown East; Breakfast/brunch/bagels)
Famous Joe's Pizza (Greenwich Village, Pizza)
Flor de Mayo (Upper West Side; Chinese, Latin)
Good Enough to Eat (Upper West Side; American, Breakfast/brunch/bagels)
Gray's Papaya (Upper West Side, Hot dogs)
Grimaldi's Pizza (Brooklyn, Pizza)
H&H Bagels (Midtown West, Upper West Side; Breakfast/brunch/bagels)
Il Laboratorio del Gelato (Lower East Side; Ice Cream)
Island Burgers and Shakes (Midtown West, Burgers)

Jacques Torres Chocolate (Brooklyn, Bakeries/hot chocolate)

John's Pizzeria (Greenwich Village, Midtown West, Upper East Side; Pizza)

Katz's Delicatessen (Lower East Side, Jewish deli)

Lombardi's (SoHo, Pizza)

Mandoo Bar (Midtown West, Korean)

Momofuku Milk Bar (East Village, Midtown West; Bakeries/hot chocolate)

Murray's Bagels (Greenwich Village, Breakfast/brunch/bagels)

New York Burger Co. (Chelsea, Flatiron District; Burgers)

Noche Mexicana (Upper West Side, Mexican)

No. 7 Sub (Flatiron District, Sandwiches/snacks)

Papaya King (Upper East Side, Hot dogs)

Patsy's Pizzeria (Harlem, Pizza)

Pho Viet Huong (Chinatown, Vietnamese)

Pinkberry (Nolita, Upper West Side; Ice cream)

P. J. Clarke's (Midtown East, Burgers)

2nd Avenue Deli (Gramercy, Jewish deli)

Shade (Greenwich Village, Sandwiches/snacks)

Shake Shack (Flatiron District, Midtown West, Upper East Side, Upper West Side; Burgers)

Soul Fixins (Midtown West, Soul food)

Sugar Sweet Sunshine (Lower East Side, Bakeries/hot chocolate)

Two Boots (Lower East Side, Pizza)

Veniero's (East Village, Bakeries/hot chocolate)

Veselka (East Village, Breakfast/brunch/bagels)

'wichcraft (Midtown East, Sandwiches/snacks)

Part IV
Exploring New York City

The 5th Wave   By Rich Tennant

"It's a play in two acts. The middle act is about to start now."

In this part . . .

How do you get to Carnegie Hall? Practice, practice, practice . . . and the N or R train! Here's where I tell you about the top attractions, the guided tours, and the shopping scene. I also offer itineraries that guarantee a good time based on how much time you have to spend or your interests.

Chapter 11

New York City's Top Sights

. . . .

In This Chapter

▶ Homing in on New York City's top sights
▶ Finding the best attractions to match your interests
▶ Taking a guided tour by bus, by boat, or on foot

. . . .

I'm certain that I've seen so many of New York's major attractions only because I've lived and hosted visiting friends and family here for years. New York offers a hundred great things to see, but you have just a few days to hit the highlights. To get in as much as possible in the time you have, consider these pointers:

✔ **Visit the more popular museums and attractions as early as possible before lines begin to form.** Check the hours of the attraction and do your best to be there when it opens.

✔ **Plan each half-day so that the sights you want to see are close by.** For example: Grab breakfast at the Chelsea Market and then make a beeline for the High Line park early. Then stroll through the Meatpacking District and Greenwich Village, followed by a shopping expedition in SoHo and a leisurely lunch.

✔ **Consider a guided bus tour or a Manhattan island cruise.** Most are around three hours long, and you get a good overview of the city's attractions. After the tour is done and you've seen all the major landmarks, you can spend more of your time concentrating on what interests you, which may include something you saw during your tour.

✔ **Buy tickets in advance.** Many attractions, like the Empire State Building, sell tickets online. If you're looking to save time waiting on a line, the couple of dollars for a "service charge" may be worth it. Purchasing a **CityPASS** saves you both money *and* ticket-buying time (see the sidebar "Save time and money with CityPASS," later in this chapter).

✔ **Savor the outer boroughs next time.** The words *New York City* are often assumed to mean "Manhattan," but Brooklyn and Queens are destinations in their own right, and Staten Island and the Bronx also offer worthwhile attractions. In this chapter, I cover some major outer-borough attractions, but consider them just a sample of what's on offer — and plan to explore more on your next trip.

New York City's Top Sights

American Museum of Natural History
Upper West Side

You need two hours to take in a sampling of this vast museum, which spans 4 city blocks. In addition to special exhibitions (for which you must buy tickets in advance for timed entry), the museum features a remarkable, if somewhat dated-looking, permanent collection of taxidermic wildlife (including a herd of African elephants); an enormous exhibition dedicated to biodiversity; interactive exhibits; and displays of gems, dinosaur fossils, and meteorites, among other treasures. It also has an IMAX theater. The **Hayden Planetarium** — a huge sphere housed in a glass box several stories tall — is part of the **Rose Center for Earth and Space.** The top half of the sphere houses the state-of-the-art Space Theater, which airs a breathtaking space show, *Journey to the Stars,* narrated by Whoopi Goldberg; the bottom half houses *The Big Bang,* a multisensory re-creation of the first moments of the universe. If your visit is between October and May, don't miss the **Butterfly Conservatory.**

See map p. 178. Central Park West (between 77th and 81st streets). ☎ *212-769-5100.* www.amnh.org. *Subway: B or C to 81st Street/Museum of Natural History, then walk south along the front to the entrance. Bus: M10 (north–south bus running on Central Park West, Eighth Avenue uptown, and Seventh Avenue downtown) and M79 (crosstown bus running on 79th Street) stop right at the museum. Suggested admission: $16 adults, $12 seniors and students, $9 children ages 2–12, free for children 1 and under. Museum admission plus space show, IMAX, and special exhibitions: $32 adults, $29 children, $25 seniors and students. Open: Daily 10 a.m.–5:45 p.m. The museum is fully accessible to wheelchairs and the hearing-impaired.*

Save time and money with CityPASS

The **New York CityPASS** (☎ **888-330-5008** or 208-787-4300; www.citypass.com) gives you admission to six major attractions: the American Museum of Natural History and Rose Center (including the space show in Hayden Planetarium), a Circle Line sightseeing cruise *or* cruise to the Statue of Liberty/Ellis Island, the Empire State Building's 86th-floor observatory, the Metropolitan Museum of Art, the Guggenheim Museum *or* Top of the Rock at Rockefeller Center, and the Museum of Modern Art (MoMA). The pass costs $79 adults and $59 children ages 6 to 17, which is around 45 percent less than you would pay if you purchased each ticket separately. (Note that the Metropolitan has a voluntary "suggested donation" admission, so this pass offers admission to an attraction you don't actually *have* to pay for.) You can buy the CityPASS online, at the first attraction you visit, or at one of the electronic kiosks maintained by NYC & Company at the Visitor Information Center, 810 Seventh Ave. (between 52nd and 53rd streets). A perk of the CityPASS is that it enables you to bypass the sometimes-lengthy ticket lines. Note that the CityPASS is good for nine days, and it doesn't include admission to the Empire State Building's 102nd-floor observatory (an extra $15) or the special exhibits at the American Museum of Natural History.

Bronx Zoo
The Bronx

With more than 4,000 animals on 265 acres, the Bronx Zoo is not only the largest metropolitan animal park in the United States, but it's also one of the city's best attractions. Visit any of the numerous exhibits scattered throughout the zoo; the best is **JungleWorld,** an indoor re-creation of an Asian rain forest, and the **Wild Asia Monorail** (Apr–Oct; $4 extra), which takes you on a narrated ride high above free-roaming Siberian tigers, Asian elephants, Indian rhinoceroses, and other nonnative New Yorkers. You can also visit the **Congo Gorilla Forest,** home to inquisitive gorillas and other African rain-forest animals. Also located within the zoo are a **Children's Zoo** (Apr–Oct), **Butterfly Garden,** camel rides, and the **Zucker Bug Carousel** (each an extra charge, $2–$5). It's too much ground to attempt to cover all in one day, so prioritize and pace yourself.

Fordham Road and Bronx River Parkway, the Bronx. ☎ **718-367-1010.** *www.bronx zoo.com. Subway: 2 or 5 to East Tremont Avenue/West Farms Square, then walk north to the zoo's Asia Gate entrance. Bus: Liberty Lines' BxM11 express bus. Admission: $15 adults, $13 seniors, $11 children ages 3–12, free for children 2 and under. Open: Nov–Mar daily 10 a.m.–4:30 p.m. (extended hours for Holiday Lights late Nov–early Jan); Apr–Oct Mon–Fri 10 a.m.–5 p.m., Sat–Sun 10 a.m.–5:30 p.m. Discounted admission Nov–Mar; pay what you wish Wed year-round. Nominal additional charges may be applied for some exhibits.*

Brooklyn Bridge
Downtown

With sweeping views of lower Manhattan, Brooklyn, and the New York Harbor, the walk across the historic stone-and-steel Brooklyn Bridge is one of my favorite New York activities; I make a point of doing it with every friend or family member I host in the city. Crossing takes between 20 and 40 minutes each way, depending on how long you linger to enjoy the views. Be careful not to meander in the bike lanes. You can sit on the benches along the way if you need a break or just want to stop for a bit to try to comprehend that you're really in New York and that this is not a movie set.

The perfect complement to your stroll over the Brooklyn Bridge is a stop for delicious homemade ice cream at the **Brooklyn Ice Cream Factory** (☎ **718-246-3963;** see map p. 132), located in the shadow of the bridge at the Fulton Ferry Fire Boat House on the river. The ice cream fortifies you for your return stroll into Manhattan.

See map p. 175. Sidewalk entrance to the Manhattan end of the bridge is on Park Row just across from City Hall, south of Chambers Street. Subway: 4, 5, or 6 to Brooklyn Bridge/City Hall; exit across the street from the entrance. Bus: M1 (north–south bus running down Broadway and up Center Street/Lafayette/Park and Madison avenues), although traffic congestion makes the subway a better choice.

Downtown Attractions

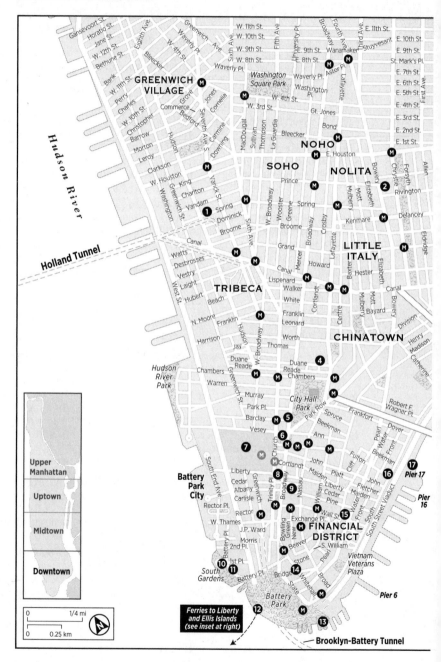

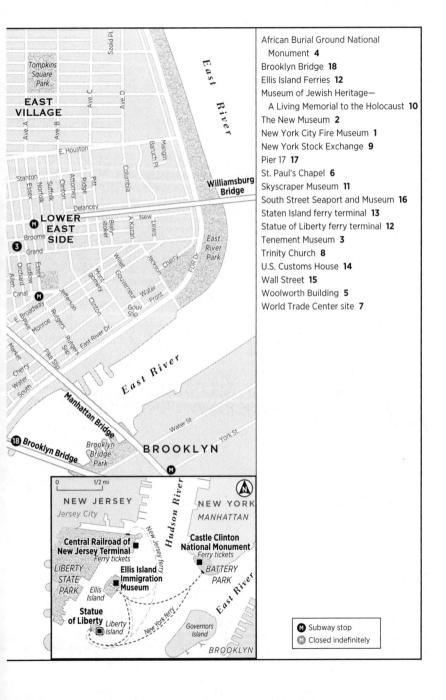

African Burial Ground National
  Monument **4**
Brooklyn Bridge **18**
Ellis Island Ferries **12**
Museum of Jewish Heritage—
  A Living Memorial to the Holocaust **10**
The New Museum **2**
New York City Fire Museum **1**
New York Stock Exchange **9**
Pier 17 **17**
St. Paul's Chapel **6**
Skyscraper Museum **11**
South Street Seaport and Museum **16**
Staten Island ferry terminal **13**
Statue of Liberty ferry terminal **12**
Tenement Museum **3**
Trinity Church **8**
U.S. Customs House **14**
Wall Street **15**
Woolworth Building **5**
World Trade Center site **7**

Midtown Attractions

American Folk Art Museum **23**
Bateaux New York **8**
Bryant Park **14**
Carnegie Hall **1**
Chelsea Piers **9**
Chrysler Building **17**
Circle Line **4**
Empire State Building **12**
Flatiron Building **11**
Grand Central Terminal **16**
Gray Line Tours **2**
The High Line **10**
Intrepid-Sea-Air-Space Museum **3**
Madison Square Garden **7**
The Morgan Library & Museum **13**
Museum of Modern Art **22**
New York Public Library **15**
New York Waterways **5**
The Paley Center for Media **24**
Radio City Music Hall **19**
Rockefeller Center **20**
St. Patrick's Cathedral **21**
Sony Wonder Technology Lab **25**
Times Square **6**
Top of the Rock **20**
United Nations **18**

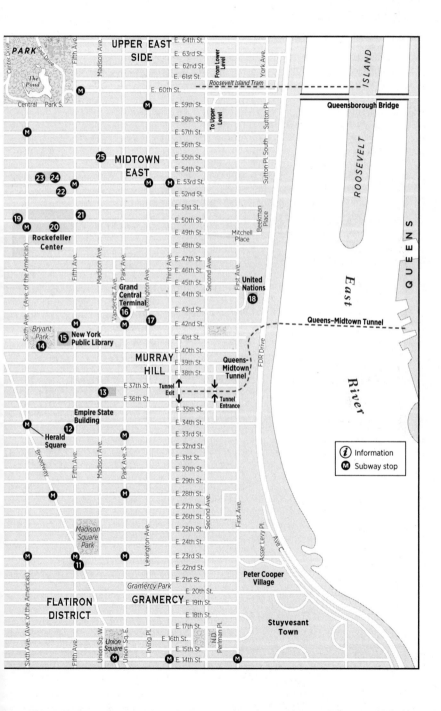

Uptown Attractions

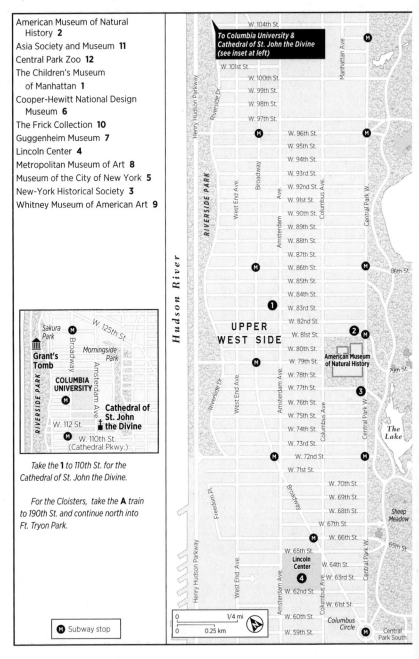

American Museum of Natural History **2**
Asia Society and Museum **11**
Central Park Zoo **12**
The Children's Museum of Manhattan **1**
Cooper-Hewitt National Design Museum **6**
The Frick Collection **10**
Guggenheim Museum **7**
Lincoln Center **4**
Metropolitan Museum of Art **8**
Museum of the City of New York **5**
New-York Historical Society **3**
Whitney Museum of American Art **9**

Take the **1** to 110th St. for the Cathedral of St. John the Divine.

For the Cloisters, take the **A** train to 190th St. and continue north into Ft. Tryon Park.

M Subway stop

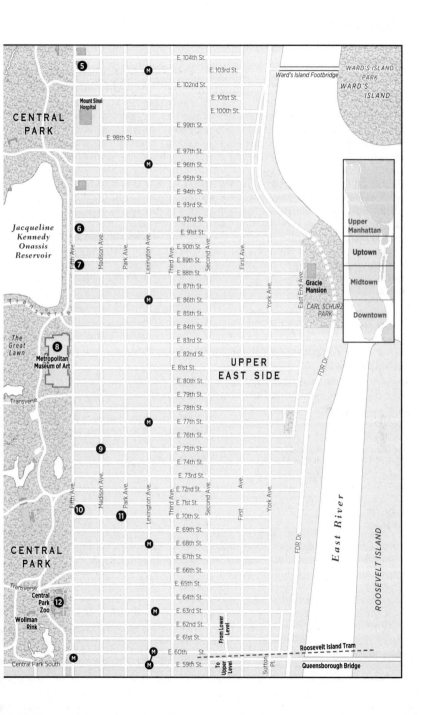

Central Park
Upper West Side, Upper East Side

This 843-acre refuge in the middle of the city is one of New York's wonders. Central Park was the first public park in the United States and is completely man-made. Throughout the year, but especially in nice weather, Central Park is a sanctuary for Manhattanites and visitors looking for a green escape from the pace of the city streets (though you can stay in touch with home or office if need be — Central Park is now wireless). You can spend hours strolling (or biking) miles of paths that wind through acres of landscaped fields and rolling hills. The park offers pleasures for kids of all ages: You and your children may enjoy taking a boat ride on the lake (call **Loeb Boathouse** [☎ **212-517-2233**; www.the centralparkboathouse.com], for rental information), skating around **Wollman Rink** just north of the pond (☎ **212-439-6900**; www.wollman skatingrink.com), or visiting the polar bears and other animals in **Central Park Zoo.** I enjoy strolling through the **Conservatory Gardens** in the springtime. In the summer, the park plays host to Shakespeare in the Park and SummerStage (see Chapter 14), a series of free concerts. For information about tours, flip to "Faring well with free walking tours," at the end of this chapter.

Even though the park has one of the lowest crime rates of any of the city's precincts, keep your wits about you, especially in the more remote northern end. Avoid spending time in the park after dark, unless you're heading to one of the restaurants for dinner or to a SummerStage or Shakespeare in the Park event.

See map p. 178. From 59th to 110th streets (between Fifth Avenue and Central Park West, the continuation north of Eighth Avenue). Information Center: ☎ **212-310-6600.** www.centralparknyc.org. *Subway: A, B, C, D, or 1 to 59th Street/Columbus Circle for the southwest main entrance; N, R, or Q to Fifth Avenue/59th Street for the southeast main entrance. Buses run along both sides of Central Park and make several stops; the M10 runs up and down Central Park West, and the M1, M2, M3, and M4 run south down Fifth Avenue on the east side of the park (they go north on Madison Avenue). Open: 24 hours.*

Chrysler Building
Midtown East

Words can hardly express how much I love the Chrysler Building. It's one of the most stunning buildings in New York: Topped by a shiny steel needle, with triangular windows that are illuminated at night, it looks like something out of Oz. Steel sculptures are poised on its battlements like gargoyles. It's my personal lighthouse in the nighttime city skyline, and I get a thrill every time I see it when I return home after a trip away. The building was designed by William Van Alen; finished in 1930, it enjoyed the title of world's tallest building until 1931, when the Empire State Building was completed. The observation deck is no longer open to the public, but peek into the lobby — an Art Deco tour de force in chrome, wood, and marble.

Central Park

Alice in Wonderland Statue **15**
Balto Statue **21**
The Bandshell **19**
Belvedere Castle **7**
Bethesda Terrace &
  Bethesda Fountain **17**
Boathouse Cafe **12**
Bow Bridge **9**
Carousel **27**
Central Park Zoo **24**
Charles A. Dana
  Discovery Center **1**
Cleopatra's Needle
  (The Obelisk) **10**
Conservatory **14**
Conservatory Garden **1**
The Dairy Information Center **26**
Delacorte Clock **23**
Delacorte Theater **8**
Diana Ross Playground **5**
Hans Christian Andersen
  Statue **13**
Harlem Meer **1**
Heckscher Ball Fields **29**
Heckscher Playground **30**
Henry Luce
  Nature Observatory **7**
Imagine Mosaic **18**
Jacqueline Kennedy Onassis
  Reservoir **3**
Lasker Rink and Pool **1**
Loeb Boathouse **16**
The Mall **20**
North Meadow Ball Fields **2**
Pat Hoffman Friedman
  Playground **11**
The Pool **2**
Rustic Playground **22**
Shakespeare Garden **9**
Spector Playground **4**
Swedish Cottage **6**
Tisch Children's Zoo **24**
Wollman Rink **25**

Information
Ⓜ Subway stop

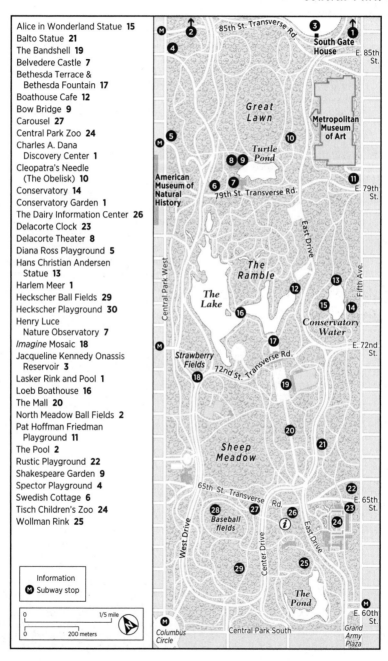

See map p. 176. 405 Lexington Ave. (at 42nd Street). Subway: S, 4, 5, 6, or 7 to 42nd Street/Grand Central, then follow the exit signs for Lexington Avenue, pass the barrier, and take the passage in front of you toward the right, which brings you right inside the Chrysler at the lower level; if you miss this exit, go up to street level and cross the street walking east. Bus: M104 from the Upper West Side (runs down Broadway and crosses town at 42nd Street) and M42 across town on 42nd Street; both stop right in front of the building. On the east side and from downtown, take the M101, M102, or M103 (running up Third Avenue and down Lexington Avenue).

The Cloisters
Upper Manhattan

At the north end of Manhattan in Fort Tryon Park, this museum is constructed from portions of medieval and early Renaissance European cloisters that were shipped across the Atlantic. The Cloisters houses an important collection of medieval art, including stained glass, metalwork, sculpture, and an impressive series of unicorn tapestries. The gardens that hug one side of the complex authentically reproduce the herbs, flowers, and other plants found in typical medieval cloisters. Both the museum and the gardens have a commanding view of the Hudson River and the New Jersey Palisades. If you choose to get here by bus, consider that, although the bus takes you right to the museum and offers a scenic, interesting ride, the ride is a long one (up to an hour or more, depending on where you start, as compared to 30 to 45 minutes on the subway). The subway is a good alternative; it takes you right to the entrance of Fort Tryon Park.

See map p. 183. At the north end of Fort Tryon Park, 1 block north of West 190th Street. ☎ 212-923-3700. www.metmuseum.org. Subway: A to 190th Street, then take the elevator to street level (don't walk up the long ramp — it takes you out of your way); once outside, you see the park entrance; walk north along Fort Washington Avenue to the entrance of Fort Tryon Park and follow the signs along the path north to the Cloisters. Bus: The M4 (north–south bus running on Madison Avenue, 110th Street, Broadway, Fort Washington Avenue uptown, and Fifth Avenue downtown) is very convenient and stops right at the museum; if you're in a hurry, you can take the subway and then catch the bus for the last part of the run. Suggested admission: $20 adults, $15 seniors, $10 students, free for children under 12 when accompanied by an adult; fee includes admission to the Metropolitan Museum. Open: Tues–Sun 9:30 a.m.–5:15 p.m.; Nov–Feb closes at 4:45 p.m.

Ellis Island
Downtown

From its opening in 1892 to its closing in 1954, more than 12 million immigrants entered the United States through the Registry Hall on Ellis Island. After a $160-million restoration in the 1980s, it reopened as a museum dedicated to the history of immigration. An enormous pile of luggage and other personal items (children's dolls, hairbrushes, clothing, and the like) remind visitors of the huddled masses who passed through. Other exhibits illustrate how these immigrants changed the demographics of the

Harlem and Upper Manhattan

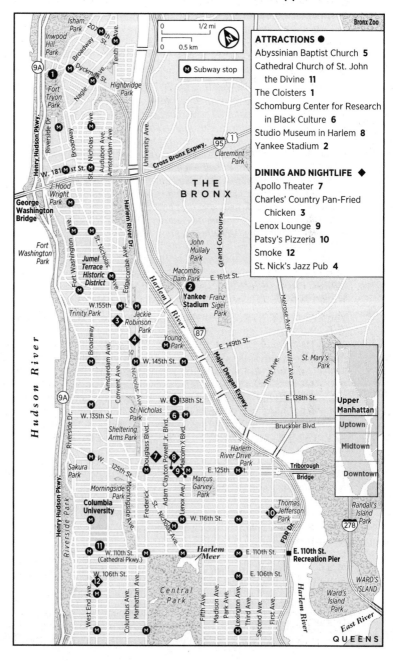

ATTRACTIONS ●
Abyssinian Baptist Church **5**
Cathedral Church of St. John
  the Divine **11**
The Cloisters **1**
Schomburg Center for Research
  in Black Culture **6**
Studio Museum in Harlem **8**
Yankee Stadium **2**

DINING AND NIGHTLIFE ◆
Apollo Theater **7**
Charles' Country Pan-Fried
  Chicken **3**
Lenox Lounge **9**
Patsy's Pizzeria **10**
Smoke **12**
St. Nick's Jazz Pub **4**

United States. The American Immigrant Wall of Honor remembers more than half a million people who came to the U.S. in search of a better life. Ellis Island offers an optional $8 audio tour (one is available for children as well, for $7.25) and a documentary film called *Island of Hope, Island of Tears.* Note that a round-trip ferry ticket to Ellis Island includes a trip to Liberty Island, the site of the Statue of Liberty. Buying your tickets in advance online is *strongly* recommended; they sell out regularly.

See map p. 175. In New York Harbor. ☎ *212-363-3200 for general information, 877-523-9849 for ticket and ferry information.* www.nps.gov/elis *or* www.statue cruises.com. *Transport: Ferry from Battery Park. Subway to ferry ticket booth: 4 or 5 to Bowling Green stop, then walk through the park heading south; the fortress-like ticket booth is at the edge of the trees by the promenade. Bus to ticket booth: M1 (running down Fifth Avenue/Park Avenue/Broadway), M6 (running down Broadway), or M15 (running down Second Avenue). Admission: Free; ferry ticket to Statue of Liberty and Ellis Island $12 adults and children 13–17, $10 seniors, $5 children ages 4–12, free for children 3 and under. Open: Daily 9:30 a.m.–5:15 p.m. Last ferry departs at 2 p.m. Note that if you want to visit both Ellis Island and the Statue of Liberty, you can't take the last ferry; taking the last ferry enables you to visit only one of the two attractions. Due to security restrictions, no backpacks, luggage, or coolers are allowed.*

Empire State Building
Midtown East

You can't see King Kong dangling from the top of the Empire State Building as he did in the 1933 and 2005 versions of *King Kong,* but you can get one of the best views of Manhattan from this 1,472-foot Art Deco structure — that is, if visibility is good. You can find a visibility rating posted in the lobby, and you should take the rating seriously — zero visibility means that you really won't see a thing except clouds and fog. The observatory is on the 86th floor and has both an outdoor and an indoor viewing area. Huge lights glow in the top of the building and are lit up in different colors at night, in honor of various holidays. On the second floor is the **NY SKYRIDE** (☎ **212-279-9777**), a simulated aerial tour of New York that I cannot wholeheartedly recommend.

Lines to visit the observation deck can be horrible at the concourse-level ticket booth, so be prepared to wait — or purchase advance tickets using a credit card, online at www.esbnyc.com. You pay slightly more — tickets were priced $2 higher on the Web site at press time — but it's worth it, especially if you're visiting during busy seasons, when the line can be frustratingly long. You're not required to choose a time or date for your tickets; they can be used on any regular open day. However, order them at a computer with a printer, because only printing them online is free. If you need them sent to you, expect to pay an additional $6 and to wait seven to ten days for the tickets to reach you ($8 and more days if you live outside the United States). With tickets in hand, you're allowed to proceed directly to the second floor — past everyone who didn't plan as well as you did!

See map p. 176. Fifth Avenue at 34th Street. ☎ **212-736-3100.** www.esbnyc.com. *Subway: B, D, F, M, N, Q, or R to 34th Street/Herald Square, then walk east on 34th Street, and turn right on Fifth Avenue to the entrance. Bus: M2, M3, M4, or M5 (all run down Fifth Avenue and stop right in front of the entrance). Admission to 86th-floor observatory: $19 adults, $17 seniors and children 12–17, $13 children 6–11, free for children 5 and under. Open: Daily 8 a.m. to 2 a.m. For security reasons, no back-packs or large parcels are allowed, and visitors are required to present a photo ID. You can buy tickets online with a surcharge at the Web site.*

Grand Central Terminal
Midtown East

Even if you're not catching one of the Metro-North commuter trains, make Grand Central part of your itinerary. You count as one of the 700,000 people who pass through the terminal daily. Finished in 1913 and beauti-fully renovated a decade ago, this Beaux Arts masterpiece features a 12-story vibrant blue ceiling on which the stars of the zodiac are traced in 24-karat gold (accidentally done backward, as a commuter testily pointed out when it was unveiled in 1913) and a central kiosk over which the land-mark brass and opal clock is perched. Aside from the gorgeous main con-course, Grand Central offers a very good dining concourse on the lower level; top restaurants including **Michael Jordan's The Steak House,** the famous **Oyster Bar & Restaurant;** the **Campbell Apartment,** a glitzy bar; and a gourmet food market, **Grand Central Market.** You can enjoy a guided tour of the terminal ($10 suggested donation), given by the Municipal Art Society (Wed 12:30 p.m.; ☎ **212-439-1049**).

See map p. 176. Main entrance on 42nd Street at Park Avenue. www.grand centralterminal.com. *Subway: S, 4, 5, 6, or 7 to 42nd Street/Grand Central. Bus: M1, M2, M3, or M4 running up Madison Avenue; M101, M102, or M103 running down Lexington Avenue. Open: 24 hours.*

High Line
Meatpacking District

In a formerly industrial area largely left to cars and highways, the High Line is an enchantingly human-scaled, nurturing park and unquestionably the best new development in Manhattan in years. The 1½-mile park — the first section opened in 2009 — is on a disused elevated freight-train track once slated for demolition. Great care has been taken in preserving the tracks while creating spaces to stroll, take photos, or sit and watch the boats on the Hudson (which I do as often as I can). The park drew more than two million visitors in its first year, and it's easy to see why: Besides the interesting plantings, the charm of walking along an elevated train track is not lost on kids (especially not my son), and adults love the many photo ops (there's a prime one around 18th Street with the Empire State Building in the background). I wish that all public-space planning in New York City could be this visionary. At press time, the second section of the park, which will include picnic areas, is expected to open sometime in 2011. Wheelchair and stroller access is at the 16th Street access point.

See map p. 176. From Gansevoort to 20th streets (between 10th and 11th avenues). Information Center: ☎ 212-500-6035. www.thehighline.org. Subway: A, C, E, or L to 14th Street. Open: Daily 7 a.m.–10 p.m. (to 8 p.m. in winter).

Intrepid Sea-Air-Space Museum
Midtown West

The USS *Intrepid*, an aircraft carrier that saw active duty in World War II, is the focal point of this large naval museum and is now a National Historic Landmark. The *Intrepid* was recently refurbished, and the visitor experience has been improved; changes include new interactive exhibits and the opening of several new areas of the ship, such as the berthing quarters and the anchor chain room. Even if warships aren't a big interest of yours, you're likely to appreciate the history of the carrier, its crew, and the aircraft — as well as the cool flight simulators ($8–$10 per ride). For the kids, the *Intrepid* is like an educational amusement park with a few thrill rides. The museum also hosts Fleet Week celebrations every year in late May.

See map p. 176. Pier 86, Hudson River at 46th Street, west of 12th Avenue. ☎ 212-245-0072. www.intrepidmuseum.org. Subway: A, C or E to 42nd Street/Port Authority Bus Terminal stop, and then continue west on 42nd Street for 4 blocks, or change to the bus. Bus: M42 crosstown bus running on 42nd Street or, even better, the M50 crosstown bus running west on 49th Street and east on 50th Street. Admission: $22 adults, $18 seniors and college students, $17 children 3–17 and veterans, free for children 2 and under and active and retired military. Open: Oct–Mar Tues–Sun 10 a.m.–5 p.m.; Apr–Sept Mon–Fri 10 a.m.–5 p.m. and Sat–Sun and holidays 10 a.m.–6 p.m. Last admission is 1 hour before closing time.

Metropolitan Museum of Art
Upper East Side

As the largest museum in the Western Hemisphere, the Met has something for everyone, from its world-famous Egyptian collection (and the Temple of Dendur) to its massive holdings of American and European masterpieces (the Impressionist works in the European-paintings section is my favorite area) to its beautiful sculpture garden. Highlights also include the Asian collection, the collection of musical instruments, and the armor collection; kids love the displays in the Costume Institute on the lower level. You're not going to fit all this into only one visit, so try to narrow your focus before you go. Tours of various parts of the collection are conducted several times an hour; you also can take a self-guided audio tour or a "highlights" tour. For schedules, check the Web site.

See map p. 178. 1000 Fifth Avenue (at 82nd Street). ☎ 212-535-7710. www.metmuseum.org. Subway: 4, 5, or 6 to 86th Street, then walk 3 blocks west to Fifth Avenue, turn left, and walk along the park to the entrance. Bus: M1, M2, M3, or M4 up Madison and down Fifth Avenue. Suggested admission: $20 adults, $15 seniors, $10 students, free for children 11 and under when accompanied by an adult; fee includes admission to the Cloisters. Open: Tues–Thurs and Sun 9:30 a.m.–5:30 p.m., Fri–Sat 9:30 a.m.–9 p.m., holiday Mon 9:30 a.m.–5:30 p.m.

Museum of Modern Art (MoMA)
Midtown West

A two-year renovation, designed by Yoshio Taniguchi, transformed MoMA into a 63,000-square-foot building that highlights space and light, with open rooms, high ceilings, and gardens — a beautiful work of architecture and a perfect complement to the art that resides within. This is where you find van Gogh's *Starry Night*, Cézanne's *Bather*, Picasso's *Les Demoiselles d'Avignon*, and the amazing sculpture by Rodin, *Monument to Balzac*. I am a bit of a design freak, so I recommend the Architecture and Design department, with examples of design for modern appliances, furniture, and even sports cars. MoMA also features edgy new exhibits (two recently much-talked about shows were by painter William Kentridge and performance artist Marina Abramovi) and a celebrated film series that attracts serious cinephiles. But the heart of the museum, as it was before the renovation, remains the **Abby Aldrich Rockefeller Sculpture Garden,** which has been enlarged; the building's design now affords additional views of this lovely space from other parts of the museum.

See map p. 176. 11 W. 53rd St. (between Fifth and Sixth avenues). ☎ *212-708-9400. www.moma.org. Subway: E or M to Fifth Avenue; B, D, or F to 47–50th streets/ Rockefeller Center. Bus: M1, M2, M3, M4, or M5 to 53rd Street. Admission: $20 adults, $16 seniors, $12 students, free for children 15 and under when accompanied by an adult. Open: Sat–Mon and Wed–Thurs 10:30 a.m.–5:30 p.m., Fri 10:30 a.m.–8 p.m.*

Rockefeller Center
Midtown West

This complex of 18 buildings includes the GE building, a 70-story Art Deco tower. The entertainment ranges from the outdoor ice-skating rink to Radio City Music Hall, where the Rockettes perform. More than 150 shops and restaurants are located around the plaza and under the concourse. Call ☎ 212-247-4777 for backstage tours, and see Chapter 14 for more information. You can tour the NBC Studios (call ☎ **212-664-3700,** or buy tickets on the center's Web site), where NBC's *Today* show tapes. Show up with your WE ♥ YOU, MATT! sign and you may get on TV. For a self-directed tour, pick up a map at 30 Rockefeller Center; if you prefer a guided tour, call ☎ **212-698-2000.** During the holiday season, you can expect huge crowds to gather and gaze upon the famous Christmas tree and the skaters on the rink, located below at Rockefeller Plaza (☎ **212-332-7654)** — expect long lines on weekends to enjoy the latter. Rink admission is $10 to $14 for adults and $7.50 to $8.50 for seniors and children 10 and under; skate rental is $8. The rink is open from mid-October to mid-April.

See map p. 176. Between Fifth and Sixth avenues and from 48th to 51st streets. Promenade main entrance between 49th and 50th streets on Fifth Avenue. ☎ *212-332-6868. www.rockefellercenter.com. Subway: B, D, F, or M to 47–50th streets/Rockefeller Center lets you out on the Sixth Avenue side of the complex. Bus: M1, M2, M3, M4, or M5 down Fifth Avenue; M5, M6, or M7 up Sixth Avenue. Center tours $15 (tickets available from Top of the Rock).*

Top of the Rock

Giving the Empire State Building some friendly competition in the spectacular-views arena is the observation deck of 30 Rockefeller Plaza, known as Top of the Rock. First constructed in 1933 to invoke the grandeur of a luxury ocean liner, the 70th-floor deck was closed in 1986 but reopened in late 2005. Though not quite as high as the Empire State Building, the deck here is more spacious and the views just as stunning. You can have just as much fun getting up to the observation deck as you will on the deck itself; the glass-ceiling Sky Shuttle elevators project images from the 1930s through present day as they zoom their way up. Reserved-time tickets help minimize the lines and are available online. The observation deck is open daily from 8 a.m. to midnight (the last shuttle to the top is at 11 p.m.); admission is $21 for adults, $19 for seniors, $14 for children ages 6 to 12, and free for children 5 and under. For more information, call ☎ 877-692-7625 or 212-698-2000, or visit www.topoftherocknyc.com.

Solomon R. Guggenheim Museum
Upper East Side

Frank Lloyd Wright designed this famous museum, whose swirling, shell-like shape reminds me of a spiraling orange peel. Inside, the exhibition space curves in a spiral; you can take an elevator to the top and work your way down if you don't want to make the hike up. Exhibits change regularly but have recently been less compelling than those at other museums such as the Whitney or MoMA. I find the building itself to be the most interesting aspect of a visit (the facade was recently restored), as well as the permanent collection of 19th- and 20th-century art, which includes works by the Impressionists and founding modernists such as Picasso. Free tours are available; check the Web site for special events including films, concerts, and lectures.

See map p. 178. 1071 Fifth Ave. (at 89th Street). ☎ *212-423-3500.* www.guggenheim.org. *Subway: 4, 5, or 6 to 86th Street, then walk 3 blocks west to Fifth Avenue, turn right, and walk 2 blocks north to the entrance. Bus: The bus is a good idea because it brings you closer — M1, M2, M3, or M4 up Madison, then walk 1 block west (it goes south on Fifth), or take the M86 crosstown on 86th Street. Admission: $18 adults, $15 seniors and students, free for children 11 and under when accompanied by an adult; pay what you wish on Sat 5:45–7:45 p.m. Open: Sun–Wed and Fri 10 a.m.–5:45 p.m., Sat 10 a.m.–7:45 p.m.*

Staten Island Ferry
Downtown

You can't beat the price of this attraction — it's free. And not only do you get an hour-long excursion (round-trip) in New York Harbor, but you get beautiful views of the Statue of Liberty. You also get to mingle with commuters: people who take this ferry every day to work in Manhattan. Your journey provides great views of Ellis Island, the Verrazano Narrows

Bridge, and Governor's Island. Returning from Staten Island, you can enjoy that very famous view of the lower Manhattan skyline.

See map p. 175. Departs from the Whitehall Terminal at the southern tip of Manhattan. ☎ **718-727-2508.** *www.siferry.com. Subway: N or R to Whitehall Street; 4 or 5 to Bowling Green; 1 to South Ferry (ride in the first 5 cars). Admission: Free. Open: 24 hours; ferries run Mon–Fri every 20–30 minutes, less frequently during off-peak and weekend hours.*

Statue of Liberty
Downtown

Lady Liberty is one of the grandest symbols of what New York and America stand for. And after years of closure in the aftermath of the terrorist attacks of September 11, 2001, you can now climb the 354 steps to the statue's crown. You can also explore the Statue of Liberty Museum, peer into the inner structure through a glass ceiling near the base of the statue, and enjoy views from the observation deck on top of the 16-story pedestal. Whether you choose to wander the grounds or just get a look via the Staten Island Ferry or on your way to Ellis Island, the Statue of Liberty is a must-see. Reserve your tickets online well in advance of your trip.

See map p. 175. On Liberty Island in New York Harbor. ☎ **212-363-3200** *for general information,* **877-523-9849** *for ticket and ferry information. www.nps.gov/stli or www.statuecruises.com. Transport: Ferry from Battery Park. Subway to ferry ticket booth: 4 or 5 to Bowling Green, then walk through the park heading south; the fortresslike ticket booth is at the edge of the trees by the promenade. Bus to ticket booth: M1 (running down Fifth Avenue/Park Avenue/Broadway), M6 (running down Broadway), or M15 (running down Second Avenue). Admission: Free; ferry ticket to Statue of Liberty and Ellis Island $12 adults and children 13–17, $10 seniors, $5 children 4–12, free for children 3 and under; $3 extra to access the Crown. Open: Daily 9:30 a.m.–5:15 p.m. Last ferry departs at 2 p.m. Note that if you want to visit both Ellis Island and the Statue of Liberty, you can't take the last ferry; taking the last ferry enables you to visit only one of the two attractions. Due to security restrictions, no backpacks, luggage, or coolers are allowed.*

Times Square
Midtown West

Times Square has evolved into something much different from what it was as recently as 20 years ago, when it had a deservedly sleazy reputation. New Yorkers still debate which incarnation was better. For New Yorkers, today's Times Square is a place we go out of our way to avoid. The crowds, even by New York standards, are stifling; the restaurants, mostly national chains, aren't very good; the shops, also mostly national chains, are unimaginative; and the attractions, like **Madame Tussaud's New York** wax museum, are kitschy. Comparisons to Vegas are made, but believe me when I say that Vegas is far more fun. Still, you've come all this way; you've got to at least take a peek at night, if only for the amazing neon spectacle of it. Efforts have been made to make the area far more pedestrian friendly as well, with the renovation of Duffy Square (and its ruby-red glass steps) and the conversion of the "Bowtie" into a car-free plaza.

 Most of the Broadway shows are centered on Times Square, so plan your visit around your show tickets. For your predinner meal, walk 2 blocks west to Ninth Avenue, where you find a number of relatively inexpensive, good restaurants. If you're with the kids, the 60-foot Ferris wheel in the Toys "R" Us store makes a visit to Times Square worthwhile — if the line to ride it isn't obnoxiously long.

See map p. 176. At the intersection of Broadway and Seventh Avenue, between 42nd and 44th streets. www.timessquarenyc.org. *Subway: N, Q, R, S, 1, 2, 3, or 7 train to Times Square/42nd Street. Bus: M6 and M7 down Seventh Avenue and M104 and M10 down Broadway all offer a perfect view of Times Square.*

United Nations
Midtown East

A guided 45-minute tour of the United Nations headquarters examines the history and purpose of the UN and takes you through the General Assembly Hall and the Security Council Chamber. You also can walk through the grounds and a beautiful garden (the rose garden is fantastic), which offers a view of the East River, Roosevelt Island, and Brooklyn. The grounds feature many sculptures that member states have given the UN, like the symbolic pistol with a knot in the barrel, a gift from the government of Luxembourg.

See map p. 176. United Nations Plaza (on First Avenue between 42nd and 48th streets; visitor entrance at 46th Street). ☎ *212-963-8687. Subway: 4, 5, 6, or 7 to Grand Central/42nd Street, then walk east on 42nd Street to First Avenue, turn left, and walk to the visitor entrance at 46th Street. Bus: Much more convenient than the subway — take the M15 down Second Avenue and up First Avenue, the M104 down Broadway and 42nd Street, or the M42 crosstown on 42nd Street. Admission: Free to the park and lobby; guided tour $16 adults, $11 seniors and students, $9 children 5–12. Children 4 and under are not allowed on the guided tours. Open: Mon–Fri 9:45 a.m.–4:45 p.m. Call ahead for tours in languages other than English (including Arabic, French, Japanese, Mandarin, Russian, and Spanish).*

Wall Street and the Stock Exchange
Downtown/Wall Street

On weekdays, Wall Street offers a glimpse into the teeming world of finance that characterizes lower Manhattan. This is where it all started; it's the historical heart of the city and its financial center today. See the skyscrapers — many among the first ever built — and throngs of people who inhabit this world. While you're here, visit the **Museum of American Finance,** 48 Wall St. (at William Street; ☎ 212-908-4110; Admission: $8 adults, $5 seniors and students, free for children 6 and under). The **Stock Exchange** building, 11 Wall St. (☎ 212-656-3000), which dates from 1903, is a classical temple for dollar worship; from the observation gallery, you can watch the world's largest stock frenzy in action. The gallery has been closed to the public for security reasons since September 11, 2001; you can always check to see if it has reopened, but don't get your hopes up. *See map p. 175. Wall Street runs between Broadway and South Street. Subway: 4 or 5 to Wall Street; N or R to Rector Street, then walk east across Broadway to Wall Street. Bus: M1 or M6 down Broadway and up Trinity Place. Admission: Free. Open: Call for information.*

World Trade Center Site
Downtown

I would never consider a place where over 3,000 people lost their lives an "attraction," but I understand why visitors would want to come to the site to pay their respects. Construction has finally begun on new skyscrapers, a memorial, and a retail and transportation hub. The most recent reports suggest that the memorial will open in 2011.

In the meantime, you can see the site from pedestrian bridges on Liberty and Vesey streets; as the construction progresses, sidewalk views will be more limited. The **Tribute WTC Visitor Center,** 120 Liberty St. (☎ 866-737-1184; www.tributenyc.org), offers guided one-hour tours of the site daily at 11 a.m., noon, 1 p.m., and 3 p.m., with additional tours at 2 p.m. and 4 p.m. on Saturdays, for $10 per person. Note that the walking tour is free for children 11 and under, but consider carefully whether it's appropriate for your child to participate, given the grave and possibly upsetting subject matter. *See map p. 175. Broadway at Fulton Street. Subway: A, C, J, M, Z, 1, 2, 4, or 5 to Fulton Street/Broadway Nassau, then walk west on Fulton. Bus: M1 and M6 run down Broadway, letting you off at the entrance to the platform. Open: Daily 24 hours. Admission: Free.*

Yankee Stadium
The Bronx

Next to the Colosseum in Rome, there were few sports arenas more famous than the House That Ruth Built. The 2008 season was the Yankees' last in their historic stadium; they now play in a new home just across from the old one. You find comfier seating, many more dining options and other ways to part with your money, and (blessedly) more restrooms. One-hour tours that include a trip to the dugout are available; check the Web site for scheduling.

The Yankees play from April until October. Tickets, which range in price from $14 to $300 for the 2010 season, are tough to snag, but if you plan in advance (and even if you don't), you should be able to score a seat by going through a broker or scalping (be careful of forgeries) the day of a game. (For more information about admission to Yankees games, see "Surveying the New York Sports Scene," later in this chapter.) *See map p. 183. 161st and River Avenue. ☎ 718-293-6000. www.yankees.com. Subway: B, D, or 4 to 161st Street. Bus: BX6, BX13, or BX55 to 161st Street and Grand Concourse, then walk 2 blocks to the stadium.*

Finding More Cool Things to See and Do

After you've seen the top sights, check out these additional attractions.

Other excellent museums

The Met and MoMA (see "New York City's Top Sights," earlier in this chapter) are probably New York's best-known art museums, but many, many others are available for you to explore.

American Folk Art Museum
Midtown West

Not only is this gorgeous, ultramodern boutique museum a stunning structure, but it also heralds American folk art's entry into the top echelon of museum-worthy art. The modified open-plan interior features an extraordinary collection of traditional works from the 18th century to the self-taught artists and craftspeople of the present, reflecting the breadth and vitality of the folk-art tradition. A splendid variety of quilts, in particular, makes the textiles collection the museum's most popular. The book and gift shop is outstanding, filled with one-of-a-kind objects.

See map p. 176. 45 W. 53rd St. (between Fifth and Sixth avenues). ☎ **212-265-1040.** *www.folkartmuseum.org. Subway: E or M to Fifth Avenue. Admission: $12 adults, $8 seniors and students, free for children 11 and under; free for everyone Fri 5:30–7:30 p.m. Open: Tues–Thurs and Sat–Sun 10:30 a.m.–5:30 p.m., Fri 11 a.m.–7:30 p.m.*

Brooklyn Museum of Art
Brooklyn

New York's second-largest museum after the Met, the Brooklyn Museum of Art is housed in a beautiful Beaux Arts building and has a collection that includes major Egyptian and African art; in fact, it lays claim to the largest collection of Egyptian artifacts in the world after London and Cairo. The museum also contains important 19th-century American and European paintings; 28 decorative art galleries and period rooms, some of them rescued from now-demolished historic buildings; and an important sculpture collection, including a Rodin gallery. The museum has built a reputation for dynamic exhibitions as well, some more hype than substance. Recent ones have included a stunning watercolor retrospective, a respectful and highly popular Jean-Michel Basquiat exhibition, and a somewhat controversial Annie Leibovitz show. You're not going to have any trouble getting here, because the museum has its own subway stop. Allow at least three hours; take some time afterward to wander through the adjacent **Brooklyn Botanic Garden** (☎ **718-623-7200**).

On the first Saturday of every month, the Brooklyn Museum of Art runs a program from 4 to 11 p.m. that includes free admission to the museum and a slate of live music, films, dancing, talks, and other entertainment that can get pretty creative — think karaoke, lesbian poetry, silent films, experimental jazz, and disco. As only-in–New York events go, **First Saturday** is a good one — you can count on a full slate of cool.

200 Eastern Parkway (at Washington Avenue). ☎ **718-638-5000.** *www.brooklyn museum.org. Subway: 2 or 3 to Eastern Parkway/Brooklyn Museum. Suggested admission: $10 adults, $6 students and seniors, free for children 11 and under. Open: Wed–Fri 10 a.m.–5 p.m., Sat–Sun 11 a.m.–6 p.m.; first Sat of each month 11 a.m.–11 p.m.*

Cooper-Hewitt National Design Museum
Upper East Side

Part of the Smithsonian Institution, the Cooper-Hewitt is in the Carnegie Mansion, built by steel magnate Andrew Carnegie in 1901. Some 11,000 square feet of gallery space is devoted to exhibits that are well conceived, engaging, and educational. Shows are both historical and contemporary in nature. Many installations are drawn from the museum's own vast collection of industrial design, drawings, textiles, wall coverings, books, and prints. On your way in, note the fabulous Art Nouveau–style copper-and-glass canopy above the entrance. And be sure to visit the garden, which is ringed with Central Park benches from various eras. Note that the museum is undergoing a renovation to expand its gallery space by an additional 6,000 feet; the work is expected to be complete in 2011.

See map p. 178. 2 E. 91st St. (at Fifth Avenue). ☎ **212-849-8400.** *www.si.edu/ndm. Subway: 4, 5, or 6 to 86th Street. Admission: $15 adults, $10 seniors and students, free for children 11 and under. Open: Mon–Fri 10 a.m.–5 p.m., Sat 10 a.m.–6 p.m., Sun 11 a.m.–6 p.m.*

The Frick Collection
Upper East Side

This museum features the splendid collection of tycoon Henry Clay Frick and is housed in his Gilded Age mansion, more or less as he organized it. The painting collection includes works by old masters of the 16th and 17th centuries, including Tiziano (also known as Titian), Vermeer, Rembrandt, and El Greco, as well as 19th-century artists, including Turner and Whistler. The furnishings and ceramic collections are also worth seeing. Enjoy some fantastic art and see how the cultured aristocracy of old New York lived. Allow at least two hours.

See map p. 178. 1 E. 70th St. (at Fifth Avenue). ☎ **212-288-0700.** *www.frick.org. Subway: 6 to Hunter College/68th Street, then walk west to Fifth Avenue, and 2 blocks north. Admission: $18 adults, $12 seniors, $5 students; admission includes audio guide. Children 9 and under not admitted; children ages 10–15 admitted only with an adult. Open: Tues–Sat 10 a.m.–6 p.m., Sun 11 a.m.–5 p.m.*

The Morgan Library & Museum
Midtown East

This New York treasure, boasting one of the world's most important collections of original manuscripts, rare books and bindings, master drawings, and personal writings, was recently extensively renovated. Those renovations included a welcoming entrance on Madison Avenue, remodeled galleries (so that more of the library's holdings can be exhibited), an auditorium, a reading room with greater capacity, and electronic resources and expanded space for collections storage.

See map p. 176. 225 Madison Ave. (at 36th Street). ☎ **212-685-0008.** www.morgan library.org. *Subway: 6 to 33rd Street. Admission: $12 adults, $8 seniors and students, free for children 11 and under. Open: Tues–Thurs 10:30 a.m.–5 p.m., Fri 10:30 a.m.–9 p.m., Sat 10 a.m.–6 p.m., Sun 11 a.m.–6 p.m.*

The New Museum
Downtown

This museum is known for its exhibitions of contemporary art, focusing on innovative art and artists. The permanent collection includes work by artists from around the world, ranging from installations to video, painting, and sculpture. The museum is now housed in a 60,000-square-foot, $35-million home on the Bowery; it's the first (and so far only) new art museum ever constructed from the ground up below 14th Street.

See map p. 175. 235 Bowery (at Prince Street). ☎ **212-219-1222.** www.newmuseum. org. *Subway: 6 to Spring Street. Admission: $12 adults, $10 seniors, $8 students, free for children 17 and under; free for everyone Thurs 7–9 p.m. Open: Wed, Sat, and Sun noon to 6 p.m., Thurs–Fri noon to 9 p.m.*

The Paley Center for Media
Midtown West

Have you ever wanted to travel back in time and "be there" during an unforgettable TV or radio moment — to watch the first moon landing, or hear Orson Welles's *War of the Worlds* radio broadcast? Now you can. Formerly known as the Museum of Television & Radio, the Paley Center has more than 140,000 radio and television programs in its permanent collection, almost all of which are available for your viewing or listening pleasure. The museum is more like a library; instead of wandering from one exhibit to the next, you "check out" recordings or programs and play them in audiovisual cubicles — anything from Sid Caesar to vintage cartoons to your favorite commercials from childhood. Several theaters and listening rooms can accommodate large groups for special screenings. "Exhibits" are thematic documentaries that cover topics as diverse as *Saturday Night Live* film shorts and "the history of presidential campaign advertising" (on second thought, maybe those two topics aren't so different after all). The place is less crowded on weekdays; on evenings and weekends, the crowds make it hard to get a viewing booth.

See map p. 176. 25 W. 52nd St. (between Fifth and Sixth avenues). ☎ **212-621-6800** or *212-621-6600.* www.mtr.org. *Subway: E or M to 53rd Street/Fifth Avenue. Admission: $10 adults, $8 seniors and students, $5 children 13 and under. Open: Wed–Sun noon to 6 p.m., Thurs noon to 8 p.m.*

Studio Museum in Harlem
Uptown

Thanks to former Whitney curator Thelma Golden, this small museum is making a big impact with its remarkable exhibitions by black artists. Chief curator Golden has given the museum a more international flavor, with recent exhibits by British artist (and Giuliani offender) Chris Ofili and African comic art creators. Other exciting recent exhibits include works by painters Barkley L. Hendricks and Kehinde Wiley, as well as the ongoing "Postcards from Harlem" series. The museum continues its long-standing tradition of featuring highly respected and under-the-radar African-American artists such as Lorna Simpson and Charles Ethan Porter.

See map p. 183. 144 W. 125th St. (at Seventh Avenue). ☎ **212-864-4500.** *www.studio museum.org. Subway: 2 or 3 to 125th Street. Suggested admission: $7 adults, $3 seniors and students, free for children 11 and under. Open: Wed–Fri and Sun noon to 6 p.m., Sat 10 a.m.–6 p.m.*

Whitney Museum of American Art
Upper East Side

The big show here is the Whitney Biennial (in even-numbered years), which highlights the good, the bad, and the ugly in contemporary art. The Whitney also has a spectacular permanent collection of modern American art, including works by Hopper, O'Keeffe, and others. Recent exhibitions include *Polaroids: Mapplethorpe* and Kara Walker's *My Complement, My Enemy, My Oppressor, My Love.* If you have any interest in modern art, allow at least three hours for your visit here.

See map p. 178. 945 Madison Ave. (at 75th Street). ☎ **212-570-3676.** *www.whitney.org. Subway: 6 to 77th Street. Admission: $18 adults, $12 students and seniors, free for children 11 and under; pay what you wish Fri 6–9 p.m. Open: Wed–Thurs 11 a.m.–6 p.m., Fri 1–9 p.m., Sat–Sun 11 a.m.–6 p.m.*

For culture and history buffs

African Burial Ground National Monument
Downtown

While excavating a building site in preparation for a new office tower in 1991, city archaeologists made a startling discovery: the remains of more than 600 free and enslaved Africans buried in the 1600s and 1700s, when New York was still New Amsterdam. (In 2003, the bodies of 419 people were reinterred, while the known remains of approximately 200 others are undisturbed. It is believed that as many as 20,000 people were buried at the site.) The striking outdoor memorial is enhanced by the works of several African-American artists, including Barbara Chase-Riboud, and a recently opened visitor's center that provides excellent and haunting context. Free 90-minute guided tours are available by reservation; call in advance.

See map p. 175. At the corner of Duane and Elk streets. ☎ 212-637-2019. www.africanburialground.gov or www.nps.gov/afbg. Subway: R, 4, 5, or 6 to Brooklyn Bridge/City Hall. Admission: Free. Open: Tues–Sat 9 a.m.–5 p.m.

Asia Society and Museum
Upper East Side

This museum was founded in 1956 by John D. Rockefeller, who donated 285 masterpieces of Asian art that form the core of the society's permanent collection. Its exhibits have expanded to include art, films, and performances. Allow at least two hours.

See map p. 178. 725 Park Ave. (at 70th Street). ☎ 212-288-6400. www.asiasociety.org. Subway: 6 to 68th Street/Hunter College, then walk 2 blocks north, turn left, and walk 1 block west to Park Avenue. Admission: $10 adults, $7 seniors, $5 students, free for children 15 and under; free for everyone Fri 6–9 p.m. Open: Tues–Sun 11 a.m.–6 p.m., Fri until 9 p.m. (except July 4–Labor Day).

Museum of Jewish Heritage — A Living Memorial to the Holocaust
Downtown

This spare, six-sided building with a six-tier roof, alluding to the Star of David and the six million people murdered in the Holocaust, recounts the unforgettable horror yet tenacious renewal of Jews from the late 19th century to the present. Through objects, photographs, documents, and videotaped testimonies, the museum tells a very powerful story of survival and faith. Recent special exhibitions include *Shalom Y'All: Images of Jewish Life in the American South* and *The Other Promised Land: Vacationing, Identity, and the Jewish-American Dream.*

See map p. 175. 36 Battery Place (at First Place), Battery Park City. ☎ 646-437-4200. www.mjhnyc.org. Subway: 4 or 5 to Bowling Green. Admission: $12 adults, $10 seniors, $7 students, free for children 11 and under; free for everyone Wed 4–8 p.m. Open: Sun–Tues and Thurs 10 a.m.–5:45 p.m., Wed 10 a.m.–8 p.m., Fri (during daylight saving time) 10 a.m.–5 p.m., and Fri (Eastern standard time and eves of Jewish holidays) 10 a.m.–3 p.m. Closed Jewish holidays and Thanksgiving Day.

Museum of the City of New York
Upper East Side

Learn about the city's history through displays packed with information. A number of decorative objects related to New York are on display, including children's toys and re-created home interiors from the 17th to early 20th centuries. Allow an hour for your visit.

See map p. 178. 1220 Fifth Ave. (at 103rd and 104th streets). ☎ 212-534-1672. www.mcny.org. Subway: 6 to 103rd Street, then walk west toward Central Park. Suggested admission: $10 adults, $6 seniors and students, $20 families. Open: Tues–Sun 10 a.m.–5 p.m.

New-York Historical Society
Upper West Side

This museum sits across the street from the American Museum of Natural History. If you have time, try to spend an hour or two browsing exhibits that feature American history, culture, and art with a focus on New York. On the fourth floor, you can find the Henry Luce III Center for the Study of American Culture, a gallery and study facility with displays of objects, such as paintings, sculptures, Tiffany lamps, textiles, and furniture.

See map p. 178. 170 Central Park West (at 77th Street). ☎ **212-873-3400.** *www.* *nyhistory.org. Subway: B or C to 81st Street; 1 to 79th Street. Admission: $12 adults, $9 seniors, $7 students, free for children 12 and under. Open: Tues–Fri noon to 8 p.m., Sat 10 a.m.–6 p.m., Sun 11 a.m.–5:45 p.m.*

Schomburg Center for Research in Black Culture
Harlem

One of the largest collections of African-American materials in the world can be found at this branch of the New York Public Library. The Exhibition Hall, the Latimer/Edison Gallery, and the Reading Room host changing exhibits related to black culture, such as *Commemorating New York's African Burial Ground: A National Monument.* A rich calendar of talks and performing-arts events is also part of the continuing program. Make an appointment for a guided tour so you can see the 1930s murals by Harlem Renaissance artist Aaron Douglas; it's worth your while. Academics and others interested in a more complete look at the center's holdings can preview what's available online.

See map p. 183. 515 Malcolm X Blvd. (Lenox Avenue between 135th and 136th streets). ☎ **212-491-2200.** *www.nypl.org. Subway: 2 or 3 to 135th Street. Admission: Free. Open: Mon–Wed noon to 8 p.m., Thurs–Fri 11 a.m.–6 p.m., Sat 10 a.m.–5 p.m.*

Tenement Museum
Downtown

This five-story tenement was home to over 10,000 people from 25 countries between 1863 and 1935. Now it's a museum and a National Trust for Historic Preservation. The museum tells the story of the immigration boom of the late 19th and early 20th centuries, when the Lower East Side was considered the "Gateway to America." The only way to see the museum is by guided tour, and you can choose from three different ones; the best is the one-hour Confino Living History Tour, given on weekends only. To ensure a spot, purchase your tickets early at ☎ **866-606-7232,** or via the museum's Web site.

See map p. 175. Visitors' Center at 108 Orchard St. (at Broome Street). ☎ **212-431-0233.** *www.tenement.org. Subway: F to Delancey Street; J, M, or Z to Essex Street. Admission: Tours $20 adults, $15 seniors and students. Open: Tours given daily 10:30 a.m.–5 p.m.*

Notable New York City architecture

You can walk the city streets with your eyes skyward and your mouth open over some of the magnificent structures scattered throughout the city. The Empire State Building and the Chrysler Building are two of the most famous buildings in New York and are also top sights (see their listings earlier in this chapter). But you may want to gawk at some of these other structures, too.

Flatiron Building
Flatiron District

The Flatiron Building (its original name was the Fuller Building) takes its name from its unusual triangular shape. Built in 1902, it was one of the first skyscrapers in Manhattan. Only 20 stories tall, it's one of the most recognized and unique buildings in the city (though it didn't stop retailer H&M from temporarily mounting a 15-story ad on the side a couple of years ago, to the ire of New Yorkers and the city's Department of Buildings). Now, the area surrounding the building, which features a number of publishing houses and modeling agencies, is known as the Flatiron District.

See map p. 176. 175 Fifth Ave. (where Fifth Avenue and Broadway cross at 23rd Street). Subway: N or R train to 23rd Street. Bus: M6 or M7 down Broadway; M2, M3, or M5 down Fifth Avenue for a magnificent view of the building (the buses stop right there, too).

New York Public Library
Midtown West

With its white Corinthian columns, allegorical statues, and the world-famous lion sculptures (their names are Patience and Fortitude) at the entrance, the New York Public Library's Humanities & Social Sciences Library is one of the country's finest examples of Beaux Arts architecture. I did a semester-long practicum here (yep, you're taking travel advice from a degreed librarian), and showing up to work never dulled the joy of approaching the entrance. Oh, and you can find a lot of good books inside, too. Don't miss the Rose Reading Room, and take some time to check out whatever special exhibit is on display — it's always worthwhile. After a $5-million restoration, what was once known only as Room 117, a Beaux Arts masterpiece with incredible views of Fifth Avenue and 42nd Street, reopened in late 2005 and is now known as the Lionel Pincus and Princess Firyal Map Division; here you find possibly the finest and most extensive collection of maps in the world.

See map p. 176. Fifth Avenue and 42nd Street. ☎ 212-930-0830. www.nypl.org. Subway: B, D, F, or M to 42nd Street; S, 4, 5, 6, or 7 to Grand Central/42nd Street. Admission: Free. Open: Mon and Thurs–Sat 10 a.m.–6 p.m., Tues–Wed 10 a.m.–9 p.m., Sun 1–5 p.m.

Skyscraper Museum
Financial District

This museum features those structures that you've craned your neck to get a good look at, and it's the first of its kind. Located in the 38-story Skidmore, Owings & Merrill tower that also houses the Ritz-Carlton New York, Battery Park, the space comprises two galleries: one housing a permanent exhibition dedicated to the evolution of Manhattan's commercial skyline, the other available for changing shows.

See map p. 175. 39 Battery Place. ☎ **212-968-1961.** *www.skyscraper.org. Subway: 4 or 5 to Bowling Green. Admission: $5 adults, $2.50 students and seniors. Open: Wed–Sun noon to 6 p.m.*

U.S. Customs House
Downtown

This 1907 National Historic Landmark houses the **National Museum of the American Indian,** George Gustav Heye Center. The granite structure features giant statues carved by Daniel Chester French (of Lincoln Memorial fame); the statues lining the front personify Asia (pondering philosophically), America (bright-eyed and bushy-tailed), Europe (decadent, whose time has passed), and Africa (sleeping). Inside, the airy oval rotunda, designed by Spanish engineer Raphael Guastavino, was frescoed by Reginald Marsh to glorify the shipping industry (and, by extension, the Customs office once housed here).

See map p. 175. 1 Bowling Green (between State and Whitehall streets). ☎ **212-514-3700.** *www.nmai.si.edu. Subway: 4 or 5 to Bowling Green; R to Whitehall. Admission: Free. Open: Daily 10 a.m.–5 p.m. (Thurs until 8 p.m.).*

Woolworth Building
Downtown

Completed in 1913, the Woolworth was the tallest building in the world for a time. Designed by architect Cass Gilbert, the Gothic tower is known for its beautifully decorated interior and exterior. Mr. Woolworth paid $15.5 million cash for the structure, and it shows. Besides the stunning exterior, this building — once known as "The Cathedral of Commerce" — has gorgeous mosaic ceilings, a marble staircase, and statues of people involved in the building's construction. Enjoy it from the outside; because of heightened security, the public is no longer allowed inside.

See map p. 175. 233 Broadway (at Park Place). Subway: 1 or 2 to Park Place; 4, 5, or 6 to Brooklyn Bridge/City Hall, then walk west across the park.

Beautiful places of worship
New York is a city known for its religious tolerance. Places of worship for just about every denomination are everywhere, and many are housed in remarkable structures worth checking out even if religion is not what you came to New York to get.

Abyssinian Baptist Church
Harlem

This Baptist church, founded in 1808 by African-American and Ethiopian merchants, is the most famous of Harlem's 400-plus houses of worship. The chamber of commerce has declared the church a "Living Treasure." Come for Sunday morning services at 11 a.m. to get a sample of the Harlem gospel tradition.

See map p. 183. 132 Odell Clark Place (West 138th Street, between Adam Clayton Powell Boulevard and Lenox Avenue). ☎ **212-862-7474.** www.abyssinian.org. *Subway: B, C, 2, or 3 to 135th Street.*

Cathedral Church of St. John the Divine
Upper West Side

Towering over Amsterdam Avenue near the edge of Harlem is an unlikely sight: the largest Gothic cathedral in the world. The cathedral, begun in 1892, is still only two-thirds complete; the towers, transepts, choir roof, and other aspects remain unfinished. The architects and builders have continually employed Gothic engineering, stone-cutting, and carving techniques. Numerous chapels throughout the cathedral commemorate various ethnic groups and traditions. You can visit the towers on Saturdays. Three services per day are held during the week (8 a.m., 12:15 p.m., and 5 p.m.), and four are held on Sunday (8 a.m., 9 a.m., 11 a.m., and 4 p.m.).

The cathedral hosts numerous concerts, including dance, choir, and classical music performances. But by far the most unforgettable special event is the **Blessing of the Animals,** held in early October as part of the Feast of St. Francis of Assisi. A procession of critters — everything from dogs and cats to camels and elephants — parades through the church; each is blessed in honor of St. Francis, the patron saint of animals. Call **212-316-7540** for tickets (advance reservations are necessary).

See map p. 183. 1047 Amsterdam Ave. (between 110th and 113th streets). ☎ **212-316-7540.** www.stjohndivine.org. *Subway: 1 to Cathedral Parkway (110th Street), then walk 1 block east to Amsterdam Avenue. Bus: M11 (running up Tenth/Amsterdam Avenue and down Columbus/Ninth Avenue). Open: Mon–Sat 7 a.m.–6 p.m., Sun 7 a.m.–7 p.m.*

St. Patrick's Cathedral
Midtown East

St. Patrick's, the largest Catholic cathedral in the United States, features Gothic spires, beautiful stained-glass windows, and an impressive white-marble facade. Mass is held seven times a day Sunday through Friday and three times a day on Saturday. It's a calm island in a busy thoroughfare, across from Rockefeller Center and next door to Saks Fifth Avenue.

See map p. 176. Fifth Avenue (between 50th and 51st streets). ☎ **212-753-2261.** www.saintpatrickscathedral.org. *Subway: B, D, F, or M to 47–50th streets/Rockefeller Center, then walk west to Fifth Avenue. Bus: M1, M2, M3, M4, or M5 down Fifth Avenue; M1, M2, M3, or M4 up Madison Avenue. Open: Daily 6:30 a.m.–8:45 p.m.*

Trinity Church
Downtown

This Wall Street house of worship — with neo-Gothic flying buttresses, beautiful stained-glass windows, and vaulted ceilings — was designed and consecrated in 1846. The historic Episcopal church stood strong while office towers crumbled around it on September 11, 2001; however, the historic pipe organ was damaged by dust and debris, and it was replaced by a digital organ in 2003. The gates to the historic church served as an impromptu memorial to the victims of the terrorist attack, with countless tokens of remembrance left by locals and visitors alike.

Also part of Trinity Church is **St. Paul's Chapel** at Broadway and Fulton Street, New York's only surviving pre-Revolutionary church and a transition shelter for homeless men.

See map p. 175. At Broadway and Wall Street. ☎ *212-602-0800, 212-602-0872, or 212-602-0747 for concert information.* www.trinitywallstreet.org. *Subway: 4 or 5 to Wall Street. Admission and tours: Free; $2 suggested donation for 1 p.m. concerts. Open: Mon–Fri 7 a.m.–6 p.m., Sat 8 a.m.–4 p.m., Sun 7 a.m.–4 p.m.; Sun service 11:15 a.m.*

Especially for kids

New York has plenty of attractions that you can enjoy with your children, and some of the city's top sights, like the Bronx Zoo, Central Park, and the Intrepid Sea-Air-Space Museum (see "New York City's Top Sights," earlier in this chapter), appeal especially to kids. Check out these other kid-friendly attractions.

The Children's Museum of Manhattan
Upper West Side

Designed for children ages 2 to 12, this museum is strictly hands-on. Its five floors include a Dora-and-Diego-themed section; PlayWorks, especially for children 4 and under; and a reading center for quiet time. The museum features special exhibits, such as *Gods, Myths, and Mortals: Discover Ancient Greece,* complete with a giant Trojan Horse for climbing. I don't think the admission price is worth it if your child is under 2 years old. Allow at least two hours.

See map p. 178. 212 W. 83rd St. (between Broadway and Amsterdam Avenue). ☎ *212-721-1233.* www.cmom.org. *Subway: 1 to 79th Street, then walk north on Broadway to 83rd and turn right. Admission: $10 adults and children, $7 seniors, free for children under 1; free for everyone first Fri 5–8 p.m. Open: Tues–Sun 10 a.m.–5 p.m.*

New York Aquarium
Brooklyn

The oldest aquarium in operation in the United States (since 1896), the New York Aquarium is huge, covering over 14 acres by the sea at Coney Island. It houses more than 350 species and 8,000 specimens, including beluga (white) whales and sharks. A top attraction is the California sea-lion show, held at the Aquatheater. Still, I don't think it's as impressive as more modern aquariums found in other cities, so I wouldn't make a special trip to visit if you aren't already out at Coney.

See map p. 132. Surf Avenue and West Eighth Street. ☎ **718-265-3474.** *www. nyaquarium.com. Subway: F or Q to West Eighth Street in Brooklyn. Admission: $13 adults, $10 seniors, $9 children 3–12, free for children 2 and under; pay what you wish Fri 3–5:30 p.m. Open: Daily 10 a.m.–5:30 p.m. (a bit later in summer, a bit earlier in winter).*

New York City Fire Museum
SoHo

Housed in a three-story 1904 firehouse, the former quarters of FDNY Engine Co. 30, this museum houses one of the country's most extensive collections of fire-service memorabilia from the 18th century to the present. Displays range from vintage fire marks to fire trucks (including the last-known example of a 1921 pumper) to the gear and tools of modern firefighters. Best of all, real firefighters are almost always on hand to share stories and fire-safety information with kids. The retail store sells authorized FDNY logo wear and souvenirs.

See map p. 175. 278 Spring St. (between Varick and Hudson streets). ☎ **212-691-1303.** *www.nycfiremuseum.org. Subway: C or E to Spring Street. Suggested admission: $7 adults; $5 seniors, students, and children. Open: Tues–Sat 10 a.m.–5 p.m., Sun 10 a.m.–4 p.m.*

New York Transit Museum
Brooklyn

Housed in a real (decommissioned) subway station, this recently renovated underground museum is a wonderful place to spend an hour or so. The museum is small but well done, with good multimedia exhibits exploring the history of the subway from the first shovelful of dirt scooped up at groundbreaking (Mar 24, 1900) to the present. Kids can enjoy the interactive elements and the vintage subway cars, old wooden turnstiles, and station mosaics of yesteryear. This museum is a minor but remarkable tribute to an important development in the city's history.

See map p. 132. Boerum Place and Schermerhorn Street. ☎ **718-694-1600.** *www. mta.info/museum. Subway: A or C to Hoyt Street; F to Jay Street; M or R to Court Street; 2, 3, 4, or 5 to Borough Hall. Admission: $5 adults, $3 seniors and children 3–17; free for children 2 and under; free for seniors Wed. Open: Tues–Fri 10 a.m.–4 p.m., Sat–Sun noon to 5 p.m.*

South Street Seaport and Museum
Downtown

The entire Seaport neighborhood is an important historical landmark that has been restored, in part by the South Street Seaport Museum and in part by private businesses. This attraction offers a look at commerce in the past and in the present. The Seaport's cobbled streets and restored brick buildings house many interesting shops (including Bowne & Co. Stationers, a 19th-century letterpress print shop still in operation at 211 Water St.), and two warehouses from the days when sailing ships ruled trade now contain indoor shopping complexes and fine restaurants. On the water-side, the museum has completed the restoration of a number of historical ships, including the *Peking,* an enormous four-master built of steel; the *Ambrose,* a lightship; and the *Lettie G. Howard,* a fishing schooner. One of the restored ships, the *W. O. Decker,* a cute wooden tugboat, takes people out for tours of the harbor on Saturdays from May to October.

 At Pier 17 of the Seaport, on the third floor there, two rows of deck chairs line the south terrace and overlook the water. These chairs are a great place to relax and take in the view of Brooklyn, the bridges, and New York Harbor. On weekends, though, the seats fill up fast.

See map p. 175. From Pearl Street to the East River; the heart of the Seaport is between John Street and Peck Slip. ☎ *212-732-7678.* www.southstreet seaport.com. *Museum: 12 Fulton St. (between Water and South streets).* ☎ *212-748-8725.* www.southstreetseaportmuseum.org. *Subway: A, C, J, M, Z, 1, 2, 4, or 5 to Fulton Street/Broadway Nassau; walk east on Fulton and you are right in the middle of it. Bus: M15 (down Second Avenue and up First) stops at Fulton and Water streets. Museum admission: $15 adults, $12 students and seniors, free for children 1 and under. Open: Apr–Dec galleries and ships Tues–Sun 10 a.m.–6 p.m.; Jan–Mar galleries Thurs–Sun 10 a.m.–5 p.m., ships 10 a.m.–4 p.m.*

New York City for teens

Don't underestimate the interests of teenagers; I know many who are much more adult than I am. I also know a few who tend toward the infantile. What appeals to both adults and kids probably also appeals to teens. Still, don't forget these options that may go over well with the teens.

Chelsea Piers
Chelsea

Jutting into the Hudson River on four huge piers between 17th and 23rd streets is a terrific multifunctional recreational facility. Among the many sports venues within this 30-acre complex are basketball courts, bowling alleys, a roller rink, an ice rink, a 30-foot indoor climbing wall, batting cages, a golf driving range, beach volleyball courts, an open toddler gym, and a 25-yard indoor pool.

See map p. 176. On the Hudson River between Battery Park and 23rd Street. ☎ *212-336-6666.* www.chelseapiers.com. *Subway: C or E to 23rd Street, then walk west to the river. Bus: M11 running up Tenth Avenue and down Ninth Avenue; M14 running east–west on 14th Street; or M23 running east–west on 23rd Street. Contact individual venues for hours and prices.*

Museum of the Moving Image
Queens

Is there a teenager who doesn't like going to the movies? I don't think so, which is why this movie-lovers' museum is also perfect for teens. *Behind the Screen,* the museum's permanent exhibit, is an interactive installation that takes you step-by-step through the process of moviemaking. The museum houses more than 1,000 artifacts, from technological gadgetry to costumes, and exhibits where you can try your own hand at sound-effects editing or create your own animated shorts, among other simulations. Teens (and overgrown teens disguised as adults, like me) also love the popular *Digital Play* exhibit of vintage, playable video games such as Donkey Kong. Film nuts should keep an eye on the calendar of programs, which has recently included conversations with directors including Wong Kar-wai and George Romero and screenings of cult gems such as *The Last Dragon* (with a personal appearance by the star, Taimak!). If I sound overly enthusiastic about the museum (not to mention Taimak), it's for good reason. *Note:* At press time, most of the museum was closed for a major expansion (the *Behind the Screen* exhibit is open); check the Web site for updates and for museum programs offered in alternate venues during the renovation.

35th Avenue at 36th Street, Astoria. ☎ *718-784-0077.* www.ammi.org. *Subway: R to Steinway Street; N to Broadway. Suggested admission: $7 adults, seniors, college students, children 8–18; free for children 7 and under. Children 11 and under admitted only with an adult 18 or older. Open: During the renovation, Tues–Fri 10 a.m.–3 p.m.*

Sony Wonder Technology Lab
Midtown East

The Apple Stores aren't the only free interactive gizmo wonderlands in Manhattan. At the Sony Wonder Technology Lab, you and your kids can explore the history of technology by enjoying several floors of gadgets, robots, and video games and installations. Thankfully, the staff limits the number of people who can use the facility at one time to avoid total chaos, so reserve tickets in advance of your visit. Plan on staying for at least two hours. The Lab is fully wheelchair accessible.

See map p. 176. 550 Madison Ave. (entrance on 56th Street). ☎ *212-833-8100.* www.sonywondertechlab.com. *Subway: E or F train to Fifth Avenue/53rd Street, then walk 1 block east to Madison, turn north, walk up to 56th Street, and turn left. Bus: M1, M2, M3, or M4 along Fifth Avenue (traveling downtown) and Madison Avenue (traveling uptown). Admission: Free. Open: Tues–Sat 10 a.m.–5 p.m., Sun noon to 5 p.m. (last admission half-hour before closing).*

Fun for TV fans
With all the sitcoms, crime series, and talk shows based in New York, the city often feels like one big set. If applauding on cue is what you'd like to do while you're visiting the city, check out these major shows where you can do just that.

One TV show you won't need a ticket for is the *Today* show. All you have to do to see Matt, Meredith, Al, and Ann is get up early and join the crowd outside the Rockefeller Center studio on 49th Street between Fifth and Sixth avenues. (The show schedules more out-of-doors segments in warmer weather, including the Friday Summer Concert Series.) You have a good chance of getting on camera if:

- ✔ You're holding up a creative sign.

- ✔ You want to propose to your significant other on the air.

- ✔ You show up and stick around during some *really bad* weather.

 For the shows listed here, it's a good idea to arrange for tickets as far in advance of your trip as possible — six months or more. Tickets are always free. For more information about getting tickets to TV tapings, contact **NYC & Company** (☎ 212-484-1222; www.nycgo.com).

- ✔ *The Daily Show with Jon Stewart:* Comedy Central's half-hour humor and news show tapes Monday through Thursday at 5:45 p.m.; the studio is at 513 W. 54th St. Tapings are often booked solid even a year out, but you can try your luck with the show's online reservation system at www.thedailyshow.com/tickets. Arrive early even if you have tickets; the show is often overbooked and ticket-holders may be *invited* to come back on another day.

- ✔ *Late Night with Jimmy Fallon:* The show's Web site (www.late nightwithjimmyfallon.com) is unusually forthcoming about how to lay hands on tickets: Call the NBC ticket office at ☎ 212-664-3056 to make a request for a maximum of four tickets once in a six-month period. You must be 17 years or older to attend. Standby tickets (that do not guarantee admission, and only one per person) are available at 9 a.m. on the day of taping at the NBC Studios sign on the 49th Street entrance to Rockefeller Center.

- ✔ *The Late Show with David Letterman:* Dave's is the hardest TV ticket in town to score. You can fill out a form on the Web site (www.cbs.com/latenight/lateshow) to be put on a list for last-minute cancellation tickets (last-minute in this case being three months or sooner). You must be 18 years or older to attend. Standby tickets are available *only* by phone, starting at 11 a.m. on taping day; call ☎ 212-247-6497. The line is answered until the tickets are gone. Tapings are Monday through Wednesday at 5:30 p.m., and Thursday at 4:30 p.m. and 7 p.m. The studio is at 1697 Broadway between 53rd and 54th streets.

- ✔ *Live with Regis and Kelly:* Kelly and Reeg tape Monday through Friday, except in the summer, when they take Fridays off. Advance tickets are hard to come by — you're looking at a year's wait — but if you didn't plan far enough ahead, you might try snagging same-day tickets. If you're determined, go early (like 7 a.m.) to the corner of 67th Street and Columbus Avenue for a standby number, and then wait to see if you score a seat. Children under 10 are not admitted, and children ages 10 to 18 can attend only with an adult. To request tickets, send a postcard to *Live with Regis and Kelly* Tickets, Ansonia Station, P.O. Box 230-77, New York, NY 10023. Include alternate dates to improve your chances of getting in. You also can try your luck with the ticket request form on the Web site (http://regisandkelly.go.com), but they're often sold out online.

✔ **Saturday Night Live:** *SNL* has enjoyed a resurgence, making tickets harder than usual to obtain. The show starts on Saturday at 11:30 p.m. (arrive by 10 p.m.), with a dress rehearsal at 8 p.m. (arrive by 7 p.m.). Children under 16 aren't admitted. To check availability, call the NBC ticket line at ☎ 212-664-3056.

Don't forget to stop by the **Paley Center for Media.** See the listing in the "Finding More Cool Things to See and Do" section, earlier in this chapter.

Surveying the New York Sports Scene

You can get a real feel for New Yorkers when you watch their hometown teams. Sitting in the bleachers or nosebleed seats at Yankee Stadium or Madison Square Garden is a (cheap) thrill, and the minor-league teams are a hit in the big city.

Yankees and Mets: Major leaguers

With two baseball teams in town, you can catch a game almost any day from opening day in April to the beginning of the playoffs in October. (Don't bother trying to get subway-series tix, though — they're the hottest seats in town. Ditto for opening day or any playoff game.)

The Amazin' **Mets** play at the new **Citi Field** in Queens (Subway: 7 to Willets Point Station). The food options — with outposts of the Shake Shack and the BBQ joint Blue Smoke — are far better than at old Shea Stadium. For tickets (which ran $11–$460 for regular-season games in the 2010 season) and information, call the Mets Ticket Office at ☎ 718-507-8499, or visit www.mets.com.

The Bronx Bombers, also known as the **Yankees,** are always a hot ticket. The Yanks play at a new **Yankee Stadium** just across the street from the original House That Ruth Built (Subway: B, D, or 4 to 161st Street/Yankee Stadium). For tickets ($14–$300 in 2010), contact **Ticketmaster (☎ 212-307-1212** or 212-307-7171; www.ticketmaster.com) or Yankee Stadium (☎ **718-293-6000;** www.yankees.com). Most of the expensive seats (field boxes) are sold out in advance to season-ticket holders. You can often purchase these very same seats from scalpers, but you pay a premium for them. Bleacher seats (the cheapest) are sold the day of the game.

Down on the farm in New York: The minors

The **Brooklyn Cyclones,** the New York Mets' A-level farm team, and the **Staten Island Yankees,** the Yanks' junior leaguers, both play in sparkling, picturesque stadiums. What's more, with bargain-basement ticket prices, these teams offer a great way to experience baseball in the city for a fraction of the major-league hassle and cost. Both teams have already developed a rabidly loyal fan base, so it's a good idea to buy your tickets in advance.

The Cyclones were a major factor in the resurgence of Coney Island; **Keyspan Park** sits right off the legendary boardwalk (Subway: D, F, N, or Q to Stillwell Avenue/Coney Island). For Cyclones info and tickets, call ☎ **718-449-8497,** or visit www.brooklyncyclones.com.

The SI Yanks play at the **Richmond County Bank Ballpark,** just a five-minute walk from the Staten Island Ferry terminal (Subway: N or R to Whitehall Street; 4 or 5 to Bowling Green; 1 to South Ferry). To reach the SI Yanks, call ☎ **718-720-9260,** or go online to www.siyanks.com.

The city game: Basketball

Though the New Jersey Nets (www.njnets.com) are expected to be moving to Brooklyn eventually (after passionate opposition failed to stop the development of a new arena near downtown), two pro teams now play in New York at **Madison Square Garden** (Seventh Avenue between 31st and 33rd streets; ☎ **212-465-6741;** www.thegarden.com; for tickets ☎ **212-307-7171** or www.ticketmaster.com; Subway: A, C, E, 1, 2, or 3 to 34th Street). MSG is the home court for the utterly dysfunctional **New York Knicks** (☎ **877-695-3865** or 212-465-5867; www.nyknicks.com). It's also the home court for the WNBA's **New York Liberty** (☎ **212-465-6080;** www.nyliberty.com), who electrify fans each summer with their tough-playing defense.

Madison Square Garden is set to undergo a massive renovation during 2011. Management says that the Knicks' and the Rangers' seasons will not be disrupted, but the Liberty will be displaced.

Back on the ice: NHL action

The **New York Rangers** also play at Madison Square Garden (see the preceding section for more on the arena). The struggling Rangers have been on an upswing, and tickets are hard to get, so plan well ahead; call ☎ **212-307-7171** or visit www.ticketmaster.com for tickets.

Seeing New York by Guided Tour

If your time is limited, and you want an overview of the city's highlights, a guided tour is the way to go. Also, because New York has tours for just about every interest, you're sure to find one that fits your needs. In this section, I list some of the best tours in the city.

Transportation alternatives

You don't want to burden that nag with a carriage ride through Central Park in the middle of the summer, do you? Better you should hire a real beast of burden: a driver of a pedicab who probably really needs the money. Pedicabs are common sights on the streets of New York. The drivers are friendly and informative, and they don't litter the streets. **Manhattan Pedicab, Inc. (☎ 212-586-9486)**, one of the two primary pedicab companies, charges $30 for a half-hour, $60 for a full hour, and $25 (minimum) for an impromptu street pickup. Tours are also available, including Upper East Side and Upper West Side Bar and Restaurant Tours, and a Central Park–Rockefeller Center Tour. Another option is the **Manhattan Rickshaw Company (☎ 212-604-4729;** www. manhattanrickshaw.com), whose fares range from $15 to $30 (and up).

If you decide to take a group tour, ask about group size when you call to reserve your spot. Generally, you want as small a group as possible to minimize the time required to get organized and move around.

Seeing the city by tour bus

Several companies offer very general city sightseeing tours, many on double-decker buses. These tours are fine for seeing the sights and orienting yourself to the city, but don't expect too much from the running commentary.

Gray Line New York Tours (☎ 800-669-0051 or 212-397-2600; www. graylinenewyork.com) offers just about every sightseeing tour option and combination you could want. You can take a bus tour by day and by night; uptown, downtown, all around town, and out of town, as well as bus combos with Circle Line cruises, helicopter flights, museum admittance, and guided visits of sights. I think you can avoid some combination tours — you don't need a guide to take you to the Statue of Liberty, for example, and you don't save any money on admission with the combo ticket. I've found that the Gray Line puts a higher premium on accuracy than the other big tour-bus operators, so this is your best bet among the biggies. The 48-hour All Loops tour is $54 for adults and $44 for children 3 to 11; buying the tickets online will save you $5.

Although they aren't tour buses, **public buses** crisscross the city. If having a tour guide isn't essential, consider taking advantage of the $2.25 "tour" that the buses afford. Try the M1 all the way down Fifth Avenue from Museum Mile to 42nd Street; then change to the M104 and go across to Times Square, up Broadway through the Theater District, past Lincoln Center, and on to the Upper West Side. Or take the M5 down Fifth Avenue from Central Park South to Greenwich Village.

Cruising around the island

✔ **Bateaux New York** (☎ 866-817-3463; www.bateauxnewyork. com) offers gourmet lunch and dinner cruises under a glass dome. The ship has a glass top with a special anti-fog system and is climate controlled, making the evening cruises quite romantic. The three-hour dinner cruise sails down the Hudson River and around to the East River and back, passing by the Statue of Liberty ($120–$133). Jackets and ties are suggested for men. Board 30 minutes before departure from Pier 61 at Chelsea Piers (see map p. 176). Via the subway, take the C or E train to 23rd Street and then the westbound M23 bus on 23rd Street.

✔ **Circle Line** (☎ 212-563-3200; www.circleline42.com) offers the famous Full Island Cruise, which sails around Manhattan in three hours (daily Mar–Dec; $35 adults, $30 seniors, $22 children ages 3–12). The cruise leaves from Pier 83 at West 42nd Street and Twelfth Avenue (see map p. 176). You see Manhattan from both sides, go under the George Washington Bridge, and pass down through Hell Gate, the murky, swirling spot where the East and Harlem rivers meet. Departing from the same location, Circle Line also offers a shorter cruise, which goes back and forth around the lower half of Manhattan and lasts two hours (daily Mar–Sept; $31 adults, $27 seniors, $20 children); and a Harbor Lights cruise, also a two-hour cruise (at dusk, call for precise schedule; $31 adults, $27 seniors, $20 children). From Pier 16 at the South Street Seaport, Circle Line has a 75-minute Liberty cruise to see the Lady and the harbor (daily Apr–Oct; $26 adults, $23 seniors, $18 children). Allow up to 45 minutes for ticketing and boarding.

✔ To get to Pier 83 via the subway, take the A, C, or E train to Port Authority or the N, Q, R, S, 1, 2, 3, or 7 to Times Square, and then take the M42 bus westbound on 42nd Street or walk west to Twelfth Avenue. To reach Pier 16 via the subway, take the A, C, J, M, Z, 1, 2, 4, or 5 to Fulton Street/Broadway Nassau and then walk east to the Seaport.

✔ **New York Waterway** (☎ 800-533-3779; www.nywaterway.com), the nation's largest privately held ferry service and cruise operator, also does the 35 miles around Manhattan but does it on faster catamaran boats, passing by all the same sights as the Circle Line in only two hours. It also offers a variety of sightseeing options, including an architecture cruise, a leaf-peepin' cruise, and a sunset cruise. The 90-minute Skyline Cruise departs from Pier 78 (see map p. 176) and focuses on Midtown and downtown Manhattan (daily year-round, but on a reduced schedule Jan–Feb, so call for info; $26 adults, $21 seniors, $15 children 3–12).

✔ To reach Pier 78, take the free shuttle (blue, red, and white; it stops at regular city bus stops and you hail it as a cab) that runs along 57th, 49th, 42nd, and 34th streets and up and down 12th Avenue; or take the hotel bus that runs twice a day (call for route and schedule).

✔ **Spirit Cruises** (☎ 866-483-3866; www.spiritcruises.com) runs year-round cabaret-style cruises, including a two-hour lunch cruise (with a narrated tour of the harbor and a buffet lunch; ranging from $40 weekdays Jan–Mar to $53 weekends Apr–Dec) and a three-hour dinner sunset cruise (with live music and a buffet; from $130 weekdays Jan–Mar, up to $176 Sat Apr–Dec). Prices include taxes and service. Cruises board 30 minutes before departure from Pier 61 at Chelsea Piers (see map p. 176). To get there via subway, take the C or E train to 23rd Street, and then take the westbound M23 bus on 23rd Street.

Broadening your mind with specialty tours

✔ **Adventure on a Shoestring** (☎ 212-265-2663) is one of the earliest entrants into the booming walking-tour market. Host Howard Goldberg has provided unique views of New York since 1963, exploring New York with a breezy, man-of-the-people style. Tours focus on behind-the-scenes views of neighborhoods. A variety of Greenwich Village tours emphasize the haunted, the picturesque, and the historic; the Historic Roosevelt Island tour includes taking the Roosevelt Island Tram. Goldberg even does theme walks, such as "Marilyn Monroe's Manhattan" and a "Salute to Katharine Hepburn." Tours are a bargain at $5 for 90 minutes and are given year-round, rain or shine.

✔ **Joyce Gold History Tours of New York** (☎ 212-242-5762; www.nyctours.com) features weekend walking tours of neighborhoods all over Manhattan, going everywhere from Harlem to Wall Street. Gold teaches New York City history at New York University and the New School. Tours are conducted on weekends from March to December and cost $15 for adults, $12 for seniors.

✔ The **Municipal Art Society** (☎ 212-439-1049 or 212-935-3960; www.mas.org) offers excellent historical and architectural walking tours aimed at individualistic travelers. Each tour is led by a highly qualified guide who gives insight into the significance of buildings, neighborhoods, and history. Topics range from the urban history of Greenwich Village to an architectural tour of Central Park. Walking tours are $15. Reservations may be required depending on the tour, so it's best to call ahead. A full schedule is also available online.

✔ **NYC Discovery Tours** (☎ 212-465-3331) offers more than 70 tours of the Big Apple, divided into five categories: neighborhood (including "Central Park" and "The Harlem You Never Knew"), theme (such as "Academy Award Weekend Famous Movie Sites"), biography ("John Lennon's New York"), tavern/food tasting ("Chinatown History and Tasting Tour"), and American history and literature ("The Charles Dickens Tours"). Tours are about two hours long and usually cost around $20 per person (more for food tastings or drinks).

Biking, singing, eating, and all-that-jazz tours

✔ **Big Apple Jazz Tours** (☎ 718-606-8442; www.bigapplejazz.
com), hosted by New York Jazz expert Gordon Polatnick, is the real
deal for jazz buffs. Polatnick's tours are small (3–10 people), and he
bases the destinations on the jazz interests of his clients. If you're
into bebop, he shows you Minton's Playhouse, the still-standing but
now defunct jazz club that was the supposed birthplace of bebop.
From there, he takes you to other active Harlem clubs that he feels
embody Minton's spirit. If you're into the bohemian Village scene,
he takes you to clubs that represent that era. Tours range from $30
to $100.

✔ **Bike the Big Apple** (☎ 201-837-1133; www.bikethebigapple.
com) offers guided half-day, full-day, and customized bike tours
through a variety of city neighborhoods, including the fascinating
but little-explored Upper Manhattan and Harlem. You don't have to
be an Ironman candidate to participate; tours are designed for the
average rider with an emphasis on safety and fun. Shorter (approximately 2½ hours) and longer versions (around 5 hours) are available. Tours are offered year-round; the price is usually $90 and
includes a bike and all gear.

✔ **Harlem Spirituals Tours** (☎ 800-660-2166 or 212-391-0900; www.
harlemspirituals.com) offers a variety of tours of Harlem,
including gospel tours, jazz tours, and soul-food tours. Tours leave
from the office at 690 Eighth Ave. (between 43rd and 44th streets).
The Sunday Gospel tour costs $55 for adults and $39 for children
5 to 11 ($99 for adults and $75 for children with brunch included);
call or check the Web site for the prices of other tours.

✔ **NoshWalks** (☎ 212-222-2243; www.noshwalks.com) guide Myra
Alperson knows all the best food in New York City, and where to
find it. Alperson leads adventurous — and hungry — walkers to
some of the city's most delicious neighborhoods. Highlights
include the Uzbek, Persian, and Russian markets of Rego Park,
Queens; as well as the West African, Ethiopian, and Jamaican food
spots in Harlem. Tours are conducted on Saturdays and Sundays,
leaving around 11:30 a.m. and 2 p.m. The preferred means of transportation is subway. The tours generally last around three hours
and are $45 (including most tastings) for adults, $16 for children
ages 6 to 12. Space is limited, so book well in advance.

Faring well with free walking tours

✔ **Big Apple Greeter** (☎ 212-669-8159; www.bigapplegreeter.
org) is a free visitors' service that matches you up with a volunteer
who shows you around town. Fill out the Visit Request Form on the
Web site at least a month before your trip; mention your language
needs (at last count, 22 languages can be accommodated) and
neighborhood preferences.

- ✔ **Central Park Conservancy (☎ 212-360-2726;** www.centralpark nyc.org) offers a slate of free walking tours of the nooks and crannies of Central Park. Call or check the Web site (click "Visit," and then click "Tours") for schedules.

- ✔ **Downtown Alliance Walking Tours (☎ 212-606-4064;** www. downtownny.com) are a great way to learn more about lower Manhattan. Past tours have included a popular Wall Street tour and an eating tour through the neighborhood. Check the Web site for the latest offerings.

Chapter 12

Shopping in New York City

. . . .

In This Chapter

▶ Scoping out the shopping scene

▶ Going big-name hunting

▶ Discovering the best buys in different neighborhoods

▶ Finding the most interesting stores

. . . .

*E*ven if you came to New York to see the sights, chances are, you also want to explore the city's amazing shopping possibilities, if only for a souvenir of your trip or a gift. When it comes to shopping, you can't do better than New York. This chapter gives you a starting point from which you can begin your New York shopping adventure.

Surveying the Shopping Scene

First, you need to know that shopping hours depend on the type of store, time of year (such as the holiday season), and day of the week (some stores extend their hours on Thursday but shorten them on Sunday). Most department stores are open Monday through Saturday from 10 a.m. to 7 or 8 p.m. and Sunday from noon to 6 p.m. The open hours of shops and boutiques vary widely, and the only way to know for sure is to call the store you want to visit.

Another happy note is that New York sales tax (8.875 percent) is not added to clothing and footwear items under $110. Your shopping dollars can go farther here because you usually won't have to ship your purchases home to avoid the sales tax.

If you're on the hunt for a specific item that I don't mention in this chapter, two excellent resources for shopping information are the weekly magazines *New York* (www.nymag.com), which spotlights sample sales (see the "Scoring at the sample sales" sidebar, later in this chapter), and *Time Out New York* (www.timeoutny.com).

Knowing the Big Names

The names that follow are surely familiar to shopaholics, but for many others (also known as the low-maintenance types), this list helps you get familiar with some of the biggest and best known of the New York stores.

✔ **Barneys,** 660 Madison Ave. (at 61st Street; ☎ **212-826-8900;** www. barneys.com; Subway: N or R to Fifth Avenue/59th Street; see map p. 220): This store sets the tone for upscale chic for both men and women. **Barneys CO-OP** is a fashion hot spot with its own strong identity, separate from the chic Madison Avenue headquarters; there are three locations: downtown in Chelsea at 236 W. 18th St. (between Seventh and Eighth avenues; ☎ **212-593-7800;** Subway: 1 to 18th Street), in SoHo at 116 Wooster St. (between Spring and Prince streets; ☎ **212-965-9964;** Subway: N or R to Prince Street), and uptown on the Upper West Side at 2151 Broadway (between 75th and 76th streets; ☎ **646-335-0978;** Subway: 1 to 79th Street). By the time you read this, Barneys CO-OP will have added a fourth location, in downtown Brooklyn at 194 Atlantic Ave. (at Court Street; Subway: 4 or 5 to Borough Hall).

✔ Twice a year, Barneys hosts its famous **warehouse sale** in its warehouse facility in Chelsea at 255 W. 17th St. (between Seventh and Eighth avenues; ☎ **212-450-8400**). Prices change daily, but markdowns are 50 percent to 75 percent off the original retail prices on all clothing and gifts. If you're planning a shopping trip to the city, check the Barneys Web site to find out when these sales occur.

✔ **Bergdorf Goodman,** 754 Fifth Ave. (at 57th Street; ☎ **800-558-1855** or 212-753-7300; www.bergdorfgoodman.com; Subway: N or R to Fifth Avenue/59th Street; see map p. 218) and **Bergdorf Goodman Men,** 745 Fifth Ave.: Bergdorf's represents the pinnacle of exclusive shopping, with prices to match.

✔ **Bloomingdale's,** 1000 Third Ave. (at 59th Street; ☎ **212-705-2000;** www.bloomingdales.com; Subway: 4, 5, or 6 to 59th Street, or N or R to Lexington Avenue/59th Street; see map p. 218): I like Bloomie's as much for its democratic spirit as for its designer boutiques. This store has just about anything you may want. The smaller downtown branch at 504 Broadway (at Broome Street; ☎ **212-729-5900;** Subway: N or R to Prince Street) is great for those who feel overwhelmed by the typical large-department-store experience.

✔ **Henri Bendel,** 712 Fifth Ave. (between 55th and 56th streets; ☎ **212-247-1100;** www.henribendel.com; Subway: N or R to Fifth Avenue; see map p. 218): The store is gorgeous and so are the goods inside — stylish accessories and expensive makeup for women with a flair for the funky and frilly.

✔ **Lord & Taylor,** 424 Fifth Ave. (at 39th Street; ☎ **212-391-3344;** www.lordandtaylor.com; Subway: B, D, F, or M to 42nd Street, or 7 to Fifth Avenue; see map p. 218): L&T, in its own way, is retro-chic, kind of the antidote to those boutiques in SoHo and Nolita. The holiday windows are always a treat.

✔ **Macy's,** Herald Square (where West 34th Street, Sixth Avenue, and Broadway meet; ☎ 212-695-4400; www.macys.com; Subway: B, D, F, M, N, Q, or R to 34th Street; see map p. 218): Macy's has something for every taste and every price range, and it's truly massive, so pace yourself. The springtime flower show in its great hall is a special event, as is the thrill of meeting Santa — just like Natalie Wood did in *Miracle on 34th Street.* The annual Thanksgiving Day parade ends here.

✔ **Saks Fifth Avenue,** 611 Fifth Ave. (at 50th Street; ☎ 212-753-4000; www.saksfifthavenue.com; Subway: E or M to Fifth Avenue/ 53rd Street; see map p. 218): Even if there's a Saks in your town, be sure to stop into this flagship location. Smaller and more lavish than some of the other department stores, Saks best typifies New York verve and spirit.

✔ **Tiffany & Co.,** 727 Fifth Ave. (at 57th Street; ☎ 212-755-8000; www.tiffany.com; Subway: N or R to Fifth Avenue/59th Street; see map p. 218): You can ogle the gems, housewares, and other shoppers just like Audrey Hepburn did in the classic movie, *Breakfast at Tiffany's.* Prepare for lots of company on the third (silver jewelry) floor.

Shopping in Open-Air Markets

New York hosts some great outdoor markets and fairs — weather permitting, of course. On weekends from spring to fall, you can catch a major New York enterprise called the street fair. The street fair is a generic fair; the food, clothes, and crafts sold by vendors are the same at every fair, and if you've seen one, you've seen them all. Even Mayor Bloomberg recently decided to cut the number of fairs (though he claims to enjoy the hot sausages, too). If you happen upon one, you might like the people-watching and indulge in some corn dogs and zeppoli.

Antiques and vintage goods are big in New York, and the locals love to browse and (sometimes) stumble upon real treasures in several markets.

✔ The **West 25th Street Market,** on West 25th Street between Broadway and Sixth Avenue (see map p. 218), is probably the most famous market of its type. It has furniture, but also a lot of bric-a-brac, and it's open Saturday and Sunday from 9 a.m. to 6 p.m.

✔ The **Hell's Kitchen Flea Market,** on West 39th Street between Ninth and Tenth avenues (see map p. 218), has been revitalized recently with a variety of vintage clothing vendors and some excellent gourmet food trucks in addition to the usual antiques sellers. It's open Saturday and Sunday from 9 a.m. to 6 p.m.

Downtown Shopping

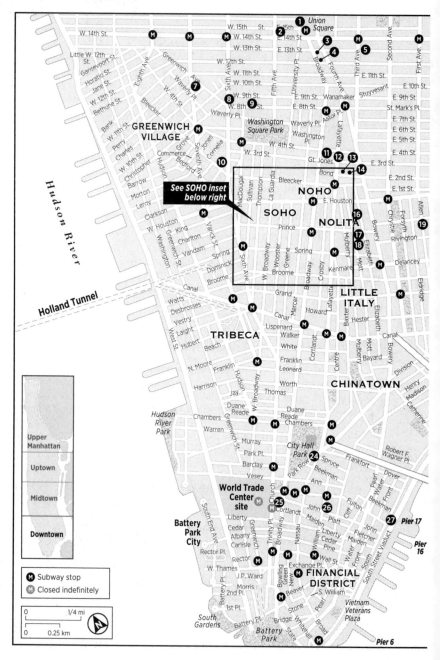

Upper Manhattan

Uptown

Midtown

Downtown

🅜 Subway stop
Ⓜ Closed indefinitely

0   1/4 mi
0   0.25 km

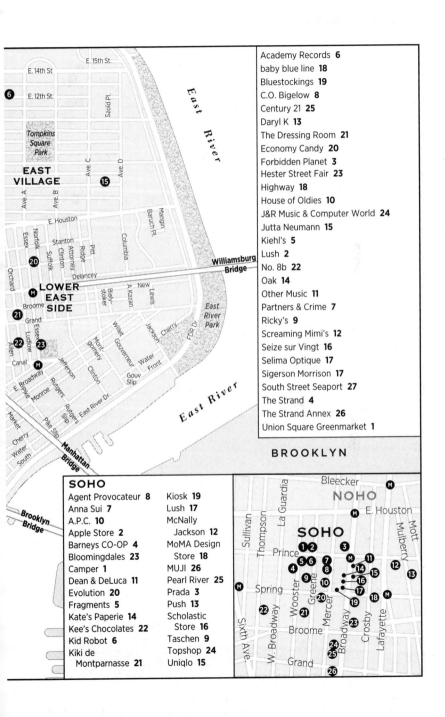

Academy Records **6**
baby blue line **18**
Bluestockings **19**
C.O. Bigelow **8**
Century 21 **25**
Daryl K **13**
The Dressing Room **21**
Economy Candy **20**
Forbidden Planet **3**
Hester Street Fair **23**
Highway **18**
House of Oldies **10**
J&R Music & Computer World **24**
Jutta Neumann **15**
Kiehl's **5**
Lush **2**
No. 8b **22**
Oak **14**
Other Music **11**
Partners & Crime **7**
Ricky's **9**
Screaming Mimi's **12**
Seize sur Vingt **16**
Selima Optique **17**
Sigerson Morrison **17**
South Street Seaport **27**
The Strand **4**
The Strand Annex **26**
Union Square Greenmarket **1**

SOHO

Agent Provocateur **8**
Anna Sui **7**
A.P.C. **10**
Apple Store **2**
Barneys CO-OP **4**
Bloomingdales **23**
Camper **1**
Dean & DeLuca **11**
Evolution **20**
Fragments **5**
Kate's Paperie **14**
Kee's Chocolates **22**
Kid Robot **6**
Kiki de
  Montparnasse **21**

Kiosk **19**
Lush **17**
McNally
  Jackson **12**
MoMA Design
  Store **18**
MUJI **26**
Pearl River **25**
Prada **3**
Push **13**
Scholastic
  Store **16**
Taschen **9**
Topshop **24**
Uniqlo **15**

Midtown Shopping

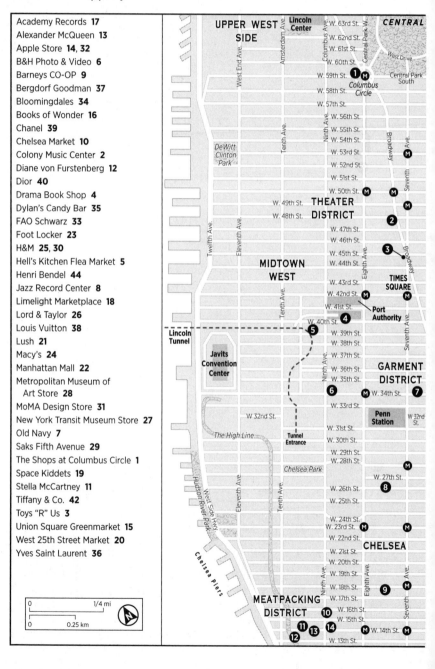

Academy Records **17**
Alexander McQueen **13**
Apple Store **14, 32**
B&H Photo & Video **6**
Barneys CO-OP **9**
Bergdorf Goodman **37**
Bloomingdales **34**
Books of Wonder **16**
Chanel **39**
Chelsea Market **10**
Colony Music Center **2**
Diane von Furstenberg **12**
Dior **40**
Drama Book Shop **4**
Dylan's Candy Bar **35**
FAO Schwarz **33**
Foot Locker **23**
H&M **25, 30**
Hell's Kitchen Flea Market **5**
Henri Bendel **44**
Jazz Record Center **8**
Limelight Marketplace **18**
Lord & Taylor **26**
Louis Vuitton **38**
Lush **21**
Macy's **24**
Manhattan Mall **22**
Metropolitan Museum of
  Art Store **28**
MoMA Design Store **31**
New York Transit Museum Store **27**
Old Navy **7**
Saks Fifth Avenue **29**
The Shops at Columbus Circle **1**
Space Kiddets **19**
Stella McCartney **11**
Tiffany & Co. **42**
Toys "R" Us **3**
Union Square Greenmarket **15**
West 25th Street Market **20**
Yves Saint Laurent **36**

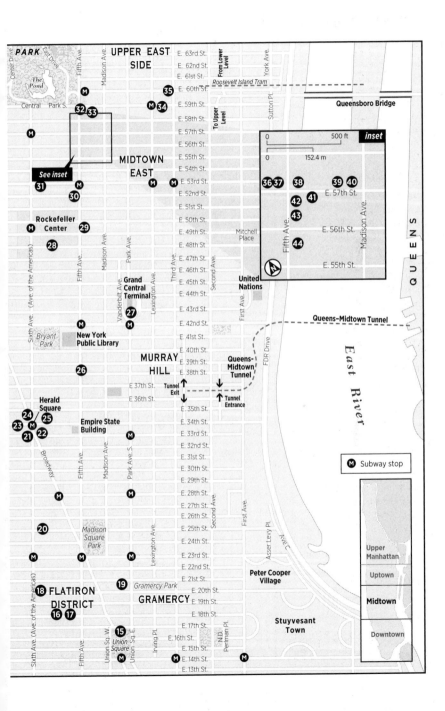

Uptown Shopping

Apple Store **6**
Barneys **8**
Barneys CO-OP **4**
Betsey Johnson **21**
Calvin Klein **9**
Carolina Herrera **18**
Chloé **16**
Dolce & Gabbana **13**
Emporio Armani **10**
Fairway **5**
Giorgio Armani **12**
Hermès **11**
Lanvin **14**
Lush **3**
Missoni **20**
Prada **15**
Ralph Lauren **17**
The Shops at Columbus Circle **7**
Zabar's **1**
Zitomer **19**

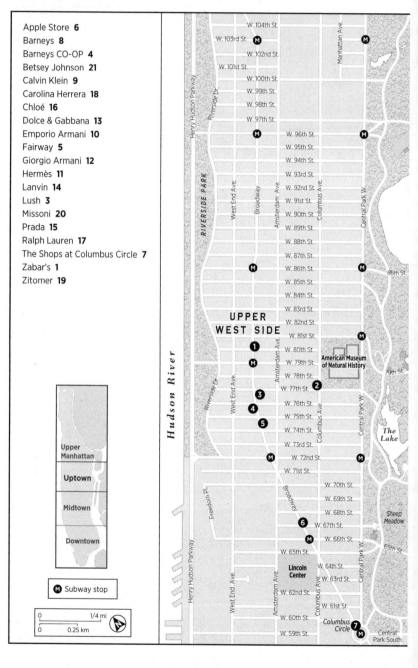

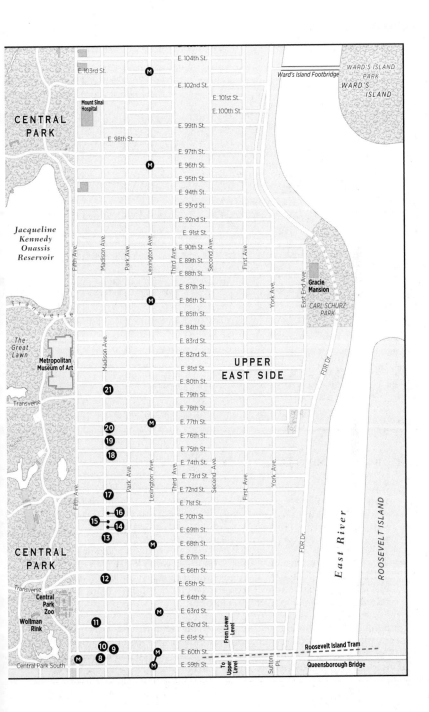

Williamsburg

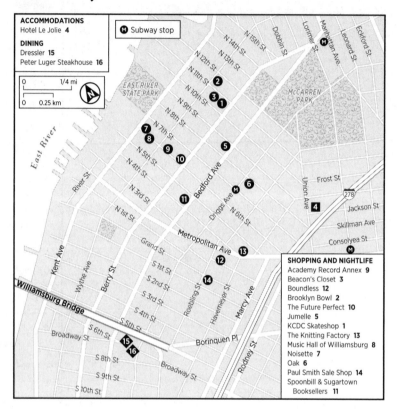

ACCOMMODATIONS
Hotel Le Jolie **4**

DINING
Dressler **15**
Peter Luger Steakhouse **16**

Ⓜ Subway stop

SHOPPING AND NIGHTLIFE
Academy Record Annex **9**
Beacon's Closet **3**
Boundless **12**
Brooklyn Bowl **2**
The Future Perfect **10**
Jumelle **5**
KCDC Skateshop **1**
The Knitting Factory **13**
Music Hall of Williamsburg **8**
Noisette **7**
Oak **6**
Paul Smith Sale Shop **14**
Spoonbill & Sugartown
  Booksellers **11**

✔ The **Hester Street Fair,** at Hester and Essex streets (www.hester streetfair.com; see map p. 216), is the relative new kid on the block (har, har), having had its inaugural season in 2010. In addition to the obligatory vintage housewares and clothing, it has a strong selection of food vendors. It's open April through December Saturday and Sunday from 9 a.m. to 6 p.m.; check the Web site to be sure its first year isn't its last.

✔ The **GreenFlea,** on Columbus Avenue between West 76th and West 77th streets, specializes in secondhand clothes, antiques, and jewelry; it's open November through March on Sundays from 10 a.m. to 5:30 p.m., to 6 p.m. April to October.

A game-changer in the market landscape has been the **Brooklyn Flea.** Just four months after blogger Jonathan Butler and former speechwriter Eric Demby shared a brainstorm over an Irish whisky in a DUMBO bar, 120 vendors and 20,000 people showed up on the 2008 opening day of what has become one of the best urban flea markets in the United States. Currently staged on Saturdays at Fort Greene's Bishop Loughlin Memorial High School yard (entrance on Lafayette Avenue between Clermont and Vanderbilt avenues), and Sundays inside the majestic landmarked lobby at One Hanson Place, across from the Atlantic Terminal, the Brooklyn Flea typically attracts 5,000 visitors daily to browse and buy vintage wares, jewelry and clothing made by local designers, and other unusual items. (Demby, who chooses the vendors, notes that more antiques and furniture can be found at the One Hanson Place location because it's indoors.) The Brooklyn Flea also set the bar for high-quality food vendors — Martha Stewart even devoted a segment of her show to the tasty treats on offer. The market has been a boon to leafy Fort Greene and prompted more than 7,000 vendor applications in its first two years. The Brooklyn Flea runs from 10 a.m. to 5 p.m. on weekends April through November, rain or shine. In the past, it has also been held in DUMBO under the Brooklyn Bridge; check the Web site at www.brooklynflea.com for the latest location details, days, times, and vendor mix.

 New York has greenmarkets at various locations throughout the city on different days, but the biggest and the best is the **Union Square Greenmarket.** You can find pickings from upstate and New Jersey farms, fresh fish from Long Island, homemade cheese and other dairy products, baked goods, plants, and organic herbs and spices. It's a true New York scene with everyone from models to top chefs poring over the bounty. The Union Square Greenmarket is open all year, but it's at its peak August through October, when the local harvest — tomatoes, corn, greens, grapes, peaches, peppers, and apples — flourishes. The greenmarket is set up on the west and north sides of the square, between 14th and 17th streets (see map p. 216), every Monday, Wednesday, Friday, and Saturday from 8 a.m. to 6 p.m. Go early for the best selection.

 New York's sidewalks are home to a plethora of street vendors, operating year-round on the streets and in subway stations of the most popular neighborhoods. Some vendors (such as those in SoHo) sell art and high-quality T-shirts, jewelry, hats, and gift items. Other vendors sell everything from socks to "preowned" Rolex watches. Sometimes you can find bargains — every winter I buy inexpensive gloves, hats, and scarves to replace the ones I've lost in a bar or a cab — but it's best to approach some of these enterprises with a healthy skepticism. (If the price sounds too good to be true, it surely is.) The thousands of street vendors who offer gold jewelry and watches at cheap prices are selling fake goods, of course — with the exception of the occasional vendor of stolen merchandise. Other hotbeds for imitation (or knockoff) designer goods and poor-quality, bootleg DVDs are the stalls along Canal Street in Chinatown.

Scoring at the sample sales

A bargain-hunter's dream, sample sales are events at which New York fashion design-ers sell — at *deep* discounts — discontinued styles, overstocks, and the sample outfits they create to show to store buyers (hence the name *sample sales*). How great are the deals? It's entirely possible to get a $300 dress from a big-name designer for $45 or less. Because the sales aren't widely publicized and may last anywhere from two days to a week, you have to hunt around to get the inside scoop. The weekly magazines *Time Out New York* and *New York* publish lists of upcoming sales; you also can try the Web site www.dailycandy.com for information.

Bring cash — credit cards are rarely accepted. You have more to choose from if you fit what designers call an "average" size — a U.S. 8 or 10 for women, a 40 for men. Items are sold as is, so try things on before you buy — and be prepared to do it in the middle of the shopping floor at the more frenzied sales.

Discovering the Best Shopping Neighborhoods

Concentrated areas for great shopping exist throughout New York. Some, however, are better than others. And new zones seem to sprout up every year, so you're hard-pressed not to find good shopping no matter where you happen to be. At the time of this writing, the neighbor-hoods below are the best for shopping.

Uptown

If you can find any bargains uptown (especially on the East Side), let me know, and I'll investigate that very rare phenomenon. You rarely score any deals here; the stores in this area are some of the most expensive in town. But that doesn't mean you can't have fun window-shopping and dreaming about what you can do with lottery winnings.

Madison Avenue

High fashion and high prices are what you find in the stores on Madison Avenue between 57th and 78th streets. (If you can't find some of these stores on the "Uptown Shopping" map, check out the "Midtown Shopping" map.) Here you can find **Barneys** (see the "Knowing the Big Names," sec-tion, earlier in this chapter) and some other high-end emporiums. To catch everything, start at one end and walk the length of this swanky strip. Take the 6 train to 77th Street and walk south; or take the 4, 5, or 6 to 59th Street or the N or R to Lexington Avenue and walk north. I've men-tioned only a few of the most notable stores along this strip; you're sure to find others along the way.

Along Madison Avenue, you find top European fashion designers' shops, such as the ultraelegant **Giorgio Armani,** 760 Madison Ave. (at 65th

Street; ☎ 212-988-9191), and his younger and less expensive line, **Emporio Armani,** 601 Madison Ave. (at 60th Street; ☎ 212-317-0800); the playfully chic **Chloé,** 850 Madison Ave. (at 70th Street; ☎ 212-717-8220); the ever-outlandish **Dolce & Gabbana,** 825 Madison Ave. (at 69th Street; ☎ 212-249-4100); and the simply gorgeous **Missoni,** 1009 Madison Ave. (at 77th Street; ☎ 212-517-9339). The classic **Yves Saint Laurent** recently folded its four-decade-old Madison Avenue flagship into its location at 3 E. 57th St. (☎ 212-980-2970).

American designers are represented, too. Browse **Calvin Klein,** 654 Madison Ave. (at 60th Street; ☎ 212-292-9000); **Carolina Herrera,** 954 Madison Ave. (at 75th Street; ☎ 212-249-6552); **Betsey Johnson,** 1060 Madison Ave. (at 80th Street; ☎ 212-734-1257); and **Ralph Lauren,** 888 Madison Ave. (at 72nd Street; ☎ 212-434-8050), among others.

If you're in search of fine Italian shoes and leather, visit **Prada,** 841 Madison Ave. (between 69th and 70th streets; ☎ 212-327-4200). Luxurious French fashion house **Lanvin** has just opened its first New York flagship at 815 Madison Ave. (at 69th Street; ☎ 646-439-0381). **Hermès** also has opened an unmissable flagship store at 691 Madison Ave. (at 62nd Street; ☎ 212-751-3181).

Midtown

From classic department stores to flagship "brand" stores like Niketown, you find a lot of variety (except in price, which is usually high) on luxury items, jewelry, clothing, and accessories in this area.

Fifth Avenue and 57th Street

Big-name shopping is the order of the day in this area, centered on Fifth Avenue south of 59th Street and East 57th Street up to Lexington Avenue. (See the "Midtown Shopping" map.) This is the area where you can find major stores like **Bloomingdale's, Tiffany & Co., Bergdorf Goodman,** and **Saks Fifth Avenue** (see "Knowing the Big Names," earlier in this chapter). To get here, take the subway to one of the nearby stops: the E or M to Fifth Avenue/53rd Street; the N or R to Fifth Avenue/59th Street; or the 4, 5, or 6 to 59th Street. From any of these points, you can explore north and south on Fifth Avenue and east and west on 57th Street.

Stores on this stretch include those of some top European haute couture designers, such as **Dior,** 21 E. 57th St. (between Fifth and Madison avenues; ☎ 212-931-2950); **Chanel,** 15 E. 57th St. (between Fifth and Madison avenues; ☎ 212-355-5050); and **Versace,** 647 Fifth Ave. (at 54th Street; ☎ 212-317-0224). The high-end names for accessories and shoes are here also, including **Ferragamo,** 725 Fifth Ave. (at 56th Street; ☎ 212-759-3822); **Gucci,** 685 Fifth Ave. (between 53rd and 54th streets; ☎ 212-826-2600); **Louis Vuitton,** 1 E. 57th St. (at Fifth Avenue; ☎ 212-758-8877); and **Fendi,** 720 Fifth Ave. (at 56th Street; ☎ 212-767-0100).

They say it's not a mall . . .

It's funny how New York developers make word pretzels to avoid using the word *mall* to describe what would be called a mall anywhere else in America, but it's true that two shopping centers (ahem) offer upscale experiences that make them exceptional.

The **Shops at Columbus Circle,** located in the Time Warner Center just off the southwest corner of Central Park, not only features some of the biggest (and most expensive) names in retail, but also offers shopping with a view of Central Park. But the picturesque view doesn't really matter to serious shoppers who are setting their sights on the goods at retailers like **A/X Armani Exchange, FACE Stockholm,** and **True Religion.** The real standouts here, though, are the world-class restaurants, including **Per Se, Landmarc** (p. 144), **Masa, Bouchon Bakery,** and **A Voce** (which I highly recommend). For more information about the Shops, you can check out the mall's Web site at www.shops atcolumbuscircle.com, or call ☎ **212-823-6300.**

In yet another recent conversion of a notorious nightlife spot (John Varvatos's takeover of the former CBGB's space was the first), the gothic church that hosted the drug-fueled antics of celebrities and club kids in the 1980s and '90s has become the **Limelight Marketplace,** 656 Sixth Ave. (at West 20th Street; ☎ **212-226-7585**). The three-story "festival of shops" (oy!), as the developer insists on calling it, includes a mix of 60 stores including **Hunter Boots, IT'SUGAR candy shop, Caswell Massey, Le Sportsac,** and **J. Sisters** (made famous by actress Gwyneth Paltrow, who once proclaimed that their Brazilian bikini wax changed her life).

Among the other big names in this area is **Niketown,** 6 E. 57th St. (at Fifth Avenue; ☎ 212-891-6453), the five-floor shoe-and-clothing emporium that appears to be one giant "Just Do It" commercial. As you enter, check out the five-story screen that unfurls periodically to show a video montage of Nike's ultrafamous pitchmen and -women. A few blocks down on Fifth Avenue is the **NBA Store,** 666 Fifth Ave. (at 52nd Street; ☎ 212-515-6221), where, in addition to all sorts of NBA and WNBA merchandise, you may catch a player at an in-store signing.

Herald Square and the Garment District

You can actually find some bargains around here, along with an actual mall. (See the "Midtown Shopping" map.)

This area is dominated by the self-proclaimed "Biggest Department Store in the World": **Macy's.** But you can also find **Lord & Taylor** here (see "Knowing the Big Names," earlier in this chapter). It's because of Macy's and Lord & Taylor that the area has attracted other big names like **Old Navy,** 150 W. 34th St. (☎ 212-594-0049), where you can outfit your extended family at bargain-basement prices; throwaway fashion temple **H&M,** 1328 Broadway (at 34th Street; ☎ 212-564-9922); and the mega-sneaker emporium **Foot Locker,** 120 W. 34th St. (☎ 212-629-4419). At

Sixth Avenue and 33rd Street is the **Manhattan Mall** (☎ 212-465-0500), where you can find such mall standards as Radio Shack and LensCrafters.

The Meatpacking District and Chelsea

Until recently, neither of these neighborhoods was known primarily for shopping; the Meatpacking District has traded the sounds of butchery for the sounds of music emanating from high-end clubs, and Chelsea has become the place for art-gallery hopping. But some major designers and the opening of the High Line have helped the area blossom, and this is the place to find fashion heavy-hitters such as **Diane Von Furstenberg,** 874 Washington St. (at 14th Street; ☎ 646-486-4800); the late and great **Alexander McQueen,** 417 W. 14th St (☎ 212-645-1797); and **Stella McCartney,** 429 W. 14th St. (☎ 212-255-1556). Another reason to come here (and with an appetite) is the **Chelsea Market,** 75 Ninth Ave. (at 15th Street; www.chelseamarket.com), a gourmet food bazaar. Take the A, C, E, or L to 14th Street to explore the area. (See the "Midtown Shopping" map.)

Downtown

Head downtown for the edgy, the alternative, the hip, the tacky, and the cheap — though sometimes it costs a lot of money to look cheap. (See the "Downtown Shopping" map.)

SoHo

New Yorkers moan that formerly artsy SoHo has become an outdoor shopping mall — and, well, we're right. Despite the complaints, SoHo is one of the best shopping neighborhoods in the city. Even the street vendors are a cut above here; my own sidewalk purchases include super-soft baby one-pieces, colorful bags, and even inexpensive silver jewelry, all sold by the crafters who made them.

SoHo is loosely bordered by Grand Street to the south, Avenue of the Americas (Sixth Avenue) to the west, Broadway to the east, and Houston to the north, forming a quadrangle. My suggested plan of attack: Enter the quadrangle at one of the four corners and walk up and down or left and right (pretend that you're hoeing a field). Take the A, C, or E to Canal Street; the C or E to Spring Street; the N or R to Canal or Prince Street; or the F or M to Broadway/Lafayette Street.

Designer shops include **Anna Sui,** 113 Greene St. (☎ 212-941-8406), and a strikingly designed **Prada** flagship at 575 Broadway (☎ 212-334-8888). Other notable boutiques include **Camper,** 125 Prince St. (☎ 212-358-1842), for highly original and highly comfortable shoes; **A.P.C.,** 131 Mercer St. (☎ 212-966-9685), a trust-fund hipster's paradise; and **Fragments,** 116 Prince St. (☎ 212-334-9588), a favorite for eye-catching jewelry. If you're in the market for something naughty, you can't go wrong at **Agent Provocateur,** 133 Mercer St. (☎ 212-965-0339), or **Kiki de Montparnasse,** 79 Greene St. (☎ 212-965-8150). For more G-rated items, the toy collectibles store **Kid Robot,** 118 Prince St. (☎ 212-966-5427), is unmissable.

International chains include **MUJI,** 455 Broadway (☎ 212-334-2002), a Japanese housewares and clothing store; **UNIQLO,** 546 Broadway (☎ 917-237-8811), a Japanese version of the Gap that I swear by for casual basics; and **Topshop,** 478 Broadway (☎ 212-966-9555), a British retailer with a devoted following.

Taschen, 107 Greene St. (☎ 212-226-2212), a publisher of eye-popping art books, is also in the area; shop there for a large selection of Taschen titles. **Kate's Paperie,** 561 Broadway (☎ 212-941-9811), features a tempting array of paper products, in spite of the generally indifferent customer service.

NoHo and Nolita

Nolita and NoHo have been hot shopping areas for more than a few years now and don't seem to be fading. Here you can find tiny boutiques specializing in high-quality fashion and design. Don't expect cheap, and, if you're an early bird, do your shopping somewhere else first; most shops don't put out the welcome mat before 11 a.m. Nolita and NoHo are on the east side of Broadway and Lafayette from SoHo. Take the N or R to Prince Street, the 6 to Bleecker Street or Spring Street, or the F or M to Broadway/Lafayette Street.

In Nolita, the buildings and shops are smaller and the atmosphere is less hyped than in SoHo. The best streets to start your explorations are Mulberry and Spring, and work your way northeast. The best places to smarten up your look include **baby blue line,** 238 Mott St. (☎ 212-226-5866), for women's clothing; **Seize sur Vingt,** 243 Elizabeth St. (☎ 212-343-0476), for menswear; **Highway,** 238 Mott St. (☎ 212-966-4388), for purses and bags; **Sigerson Morrison,** 28 Prince St. (☎ 212-219-3893), for fine footwear; **Selima Optique,** 25 Prince St. (☎ 212-334-8484), for eyeglasses; and **Push,** 240 Mulberry St. (☎ 212-965-9699), for jewelry. Come with money to burn.

NoHo is home to cutting-edge designers such as **Daryl K,** 21 Bond St. (at Lafayette; ☎ 212-529-8790). Also found in this area are the achingly hip clothing shop **Oak,** 28 Bond St. (near Lafayette; ☎ 212-677-1293), and vintage-wear veteran **Screaming Mimi's,** 382 Lafayette St. (between Great Jones and East 4th streets; ☎ 212-677-6464). And if you need any more proof of New York's transformation from punk paradise to consumers' delight, designer **John Varvatos** (formerly of Polo Ralph Lauren and Calvin Klein) has taken over the former CBGB's space at 315 Bowery (at Bleecker Street; ☎ 212-358-0315; see the "They say it's not a mall . . ." sidebar, earlier in this chapter).

Chinatown and the Lower East Side

The heart of Chinatown's commercial zone runs along Canal Street, from West Broadway to the Bowery. (See the "Downtown Shopping" map.)

Here, interspersed with more fruit, vegetable, and fish markets than you can imagine, you pass store after store — most hallway-sized stalls — selling "designer" sunglasses, watches, and handbags (Gucci, Coach, Louis Vuitton, and Kate Spade, for example), as well as bootleg CDs and DVDs. The film quality of these bootlegs is so bad that you feel as if you're watching a movie through a screen door. No matter what you find here, don't expect quality; still, it can be fun to browse, and after you get a sense of the prices, haggle a bit.

Alongside this extravaganza of fake merch is the *other* Chinatown, where you can find quirky, one-of-a-kind Asian-inspired gifts at bargain-basement prices. **Mott Street,** south of Canal Street, has a stretch of knickknack and housewares shops that sell everything from lacquered jewelry boxes and toys to embroidered silk pajamas and pottery dinner-ware. If you prefer one-stop shopping, try **Pearl River,** 477 Broadway (between Grand and Broome streets; ☎ 212-431-4770); technically in SoHo, this is a department store complete with a waterfall and specializ-ing in all things Chinatown — food, music, movies, clothing, and more.

The Lower East Side's main shopping is on Orchard Street, now known as the **Historic Orchard Street Shopping District,** which basically runs from Houston to Canal along Allen, Orchard, and Ludlow streets, spread-ing outward along both sides of Delancey Street. The bargains aren't quite what they used to be, but prices on leather bags, shoes, luggage, and fabrics on the bolt are still quite good. Be prepared for the hard sell and don't worry about saying no.

There are a number of fun boutiques in the neighborhood for the adven-turous shopper; note that many don't open before noon or 1 p.m. Among the funky stores I recommend is **Bluestockings,** 172 Allen St. (between Stanton and Rivington streets; ☎ 212-777-6028), one of the city's last remaining radical bookstores. **The Dressing Room,** 75A Orchard St. (between Grand and Broome streets; ☎ 212-966-7330), is a boutique-cum-bar where you find collections by young designers. One of the best menswear shops is **No. 8b,** 38 Orchard St. (☎ 212-925-5599). Lower East Side mainstay **Jutta Neumann** has moved to the far East Village at 355 E. Fourth St. (between avenues C and D; ☎ 212-982-7048); it's worth the trek for her handcrafted leather goods.

Lower Manhattan and the Financial District

The shopping isn't as exciting in Lower Manhattan or the Financial District, but you will find a few excellent stores like **Century 21,** 22 Cortlandt St. (☎ 212-227-9092). This king-of-discount department stores is across the street from the World Trade Center site, along with the city's best electronics retailer, **J&R Music & Computer World,** Park Row (☎ 800-426-6067 or 212-238-9000), which is a block-long emporium where you can find great prices on everything from cameras and com-puters to CDs and software.

The most concentrated shopping in this area is at the **South Street Seaport** (☎ 212-732-8257; www.southstreetseaport.com). Familiar names like Abercrombie & Fitch and Bath & Body Works line Fulton Street, which is the Seaport's main cobbled drag; similar shops fill the levels at **Pier 17,** a waterfront barge turned shopping mall. Come anyway — for both the historical ambience and the wonderful harbor views.

Brooklyn

As Brooklyn's star has risen, so it has also become a worthwhile shopping destination. You shouldn't miss the **Brooklyn Flea** (see "Shopping Open-Air Markets," earlier in this chapter), and after you've crossed the river, you should also explore the borough's eclectic shops.

In the Fort Greene neighborhood that's home to the Brooklyn Flea, you find **Greenlight Bookstore,** 686 Fulton St. (at South Portland Street; ☎ 718-246-0200; http://abookstoreinbrooklyn.blogspot.com). This gem was opened with the support of local resident writers (including Nelson George, Jennifer Egan, and Jhumpa Lahiri), and it's a great place to find signed editions. For women's (and occasionally small children's) clothing, I highly recommend **Cloth,** 138 Fort Greene Place (near Hanson Place; ☎ 718-403-0223; www.clothclothing.com), and, for unusual gifts and vintage items, **Saffron,** 31 Hanson Place (between Fort Greene Place and St. Felix Street; ☎ 718-852-6053; www.saffron-brooklyn.com); both stores are in the shadow of the hulking Atlantic Terminal.

Not far from Fort Greene and in between Brooklyn Heights and Cobble Hill is a great shopping strip along Atlantic Avenue, where Barneys CO-OP is also setting up shop. (Just be careful — Atlantic Avenue is rated as one of the worst streets for pedestrians in the city; cars tend to treat it like a highway.) I love quite a few boutiques here, including **Acorn,** 323 Atlantic Ave. (☎ 718-522-3760), for children's toys and clothing; **Steven Alan,** 349 Atlantic Ave. (☎ 718-852-3237), for men's and women's clothing; and **Hollander & Lexer,** 358 Atlantic Ave. (☎ 718-797-9190), for men's clothing.

Williamsburg now offers some of the city's best shopping. Favorite clothing stores include **Oak,** 208 N. Eighth St. (☎ 718-782-0521); **Jumelle,** 148 Bedford Ave. (☎ 718-388-9525), and **Noisette,** 54 N. Sixth St. (☎ 718-388-5188), both for women; vintage temple **Beacon's Closet,** 88 N. 11th St. (☎ 718-486-0816); and the **Paul Smith Sale Shop,** 280 Grand St. (☎ 718-218-0029). Art and architecture buffs should browse the selection at **Spoonbill & Sugartown Booksellers,** 218 Bedford Ave. (☎ 718-387-7322). Design addicts (and anyone with a sense of humor) will like **The Future Perfect,** 115 N. Sixth St. (☎ 718-599-6278). Skate rats will be thrilled by **Boundless,** 143 Roebling St. (☎ 718-821-9690; www.boundlessny.com), and **KCDC Skateshop,** 90 N. 11th St. (☎ 718-387-9006; www.kcdcskateshop.com), where you buy a new deck and then drop in on the ramp.

Other shopping areas

A host of other shopping zones exist all around Manhattan. If you're looking for something specific, chances are there's a part of town that sells nothing but what you want. The most famous is probably the **Diamond District,** a conglomeration of jewelry and gem stores along West 47th Street (between Fifth and Sixth avenues; www.47th-street.com). If you're after **beads, crafts, and notions,** the area between 35th and 39th streets, between Fifth and Sixth avenues, is the place to go. In the Village, Bleecker Street, between Sixth and Seventh avenues, is home to a dwindling number of **used CD stores;** check out St. Mark's Place, between Second and Third avenues, as well.

Teenagers and those striving for a younger look love the **shoes, clothing, and leather shops** that populate Eighth Street from Second to Sixth avenues (east of Broadway, Eighth Street is known as St. Mark's Place). Clothes and accessories for trendsters are also to be found on Seventh and Ninth streets.

The Best of New York Shopping A to Z

If your shopping intentions are less of the browsing variety, here are some of New York's specialized shopping options.

Beauty

✔ **C.O. Bigelow,** 414 Sixth Ave. (between 8th and 9th streets; ☎ **212-533-2700;** www.bigelowchemists.com; Subway: A, C, E, F, or M to West 4th Street; see map p. 216): Who'd think that a 168-year-old apothecary would carry the city's most eclectic, enjoyable, and international collection of healthy-skin and personal-care products? The goods run the gamut from Kusco-Murphy hair creams to French Elgydium toothpaste; they tend to be overpriced but sometimes too good to pass up.

✔ **Kiehl's,** 109 Third Ave. (between 13th and 14th streets; ☎ **212-677-3171;** www.kiehls.com; Subway: L, N, R, 4, 5, or 6 to 14th Street/ Union Square; see map p. 216): More a cult than a store, where the staff usually have flawless skin. Everyone from models to stockbrokers stop by this always-packed old-time apothecary.

✔ **Lush,** 531 Broadway (near Spring Street; ☎ **212-925-2323;** www.lush.com; Subway: N or R to Prince Street; see map p. 216): The super-fresh, all-natural, handmade bath and beauty products are irresistible here, and I'm not the only one who thinks so, judging by the number of outposts that keep opening around the city. The SoHo location often offers free in-store treatments; an Ocean Salt scrub followed by a dose of Dream Cream left my winter-roughened hands baby soft for days. Also at 7 E. 14th St. (at Fifth Avenue; ☎ **212-255-5133;** see map p. 216); 1293 Broadway at 34th St.

(☎ **212-564-9120;** see map p. 218); and 2163 Broadway (between 76th and 77th streets; ☎ **212-787-5874;** see map p. 220).

✔ **Ricky's,** 44 E. 8th St. (at Greene Street; ☎ **212-254-5247;** www. rickys-nyc.com; Subway: N or R to 8th Street; see map p. 216): This chain of funky drugstores also features a wide range of beauty products. If you're just dying for a multicolored wig, rainbow-colored lipstick, glitter galore, more than 80 kinds of hair brushes, or even edible undies, this is the store for you. At numerous other locations as well.

✔ **Zitomer,** 969 Madison Ave. (at 76th Street; ☎ **212-737-2016;** www. zitomer.com; Subway: 6 to 77th Street; see map p. 220): This three-story drugstore is more a mini department store than a pharmacy. It has its own very good line of cosmetics called **Z New York.** Big Apple lip gloss makes a wonderful souvenir — something you won't find in your local Walgreens.

Books

✔ **Books of Wonder,** 16 W. 18th St. (between Fifth and Sixth avenues; ☎ **212-989-3270;** www.booksofwonder.net; Subway: L, N, R, 4, 5, or 6 to 14th Street/Union Square; see map p. 218): This store is beloved by kids (the addition of cupcakes for sale in the adjoining cafe helps), though the selection isn't as extensive as you might hope. It's a particularly good stop if you're looking for a signed book (my nephew still thanks me for his Tiki Barber–autographed copy of *By My Brother's Side*) or a collectible children's book (such as vintage Nancy Drew).

✔ **Drama Book Shop,** 250 W. 40th St. (between Eighth and Ninth avenues; ☎ **212-944-0595;** www.dramabookshop.com; Subway: A, C, or E to 42nd Street; see map p. 218): You can often hear staged readings or authors reading from their own works here. Offering thousands of plays, from translations of Greek classics to this season's biggest hits, the shop also carries books, magazines, and newspapers on the craft and business of the performing arts.

✔ **Forbidden Planet,** 840 Broadway (at 13th Street; ☎ **212-473-1576;** www.fpnyc.com; Subway: L, N, R, 4, 5, or 6 to 14th Street/Union Square; see map p. 216): Here's the city's largest collection of sci-fi, comics, and graphic-illustration books. The proudly geeky staff really knows what's what.

✔ **McNally Jackson,** 52 Prince St. (between Lafayette Avenue and Mulberry Street; ☎ **212-274-1160;** www.mcnallyjackson.com; Subway: N or R to Prince Street; see map p. 216): I appreciate this compact, well-organized bookstore for its carefully considered selection of books, including Canadian and British titles. The store is staffed by true book lovers and is known for its special events.

✔ **Partners & Crime,** 44 Greenwich Ave. (at Charles Street; ☎ **212-243-0440;** www.crimepays.com; Subway: 1 to Christopher Street;

see map p. 216): This is not only the largest mystery and crime-focused bookshop in the city, but also the best. The staff readily offers recommendations, and rare and first editions are also available.

✔ The **Strand,** 828 Broadway (at 12th Street; ☎ **212-473-1452;** www. strandbooks.com; Subway: L, N, R, 4, 5, or 6 to 14th Street/Union Square; see map p. 216): A New York legend, the Strand is worth a visit for its staggering "18 miles of books," as well as its extensive inventory of review copies and bargain titles at up to 85 percent off list price. Also, check out the **Strand Annex,** 95 Fulton St. (between William and Gold streets; ☎ **212-732-6070;** Subway: 4, 5, or 6 to Fulton Street).

Edibles

✔ **Dean & DeLuca,** 560 Broadway (at Prince Street; ☎ **212-226-6800;** www.dean-deluca.com; Subway: N or R to Prince Street; see map p. 216): This upscale gourmet store in the heart of SoHo is a symbol of that area's prosperity. The store features premier quality, across the board, at premium prices. A small cafe in the front of the store makes this place a great stop for a cappuccino break.

✔ **Dylan's Candy Bar,** 1011 Third Ave. (at 60th Street; ☎ **646-735-0078;** www.dylanscandybar.com; Subway: N, R, 4, 5, or 6 to 59th Street; see map p. 218): Dylan (daughter of Ralph) Lauren is one of the co-owners of this wonderland that might make Willy Wonka proud. Located across the street from Bloomingdale's, Dylan's stocks candy classics like Necco wafers and Charleston Chews. Kids love this place — it's always a total zoo.

✔ **Economy Candy,** 108 Rivington St. (between Delancey and Norfolk streets; ☎ **212-254-1531;** www.economycandy.com; Subway: F to Delancey Street; see map p. 216): Although Dylan's is the new generation of candy store, Economy Candy, open since 1937 in the Lower East Side, is a blast from the past and my preferred place to stock up on childhood treats such as Hot Tamales, Bit-O-Honeys, rock candy, and Atomic Fireballs.

✔ **Fairway,** 2127 Broadway (between 74th and 75th streets; ☎ **212-595-1888;** www.fairwaymarket.com; Subway: 1, 2, or 3 to 72nd Street; see map p. 220): You won't find a better all-in-one market in Manhattan. Here you can buy the best and most modestly priced vegetables and cheeses in the city. Fairway also carries gourmet items you may find at Dean & Deluca, but at a fraction of the cost. The Harlem store is huge and features a walk-in freezer complete with down jackets provided for customers. Also at 2328 12th Ave. (at 132nd Street; ☎ **212-234-3883;** Subway: 1 to 125th Street).

✔ **Kee's Chocolates,** 80 Thompson St. (between Spring and Broome streets; ☎ **212-334-3284;** www.keeschocolates.com; Subway: C or E to Spring Street; see map p. 216): I am a serious chocoholic, and I'm limiting myself to this one recommendation. Kee Ling Tong makes her chocolates right next door to her spare shop, where only a small glass case stands between you and heaven. The crème brûlée bonbon is a fan favorite, but the green-tea truffle and the champagne ganache are also satisfying. New flavors are always under development; two recent ones are black rose and mirabelle plum. The Key lime macarons (not to be confused with macaroon candies) are also divine.

✔ **Zabar's,** 2245 Broadway (at 80th Street; ☎ 212-787-2000; www. zabars.com; Subway: 1 to 79th Street; see map p. 220): More than any other New York gourmet food store, Zabar's is an institution. This giant deli sells prepared foods, packaged goods from around the world, coffee beans, fresh breads, and much more (no fresh veggies, though). You can also find an excellent — and well-priced — collection of housewares and restaurant-quality cookware. Brace yourself for crowds.

Electronics

✔ **Apple Store,** 767 Fifth Ave. (at 59th Street; ☎ 212-336-1440; www. apple.com/retail; Subway: N or R to Fifth Avenue; see map p. 216): Mac-heads now have four temples in Manhattan for new gear and Genius Bar visits. The largest is the most touristed. The entrance is a transparent glass cube at the corner of 59th Street and Fifth Avenue, with the store itself below street level. It's open 24/7 and usually packed, though the design of the space doesn't make browsing insufferable and the employees are helpful. If you think coming after midnight will enable you to play with the floor samples in peace, think again; as one employee told me with a sigh, it's always nuts. Also at 103 Prince St. (at Greene Street; ☎ 212-226-3126; Subway: N or R to Prince Street); 401 W. 14th St. (at Ninth Avenue; ☎ 212-444-3400; Subway: C or E to 14th Street); and 1981 Broadway (at 67th Street; ☎ 212-209-3400; Subway: 1 to 66th Street/Lincoln Center).

✔ **B&H Photo & Video,** 420 Ninth Ave. (at 34th Street; ☎ 800-606-6969 or 212-444-6615; www.bhphotovideo.com; Subway: A, C, or E to 34th Street; see map p. 218): Looking for a digital camera at a good price? You really can't do any better than B&H, the largest camera store in the country. This camera superstore has everything from lenses to darkroom equipment. The store can be somewhat intimidating, but service is helpful. Just follow the signs to find whatever you're seeking. B&H closes early on Fridays (2 p.m.) and isn't open at all on Saturdays or major Jewish holidays.

✔ **J&R Music & Computer World,** Park Row at Ann Street (opposite City Hall Park; ☎ 800-426-6027 or 212-238-9000; www.jandr.com; Subway: 2 or 3 to Park Place, or 4, 5, or 6 to Brooklyn Bridge/City Hall; see map p. 216): This block-long, Financial District emporium is the city's top discount computer, electronics, small-appliance, and office-equipment retailer.

Gifts

✓ **Kiosk,** 95 Spring St., second floor (near Broadway; ☎ 212-226-8601; www.kioskkiosk.com; Subway: N or R to Prince Street; see map p. 216): You may worry that you're walking into the back entrance of a Chinese restaurant when you come here, but you're in the right place. Kiosk is a gallery boutique that showcases elegant, functional everyday items from foreign countries: Think Japanese notebooks with satiny recycled paper, single-use packets of Pustefix bubbles, or a German vegetable peeler with a special nib for cutting out potato eyes. Recent finds are from Portugal, and none has been previously available in the United States. It's perfect for an unusual yet useful gift. The shop is closed in August.

✓ **Evolution,** 120 Spring St. (between Greene and Mercer streets; ☎ 212-343-1114; www.theevolutionstore.com; Subway: C or E to Spring Street; see map p. 216): When my 4-year-old son needed a blue morpho butterfly specimen to call his very own, my first and only stop was Evolution, a science and natural-history nerd's dream. In stock is everything from taxidermied animals to human skulls. If you're squeamish about bugs, you won't get far into the door, but the staff is quite helpful.

Museum stores

✓ **Metropolitan Museum of Art Store,** 1000 Fifth Ave. (at 82nd Street; ☎ 212-570-3894; www.metmuseum.org/store; Subway: 4, 5, or 6 to 86th Street; see map p. 218): Treasures from the museum's collection have been reproduced as jewelry, china, and other objets d'art and sold in the museum's stores. The range of art books is dizzying, and upstairs is an equally comprehensive selection of posters and inventive children's toys. At numerous other locations as well, including 15 W. 49th St. (☎ 212-332-1360; Subway: B, D, F, or M to 47–50th streets/Rockefeller Center).

✓ **MoMA Design Store,** 44 W. 53rd St. (between Fifth and Sixth avenues; ☎ 212-767-1050; www.momastore.org; Subway: E or F to Fifth Avenue, or B, D, F, or Q to 47–50th streets/Rockefeller Center; see map p. 216): Across the street from the Museum of Modern Art is this terrific shop, whose stock ranges from museum posters and clever toys for kids to licensed reproductions of many of the classics of modern design. The SoHo store is equally fabulous. Also at 81 Spring St. (at Crosby Street; ☎ 646-613-1367; Subway: 6 to Spring Street).

✓ **New York Transit Museum Store,** Grand Central Terminal (on the main level, in the shuttle passage next to the Station Masters' office), 42nd Street and Lexington Avenue (☎ 212-878-0106; www.transitmuseumstore.com; Subway: S, 4, 5, 6, or 7 to 42nd Street/Grand Central; see map p. 218): My son can spend hours here, gazing at all this train-related stuff. (He has managed to accumulate the full set of miniature subway cars.) You can own a piece of the recently retired "Redbird" subway car fleet. Also at Boerum Place at Schermerhorn Street, Brooklyn (☎ 718-694-5100; Subway: 4 or 5 to Borough Hall).

Music

✔ **Academy Records,** 12 W. 18th St. (between Fifth and Sixth avenues; ☎ 212-242-3000; www.academy-records.com; Subway: F or M to 14th Street, or L to Sixth Avenue; see map p. 216): Classical and jazz devotees will be in heaven at this well-respected shop. Those looking for pop and rock should go to the East Village location at 415 E. 12th St. (between First Avenue and Avenue A; ☎ 212-780-9166; Subway: L to First Avenue). The **Academy Record Annex** in Williamsburg at 96 N. Sixth St. (between Berry and Wythe streets; ☎ 718-218-8200; www.academyannex.com; Subway: L to Bedford Avenue) is one of the best places in New York for new and used LPs.

✔ **Colony Music Center,** 1619 Broadway (at 49th Street; ☎ 212-265-2050; www.colonymusic.com; Subway: N or R to 49th Street, or 1 to 50th Street; see map p. 218): Housed in the legendary Brill Building, the Tin Pan Alley of '50s and '60s pop, this place has been around since 1948. You can find a great collection of Broadway scores and cast recordings; decades worth of recordings by pop-song stylists both legendary and obscure; the city's best collection of sheet music; and a great selection of original theater and movie posters.

✔ **House of Oldies,** 35 Carmine St. (at Bleecker St.; ☎ 212-243-0500; www.houseofoldies.com; Subway: A, C, B, D, F, or M to West 4th Street; see map p. 216): This musty old store has over one million records in stock in everything from R&B to surf music. A dream come true for fans of vinyl oldies.

✔ **Jazz Record Center,** 236 W. 26th St., eighth floor (between Seventh and Eighth avenues; ☎ 212-675-4480; www.jazzrecordcenter.com; Subway: 1 to 28th Street; see map p. 218): Jazz heads swear this is the best place to find rare and out-of-print jazz records. In addition to the extensive selection of CDs and vinyl (including 78s), the store offers videos, books, posters, magazines, and photos.

✔ **Other Music,** 15 E. 4th St. (between Broadway and Lafayette; ☎ 212-477-8150; www.othermusic.com; Subway: F to Broadway-Lafayette; see map p. 216): This small shop has long been the place to come for independent label and international music. Take a chance on anything with a cover that piques your interest — it'll broaden your musical horizons. Sign up on the Web site for e-mail updates of new releases.

Toys

✔ **FAO Schwarz,** 767 Fifth Ave. (at 58th Street; ☎ 212-644-9400, ext. 4242; www.faoschwarz.com; Subway: N or R to Fifth Avenue; see map p. 218): This legend carries those hard-to-find and expensive items like Vespa scooters, mini luxury cars such as Hummers and Jaguars, and karaoke machines.

✔ **Scholastic Store,** 557 Broadway (between Spring and Prince streets; ☎ **212-343-6187;** www.scholasticstore.com; Subway: N or R to Prince Street; see map p. 216): Despite the name, the Scholastic Store sells high-quality books and toys (such as Montgomery Schoolhouse wooden trucks and trains) alongside its own branded products. Everything is organized in age-appropriate sections for easier browsing. The giant stuffed dinosaur and Magic School Bus are big hits with the kids.

✔ **Space Kiddets,** 46 E. 21st St. (at Park Avenue; ☎ **212-614-3235;** www.spacekiddets.com; Subway: 6 to 23rd Street; see map p. 218): This store is well known around town for its trendy kids' threads, but the clothing has been moved a block up to 26 E. 22nd St. (☎ **212-420-9878**), to make way for an excellent collection of educational toys.

✔ **Toys "R" Us,** 1514 Broadway (at 44th Street; ☎ **800-869-7787;** Subway: 1, 2, 3, 7, or 9 to 42nd Street; see map p. 218): You have a Toys "R" Us in the mall back home, but does your local store have its own full-scale Ferris wheel where your kids can ride for free? Don't miss it if you're traveling with kids.

Chapter 13

Following an Itinerary: Five Great Options

In This Chapter

▶ Exploring the best of New York in three to five days
▶ Making the most of many museums
▶ Following the paths of history

I first visited New York as a teenager and have lived here for much of my adult life, and I still haven't seen it all. That's not because I don't have the *desire* to see it all; it's just that in New York, you *can't* see it all, if only because the rate of change is always faster than you are. So, if you feel a bit overwhelmed by all the options, I've laid out a few itineraries in this chapter that help you focus on your interests and use your time most efficiently, while also giving you a good sampling of what New York has to offer. Feel free to tailor these itineraries to suit your own schedule and taste.

New York in Three Days

Although your three-day visit may take place in the middle of the week, I'm writing this section as if your three days are part of a long weekend. Even if you're constantly on the move, you just can't cover all of New York in 72 hours. This itinerary enables you to get a taste of New York — just enough to make you want to come back for more.

Day one

Okay, start by getting a big picture of Manhattan. The best way to do this is to take either a three-hour **Circle Line Cruise** or the two-hour **New York Waterways** (see Chapter 11) full-island cruise. Both encircle Manhattan from the water. You pass by the Statue of Liberty and Ellis Island; see the lower Manhattan skyline; go up the East River, where you cruise under the Brooklyn Bridge; view the United Nations; cruise around to the Hudson River, where you pass the George Washington Bridge; and then head back to dock on the West Side piers.

The ride on both cruises is generally calm, but if you're prone to seasickness like me (and Dramamine isn't an option), you may want to consider the land alternative: a double-decker bus tour. **Gray Line New York** (see Chapter 11) offers many tour options, but the one that passes most of the major attractions is the downtown loop. The tour takes approximately two hours and shows you Times Square, the Empire State Building, the Flatiron Building, Rockefeller Center, Greenwich Village, the Lower East Side, and Chinatown.

Be aware that the tour is only as good as the tour guide, and, unfortunately, some of the Gray Line double-decker bus tour guides will fill you with misinformation. Also, if you're here for a three-day weekend, do this tour on either Saturday or Sunday morning. The double-decker buses get stuck in traffic just like anything else on wheels. Traffic is relatively light on Saturday and Sunday mornings, and you should cruise through the tour without any traffic hiccups.

You're deposited on the West Side Highway around 42nd Street after your morning boat tour, or in Times Square if you took the Gray Line downtown loop bus tour. Head over a couple of blocks to Ninth Avenue and have lunch at one of Hell's Kitchen's inexpensive ethnic restaurants. (See Chapter 10 for some restaurant suggestions.)

After lunch, you can walk east across 42nd Street to see more sights. You pass through the most famous crossroads in the world, 42nd and Broadway. Make your way through the crowds and continue east where you hit **Bryant Park;** on Fifth Avenue at 42nd Street, you'll see one of New York's great structures: the **New York Public Library.** As you walk farther east between Park Avenue and Lexington Avenue, you see Grand Central Station, another of New York's architectural treasures, and at Lexington Avenue, the city's most magnificent Art Deco building (and my personal favorite), the **Chrysler Building.** Finally, make your way back to Fifth Avenue and walk 8 blocks south to 34th Street. Look up — all the way to the top of the Empire State Building. You've got your tickets already (order them online before you leave), so you don't have to wait in line to get to the 86th-floor observatory and check out the view from the tallest building in New York.

You've done a lot of walking, so head back to your hotel and rest for a bit before setting out again. It's Friday night and that means museums are usually open late. You don't have time to hit them all, so I recommend the **Metropolitan Museum of Art** (see Chapter 11), where you'll be in one of the world's greatest museums and (Fri–Sat) have an opportunity to visit the Met's beautiful Great Hall Balcony Bar, which is open for cocktails and features classical music from a string quartet. From May to October in good weather, the lovely open-air Roof Garden Cafe overlooking Central Park is also open. I find people-watching on the front steps to be enjoyable, too.

After the museum and cocktails, you've got reservations at one of those 4-star restaurants run by a chef you've seen on television or on the cover of a famous magazine. Now you can judge for yourself what all the fuss is about.

Day two

Have your hotel give you a wake-up call — you have plenty of time to sleep on the flight home. Grab a quick, light breakfast, and then head down to Chinatown in the morning and watch as the fish markets (and there are a lot of them) prepare the day's catch (sometimes still flopping in the ice). Canal Street is the area's major thoroughfare, and by 11 a.m. on most days, especially on Saturdays, the sidewalk is absolutely teeming; so the earlier you get to Chinatown, the better.

Next, walk or get on the no. 6 train at the Canal Street station and take it one stop downtown to the Brooklyn Bridge/City Hall stop. You're going to see New York's City Hall, but it's the **Brooklyn Bridge** that you want. If the weather is decent, follow the signs to the walkway that takes you across that amazing structure; this walk is one I take with every one of my visiting friends and relatives. Don't forget to turn around for photo ops with the New York skyline behind you. After you reach Brooklyn and you've worked up an appetite, you deserve a reward; head to the foot of the bridge and fill up with a real New York pizza at **Grimaldi's,** and then walk to the river's edge to treat yourself to an ice cream at the **Brooklyn Ice Cream Factory** (see Chapter 10). Browse through the shops in DUMBO to work off lunch.

If you don't want to walk back across the bridge, take the C train at High Street back into Manhattan and get off at Spring Street. At Spring Street, you've entered the outdoor shopping parade known as **SoHo.** Traverse Spring Street and then up West Broadway to Prince Street. With all the designer boutiques and funky (but expensive) stores to explore, the going is going to be slow. (I don't normally recommend this on a Saturday, but you should see it while you're here.)

Walking north across Houston, you enter Greenwich Village. Its narrow streets and numerous cafes are often overrun with tourists, but it retains its charm. Have a cappuccino at one of the cafes, or eat an early dinner (look for early-bird and prix-fixe specials!), and then head back to your hotel to freshen up.

Tonight's the night you've got tickets to that Tony Award–winning show on Broadway. This is also your chance to take a peek at the neon spectacle of Times Square. After the show, if you're still itching to move, hit one of the downtown dance clubs (see Chapter 15), or if you're hungry and you just want a late bite, you have numerous options.

Day three

For some reason, you wake up and miss hearing the sounds of birds chirping like you hear back home. Not to worry — get on the subway and make your way to New York's green oasis, Central Park. But first, pick up some bagels and coffee for a breakfast alfresco. For hints on where you can get the best bagels, see Chapter 10. The park is vast with much to explore (see Chapter 11 for ideas); then amble over to the **Museum of Natural History,** on Central Park West. The museum opens at 10 a.m.; if you get there much later on a Sunday, expect to wait in line. The "must-sees" are numerous, but make sure you check out the dinosaurs or maybe the space show at the Rose Center for Earth and Space. (For more on what to see, turn to Chapter 11.)

After the museum, you may still have time to catch a gospel service (assuming this is Sunday) in Harlem, which you can follow up with a soul-food lunch (see Chapters 10 and 11). Or head across the park to the East Side and walk Museum Mile, where you can see museums like the **Guggenheim,** the **Frick,** and the **Whitney** to name just a few (see Chapter 11). You won't have time to explore all of them, but find one that interests you and make it your afternoon destination. An alternate plan: Head downtown to the Meatpacking District to have lunch at Chelsea Market, savor the views from the **High Line,** and shop in the neighborhood's boutiques.

Have a light dinner at one of the city's very good pizzerias or anywhere else you like, and then cap off your whirlwind New York weekend listening to some live music at a club or relaxing in a cozy bar. (See Chapter 15 for tips on where to find them.)

New York in Five Days

Compared to three days in New York, you're going to feel like five days is a lifetime — until all the things you want to do begin to add up and you realize that even in five days you can't do it all. Try not to stress. *Remember:* You're never going to do it all. But the following itinerary gives you an idea of what you can do, and it will be plenty.

Day one

Start your day and your visit at the beginning, where the city was born: Manhattan's southern tip, New York's oldest and most historic precincts. Leave early to catch the morning's first ferry to the **Statue of Liberty** and **Ellis Island** (see Chapter 11). This ride will take up most of your morning.

After you're back on the island, if you didn't arrange for tickets before you left home, pop over to the downtown **TKTS booth** at South Street Seaport (the line is usually much shorter than at the Times Square location) to pick up some discounted tickets for a **Broadway** or **Off-Broadway show** (something's always available for the evening; see Chapter 14).

By now, you're sure to need lunch, if you haven't succumbed to your hunger already. Do you want a leisurely meal or a quick snack? Check the options listed in Chapter 10. Or hop the subway over to Brooklyn (the A or C line will whisk you from lower Manhattan over to the High Street stop in minutes), and stroll back to Manhattan over the majestic **Brooklyn Bridge.** The bridge and the views from it beg to be photographed. Or, if you prefer, use the time to enjoy one of lower Manhattan's many historic or cultural attractions, such as the insightful and moving **Museum of Jewish Heritage, a Living Memorial to the Holocaust;** surprisingly diminutive **Wall Street;** the **African Burial Ground National Monument** and its recently opened visitor's center; or the **National Museum of the American Indian,** housed in the stunning, 1907 Beaux Arts **U.S. Customs House,** which is worth a visit for the architecture alone. (See Chapter 11 for more information on the city's best architecture.) Or just wander **Battery Park,** with its many memorials and stunning views of New York Harbor.

Head back to your hotel to freshen up so you can enjoy dinner at one of the city's hundreds of fantastic restaurants, see a Broadway show, or stop at a club for some dancing or to listen to some jazz.

Day two

Spend most of the day at one of the big museums: either the **Metropolitan Museum of Art** or the **American Museum of Natural History.** Both can fill days of browsing, so you may want to begin with a Highlights Tour. Don't miss the dinosaurs, the Butterfly Conservatory (if you're here at the right time of year), or the Space Show at the Natural History Museum's **Rose Center for Earth and Space.**

After you've had enough of the museum, head into **Central Park** (see Chapter 11) to see some of its many highlights; both museums sit on its fringe. You've worked up a big appetite with all that walking, so plan for another special dinner followed by the nightlife of your choice; the options are limitless.

Day three

Start your morning with a full-island cruise with either **Circle Line** (three hours) or **New York Waterways** (two hours), which circumnavigate Manhattan and offer a fascinating perspective on the island. If you're strapped for time, opt for the 1½-hour cruise around New York Harbor and halfway up the East River.

Spend the afternoon roaming some of the city's downtown neighborhoods: Bustling **Chinatown,** shopping meccas **SoHo** and **Nolita,** the 19th-century streets of **Greenwich Village,** and the revitalized **Meatpacking District.** Walk the prime thoroughfares, poke your head into shops, enjoy the views from the **High Line,** or park yourself at a street-side cafe and just watch the world go by. If you prefer to have a knowledgeable guide as you explore, schedule a **guided walking tour** (see Chapter 11 for a list of various tours, including free ones).

Stay downtown for the evening; catch dinner in a stylish (or authentically old-world) restaurant and follow dinner up with a trip to a dance club or cocktail lounge. (See Chapter 15 for recommendations.) Or if you've had enough of downtown, head back to your hotel and freshen up, and then head uptown for dinner; maybe order up some down-home cooking in Harlem and wander over for some jazz at the **Lenox Lounge** or **St. Nick's Pub.**

Day four

Head over to Rockefeller Center and see if you can get on one of the early NBC Tours (for information on times, ticket prices, and reservations, call ☎ **212-664-7174**). While you're waiting for the tour to begin, zip up to the **Top of the Rock,** where views, many people feel, are better than, or comparable to, those from the Empire State Building. Then make your way to nearby MoMA. If it's a weekday morning, you may actually see the works on exhibit at this amazing and popular museum instead of having to peer around a mass of bodies for a peek.

After you're done, walk 8 blocks to **Grand Central Terminal** (the walk is pleasant on a nice day) to admire that marvelous Beaux Arts monument to modern transportation. The dining concourse on the lower level gives you some very good lunch options.

If you never made it to the Top of the Rock, head down to the **Empire State Building** (flip to Chapter 11 for details) to see the view from the 86th-floor observation deck of New York's tallest building and ultimate landmark skyscraper. Spend the rest of the afternoon browsing a few of the Big Apple's brilliant smaller museums. Take in the **Frick Collection,** the **Whitney,** or the recently renovated **Morgan Library.** Or, if you prefer, use the afternoon to stroll up Madison Avenue and gawk, or exercise your credit line, at the staggeringly expensive shops.

Enjoy another evening at the theater, or catch a performance at **Lincoln Center, Carnegie Hall,** or one of the city's other terrific performing-arts institutions. Don't forget the innovative **Brooklyn Academy of Music;** it's easy to get to by subway with many of the major lines stopping nearby (see Chapter 14).

Day five

Use the morning to explore one of the major attractions you've missed thus far. If you spent day two at the Met, spend today at the **American Museum of Natural History.** If you made it to the top of the **Empire State Building,** but not to the **Top of the Rock,** now's your chance to compare views. Or go see Frank Lloyd Wright's iconic **Guggenheim Museum.** Tour the nerve center of international relations: the **United Nations.** If you haven't seen **Central Park** yet, go now; you can't leave New York without visiting it. If you've already done all the above, maybe today is the day you leave Manhattan for the Bronx and make a stop at the fabulous **Bronx Zoo** or the **Bronx Botanical Garden.** Or head to

Brooklyn for the **Brooklyn Museum of Art** and the **Brooklyn Botanic Gardens** (see Chapter 11).

In the evening, celebrate the end of a great vacation with some live music. A night of jazz at the **Village Vanguard,** rock at the **Bowery Ballroom,** or maybe some Haitian compass music at **S.O.B.'s** makes a very festive close, as does a night of laughs at one of the city's legendary comedy clubs, such as **Carolines** or the **Comedy Cellar.** Or, for the ultimate in New York elegance, dress to the nines and opt for a night of champagne and cabaret at the venerable **Cafe Carlyle** or **Feinstein's at the Regency.** If you want the velvet-rope experience, head to one of the city's dance clubs. This is your last night, so make it memorable. (Flip to Chapter 15 for a rundown of the city's nightlife offerings.)

New York for Museum Mavens

New York has so many museums and galleries, you could spend your entire vacation seeing them. But even if you're a maven, that's a bit extreme. Here's a stress-free two-day museum itinerary.

Start at the busiest and most extensive museum, the **Metropolitan Museum of Art.** Plan to arrive around opening time (9:30 a.m.) to avoid the crowds. Give yourself a minimum of two hours for your visit, and pace yourself — choose the galleries of most interest to you. (***Remember:*** The Met is closed on Monday.) From the Met, stroll up Museum Mile and try to decide if you want to go inside that funny-looking building (the **Guggenheim**), or head south to the **Frick** or the **Whitney** or any of the other fine museums in the area. But you won't have time to visit more than one before your hunger wins out. Head to Midtown for lunch; see Chapter 10 for more restaurant information.

After lunch, head to 53rd Street, between Fifth and Sixth avenues, and visit the jewel-like **Museum of Modern Art** (MoMA; see Chapter 11). If you have the time and energy, head just up the street to the **American Folk Art Museum** (also detailed in Chapter 11). If you're truly dedicated, you can try to make it to west Chelsea in time to hit the galleries there, and then eat at one of the innumerable restaurants nearby.

After a night dreaming of gilded treasures, take the subway to Brooklyn for part two of your museum-going adventure and the second-largest museum after the Met, the **Brooklyn Museum of Art.** You're in Brooklyn and you've got all morning, so give yourself three hours at this museum, and if the weather's nice, take a stroll in the **Brooklyn Botanic Gardens.**

Take the train back to Manhattan and, if you didn't get to Chelsea for a bit of gallery hopping, now's your chance. Wander from 13th Street to the south and 29th Street to the north between Seventh and Eleventh avenues; some of the big names here include the Gagosian Gallery, Marlborough, Annina Nosei, and the Pace Gallery. Or check out the

Studio Museum of Harlem. (For more information about museums in New York, see Chapter 11.)

New York for Families with Kids

New York has become a wonderland for children. Start your family vacation at the great **Museum of Natural History.** Take the little ones directly to the fourth floor and the dinosaur exhibit. After they've had enough dinosaurs, steer the brood to the **Rose Center for Earth and Space,** whose four-story-tall planetarium sphere hosts the Robert Redford–narrated space show that will awe all of you. Or, if your timing is right, the **Butterfly Conservatory** is a wonderful chance to see these delicate, beautiful creatures up close. The museum is across from Central Park, the perfect place for a picnic lunch with the family. Children can explore much in Central Park: playgrounds galore, boat rides, the Central Park Zoo, the carousel, and ice-skating. To do it all takes a day in itself.

After lunch, take the C train at Central Park West and 81st Street downtown to Times Square, where the kids can gawk at all the lights, familiar stores, arcades, and junk food that the flashy tourist zone has to offer. If you have little ones, take them to the **Toys "R" Us** superstore (see Chapter 12) where they can get a ride on the store's indoor Ferris wheel. (If the lines are too long, they may be just as amused by riding the store's escalators.) You're all probably famished by now, so treat the family to dinner at **Virgil's Real Barbecue** or **Carmine's,** both extremely kid-friendly (see Chapter 10).

The next day, head over to the Hudson River piers in the West 40s and take either the three-hour **Circle Line** cruise around Manhattan or the 90-minute **New York Waterways** Harbor Cruise. Both offer a different perspective on some of the city's greatest attractions like the Statue of Liberty, Ellis Island, the Brooklyn Bridge, and the United Nations.

For lunch, the pizza at **John's Pizzeria,** just off Times Square, can make any kid happy. After lunch, work your way to 34th and Fifth and the **Empire State Building.** Because you've already bought tickets (see Chapter 11), you won't have to wait in line, and you and your family are quickly whizzed up to the 86th-floor observatory where you experience the same view King Kong had when he climbed to the top. From the observation deck, look downtown and tell the kids that's where they're going for dinner: to Chinatown where the constant commotion, street vendors, flopping fish, and all-around exotic feel may excite the children as much as they do you. After the excitement of the day, you're all going to be famished and ready for a big, communal, and inexpensive dinner at one of Chinatown's many restaurants.

After dinner, take the 6 train uptown to 14th Street/Union Square where you'll switch to the no. 4 express train. Stay on the train until you come out of the tunnel and see the bright lights of Yankee Stadium. Your stop is **Yankee Stadium,** and you're here to see one of the most celebrated franchises in all sports.

If you have another day with the family, take a poll from the kids on what they want to do. Return to Central Park? Head up to the **Bronx Zoo?** Or out to Queens and the **New York Hall of Science?** Visit a few museums like the New York Transit Museum, the Skyscraper Museum, or the Children's Museum? Check out South Street Seaport? Explore the activities of Chelsea Piers? You'll have fun, whatever you decide.

It's always good to have a Plan B in case it rains (or snows). The weather may very well determine how much walking you can do (or want to do).

New York for History Buffs

The history of most cities is written in its neighborhoods. New York is no exception. Try this itinerary and visit some of the city's historic neighborhoods to get a feel for the character and growth of New York.

Start in lower Manhattan, at the extreme southern tip of the island of Manhattan. At Battery Park, you can see **Castle Clinton,** completed in 1808. Just a short walk away is the gorgeous **U.S. Customs House,** built in 1907, which houses the **National Museum of the American Indian at the George Gustav Heye Center.**

Though most of the lower Manhattan historic sights are within walking distance, the Alliance for New York offers free bus service on its **Downtown Connection** bus (see Chapter 8 for details).

Next on your walking/bus tour should be historic Wall Street and the **Federal Hall National Monument** (circa 1842), along with the famous statue of George Washington. Also on Wall Street is **Trinity Church,** built in 1846 and beautifully preserved.

For a taste of modern and very tragic history, a few blocks up from Trinity Church you can see the huge construction site that, before September 11, 2001, was the **World Trade Center.** Almost directly across the street, and miraculously spared from the terrorist attacks, is **St. Paul's Chapel,** built in 1766 and part of Trinity Church, where George Washington was a frequent worshiper.

From here, you want to get on one of those free buses and take it east to the **South Street Seaport and Museum,** where the 18th- and 19th-century buildings lining the cobbled streets and alleyways have been impeccably restored. You can also hit the very modern mall-like shopping center and numerous restaurants here if you've had too much history or you just want to take a lunch break.

After lunch, head to another historic downtown neighborhood, the Lower East Side, which is a tenement neighborhood where many immigrants — notably Eastern European Jews — settled back in the mid– to late 19th century. **Delancey Street** and historic **Orchard Street** are the main thoroughfares to explore. And to get the best taste of what life was like for the immigrants in the late 19th and early 20th centuries, visit the **Lower East Side Tenement Museum** (see Chapter 11). Then treat yourself to some great ice cream at **Il Laboratorio del Gelato** next door, or head to Houston Street or **Katz's Delicatessen** for a genuine New York egg cream (see Chapter 10).

Take a break and rest a bit before heading out to your next neighborhood, **Greenwich Village.** The Village has always been the domain of the unconventional; the place for radical thinkers; the haunt of literary figures like Henry James, Eugene O'Neill, and Dylan Thomas. Artists like Edward Hopper and Jackson Pollack, and the famous beatniks Allen Ginsberg, Jack Kerouac, and William Burroughs, lived and hung out in Greenwich Village. Unlike other parts of the city, the Village is not laden with historical landmarks. Its landmarks are its streets, alleyways, and brownstone blocks.

The physical center of the Village is **Washington Square Park,** located in the heart of New York University, where, along with some serious chess players, some entertaining street performers, and a few determined drug dealers, you can see the famous Washington Square Arch. The heart of beatnik society was centered on Bleecker and MacDougal streets. Stop and have an espresso at one of the many cafes in the area; the people-watching doesn't get any better. The West Village around Christopher Street is the center of the pioneering gay community, where you find some quaint boutiques and more cafes.

Dinnertime should be approaching, and maybe you've planned ahead and have reservations, or maybe you just want to try one of those pizzas from **Lombardi's,** believed to be one of the city's first pizzerias. (For more ideas on restaurants, see Chapter 10.) No matter when you get out of dinner, the Village will still be buzzing with activity. You may want to hear some jazz at the venerable **Village Vanguard** club or catch a comedy show at the **Comedy Cellar.** (See Chapter 15 for more on clubs and bars.)

Continue your historic neighborhood itinerary the next day on the Upper West Side. The Upper West Side has a history of liberalism and of being a home to musicians. The great performing arts venue **Lincoln Center,** at 64th Street and Broadway, is the unofficial gateway to the Upper West Side.

From Lincoln Center, cut over to Central Park West and you see the grandeur of that boulevard lined with Beaux Arts apartment houses, the oldest being the **Dakota,** built in 1884 on Central Park West and 72nd Street. The Dakota has the infamous distinction of being not only the location for the Roman Polanski film *Rosemary's Baby,* but also where John Lennon, who lived there with Yoko Ono, was shot and killed. Other famous residents of the Dakota have included Leonard Bernstein, Lauren Bacall, and Judy Garland.

Walk west across 72nd Street to Broadway, where you can see the area's other magnificent residence, the **Ansonia** at 73rd and Broadway. Musicians such as Caruso, Toscanini, and Igor Stravinsky, to name just a few, have called this building home.

If you're hungry, grab some lunch at **Zabar's** (see Chapter 12), the area's most famous gourmet-food store, and take it to Riverside Park for a picnic lunch overlooking the Hudson River, or walk a few blocks east to Central Park. If you choose to go east, you may want to stop at the **New-York Historical Society** at Central Park West and 77th Street (see Chapter 11 for details). If you choose west, stroll up **Riverside Drive,** which features some of the city's most stately apartment houses.

After lunch, head up to Harlem, where the wealthiest New Yorkers lived in the late 19th and early 20th centuries. Many of the Harlem mansions still stand and are impeccably preserved. On 130th Street, between Fifth and Lenox avenues, you can see a series of 28 redbrick town houses, known as the **Astor Row Houses,** which date back to the early 1880s. On 139th Street, between Adam Clayton Powell, Jr., and Frederick Douglass boulevards, sits the impressive **Strivers' Row,** where hardly a brick has changed among the gorgeous neo–Italian Renaissance town houses that were built in 1890. After the original white owners moved out, these lovely houses attracted the cream of Harlem, "strivers" like such as Eubie Blake and W. C. Handy.

Handsome brownstones, limestone town houses, and row houses are sprinkled atop **Sugar Hill,** 145th to 155th streets between St. Nicholas and Edgecombe avenues, named for the "sweet life" enjoyed by its residents. Finally, head up to 160th Street, east of St. Nicholas Avenue, to see Manhattan's oldest surviving house, the 1765-built **Morris-Jumel Mansion,** 65 Jumel Terrace (☎ **212-923-8008;** www.morrisjumel.org; Open: Wed–Sun 10 a.m.–4 p.m. for tours).

Taking in all that history works up a major appetite, so stay in Harlem for dinner; you can't go wrong with the soul-food buffet at **Charles' Country Pan-Fried Chicken** (see Chapter 10).

Part V
Living It Up After Dark: New York City Nightlife

The 5th Wave   By Rich Tennant

I enjoyed yelling out
improvisational situations
at Upright Citizens Brigade
last night, too. But this is
the New York Philharmonic.

In this part . . .

Though it's tamer than it used to be, New York remains "the city that never sleeps." With such an assortment of nightlife riches to choose from, New York is a night owl's dream. In this part, I go over some of the venues for theater, dance, and live music that you may want to visit. I also give you a roundup of clubs and bars where you can kick back, hook up, or dance until the break of dawn.

Chapter 14

Applauding the Cultural Scene

In This Chapter

▶ Finding out what's going on around the city

▶ Getting dramatic (and where you can do it)

▶ Listening to all sorts of music

▶ Leaping from modern dance to ballet

*N*o other city rivals New York in the breadth and scope of the performing arts offered. From the incredible range of theater, opera, dance, and symphony to live rock and jazz, the bounty is almost too full. Your biggest problem is choosing among the many temptations.

Getting the Inside Scoop

For the latest, most comprehensive nightlife listings, from theater and performing arts to live rock, jazz, and dance club coverage, *Time Out New York* (www.timeoutny.com) is my preferred weekly source; a new issue hits newsstands every Thursday. *The New York Times* (www.nytimes.com) features excellent entertainment reviews and listings, particularly in the Friday "Weekend" section. The cabaret, classical music, and theater guides are particularly useful. The city's legendary weekly alterna-paper, the free *Village Voice* (www.villagevoice.com), isn't as revered as it used to be, but the arts-and-entertainment coverage is still worthwhile. Other great weekly sources are *The New Yorker* (www.newyorker.com), in its "Goings on about Town" section, and *New York* magazine (www.nymag.com), with an "Agenda" that features the latest happenings. I also recommend **Flavorpill,** a carefully curated list of the most intriguing cultural events around town; check the Web site or subscribe to the weekly e-mails at www.flavorpill.com.

Theatre Development Fund's **Show Search** (www.tdf.org; look under "Audience Info") provides schedules, descriptions, and ticket information for theater and the performing arts.

A little research can get you an array of information and reviews of current shows. *The New York Times* is a good source for the scoop on big theater shows, and *The Village Voice* is still strong on alternative culture. The listings in *New York* magazine, *The New Yorker,* and *Time Out New York* regularly offer information about both mainstream and of-the-beaten-path shows. The following Web sites also offer valuable theater information, and the opportunity to purchase tickets.

- ✔ **Applause:** www.applause-tickets.com
- ✔ **I Love New York Theater:** www.ilovenytheater.com
- ✔ **NYC & Company:** www.nycgo.com
- ✔ **Off-Broadway Theater:** www.offbroadway.com
- ✔ **Ticketmaster:** www.ticketmaster.com
- ✔ **Theatermania:** www.theatermania.com

Taking in New York Theater

New York's theater scene is second to none. With so much breadth and depth, and so many wide-open alternatives, just keeping up with it is exhausting, as well as exhilarating, especially for theater buffs. Broadway, of course, gets the most ink and the most airplay. Broadway is where you find the big stage productions, from crowd-pleasing warhorses like *The Lion King* and *Mamma Mia!* to the phenomenally successful shows like *Wicked* and *Avenue Q.* But smaller "alternative" theater has become popular both commercially and critically, too. With bankable stars on stage, crowds lining up for hot tickets, and hits popular enough to generate major-label cast albums, Off-Broadway isn't just for culture vultures.

Helping to assure the recent success of the New York theater scene is the presence of Hollywood stars like Jude Law, Julia Roberts, Morgan Freeman, and Hugh Jackman. But keep in mind that stars' runs on stage are often limited, and tickets for their shows tend to sell out fast.

If you hear that an actor you'd like to see is coming to the New York stage, don't put off your travel and ticket-buying plans. (The box office can tell you how long a star is contracted for a role.)

Figuring out the Broadway basics

The terms **Broadway, Off-Broadway,** and **Off-Off-Broadway** refer to theater size, pay scales, and other details, not location — or, these days, even star wattage. Most of the Broadway theaters are in Times Square, around the thoroughfare the scene is named for, but not directly on it. Instead, you can find theaters dotting the side streets that intersect Broadway, mostly in the mid-40s, between Sixth and Eighth avenues (44th and 45th streets in particular), but also running north as far as 53rd Street.

Culture for free: Shakespeare in Central Park

A New York institution since 1957, Shakespeare in the Park is as much a part of a New York summer as fireworks on the Fourth of July. Shakespeare in the Park is the brainchild of the late Joseph Papp, founder of the Public Theater, who came up with the idea of staging two Shakespeare plays each summer at the open-air Delacorte Theater in Central Park. Best of all, and the reason Shakespeare in the Park has become an institution, is that the performances are free.

Two shows are offered (though it's sometimes reduced to one in years when budgets are tight), usually a Shakespeare play featuring a large company and a more modern theater classic, including at least one or more "names" from film and television. The productions run from June to August. Depending on the star power of the cast, tickets can be quite scarce. The program for 2010 included *The Merchant of Venice* with Al Pacino.

Roughly 1,800 tickets are distributed at the Delacorte on a first-come, first-served basis (two per person) for the plays, starting at 1 p.m. on the day of each performance. But keep in mind that people start lining up hours in advance, so bring a book or some refreshments and be prepared to wait. Tickets are also available between 1 and 3 p.m. on the day of the performance at the Public Theater, 425 Lafayette St. (between Astor Place and East 4th Street in the East Village); the lines get long there, too. You can also try getting tickets in an online lottery on the Public Theater's Web site.

For more information about Shakespeare in the Park, contact the Public Theater (☎ 212-539-8500; www.publictheater.org).

Off-Broadway, on the other hand, can be anywhere. Off-Off-Broadway shows tend to be more avant-garde, experimental, and/or nomadic (and also have the cheapest ticket prices). Off- and Off-Off-Broadway productions tend to be based downtown, but mini theater districts exist in Midtown and on the Upper West Side as well. Broadway shows tend to keep regular **schedules.** Eight performances a week is the norm, with evening shows Tuesday through Saturday, plus matinees on Wednesday, Saturday, and Sunday. Evening shows usually start at 8 p.m., while matinees are usually at 2 p.m. on Wednesday and Saturday and 3 p.m. on Sunday, but schedules can vary. Broadway and Off-Broadway shows usually start exactly on time; if you arrive late, you may have to wait until after the first act to take your seat — so be on time and you won't miss any of the show.

Getting theater tickets

Ticket prices for Broadway shows vary dramatically. Expect to pay a lot for good seats; you're looking at $100 to $150 or more for full-price tickets to any given show. The cheapest end of the price range can be around $35 to $55, depending on the theater configuration. If you're buying tickets at the low end of the available range, be aware that you may be buying obstructed-view seats. If all tickets are the same price or the range is small, you can pretty much count on all the seats being pretty good.

Two pet peeves of mine: Despite having to pay so much for a show, many theaters haven't installed more comfortable seating (especially in the older theaters, which can date from the early 20th century). Even if you're of modest build, you may feel uncomfortably close to your fellow theatergoers and as though your knees are up to your chest — and those are orchestra seats. Consider yourself forewarned. Also, the days are long gone when people actually dressed up for live theater, but where's the harm in making a little effort to look pulled together? If your usual uniform is jeans and sneaks, upgrade to business casual for the evening — because you're shelling out for the tickets, you may as well feel special.

Kids like theater, too!

And they have lots of venues and shows to choose from in New York City.

✔ **The New Victory Theater,** 229 W. 42nd St. (between Seventh and Eighth avenues; ☎ 646-223-3020; www.newvictory.org), is a full-time, family-oriented performing-arts center and has hosted companies ranging from Aeros, a Romanian gymnastics troupe, to the astounding Flaming Idiots, who juggle everything from fire and swords to beanbag chairs.

✔ Called "the most original children's theater group in the country" by *Newsweek,* **The Paper Bag Players** (☎ 212-663-0390; www.paperbagplayers.org), perform funny tales for children ages 4 to 9 in a set made from bags and boxes at venues around town including the Kaye Playhouse at Hunter College, 68th Street between Park and Lexington avenues (☎ 212-772-4448).

✔ **TADA! Youth Theater,** 15 W. 28th St. (between Fifth Avenue and Broadway; ☎ 212-252-1619; www.tadatheater.com), is a youth ensemble that performs musicals and plays with a multiethnic perspective for kids, teens, and their families.

✔ The **Swedish Cottage Marionette Theater** (☎ 212-988-9093; http://central park.org/index.php/attractions/swedish-cottage) puts on marionette shows for kids at its 19th-century Central Park theater throughout the year. Reservations are a must.

✔ Yes, it's the same David Mamet who writes those hard-boiled movies and plays, but he shows his softer side with acclaimed twice-yearly youth productions as part of his **Atlantic Theater Company,** 336 W. 20th St. (between Eighth and Ninth avenues; ☎ 212-691-5919; www.atlantictheater.org).

Off-Broadway and Off-Off-Broadway shows tend to be cheaper than Broadway shows, with tickets often as low as $20. However, seats for the most established shows and those with star power can command much higher prices, from $60 and up.

If you've decided on a show to see before you leave, have your credit card in hand and contact any of the ticket agencies by phone or on the Web. (You'll usually have to pay a service fee in addition to the cost of the tickets, ranging from a few dollars to a *lot* more for premium seats to a hit show.)

Some of these organizations have lists of discounted shows, the latest theater news and reviews, and member bulletin boards where you can ask for recommendations. If you're planning to get to as many shows as you can, it's worth it to register with a service like **TheaterMania.com, Playbill.com,** or **Broadway.com** to get discounts and subscribe to their e-mail newsletters.

- ✔ **Applause** (www.applause-tickets.com): Also offers discounts.

- ✔ **Broadway.com** (www.broadway.com): Also offers dinner packages and gift certificates.

- ✔ **Manhattan Concierge** (☎ **800-697-4697** or 888-675-3669; www. manhattanconcierge.com): A ticket broker that can sell you good tickets to almost anything (including concerts and sporting events). Expect to pay a service charge.

- ✔ **Playbill.com** (www.playbill.com): The online presence of the company that distributes the familiar programs with the yellow logo in theaters. Also offers packages, industry news, and photos and videos of shows. Has a regular list of discounts if you sign up as a member.

- ✔ **Telecharge** (☎ **800-432-7250** or 212-239-6200; www.telecharge.com).

- ✔ **TheaterMania.com** (☎ **866-811-4111** or 212-352-3101; www. theatermania.com): An excellent source for Off- and Off-Off-Broadway, as well as full-price and discounted Broadway tickets.

- ✔ **Ticketmaster** (☎ **866-448-7849** or 212-307-7171; www.ticket master.com).

You can buy same-day tickets at the following outlets:

- ✔ **TKTS** (☎ **212-221-0013**) sells discounted (up to 50 percent) Broadway and Off-Broadway tickets as they become available from theaters. For the most up-to-date ticket information, consult www. tdf.org. Before you visit a physical ticket booth, keep in mind that long lines are the norm (especially when the booths open for the day), and you're not guaranteed to get tickets for a specific show. Also, note that tickets for a popular show may be available because the cast for that day changed, which is not the best scenario if you have your heart set on seeing a particular production or actor.

✔ The newly renovated main booth — utterly unmissable with its signature red-glass steps overhead — is in the heart of the Theater District in Duffy Square at 47th and Broadway (Open: For evening performances Mon, Wed–Sat 3–8 p.m., Tues 2–8 p.m., and Sun 3 p.m. to half-hour before latest curtain time; for matinees, Wed and Sat 10 a.m.–2 p.m., Sun 11 a.m.–3 p.m.). A booth is also open downtown at the South Street Seaport on the corner of Front and John streets (Open: Mon–Sat 11 a.m.–6 p.m., Sun 11 a.m.–4 p.m.; at this location and in Brooklyn, matinee tickets can be purchased the day before the show). There's also a TKTS booth in Brooklyn, in 1 MetroTech Center at the corner of Jay Street and Myrtle Street Promenade (Open: Tues–Sat 11 a.m.–3 p.m. and 3:30–6 p.m.); it tends to have the shortest lines of all the locations.

✔ For same-day advance tickets at regular prices for most shows, visit the official booth run by the Broadway League: the **Broadway Ticket Center** inside the Times Square Information Center, 1560 Broadway (at 46th Street; ☎ **888-276-2392;** Open: Mon–Sat 9 a.m.–7 p.m., Sun 10 a.m.–6 p.m.).

Catching a little pre-theater dinner

For a number of reasons, you want to eat before you go to the theater. If you try to hold out until after the show, your hunger may distract you from the drama in front of you. Also, you don't want to disturb other theatergoers with the rumblings of your stomach! So plan to eat before you go. Many restaurants in the Theater District have pre-theater prix-fixe specials, and all of them are expert at serving you quickly. Consider these suggestions:

✔ **db Bistro Moderne,** 55 W. 44th St. (between Fifth and Sixth avenues; ☎ 212-391-2400), is the home of a famously rich hamburger made with braised short ribs, foie gras, and shaved black truffles. The restaurant also offers a three-course pre-theater dinner for $45.

✔ **La Bonne Soupe,** 48 W. 55th St. (between Fifth and Sixth avenues; ☎ 212-586-7650), is just a short stroll to almost everything: Lincoln Center, Carnegie Hall, the theaters, and Rockefeller Center. The French bistro fare is solid.

✔ **Molyvos,** 871 Seventh Ave. (between 55th and 56th streets; ☎ 212-582-7500), is a great option for a Greek meal before a concert at nearby Carnegie Hall. The three-course pre-theater prix fixe at Molyvos is $37.

✔ **Virgil's Real Barbecue,** 152 W. 44th St. (between Sixth and Seventh avenues; ☎ 212-921-9494), is just a short stroll from most Broadway theaters. Because of the pre-theater dining rush, reservations are an absolute must.

Always inform the staff at sit-down restaurants that you have theater tickets; they'll make sure you're out the door in time to make the opening curtain.

You also can get tickets after you arrive in the city by calling one of the telephone services listed earlier in this chapter, by asking the concierge at your hotel, or by using one of the numerous ticket brokers, whose listings you can find in newspapers and in the phone book. According to New York City law, these brokers are supposed to charge only a $5 fee or a 10 percent commission, whichever is less. However, New Jersey has no such law, and a lot of the brokers are based there. Ask about the fee upfront, because tickets to a very hot show can go for as much as double or more the face value.

Another option is to call the box office of the theater where the show is playing to ask whether they have any tickets available, because they often do. Some long-running shows run special promotions, so it pays to inquire when you call. As a last resort, remember that a cheap way to get a seat is not to have one: Standing room is available at some shows for $20 to $35.

 Make the rounds of Broadway theaters at about 6 p.m., when unclaimed house seats are made available to the public. These tickets — reserved for VIPs, friends of the cast, the press, or industry professionals — offer great seats and are sold at face value. (If you're with someone, tell the box-office staff that you don't want to sit together. Single seats are usually easier to come by than pairs at the last minute).

Also, note that **Monday** is often a good day to score big-name show tickets. Although many theaters are dark that day, some of the most sought-after choices aren't. Locals are likely to stay at home the first night of the workweek, so the odds of getting tickets are in your favor. Your chances of getting tickets are always better on weeknights or for Wednesday matinees, rather than on weekends (but do check and see if the Big Star is on, rather than the understudy).

Venues That Set the Standard

New York is blessed with a number of amazing venues to hear and see the performing arts. Some, like Lincoln Center and Carnegie Hall, are so famous that they're household names around the globe, while the Brooklyn Academy of Music, though not quite as famous worldwide, certainly should be.

The Lincoln Center for the Performing Arts

This celebrated complex (www.lincolncenter.org) extends over 4 blocks on the Upper West Side. It hosts an extraordinary range of productions, from opera to film to dance to classical music, in the following performance spaces:

- **Metropolitan Opera House** (☎ 212-362-6000; www.metopera.org) is home to the Metropolitan Opera Company (see the "Opera" section, later in this chapter) and the American Ballet Theatre (see

"Dance," later in this chapter). It also showcases visiting ballet performers from around the world.

✔ **Avery Fisher Hall** (☎ 212-721-6500) is the seat of the New York Philharmonic (see "Classical Music," later in this chapter), but it also hosts many seasonal musical events organized by Lincoln Center, such as Mostly Mozart, and concerts by students from the Juilliard School.

✔ **David H. Koch Theater** (☎ 212-870-5570) is home to the New York City Opera (see "Opera") and the New York City Ballet (see "Dance").

✔ **Alice Tully Hall** (☎ 212-875-5050), recently renovated, hosts the Chamber Music Society of Lincoln Center (☎ 212-875-5775; www.chambermusicsociety.org).

✔ **Walter Reade Theater** (☎ 212-875-5600) is home to the Film Society of Lincoln Center (www.filmlinc.com), which sponsors the New York Film Festival and other events.

✔ The **Juilliard School** (☎ 212-769-7406; www.juilliard.edu) hosts many concerts — mostly classical — as well as other performances. The quality is excellent and the prices are attractive — many concerts are free. Check the bulletin board in the hall, or call for current productions. The school also sponsors many free outdoor concerts in the summer.

✔ **Vivian Beaumont Theater** (☎ 212-362-7600) is the city's northernmost Broadway theater and shares a building with **Mitzi E. Newhouse Theater,** an Off-Broadway venue. They host a variety of shows. Together, they form the **Lincoln Center Theater** (www.lct.org).

Jazz at Lincoln Center

Despite its name, **Jazz at Lincoln Center** (JALC) is not *at* Lincoln Center: JALC is 4 blocks south in the Time Warner Center at Broadway and 60th Street on Columbus Circle (☎ 212-258-9800; www.jalc.org). Though the move was slightly downtown, the facility change was definitely a step up. Its complex on the fourth floor of Time Warner's northern tower features two amazing performance spaces, a jazz club **(Dizzy's Club Coca-Cola),** a mini jazz Hall of Fame, and a 7,000-square-foot atrium with views of Central Park.

The largest of the venues is **Rose Hall** (also known as "The House of Swing"), where you may see the Lincoln Center Jazz Orchestra, led by Wynton Marsalis. Acoustics are perfect and seating is spacious. The glittering jewel of the Center is the **Allen Room,** with its 4,500-square-foot glass backdrop behind the main stage offering glittering views of Central Park and the Manhattan night sky. It's hard to believe that what was once played in smoky basements is now presented in venues as spectacular and opulent as these.

The Center also has two outdoor spaces: a central plaza with a huge fountain and Damrosch Park toward the back. In summer, the outdoor spaces host some great series, such as Midsummer Night Swing in July and Lincoln Center Out of Doors in August, as well as many free concerts. Summer is the season of special series indoors, too — such as the JVC Jazz Festival, Mostly Mozart, and the Lincoln Center Festival — because it's the resident companies' time off.

If you want to use public transportation to get to the Center, take the 1 train to 66th Street/Lincoln Center, or take one of the following buses: M104 (running east–west on 42nd Street, north on Sixth Avenue, and south on Broadway), M5 and M7 (running up Sixth Avenue and Broadway), or M66 (across town running west on 67th Street).

Carnegie Hall

Perhaps the world's most famous performance space, **Carnegie Hall** offers everything from grand classics to the music of Ravi Shankar. The **Isaac Stern Auditorium,** the 2,804-seat main hall, welcomes visiting orchestras from across the country and around the world. Many of the world's premier soloists and ensembles give recitals here. The legendary hall is both visually and acoustically brilliant; don't miss an opportunity to experience it if there's something on the schedule that interests you.

Also part of Carnegie Hall is the intimate 268-seat **Weill Recital Hall,** usually used to showcase chamber music and vocal and instrumental recitals. Carnegie Hall has also reclaimed the ornate underground 599-seat **Zankel Hall,** which was occupied by a movie theater for 38 years.

Carnegie Hall is at 881 Seventh Ave. (at 57th Street). For schedule and ticket information, check the Web site (www.carnegiehall.org), or call ☎ 212-247-7800. Besides practice, practice, practice, another way to get to Carnegie Hall is by taking the N, Q, or R train to 57th Street.

Brooklyn Academy of Music

The city's most renowned contemporary arts institution, **Brooklyn Academy of Music** (BAM) is often at the forefront of cutting-edge theater, opera, dance, and music. Cate Blanchett, Sir Ian McKellan, Yoko Ono (with surprise guest Eric Clapton), and Patrick Stewart are just a few of the high-profile, respected performers who have sold out productions here in the past several years.

Like Lincoln Center, BAM sponsors many special series, including the prestigious Next Wave Festival in the fall, a showcase for experimental American and international artists; and DanceAfrica in spring, a choice of productions with an African heritage, ranging from traditional to modern. BAMcinématek offers some of the city's best film programming; past Cinema Club Chairs have included actors (and Brooklyn residents) Paul Giamatti and Marisa Tomei. BAM also sponsors several youth series during the year and free outdoor concerts throughout the city in the summer.

BAM is at 30 Lafayette Ave. (between Ashland Place and Felix Street; ☎ 718-636-4100; www.bam.org); the BAM Harvey Theater is nearby at 651 Fulton St. (between Ashland and Rockwell places). If you want to take public transportation, take the C to Lafayette Avenue; the Q, 2, 4, or 5 to Atlantic Avenue; or the M, N, or R to Pacific Street. If you reserve tickets 24 hours in advance at ☎ 718-636-4100 and pay $7, you can take the BAMbus, which makes multiple stops in Manhattan.

Other major concert spaces

Live music is always in the air in New York City. Here are some other venues where you can hear and see a wide variety of performing arts:

- ✔ **Radio City Music Hall,** 1260 Sixth Ave. (at 50th Street; ☎ 212-247-4777; www.radiocity.com; see map p. 176), is a gorgeous venue to see a roster of renowned artists, from Peter Gabriel to Willie Nelson.

- ✔ **Madison Square Garden,** Seventh Avenue at 32nd Street (☎ 212-465-6741; www.thegarden.com; see map p. 176), proves that only the biggest stage is appropriate for the biggest names — Pearl Jam, Lady Gaga, Jay-Z, and Bruuuuuuuce (Springsteen, that is). Bring your binoculars — that speck on the stage really is Tom Petty. Adjacent to the Garden is the **Theater at MSG** (www.theateratmsg.com), a smaller space that features a variety of acts, such as comedian Ricky Gervais and singer Teena Marie, as well as boxing matches.

- ✔ **Town Hall,** 123 W. 43rd St. (between Sixth Avenue and Broadway; ☎ 212-840-2824; www.the-townhall-nyc.org), is a lovely, medium-size theater that hosts a wide range of events — everything from world music to modern dance to solo shows to appearances by musicians and performers of every genre, ranging from Joan Baez to Garrison Keillor to Henry Rollins.

- ✔ Harlem's legendary **Apollo Theater,** 253 W. 125th St. (between Adam Clayton Powell and Frederick Douglass boulevards; ☎ 212-531-5305; www.apollotheater.org; see map p. 183), was the ultimate stage for musical legends like Smokey Robinson and the Miracles, the Temptations, and James Brown. These days, a steady stream of hip-hop, pop, and R&B acts perform at this beautifully restored theater; recent headliners have included Sharon Jones & the Dap Kings and Morrissey (yes, Morrissey). Wednesday night is the famous (and gleefully unforgiving) Amateur Night.

- ✔ An Upper West Side institution, **Symphony Space,** 2537 Broadway (at 95th Street; ☎ 212-864-1414; www.symphonyspace.org), has offered an eclectic mix of performing arts for more than three decades. The variety of shows at the **Peter Jay Sharp Theater** includes series by the World Music Institute as well as classical, rock, blues, and dance. Adjacent to the Peter Jay Sharp Theater is the **Leonard Nimoy Thalia Theater;** the film revival house known for its quirky sightlines was rescued by none other than the original Mr. Spock and has been totally renovated.

Classical Music

The **New York Philharmonic** at Avery Fisher Hall in Lincoln Center, at Broadway and 64th Street (☎ **212-875-5656;** www.nyphilharmonic. org), offers what many consider to be the city's best concerts. Ticket prices generally range from $30 to $110.

Carnegie Hall, at 57th Street and Seventh Avenue (☎ **212-247-7800;** www.carnegiehall.org; see map p. 176), is a gem in the crown of New York's music community. The price of a ticket depends on the performance; call or check the Web site for information.

The **Brooklyn Academy of Music** hosts performances of outstanding quality, some of them experimental or cutting edge. Don't let the location of this venue dissuade you from going to a show — it's quite easy to reach. See the "Brooklyn Academy of Music" section, earlier in this chapter, for specifics.

Bargemusic, in Brooklyn, at Fulton Ferry Landing, just south of the Brooklyn Bridge (☎ **718-624-2083** or 718-624-4061; www.bargemusic. org), is an internationally renowned recital room located, yes, on an actual barge. This venue boasts more than 200 first-rate chamber-music performances a year. Shows take place Wednesday through Saturday at 8 p.m. and Sunday at 3 p.m. The musicians perform on a small stage in a cherry-paneled, fireplace-lit room that holds 130 people. The music rivals what you can find in almost any other New York concert hall — and the panoramic view of Manhattan through the glass wall behind the stage can't be beat. Tickets are just $35 ($15 for students), or $40 ($20 for students) for performances by larger ensembles. Reserve *well* in advance. To get to Bargemusic, take the 2 or 3 train to Clark Street or the A or C to High Street.

Opera

The **Metropolitan Opera Company,** at the Metropolitan Opera House at Lincoln Center, Broadway and 64th Street (☎ **212-362-6000;** www.met opera.org), stages classic operas and is the world's premier opera company. The sets are works of art, and the performers are among the most famous in the world. Ticket prices range from $20 to $375.

The **New York City Opera,** in the David H. Koch Theater at Lincoln Center, Broadway and 64th Street (☎ **212-870-5570;** www.nycopera. com), stages less elaborate shows than the Metropolitan Opera Company (but from the same classic repertoire), with lower ticket prices — seats range in price from $16 to $130.

The Amato Opera Company, a Bowery fixture known for its affordable tickets, closed in 2009. However, devotees of the former company came together to form the **Amore Opera** (www.amoreopera.org). Check the Web site for the latest performance schedule and venue.

Dining after the show

It's a well-known fact that classical music and opera can make you hungry. The good news: You're in New York, and many restaurants are open past 10 or 11 p.m.

If you're in the Theater District and you don't mind being weighted down before bedtime, finish off an enormous Reuben sandwich and a slice of cheesecake at the **Carnegie Deli,** 854 Seventh Ave. (at 55th Street; ☎ 800-334-5606 or 212-757-2245).

For most after-hours dining, you may want to head downtown. The authentic bistro **Pastis,** 9 Ninth Ave. (at Little West 12th Street; ☎ 212-929-4844), is an excellent choice. In SoHo, there's raucous **Balthazar,** 80 Spring St. (at Crosby Street; ☎ 212-965-1414), and — my favorite — **Blue Ribbon,** 97 Sullivan St. (between Spring and Prince streets; ☎ 212-274-0404), which is open to 4 a.m.

In the East Village, head to **Veselka,** 144 Second Ave. (at 9th Street; ☎ 212-228-9862), a comfortable and appealing diner offering Ukrainian fare at rock-bottom prices 24/7, and **Katz's Delicatessen,** 205 E. Houston St. (at Ludlow Street; ☎ 212-254-2246), for first-class Jewish deli eats served Friday and Saturday until 3 a.m. In Chinatown, many restaurants are open late or even all night.

Music Alfresco

With summer also comes the sound of music to Central Park, where the **New York Philharmonic** and the **Metropolitan Opera** regularly entertain beneath the stars; for the current schedule, call ☎ 212-362-6000, 212-360-3444, or 212-875-5709; or visit www.lincolncenter.org.

The most active music stage in Central Park is **SummerStage,** at Rumsey Playfield, midpark around 72nd Street. SummerStage has featured everyone from James Brown to Patti Smith; recent offerings have included the Black Keys, the Beastie Boys, and Marianne Faithfull; "Viva, Verdi!" festival performances by the New York Grand Opera; cabaret nights; and more. The season usually lasts from June to August. Though most big-name shows charge admission, there are always a number of free shows (donations are always accepted). Call the hot line at ☎ 212-360-2777, or visit www.summerstage.org.

In Brooklyn, the **East River State Park** (a.k.a. the Williamsburg Waterfront, 70 Kent Ave., at North Eighth Street) has become the site of some of the most talked-about summer concerts in town. (Even Jay-Z and Beyoncé rocked out at a recent Grizzly Bear concert.) Typically, shows are scheduled in July and August; 2010 acts included the reunited Faith No More and rapper Nas. Check Ticketmaster (www.ticketmaster.com) for scheduling and tickets.

Most of the city's top museums offer monthly parties after regular hours on select nights. The **American Museum of Natural History** has generated a lot of buzz with its One Step Beyond party, co-sponsored by *The Fader* magazine at the Rose Center for Earth and Space. The **Brooklyn Museum of Art** hosts the remarkably eclectic **First Saturday** program — and it's free. You can have lots of fun at other museums as well, including the **Guggenheim's Art after Dark First Fridays** and the **Metropolitan Museum of Art** (which hosts classical performances in choice spots such as the Temple of Dendur). Check the museums' calendars for the latest events and ticket information.

Dance

The **New York City Ballet** (☎ 212-870-5570; www.nycballet.com) performs at the New York State Theater, sharing this space with the New York City Opera. The leading dance company in the world, it presents wonderfully staged productions featuring world-class dancers. New works of choreography use both classical and modern music. Their performance of *The Nutcracker* is a highlight of the Christmas season.

The **American Ballet Theater** (☎ 212-477-3030; www.abt.org) performs at the Metropolitan Opera House and shares its space with the Metropolitan Opera. The guest companies and dancers are of international renown in the world of dance.

City Center, 131 W. 55th St. (between Sixth and Seventh avenues; ☎ 877-247-0430; www.citycenter.org), hosts premier companies, such as the Alvin Ailey American Dance Theater, the Kirov Ballet, and Paul Taylor Dance Company. To get there, take the B, D, or E train to Seventh Avenue.

The **Joyce Theater,** 175 Eighth Ave. (at 19th Street; ☎ 212-242-0800; www.joyce.org), boasts performances by the likes of the Martha Graham Dance Company, Savion Glover, and MOMIX. To get there, take the C or E train to 23rd Street or the 1 to 18th Street.

Radio City Music Hall (see "Other major concert spaces" earlier in this chapter) is home to a long-standing tradition that's popular with children of all ages: the Rockettes. The renowned **Radio City Christmas Spectacular** (☎ 212-307-1000; http://christmas.radiocity.com), which runs from late November to mid-January each year is a one-of-a-kind treat. You can even take a one-hour Stage Door Tour guided by one of the famed leggy beauties!

Chapter 15

Hitting the Clubs and Bars

. . . .

In This Chapter

▶ Listening to the music

▶ Yukking it up at the comedy clubs

▶ Quenching your thirst at the hottest bars

. . . .

*I*n this chapter, I dig into the entertaining playtime options in New York City. Whether it's live jazz, rock, comedy, or cabaret, or sweating on a dance floor, sipping a martini while lounging on a plush couch, or just people-watching in a neighborhood pub, New York has plenty of choices for your evening's entertainment.

To find out what's happening and where, check out these print and online sources. *Village Voice* (www.villagevoice.com) is a free weekly that has a very good calendar with listings of the latest entertainment. Rivaling the *Voice* in quality is the weekly magazine *Time Out New York* (www.timeoutny.com). Another worthwhile resource is **Flavorpill,** available online at www.flavorpill.com (or you can sign up to receive the weekly e-mail).

A good source for information about bars is **New York on Tap** (www.newyorkontap.com), which lists and maps nearly 2,000 bars around town; it's also available as an iPhone app. Another online bar source is **www.murphguide.com**. This Web site has the latest happy-hour information and is a useful source if you're seeking out an Irish pub, of which there are many in New York.

All About the Music

From garage bands at holes in the wall with no cover charge to the world's greatest musicians onstage at Jazz at Lincoln Center, you can find something for every taste every night of the week in New York.

All that jazz

People come from all over the world to experience jazz in New York at the city's many celebrated clubs. No matter when you come, you're guaranteed to find top talent playing at a city venue. The best of New York's jazz clubs include

✔ **Birdland,** 315 West 44th St. (between Eighth and Ninth avenues; ☎ 212-581-3080; www.birdlandjazz.com; see map p. 268): This legendary club is one of the city's premier jazz spots. The big room is spacious, comfy, and classy, with an excellent sound system and top-notch talent roster any night of the week. Expect lots of accomplished big bands and jazz trios, but you can't go wrong with the Sunday night show, starring Chico O'Farrill's smokin' Afro-Cuban Jazz Orchestra.

✔ **Blue Note,** 131 W. 3rd St. (at Sixth Avenue; ☎ 212-475-8592; www.bluenote.net; see map p. 266): This Greenwich Village institution attracts some of jazz's biggest names, including Dave Brubeck, Nancy Wilson, and Chick Corea. Lately, the club seems to book more popular vocalists such as Madeleine Peyroux and smooth-jazz acts (Fourplay and Chuck Mangione, anyone?), and prices can be astronomical. The Late Night Groove Series is more interesting; Burnt Sugar was a recent act.

✔ **Dizzy's Club Coca-Cola,** Time Warner Center, 60th Street and Broadway (☎ 212-258-9595; www.jalc.org; see map p. 270): This beautiful, cozy jazz club is part of the Jazz at Lincoln Center complex in the Time Warner Center on Columbus Circle. The club attracts an interesting mix of both up-and-coming and established bands.

✔ **Lenox Lounge,** 288 Malcolm X Blvd. (Lenox Avenue; between 124th and 125th streets; ☎ 212-427-0253; www.lenoxlounge.com; see map p. 266: The club's history includes performances by such artists as Billie Holliday and Dinah Washington. Now, at this beautifully restored club, you just may hear the *next* Billie or Dinah.

✔ **Smalls,** 183 W. 10th St. (near Seventh Avenue; ☎ 212-252-5091; www.smallsjazzclub.com; see map p. 183): Jazz lovers were crestfallen when this tiny subterranean club shut down in 2002 — so much so that musicians rallied and partnered with owner Mitch Borden to reopen it five years later. Renovated but still intimate, Smalls is for dedicated jazz heads. Pay the $20 cover and stay as long as you like; you may not emerge 'til daybreak.

✔ **Smoke,** 2751 Broadway (between 105th and 106th streets; ☎ 212-864-6662; www.smokejazz.com; see map p. 270): This intimate Upper West Side club feels like a welcome throwback to more informal clubs of the past, though it's not as inexpensive as it used to be. On weekends, music covers never exceed $30; during the week after 10:30 p.m., there's usually just a $20 food and drink minimum.

✔ **St. Nick's Jazz Pub,** 773 St. Nicholas Ave. (at 149th Street; ☎ 212-283-9728; www.stnicksjazzpub.net): As unpretentious a club as you'll find, St. Nick's in Harlem's Sugar Hill district is the real deal, with live entertainment every night and never a cover. This is where Miles and Coltrane used to hang out after their own gigs. The tradition continues with Monday night jam sessions and African music on Saturday nights.

Downtown Arts and Nightlife

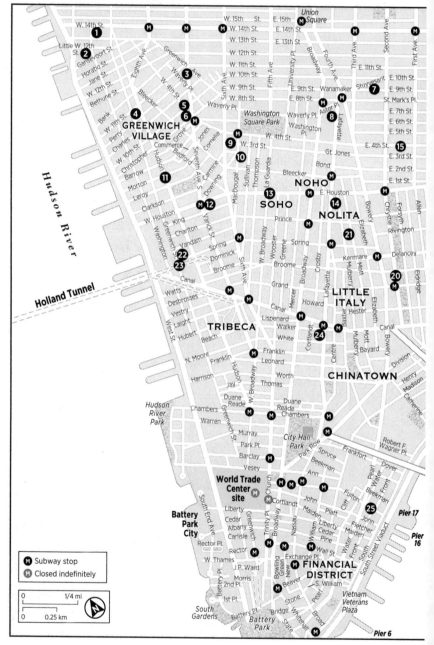

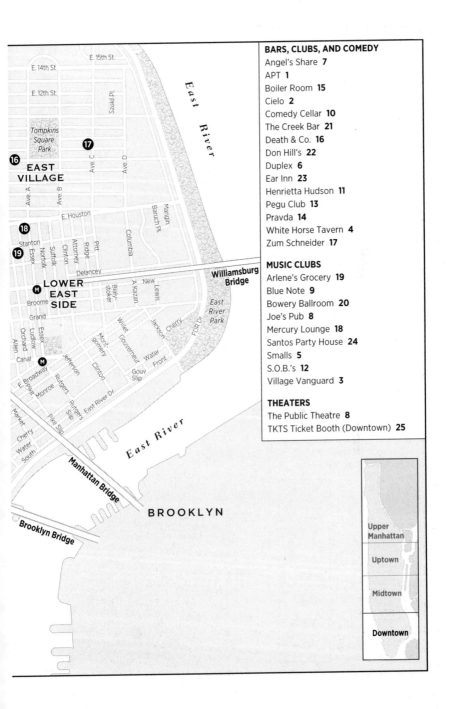

Midtown Arts and Nightlife

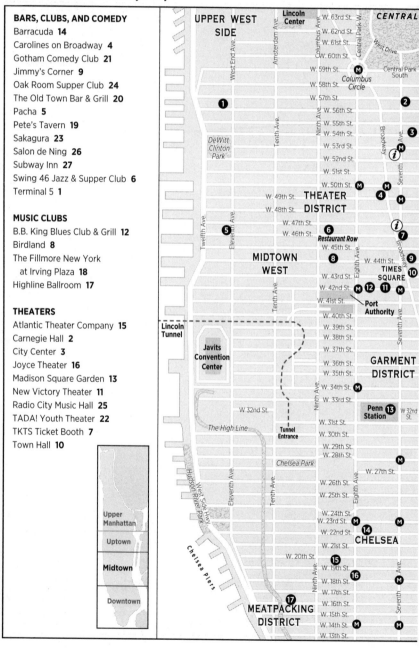

BARS, CLUBS, AND COMEDY
Barracuda **14**
Carolines on Broadway **4**
Gotham Comedy Club **21**
Jimmy's Corner **9**
Oak Room Supper Club **24**
The Old Town Bar & Grill **20**
Pacha **5**
Pete's Tavern **19**
Sakagura **23**
Salon de Ning **26**
Subway Inn **27**
Swing 46 Jazz & Supper Club **6**
Terminal 5 **1**

MUSIC CLUBS
B.B. King Blues Club & Grill **12**
Birdland **8**
The Fillmore New York
   at Irving Plaza **18**
Highline Ballroom **17**

THEATERS
Atlantic Theater Company **15**
Carnegie Hall **2**
City Center **3**
Joyce Theater **16**
Madison Square Garden **13**
New Victory Theater **11**
Radio City Music Hall **25**
TADA! Youth Theater **22**
TKTS Ticket Booth **7**
Town Hall **10**

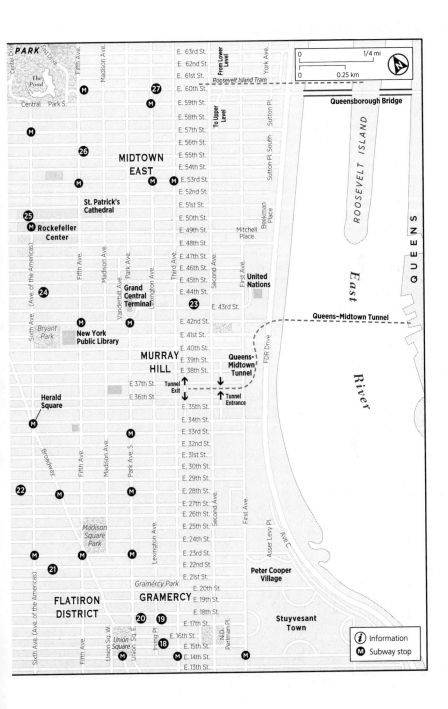

PARK

East Drive

Central Drive

The Pond

Central   Park S.

Fifth Ave.

Madison Ave.

E. 63rd St.
E. 62nd St.
E. 61st St.

From Lower Level

Roosevelt Island Tram

E. 60th St.
E. 59th St.
E. 58th St.
E. 57th St.

To Upper Level

York Ave.

Queensborough Bridge

27

E. 56th St.
E. 55th St.
E. 54th St.

Sutton Pl. South

Sutton Pl.

MIDTOWN EAST

26

E. 53rd St.
E. 52nd St.
E. 51st St.

St. Patrick's Cathedral

E. 50th St.
E. 49th St.

Beekman Place

Mitchell Place

25

Rockefeller Center

E. 48th St

Fifth Ave.

Madison Ave.

Park Ave.

Vanderbilt Ave.

Lexington Ave.

Third Ave.

E. 47th St.
E. 46th St.
E. 45th St.
E. 44th St.

Second Ave.

First Ave.

United Nations

(Ave. of the Americas)

24

Grand Central Terminal

23

E. 43rd St.

ROOSEVELT ISLAND

East

QUEENS

Sixth Ave.

Bryant Park

New York Public Library

E. 42nd St.
E. 41st St.
E. 40th St.

MURRAY HILL

E. 39th St.
E. 38th St.

Queens-Midtown Tunnel

FDR Drive

Queens-Midtown Tunnel

River

E. 37th St.
E. 36th St.

Tunnel Exit

Tunnel Entrance

Herald Square

E. 35th St.
E. 34th St.
E. 33rd St.
E. 32nd St.
E. 31st St.
E. 30th St.
E. 29th St.

Broadway

Fifth Ave.

Madison Ave.

Park Ave. S.

22

E. 28th St.
E. 27th St.
E. 26th St.
E. 25th St.

Second Ave.

First Ave.

21

Madison Square Park

E. 24th St.
E. 23rd St.
E. 22nd St.

Lexington Ave.

E. 21st St.

Asser Levy Pl.

Ave. C

Peter Cooper Village

Sixth Ave. (Ave. of the Americas)

FLATIRON DISTRICT

Gramercy Park

GRAMERCY

E. 20th St.
E. 19th St.
E. 18th St.
E. 17th St.

20 **19**

18

Stuyvesant Town

Fifth Ave.

Union Sq. W.

Union Square

Union Sq. E.

Irving Pl.

N.D. Perlman Pl.

E. 16th St.
E. 15th St.
E. 14th St.
E. 13th St.

i Information

M Subway stop

0   1/4 mi

0   0.25 km

Uptown Arts and Nightlife

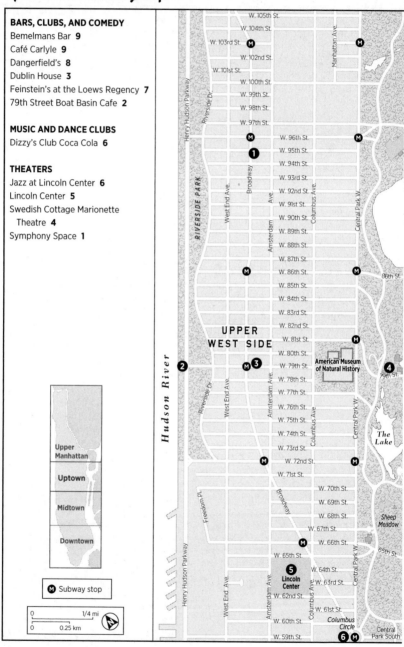

BARS, CLUBS, AND COMEDY
Bemelmans Bar **9**
Café Carlyle **9**
Dangerfield's **8**
Dublin House **3**
Feinstein's at the Loews Regency **7**
79th Street Boat Basin Cafe **2**

MUSIC AND DANCE CLUBS
Dizzy's Club Coca Cola **6**

THEATERS
Jazz at Lincoln Center **6**
Lincoln Center **5**
Swedish Cottage Marionette
   Theatre **4**
Symphony Space **1**

Upper Manhattan
Uptown
Midtown
Downtown

Ⓜ Subway stop

0   1/4 mi
0   0.25 km

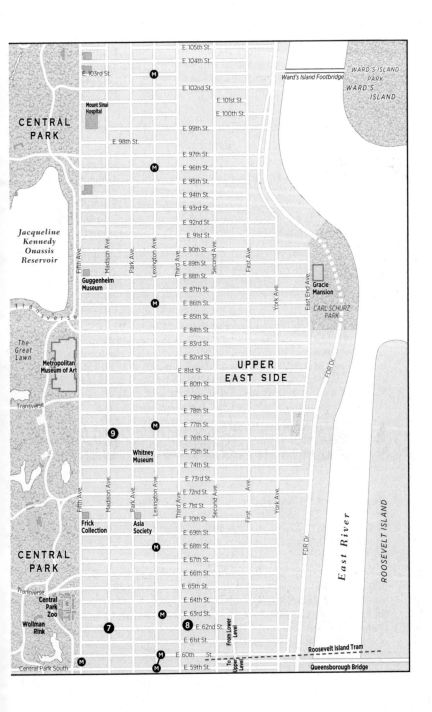

✔ **Village Vanguard,** 178 Seventh Ave. S. (☎ 212-255-4037; www.villagevanguard.com; see map p. 266): The Vanguard, established in 1935, is a New York legend. All the greats, from Miles to Monk, have played here, and their spirits live on in the high-quality talent of frequent performers such as Roy Hargrove and Bill Frisell.

It's only rock 'n' roll

Rock 'n' roll abounds in New York; here are just a few of the countless offerings:

✔ **Arlene's Grocery,** 95 Stanton St. (between Ludlow and Orchard streets; ☎ 212-995-1652; www.arlenesgrocery.net; see map p. 266): This funky little Lower East Side club has become a big name in the intimate rock club scene. With covers that rarely peak beyond $10, it's a bargain as well. Need to unleash your inner rock star? Monday night's Live Rock and Roll Karaoke is for you.

✔ **Bowery Ballroom,** 6 Delancey St. (at Bowery; ☎ 212-533-2111; www.boweryballroom.com; see map p. 266): There's plenty of room in this club, but it still has the feel of a more intimate venue. With great sightlines and sound, the Bowery Ballroom attracts excellent alt-rock talent.

✔ **The Fillmore New York at Irving Plaza,** 17 Irving Place (at 15th Street; ☎ 212-777-6800; www.irvingplaza.com; see map p. 268): Corporate concert promoter Live Nation changed the name and made some upgrades, but this midsize music hall is still a prime stop for national-name rock bands. Recent shows include Baaba Maal, Echo & the Bunnymen, and, er, Ratt. The best seats can be found in the upstairs balcony, but come early for a spot.

✔ **Mercury Lounge,** 217 E. Houston St. (at Essex Street and Avenue A; ☎ 212-260-4700; www.mercuryloungenyc.com; see map p. 266): Another excellent intimate spot for good-quality, hard-edge rock 'n' roll, and it doesn't cost a fortune. As a result, the Merc is always packed.

✔ **Music Hall of Williamsburg,** 66 N. 6th St. (between Wythe and Kent avenues; ☎ 718-486-5400; www.musichallofwilliamsburg.com; see map p. 222): Consider it the Bowery Ballroom across the East River, drawing performers such as Broken Social Scene and Corinne Bailey Rae.

✔ **Terminal 5,** 610 W. 56th St. (between 11th and 12th avenues; ☎ 212-260-4700; www.terminal5nyc.com; see map p. 268): The baby jewel in the Bowery Presents crown, this sister to the Bowery Ballroom and the Mercury Lounge is more than three times larger than the two of them put together. With three floors and a capacity of 3,000, Terminal 5 hosts the bigger draws on the alt-rock scene, such as the Gossip, Dirty Projectors, and Massive Attack.

The best of the rest

What follows are clubs that are tough to classify; on one night they may feature jazz or blues, and on another night you may hear cutting-edge rock or world music.

- ✔ **B.B. King Blues Club & Grill,** 237 W. 42nd St. (between Seventh and Eighth avenues; ☎ 212-997-4144; www.bbkingblues.com; see map p. 268): Despite its name, B.B. King's rarely sticks to the blues. Here you can find big-name talent from pop, funk, soul, and rock, more from the past than from the present. Take your pick of brunches: Saturday Beatles or Sunday gospel?

- ✔ **Brooklyn Bowl,** 61 Wythe St. (between North 11th and 12th streets, in Williamsburg; ☎ 718-963-3369; www.brooklynbowl.com; see map p. 222): Believe me when I say that you've never seen a bowling alley like this. Not only does it have 16 state-of-the-art lanes and bar food by Blue Ribbon (see p. 134), you can also catch shows by a variety of rock, pop, and hip-hop acts. Beloved emcee Q-Tip and Roots drummer ?uestlove often show up to move the crowd from behind the DJ decks, and Hip Hop Karaoke (www.hiphopkaraoke nyc.com) is every Friday night.

- ✔ **Highline Ballroom,** 431 W. 16th St. (between Ninth and Tenth avenues; ☎ 212-414-5994; www.highlineballroom.com; see map p. 268): This bi-level, midsize venue offers table seating upstairs (first-come, first-seated basis, with a $10 food-and-drink minimum) and solid sightlines from everywhere. The diverse roster of acts ranges from the B-52s and the Brand New Heavies (yes, I know it's not the 1990s anymore) to hip-hop artists such as the Roots and Common.

- ✔ **The Knitting Factory,** 361 Metropolitan Ave. (between North Fourth and Fifth streets; ☎ 347-529-6696; http://bk.knittingfactory.com; see map p. 222): In perhaps another marker of Brooklyn's elevation to the cool place to be, this premier avant-garde music venue recently moved to Williamsburg. Expect the gamut, from experimental jazz to acoustic folk to bleeding-edge rock.

- ✔ **S.O.B.'s** 204 Varick St. (at Houston Street; ☎ 212-243-4940; www.sobs.com; see map p. 266): If you think music is for dancing, visit S.O.B.'s, the city's top global-music venue, specializing in Brazilian, Caribbean, and Latin sounds. The packed house dances and sings along to calypso, samba, mambo, Afrobeat, reggae, or other grooves. It's very popular, so book in advance, especially if you want table seating. DJ Rekha's bangin' Basement Bhangra packs 'em in on the first Thursday of every month. If you want a mellower vibe, there's a family-friendly Bossa Nova Brunch on Sundays.

Life is a cabaret

Want the quintessential New York night-on-the-town experience? Take in a cabaret. But be prepared to part with your greenbacks; covers can range from $10 to $75 along with a two-drink or dinner-check minimum. Always reserve ahead. New York's top cabarets include

- ✔ **Café Carlyle,** at the Carlyle, 781 Madison Ave. (at 76th Street; ☎ 212-744-1600; see map p. 270): The recently renovated club features classy acts such as Betty Buckley and Elaine Stritch. Woody Allen also shows up to jam with the Eddy Davis New Orleans Jazz Band on Monday nights. The room is intimate and as swanky as they come. Expect a high tab: Music charges are a minimum of $75; with dinner, two people can easily spend upwards of $300. But if you're looking for the best of the best, look no further.

- ✔ **Feinstein's at the Loews Regency,** at the Loews Regency Hotel, 540 Park Ave. (at 61st Street; ☎ 212-339-4095; www.feinsteinsat theregency.com; see map p. 270): If you don't catch song impresario Michael Feinstein playing here at the club he opened, don't despair — high-wattage talent is always on tap. Recent performers include Alan Cumming, Jane Krakowski, and Bob Dorough.

- ✔ **Joe's Pub,** at the Public Theater, 425 Lafayette St. (between Astor Place and 4th Street; ☎ 212-539-8778 or 212-967-7555; www.joes pub.com; see map p. 266): This isn't exactly your daddy's cabaret. Still, this beautiful and popular club, named for the legendary Joseph Papp, is everything a New York cabaret should be. The multilevel space serves up an Italian menu and top-notch entertainment from a more eclectic mix of talent than you'll find on any other cabaret calendar.

- ✔ **Oak Room Supper Club,** at the Algonquin Hotel, 59 W. 44th St. (between Fifth and Sixth avenues; ☎ 212-840-6800; see map p. 268): The Oak Room is one of the city's most elegant and sophisticated spots for cabaret, and that's saying a lot. You can almost always be sure that top-rated talent is headlining here.

New York Comedy Is No Joke

Something about New York makes it a ripe breeding ground for comedians. The names of those who got their start here, from Dangerfield to Seinfeld, are like a "who's who" of comedy. And you never know, the nebbishy guy or girl at the mic may be the next Richard Pryor or Ellen DeGeneres. New York's top comedy clubs include

- ✔ **Carolines on Broadway,** 1626 Broadway (between 49th and 50th streets; ☎ 212-757-4100; www.carolines.com; see map p. 268): New York's biggest and highest-profile comedy club attracts the hottest headliners, including Charlie Murphy (brother of Eddie), Paul Mooney, and Gilbert Gottfried.

- ✔ **Comedy Cellar,** 117 Macdougal St. (between Minetta Lane and West 3rd Street; ☎ 212-254-3480; www.comedycellar.com; see map p. 266): This intimate, subterranean comedy club is a throwback to the days of the raw, hard-edge stand-up comedy that spawned Lenny Bruce and Richard Pryor. Big-name unscheduled drop-ins are frequent; think Dave Chappelle, Dave Attell, and Chris Rock.

✔ **Dangerfield's,** 1118 First Ave. (between 61st and 62nd streets; ☎ **212-593-1650;** www.dangerfieldscomedyclub.com; see map p. 270): If Tony Soprano were a comedy fan, this would be his kind of place. Slick, mature, and Vegas-like, Dangerfield's gets plenty of respect.

✔ **Gotham Comedy Club,** 208 W. 23rd St. (between Seventh and Eighth avenues; ☎ **212-367-9000;** www.gothamcomedyclub.com; see map p. 268): This is New York's comedy club of the moment. The luxurious Art Deco–style club provides the backdrop for TV shows such as Comedy Central's *Live at Gotham*.

Hanging Out in New York's Best Bars

You won't have to search far to find a place to have a cocktail in New York. On every block you'll find bars, sometimes two or three. And they come in just about every variety, from sleek and hip to dark and gritty. Check out this small sampling of some of my favorite New York bars.

For creative cocktails

✔ **Angel's Share,** 8 Stuyvesant St., second floor (☎ **212-777-5415;** see map p. 266): Once upon a time, I would never have revealed this tucked-away bar in a guidebook. But the secret's long been out, and you may as well slip into this gem to see what the fuss is about. (Walk though the unmarked door to your left as you reach the top of the stairs, in the restaurant Village Yokocho.) Cocktails are made with care here, and service is classy. Bring a date.

✔ **Bemelmans Bar,** in The Carlyle, A Rosewood Hotel, 35 E. 76th St. (at Madison Avenue; ☎ **212-744-1600;** see map p. 270): The bar is a beauty with its whimsical murals painted by children's book illustrator Ludwig Bemelmans, who created the Madeline books. And they make beautiful (and pricey) cocktails to match the creative setting; some date from the 1860s.

✔ **Death & Co.,** 433 E. 6th St. (between First Avenue and Avenue A; ☎ **212-388-0882;** www.deathandcompany.com; see map p. 266): This speakeasy-style bar is currently *the* place to get schooled in mixology. If you can get a seat, the trick will be to stay on it after you've had one or two Strange Brews or (heaven help you) Electric Kool-Aid Acid Tests.

✔ **Pegu Club,** 77 W. Houston St. (between Wooster Street and West Broadway; ☎ **212-473-7348;** www.peguclub.com; see map p. 266): Mixologist and owner Audrey Saunders, formerly of Bemelmans Bar in The Carlyle, makes magic with cocktails. Pegu Club is her own little downtown gathering spot where she can even better showcase her immense talents. The cocktails — perfectly poured, stirred, and shaken — change seasonally and will astound you with their creativity.

Smoking has been illegal in all restaurants and bars in New York City (except for a few cigar bars) for the better part of a decade. So, if you get the urge, join the huddled (and shivering, in the winter) masses outside the bar, in what some not-so-fondly call the "Bloomberg Lounge" (after Mayor Mike, who pushed through the antismoking laws).

For old-world charm

✔ **Dublin House,** 225 W. 79th St. (between Broadway and Amsterdam Avenue; ☎ 212-874-9528; www.dublinhousenyc.com; see map p. 270): For years, like a welcoming beacon, the Dublin House's neon harp has blinked invitingly. This old pub is a no-frills Irish saloon and the perfect spot for a drink after visiting the Museum of Natural History or Central Park. The Guinness is cheap and drawn perfectly by the very able and sometimes crusty bartenders.

✔ **Ear Inn,** 326 Spring St. (between Greenwich and Washington streets; ☎ 212-431-9750; www.earinn.com; see map p. 266): This cluttered old, 1870-established pub is a cranky relief in super-chic SoHo.

✔ **The Old Town Bar & Grill,** 45 E. 18th St. (between Broadway and Park Avenue; ☎ 212-529-6732; www.oldtownbar.com; see map p. 268): The bar where food (get the burger) is shuttled to customers via a dumbwaiter from the basement kitchen has been featured on film and TV (the opening credits of Letterman in his NBC days).

✔ **Pete's Tavern,** 129 E. 18th St. (at Irving Place; ☎ 212-473-7676; www.petestavern.com; see map p. 268): This place is so old it's said to have opened when Lincoln was still president.

✔ **White Horse Tavern,** 567 Hudson St. (at 11th Street; ☎ 212-243-9260; see map p. 266): This circa-1880 pub is where Dylan Thomas supposedly had his very last drink before becoming a bar legend.

For cultural exchange

✔ **The Creek Bar,** 240 Mulberry St. (between Spring and Prince streets; ☎ 212-431-4635; www.eightmilecreek.com; see map p. 266): Located below Australian restaurant Eight Mile Creek, this bar serves up Aussie beer, wine, music, and rugby and cricket matches.

✔ **Pravda,** 281 Lafayette St. (between Houston and Prince streets; ☎ 212-226-4944; www.pravdany.com; see map p. 266): You can find more than 70 vodkas here, served with caviar and chicken Kiev. Don't overlook the specialty cocktails; the pear martini is a winner.

✔ **Sakagura,** 211 E. 43rd St. (between Second and Third avenues; ☎ 212-953-7253; www.sakagura.com; see map p. 268): Sake bars are popping up all over town, but few are as fun to find as this one. Make your way through a standard office-building lobby and down a staircase; your reward will be a peaceful place with a treasure-trove of 200 sakes.

✔ **Zum Schneider,** 107 Avenue C (at 7th Street; ☎ **212-598-1098;** www.zumschneider.com; see map p. 266): This authentic indoor German beer garden is best enjoyed on a spring day, when you can sit on the benches and catch a breeze. Somehow steins of beer go down very easily here.

For dive-bar aficionados

✔ **Jimmy's Corner,** 140 W. 44th St. (between Broadway and Sixth Avenue; ☎ **212-221-9510;** see map p. 268): Jimmy's is a tough guy's joint that has happily survived the Disney-fication of Times Square. Beer is cheap and drinks aren't fancy, so skip the theme bars and restaurants in the area and go for an after-theater pop at Jimmy's instead.

✔ **Subway Inn,** 143 E. 60th St. (at Lexington Avenue; ☎ **212-223-8929;** see map p. 268): This dive has been around for more than 70 years, and it has the layers of funk to prove it. No matter what time of day, it's always as dark as midnight inside the Subway Inn.

For drinks with a view

✔ **Salon de Ning,** at the Peninsula Hotel, 700 Fifth Ave. (at 55th Street; ☎ **212-956-2888;** www.salondening.com; see map p. 268): The views of midtown Manhattan are awesome here and make the steep price of the drinks easier to take.

✔ **79th Street Boat Basin Cafe,** 79th Street at the Hudson River (☎ **212-496-5542;** see map p. 270): As you sip your cocktail, enjoy a beautiful sunset and watch boats bob on the river; you may just forget you're in New York for a moment. Open from May to September.

For gay and lesbian nightlife

✔ **Barracuda,** 275 W. 22nd St. (between Seventh and Eighth avenues; ☎ **212-645-8613;** see map p. 268): In the heart of Chelsea, this bar is regularly voted best gay bar in New York by the various local GLBT publications.

✔ **Boiler Room,** 86 E. 4th St. (between First and Second avenues; ☎ **212-254-7536;** see map p. 266): This is New York's favorite gay dive bar and a fun East Village hangout.

✔ **Duplex,** 61 Christopher St. (at Seventh Avenue; ☎ **212-255-5438;** www.theduplex.com; see map p. 266): High camp is the norm at this gay cabaret and piano bar, still going after 50 years. It once hosted the likes of Woody Allen and Joan Rivers in their early stand-up careers.

✔ **Henrietta Hudson,** 438 Hudson St. (at Morton Street; ☎ **212-924-3347;** www.henriettahudsons.com; see map p. 266): This popular lipstick lesbian hangout has a great jukebox and a DJ on weekends.

Some of the hottest "clubs" are actually traveling parties that alight in various spots depending on the day, making them hard for visitors to find. Various publications — *Time Out New York* and the *Village Voice,* as well as the GLBT-specific *Next Magazine* (www.nextmagazine.com), lesbian magazine *GO Magazine* (www.gomag.com), and others I list in Chapter 6 — provide the best up-to-the-minute club information. Another source is the Lesbian, Gay, Bisexual & Transgender Community Center site at www.gaycenter.org.

Hitting the Dance Clubs and Getting Beyond the Velvet Rope

Dance-club fame is transient; one year a club can be white hot, and the next year it's not even good enough for the bridge-and-tunnel crowd. These dance clubs, as of this writing, are closer to the hot variety. Keep in mind that many clubs have dress codes; leave your sneakers, shorts, flip-flops, and T-shirts at the hotel. Well-dressed folks will always slide past the velvet ropes first.

✔ **APT,** 419 W. 13th St. (near Washington Street; ☎ **212-414-4245;** www.aptnyc.com; see map p. 266): Since 2000, APT has been holding it down with dope beats in a swanky unmarked space. (Ring the buzzer.) It's become a little hit-or-miss, but if the names DJ Premier, Prince Paul, or Bobbito Garcia mean anything to you, this is your kind of club. Check the Web site to see who's behind the decks before you go.

✔ **Cielo,** 18 Little W. 12th St. (between Ninth Avenue and Washington Street; ☎ **212-645-5700;** www.cieloclub.com; see map p. 266): At Cielo, you'll find the best sound system of any small club in New York. House is big here, and they bring in some of the best DJs from around the globe. The renowned Louis Vega spins on Wednesdays. An authentic disco ball rotates above a sunken dance floor.

✔ **Don Hill's,** 511 Greenwich St. (at Spring Street; ☎ **212-219-2850;** www.donhills.com; see map p. 266): This is a long-standing dive that pulls a crowd as sexually and ethnically diverse as the music and campy parties it features. Mondo Indie Dance Party? Reggaeholics? Metal Meltdown? Truly something for everyone.

✔ **Pacha,** 618 W. 46th St. (near 11th Avenue; ☎ **212-209-7500;** www.pachanyc.com; see map p. 268): It doesn't get any hotter than Pacha, a four-floor megaclub that hosts a revolving door of world-class DJs such as Carl Cox and Victor Calderone.

- ✔ **Santos Party House,** 96 Lafayette St. (between White and Walker streets; ☎ **212-584-5492;** www.santospartyhouse.com; see map p. 266): It delivers exactly what the name promises: a party, especially if you like hip-hop, reggae, and old-school R&B. The industry's freshest DJs think so, too. Expect an eclectic, fun-loving crowd.

- ✔ **Swing 46 Jazz & Supper Club,** 349 W. 46th St. (between Eighth and Ninth avenues; ☎ **212-262-9554;** www.swing46.com; see map p. 268): As its name suggests, the music here, mostly live, is swing. And if swing dancing is new to you, lessons are offered.

New York nightlife starts late and finishes *really* late. Things don't get going until at least 11 p.m. Most places don't take credit cards, so bring cash (or be prepared to fork over a high transaction charge at an in-house ATM). Cover charges can range from $7 to $30 and often increase as the night goes on. The best source for club information is the weekly *Time Out New York* magazine. It lists cover charges for the week's big events and gives sound advice on the type of music *and* the type of crowd each event attracts. (Refer to this chapter's introduction for additional sources of entertainment information.)

Part VI
The Part of Tens

"Ooo — look at this — we've got a perfect view of
the Chrysler Building, the Buick Building and
the Chevy Building."

In this part . . .

1 give you a heads-up about some New York experiences you should avoid and some you should definitely seek out. I also offer the lowdown on some of the city's iconic foods and eating experiences.

Chapter 16

The Top Ten Cheap New York City Experiences

In This Chapter
- Riding the subway from New York to Thailand
- Feasting your eyes and feeding your head
- Biking the Hudson

As I mention in Chapter 4, New York is a spendy town, but there are some strategies you can use to have a wallet-friendly trip. Just as there are many opportunities to empty your bank account, you can also find many unique things to do that are rich in fun but not in price. Check out some of my favorite inexpensive (and free!) New York experiences.

Befriend a New Yorker

Don't be bashful. New Yorkers are friendlier and more helpful than their reputations suggest. One of the best ways to find out is to take a free walking tour with a **Big Apple Greeter** (☎ **212-669-8159;** www.big applegreeter.org). This visitor welcome program matches one of its 300 volunteers (who conduct tours in 22 languages) with visitors who submit requests at least a month in advance of their arrival. Tours typically last two to four hours, and your new New York buddy can show you around specific neighborhoods at your request, make personal recommendations, and take you off the beaten path to highlight the everyday things that makes the city so great.

Ride the International Express

The no. 7 train is sometimes referred to as the "International Express." Take it out of Manhattan and through the borough of Queens, and you pass through one ethnic neighborhood after another, from Indian to Thai, from Peruvian to Colombian, from Chinese to Korean. Get off at any stop along the way and sample the local cuisine; it's the cheapest round-the-world trip you can take. Built by immigrants in the early

1900s, the no. 7 Interborough Rapid Transit (IRT) brought those same immigrants to homes on the outer fringes of New York City. That tradition has continued as immigrants from around the world have settled close by the no. 7's elevated tracks.

In 1999, the Queens Council on the Arts nominated the no. 7 for designation of a National Millennium Trail, and it was chosen as representative of the American immigrant experience by the White House Millennium Council, the U.S. Department of Transportation, and the Rails-to-Trails Conservancy. For more about the International Express, visit the **Queens Council on the Arts** Web site at www.queenscouncilarts.org; for details about the annual springtime art festival along the line, check the **Queens Art Express** Web site at www.queensartexpress.com.

Party at the Brooklyn Museum

Museum parties have become pretty popular in New York; a few of the largest museums host monthly blowouts that rival some of the city's better nightclubs. (DJ Kid Koala recently rocked the house at the American Museum of Natural History's One Step Beyond party, cosponsored by *The Fader* magazine.) But one of the first parties in town — and still consistently the most eclectic — is First Saturdays at the **Brooklyn Museum,** 200 Eastern Parkway (☎ **718-638-5000;** www.brooklynmuseum.org; Subway: 2 or 3 to Eastern Parkway/Brooklyn Museum). From 4 or 5 to 11 p.m. on the first Saturday of every month, the museum presents a slew of free programs, including concerts and dance parties. A recent First Saturday marked the opening of an exhibition by Japanese pop artist Takashi Murakami with a "cosplay" photo contest (competitors dressed as anime and manga characters), traditional Japanese drumming, Brooklyn-based Japanese rock bands, Japan's top hip-hop DJ, and screenings of the anime film *Kiki's Delivery Service.* Family-friendly First Saturdays offer something for everyone, which is why it's perhaps the most beloved museum party in the city.

Explore the (Free) Art in Queens

Most city museums offer hours when admission is free to all, but if you're visiting for just a few days, your trip plans may not coincide with those times. Want your fix of modern and contemporary art but *don't* want to shell out $20 for MoMA, the Guggenheim, or the Whitney? For no more than the cost of subway fare, you can get it at the **Fisher Landau Center for Art,** 38–27 30th St. (☎ **718-937-0727;** www.flcart.org; Subway: N to 39/Beebe Avenue), in Long Island City, Queens. Just ten minutes from Midtown and open Thursday through Monday from noon to 5 p.m., this little-known free exhibition space features many boldface names from the personal collection of Emily Fisher Landau. Recent shows have presented works by Jasper Johns, Matthew Barney, Jenny Holzer, Cy Twombly, and Kiki Smith.

Long Island City is also home to the **P.S. 1 Contemporary Art Center,** 22–25 Jackson Ave. (www.ps1.org), where the suggested admission is $5 and hours are similar to the Fisher Landau Center's. Or, if the weather is fine, visit outdoor **Socrates Sculpture Park,** Broadway at Vernon Boulevard (☎ **718-956-1819;** www.socratessculpturepark.org; Subway: N to Broadway), in Long Island City, where there's no admission charge to see the exhibits or the fabulous view of the East Side of Manhattan. You also find free concerts, exercise classes, children's art classes, and outdoor movie screenings there in the summer.

Be a Culture Vulture

Art isn't the only cultural experience you can enjoy on the cheap in New York. During the summer, you have lots of choices for free outdoor music (Central Park SummerStage) and theater (Shakespeare in the Park) performances (see Chapter 14 for more details).

Film fans are also well provided for with a number of free outdoor screenings in the city's parks. Bryant Park is the site of a popular summer film festival, usually featuring classic movies; check www.bryantpark.org for the calendar and plan to grab a spot early and eat sandwiches from 'wichcraft (see Chapter 10) for dinner.

New York is also a great literary town, and the number of free readings and author signings is mind-boggling. Bookstores such as **McNally Jackson** (see Chapter 12) and several **Barnes & Noble** branches are known for their author appearances; free (or nearly free) readings and lectures are also offered everywhere from the New York Public Library to downtown bars. Check *Time Out New York* (www.timeoutny.com) or *New York* magazine (www.nymag.com) for listings.

Roller-Skate Like It's 1979

New York has changed tremendously in the past three decades, but artifacts of the past lurk around every corner . . . or roller-boogie past you in plain sight. You can get a taste of what it was like when Michael Jackson was still living off the wall and even Rod Stewart was prancing around in spandex and gold lamé by joining the free summer skate circle in Central Park, a New York institution since it began in 1977. Mid-April through late October on weekends from 2:30 to 6:30 p.m., head to the middle of the park from 72nd Street — your ears will guide you to the action. You see some people whizzing around on Rollerblades, but you are more impressed by the old-schoolers on four-wheel skates, seemingly oblivious to the passage of time and jamming like it's still 1979. This is the last refuge for those who still like to shake their groove thang on wheels. Check it out before this, too, is legend.

Tour Little Italy in the Bronx

Taking a trip to Little Italy in the Bronx has grown in popularity. Since the downsizing of Little Italy in Manhattan, the area centered on Arthur Avenue is the place to go for old-fashioned Italian charm, food, and ambience. You know you've arrived on Arthur Avenue when you smell the fresh-baked bread, stacks of *bacala* (dried salt cod), aromatic sausages and cheeses, and tomato sauce. Browse the markets and have lunch at one of the local restaurants or pizzerias followed by cappuccino or espresso at a cafe. You can combine your visit with a trip to the nearby Bronx Zoo. To get to Arthur Avenue, take the D or 4 train to Fordham Road, and then the 12 bus east; or take the 2 or 5 train to Pelham Parkway, and then the 12 bus west; or take the Metro North Harlem Line to Fordham Road followed by the shuttle bus to Belmont and Bronx Zoo.

Take the High Line

Not all the boom-time development in New York was commercially oriented. One space that was transformed for the public good is the **High Line,** an abandoned elevated 1930s railway line that runs from Gansevoort Street to 34th Street. The High Line District was created in 2002 to transform it into a free public promenade, similar to Paris's promenade plantée (also a former elevated rail viaduct, now one of that city's most popular parks). Since the first section of the park (from Gansevoort to 20th Street) opened in June 2009, it has become one of the city's most beloved attractions, drawing more than two million visitors in its first year. Its success is well deserved, as it is an incredibly special way to view the city. At press time, construction was underway on the second section, which is expected to open sometime in 2011. Check the Web site (www.thehighline.org) for updates.

Bike along the Hudson River

If walking is just not enough exercise for you, rent a bike and ride the length of Manhattan via the Hudson River Park. You can bike from Battery Park to Fort Tryon Park near the George Washington Bridge. Although detours along the way may take you on and off bike paths, don't let them deter you from a remarkable bike ride. Along the route, you pass the World Trade Center site, the far West Village, Chelsea Piers, the USS *Intrepid,* Riverside Park, and the George Washington Bridge. You can rent bikes from **Bike and Roll,** 557 12th Ave. (at 43rd Street; Pier 84, Hudson River Park; ☎ **866-736-8224** or 212-260-0400; www.bikeandroll.com); they cost $8 to $20 per hour, $25 to $69 per day.

Wander the Streets on Sunday Morning

I've saved the best for last. The city has a special feel on Sunday mornings. You may spot some jet-lagged tourists, a few college kids doing the walk of shame, and smeared-mascara clubbers who've broken dawn, but the streets are generally deserted. Things are so quiet, it's almost eerie. I feel as if I have the city to myself, which is exhilarating. Is it worth getting an early wake-up call? You decide. Or it may be easier to join the clubbers and not go to bed at all on Saturday night. . . .

Chapter 17

The Top Ten Essential New York City Eating Experiences

In This Chapter

▶ Noshing New York's surf, turf, and dessert

▶ Eating a slice standing up

▶ Having your chicken . . . and waffles, too

*N*o matter what your budget, you find it almost impossible to go hungry in New York. But do you want to eat what you can eat any day of the week back home, or do you want a uniquely New York eating experience? Read on for ten essential New York eating experiences.

A Slice of Pizza

The best classic slice in New York is a matter of perpetual debate, but most reasonable people agree that it's meant to be eaten standing up, folded to capture the grease before it stains your clothes. In Manhattan, the quintessential New York slice is served at **Famous Joe's Pizza,** 7 Carmine St. (☎ **212-366-1182**), in Greenwich Village; the joint is open until the wee hours, so it's particularly satisfying for late-night cravings.

Bagel with a Schmear

If there's anything more simply satisfying than a fresh, piping-hot bagel topped with a schmear of cream cheese, I don't know what it is. Many people love it with lox, tomato, and onion; it's one of the most popular breakfast items in New York. You can find bagels and lox in diners and delis all over the city, but the quality isn't assured; go to the specialists to get it right. Head to **Ess-a-Bagel,** downtown at 359 First Ave. (☎ **212-260-2252**), and in Midtown at 831 Third Ave. (☎ **212-980-1010**); the bagels are so hefty that I rarely make it through an entire one, but I love to try. If you need it with lox, though, your spot is **Barney Greengrass,** 541 Amsterdam Ave. (at 86th Street; ☎ 212-724-4707), if you're uptown, or **Russ & Daughters,** 179 E. Houston St. (between Allen and Orchard streets; ☎ 212-475-4880), if you're downtown.

Chicken and Waffles

You're out late, the sky is getting lighter, and you can't decide whether you want dinner or breakfast. You can't resist the fried chicken, but waffles sound good, too. So you try a little of both together — maple syrup melding with hot sauce, sweet with savory. And that is the purported legend behind this funky combination. If you're visiting from Chicago, Los Angeles, or Atlanta, where you can also find chicken and waffles, you may wonder what claim New York has to this dish. Try its origins: Its birthplace is said to be Wells Chicken and Waffles in Harlem in 1938. Wells is long gone, but a number of Harlem restaurants continue what Wells started. The most popular is **Amy Ruth's,** 113 W. 116th St. (☎ 212-280-8779), where you can get not only chicken and waffles but also other novel combinations such as catfish and waffles and steak and waffles.

Chino-Latino

There used to be countless Cuban-Chinese restaurants in Manhattan, most found on the Upper West Side. The boom began in the late 1950s after the Cuban revolution and the beginning of the Castro regime. Chinese Cubans immigrated to New York and opened up restaurants serving both Cantonese-style Chinese food and traditional Cuban food. A few are left, some pairing Chinese dishes with other Latin American cuisines. Two of the most popular are the old-school **La Caridad 78,** 2199 Broadway (☎ 212-874-2780), setting the standard since the '60s, and **Flor de Mayo,** 484 Amsterdam Ave. (☎ 212-787-3388), where you can order an egg roll followed by Peruvian *seco de res* (beef stew). Try one before they disappear.

Dining in a Diner

Yes, I realize that the diner is an American institution, not just a New York one. But New York diners are a breed apart. Largely owned and operated by Greek immigrants since the 1940s (which explains the inclusion of menu items such as gyros and spanakopita alongside the standard pancakes and BLTs), diners in the city are the definition of democratic, equally welcoming to the well-heeled and the round-heeled. The food is reliably cheap and filling; the ambience is "only in New York." They're also a dying breed. I enjoy stopping into wherever looks clean and appealing, but two to check out are **Eisenberg's Sandwich Shop,** 174 Fifth Ave. (between 21st and 22nd streets; ☎ 212-675-5096), a luncheonette where time has slowed to a crawl, and **Waverly Restaurant,** 385 Sixth Ave. (at Waverly Place; ☎ 212-675-3181), in Greenwich Village, which is a bit pricey and hipsterish for a classic diner but still retains some old charm.

The Hot Dog

Let me be frank with you: I am not a fan of the street-cart hot dog. But you can find the carts all over town and you may be tempted to try one just to say you did, so go for it — it's definitely a New York experience. For a more memorable meal, however, take the subway out to Coney Island and sample a **Nathan's Famous** dog right on the boardwalk at 1310 Surf Ave. (☎ 718-946-2202). Just don't do it during the Fourth of July hot-dog-eating contest — otherwise, it may be memorable for all the wrong reasons. If you can't make it to Coney, another option is **Gray's Papaya,** 2090 Broadway (at 72nd Street; ☎ 212-799-0243), on the Upper West Side, or at the corner of Sixth Avenue and 8th Street (☎ 212-260-3532), in Greenwich Village. The "Recession Special," two hot dogs with unlimited toppings and a drink, is the special whether the country is in a recession or not.

The New York Cheesecake

The classic New York cheesecake is harder to find than you may expect. Many city dessert makers have claimed to bring together the requisite qualities — creaminess, lightness, the right level of sweetness — but as with bagels and pizza, there's a great diversity of opinion when it comes to crowning the best. I have to disagree with the most common answer, **Junior's,** 1515 Broadway (at West 45th Street; ☎ 212-302-2000); the cheesecake is fine but not spectacular. A better contender is **Eileen's Special Cheesecake,** 17 Cleveland Place (between Spring and Kenmare streets; ☎ 212-966-5585).

The New York Oyster

There was a time when New York was more the Big Oyster than the Big Apple. The local harbor beds were overflowing with oysters and the mollusk helped feed the city. But you don't want to eat an oyster from New York Harbor these days (for obvious reasons). Instead, head to the **Grand Central Oyster Bar & Restaurant,** in Grand Central Station (☎ 212-490-6650), where, since 1913, oysters have been the specialty. Order oysters on the half shell from Rhode Island, Oregon, Baja California, British Columbia, or even the waters of Long Island Sound. With the Metro North commuter trains rumbling in the station along with the cacophonous din of other diners and the magnificent tiled ceiling of the restaurant above, try to imagine that you're sucking down a New York oyster in the days when you could actually *eat* a New York oyster. It's not as big a reach as you may think.

The New York Strip

The restaurant scene in New York is extremely volatile, but one constant is the steakhouse. The steakhouse doesn't have to worry about trends or gimmicks. Sure, there were some rocky moments when red meat was considered a no-no by the diet police, but the steakhouse weathered the storm and not only survived but thrived. Some of New York's oldest restaurants are steakhouses, and for good reason: They keep it simple. They serve quality, properly aged meat, cooked perfectly and presented in a no-nonsense, no-frills manner. Places like **Keens,** 72 W. 36th St. (☎ **212-947-3636**), established in 1885; **Peter Luger,** 178 Broadway (☎ **718-387-7400**), in Williamsburg, Brooklyn, established in 1887; and **Frankie & Johnnie's,** 269 W. 45th St. (☎ **212-997-9494**), established in 1926, all have their loyal fans. Visit any of the above, and your New York steakhouse obligation will be more than fulfilled.

Ice Cream with a View

The Brooklyn Bridge is surely on your New York itinerary. You can time your walk to coincide with lunchtime (to eat at Grimaldi's Pizzeria), or you can wait until closer to dusk. Once over the bridge on the Brooklyn side, head down to the river until you get to what appears to be an old fireboat house right on the waterfront. Inside that structure you find the best ice cream in the city at the **Brooklyn Ice Cream Factory,** 1 Water St. (☎ **718-246-3963**). All the ice cream is homemade, and you won't be challenged by too many exotic choices. Keep it simple and just add some of the amazing hot fudge to whatever you get. If you wait until sunset, you can eat your ice cream with the visual treat of the twinkling lights on the buildings of Manhattan across the river. Not that it needs the enhancement, but your ice cream will taste even better with that view.

Chapter 18

Ten New York City Experiences to Avoid

● ●

In This Chapter

▶ Ringing in the New Year in Times Square (stay away!)

▶ Falling for a sidewalk sob story (scam!)

▶ Trusting the subway on the weekends (don't!)

▶ Experiencing a horse-drawn carriage ride (avoid it!)

● ●

*N*ew York offers plenty of excellent adventures that you may want to experience (see Chapter 16 for a rundown). Here's the flip side: things, events, and places to avoid. Some of the experiences I list here are commonly considered quintessential New York experiences. You may, in fact, have a lifelong dream of ringing in the New Year in Times Square or taking a carriage ride through Central Park. I hate to be a curmudgeon and burst your bubble, but I give you the straight story here, and leave it to you to decide.

New Year's Eve in Times Square

You see it on television every year, and now you're here. This is your chance to be one of the hundreds of thousands of revelers packed tightly together in the cold to watch the ball drop. *Spare yourself the misery.* Despite the happy faces you see on TV, it's not worth the hours spent on your feet ignoring your bladder and holding your ground in freezing temperatures; the forced elation of blowing on a noisemaker at midnight with half a million others; and dodging piles of trash and puddles of puke after it's over. Instead, make like the natives: Find a restaurant or bar to celebrate in. Or, better yet, have room service deliver a delicious meal and some bubbly for you and a loved one, and don't go out at all.

Chain Stores and Restaurants

Oh, yes, they're here — and more seem to come every month. I'm referring to those restaurants with familiar names such as Applebee's, Red

Lobster, and Domino's. And yes, that was a Gap, Banana Republic, and Old Navy you just passed . . . and another . . . and another. Chains aren't always such a bad thing; international brands (including MUJI, Topshop, and UNIQLO) are fond of opening New York flagships, often one of their only stores on U.S. soil. But when you begin to feel the pangs of hunger or need a new pair of jeans, ask yourself: Did I come to New York to eat and buy exactly what I can eat and buy in every city or town in this country? Or did I come here to experience what makes New York so unique? And that includes the amazing variety of nonchain stores and restaurants, including bargain-priced ethnic cuisine and hole-in-the-wall shops opened by upstart designers. Bypass the old standards and try something homey, glamorous, or new. You won't regret it.

Street Scams

If you see a crowd gathered around a cardboard box with one man flipping cards, madly enticing innocent rubes into his game while another guy scans the crowd for undercover cops, you may already know to keep on walking. Three-card Monte is one of the most recognizable New York street scams, so much so that I can't believe anyone bothers anymore (but they do — look for it in Chinatown). Beware of other petty hustles in this striving city that bilk unsuspecting newcomers on a daily basis. The peddler who asks your name, writes it on a poster or CD, and then demands that you pay $10 for it? That guy you bumped into who insists you give him cash to replace the food/eyeglasses/bottle of beer you "made" him drop? That girl with a sob story about being stuck in New York, telling you that your $20 can help get her home? Scammers, hon. Harden your heart and keep your wallet in your pocket. Hey, you still have it, right?

Weekend Subway Rides

If you're in New York over the weekend, you can count only on taxis and your toes to get you around with certainty. Why? Because the Metropolitan Transit Authority saves its most disruptive subway track work for the less-trafficked weekends. Hey, it's a 24/7 system and repairs have to happen sometime. Don't expect to zip around town by train in a timely fashion. Instead, you may head into a subway entrance only to discover that the station is being skipped, so you have to choose a different train line or take an uptown train in order to go downtown (or vice versa). You may board an F train at West 4th Street and find yourself following the Eighth Avenue A/C line until Brooklyn, where it switches back to F-train behavior at Jay Street. Or you may have planned to take the express 4 or 5 from downtown to the Upper East Side for a brunch date, and wind up late because only the local 6 is running. On weekends, if time is of the essence, take a cab.

SoHo on Saturdays

I suppose there's an argument to be made for shopping in SoHo on a Saturday, but having done it more times than I wish, I cannot imagine what it is. SoHo's skinny sidewalks become jammed with tourists and bridge-and-tunnel teenagers; the must-see stores (Apple, Prada, H&M, to name a few) are completely crowded, with crazy-long lines; and whatever charm that's left in the area is totally lost as you elbow through and dodge cars and cabs. Sundays are usually better, but brace yourself if it's exceptionally pretty outside. If you're visiting on a weekend, you can make the best of it by coming as early as the shops open (usually around 10 or 11 a.m. on Sat and noon on Sun); you also have first crack at the more unusual street-vendor wares. Otherwise, save your serious SoHo shopping for a weekday, when you can actually enjoy browsing and buying. Many shops are open later on Thursdays, anyway, and Fridays still have a festive feel without the crush.

The St. Patrick's Day Parade

On March 17, packs of suburban teenagers (with cases of beer between them) begin arriving early via the Long Island Rail Road, Metro North, or New Jersey Transit. By the time the parade kicks off, they — along with a few off-duty policemen — are sloshed. Midtown becomes exasperating to navigate, with parade crowds and blockades slowing down all public transportation. The pubs are packed, and the already-high price of drinks gets even higher. If you truly yearn for a bit of the Irish on this day, for your own good, stay in, order a pint of Guinness from room service, and listen to the Irish Tenors sing "Danny Boy."

Electronics Stores

You may notice a wealth of "electronics stores" in and around Times Square and Fifth Avenue or wherever gullible tourists frequent. Some of the stores post banners advertising a going-out-of-business sale. These guys have been going out of business since the Stone Age. That's the bait and switch; pretty soon you've spent too much money for digital cameras or MP3 players in questionable working order. The people who work at these stores are a special breed of shark; they work you hard to take their "deal." Don't even get close enough to let them sink their fangs into you because, after they do, you're usually theirs for the taking.

Driving in the City

I warn you about driving in the city in Chapter 7, but it bears repeating. If you want a world of aggravation, rent a car, grit your teeth in the traffic, play chicken with the taxis, and try, just try, to find a parking place.

And when you do, make sure it's a legal one (read the fine print on the street signs). Or put the car in a garage and watch your vacation budget fritter away. (If you *must* drive your car to get here, at least stay in a hotel that offers free or discounted parking.) New York has the best and fastest public transportation in the country. A car is a luxury you want no part of.

Horse-Drawn Carriage Rides

Pity those poor beasts of burden. They get dragged out in the heat and cold with a buggy attached to them just to give the passenger the feel of a romantic buggy ride through Central Park. But the horses look totally forlorn, as if contending with Midtown traffic is the last thing they want to do. (Can you blame them?) And they don't even get a cut of the generous take: $50 for a 20-minute ride, excluding tip. If you want a slow, leisurely ride through Central Park, minus the smell of horse poop, consider an alternative called **Manhattan Rickshaw Company** (☎ 212-604-4729). The beast of burden behind the rickshaw has two legs, and the rate is about $1 a minute.

Getting your car out of the pound

If you come back to the spot on the street where you left your car and it's not there, it *probably* hasn't been stolen — more than likely, it's been towed. You can call the city information number (☎ 311) or call the car pound directly at ☎ 212-971-0770, and the personnel there can help you track your car in the system. Or just head for the Manhattan car pound at Pier 76 on the far West Side (12th Avenue and 38th Street). Take a cab; it's on the other side of the busy West Side Highway. The pound is open 24 hours a day, except from Sunday at 6 a.m. to Monday at 7 a.m., when it's closed.

If your car is towed, you should get it out as quickly as possible because they charge you $15 a day for storage after the first day. Granted, this may be cheaper than what you're paying at a parking lot, but don't forget that big fine you already have to cover.

When you go to the car pound, bring the car's registration (if it's not in the glove box) or rental agreement and your driver's license. Pound personnel will escort you to the car, if necessary, to identify it if you don't have all the required documentation. Oh, and bring cash (or traveler's checks). You'll pay a minimum of $185 to claim your car, and they don't take credit cards or personal checks. You don't have to pay the (additional) $55 parking ticket when you claim your car.

The Feast of San Gennaro

At one time, this was a distinctive and genuine Italian feast (see the films *Godfather II* and *Mean Streets* for the Feast in the good old days). Its decline has pretty much coincided with the decline of Little Italy, a neighborhood that barely exists anymore. Now, the Feast is just another overblown and overcrowded street fair with bad food (well, except for the *zeppole,* which you can get at any city street fair), cheap trinkets (KISS ME, I'M ITALIAN buttons come to mind), and games of chance you have no chance of winning. Most of the original Little Italy residents have left, but the ones who are still there make sure to clear out during the Feast and let the bridge-and-tunnel expats take over.

Appendix

Quick Concierge

Fast Facts

Ambulance

Call ☎ 911.

American Automobile Association (AAA)

The general number is ☎ 212-757-2000; emergency road service, ☎ 800-222-4357.

American Express

Several locations, including Macy's in Herald Square, Sixth Avenue at 34th Street (☎ 212-695-8075), and the World Financial Center at 200 Vesey St. (☎ 212-640-5130). For other New York branches, call ☎ 800-528-4800, or check www.amextravel resources.com.

Area Codes

The area codes for Manhattan are **212** and **646**. The area code for the Bronx, Brooklyn, Queens, and Staten Island is **718**. Also common are the **917** and **347** area codes, which are usually assigned to cellphones. All calls between these area codes are local calls, but you have to dial 1 plus the area code plus the seven digits for all calls, even ones made within your area code.

ATMs

ATMs are virtually everywhere in New York — even inside small shops, delis, drugstores, and some restaurants. Banks are on almost every corner in Manhattan; full-service locations are less ubiquitous in the outer boroughs. Most ATMs accept cards on both the PLUS and Cirrus networks. For information about PLUS ATM locations, call ☎ 800-847-2911, or try www.visa.com. For Cirrus locations, call ☎ 800-627-8372, or try www.mastercard.com.

Baby Sitters

Both the Baby Sitters Guild (☎ 212-682-0227; www.babysittersguild.com) and Pinch Sitters (☎ 212-260-6005) are frequently recommended by local moms.

Camera Repair

Try Berry Camera Repair, 844 Sixth Ave., Rm. 704 (between 29th and 30th streets; ☎ 212-685-9334; www.berrypro camera.com).

Doctors

For an emergency, go to a hospital emergency room (see the "Hospitals" listing, later in this section). Walk-in clinics can handle minor ailments; one example is DOCS at New York Healthcare, 55 E. 34th St. (between Park and Madison avenues; ☎ 212-252-6001), open Monday through Friday 8 a.m. to 7 p.m., Saturday and Sunday 9 a.m. to 2 p.m. The charge is $100 for a visit. A Times Square branch of Duane Reade pharmacy at 1627 Broadway (at 50th Street; ☎ 888-535-6963), open daily from 8 a.m. to 8 p.m., is one of several Manhattan locations offering urgent care for non-life-threatening afflictions; see www.drwalkin.com for other branches.

Drinking Laws

The minimum legal age to buy and consume alcoholic beverages in New York is 21; proof of age is required and often requested at bars, nightclubs, and restaurants, so it's always a good idea to bring ID when you go out. Liquor and wine are sold only at licensed stores, which are open six days a week; most are closed Sundays and holidays. You can purchase beer at grocery stores, delis, and supermarkets 24 hours a day, except on Sundays before noon.

Electricity

Like Canada, the United States uses 110 to 120 volts AC (60 cycles), compared to 220 to 240 volts AC (50 cycles) in most of Europe, Australia, and New Zealand. Downward converters that change 220 to 240 volts to 110 to 120 volts are difficult to find in the United States, so bring one with you.

Embassies and Consulates

All embassies are in the nation's capital, Washington, D.C. Some consulates are in major U.S. cities, and most nations have a mission to the United Nations in New York City. If your country isn't listed below, call for directory information in Washington, D.C. (☎ 202-555-1212), or check www.embassy.org/embassies.

The embassy of Australia is at 1601 Massachusetts Ave. NW, Washington, DC 20036 (☎ 202-797-3000; http://australia.visahq.com). An Australian consulate is in New York.

The embassy of Canada is at 501 Pennsylvania Ave. NW, Washington, DC 20001 (☎ 202-682-1740; www.canadainternational.gc.ca/washington). A Canadian consulate is in New York.

The embassy of Ireland is at 2234 Massachusetts Ave. NW, Washington, DC 20008 (☎ 202-462-3939; www.embassyofireland.org). An Irish consulate is in New York.

The embassy of New Zealand is at 37 Observatory Circle NW, Washington, DC 20008 (☎ 202-328-4800; www.nzembassy.com). New Zealand consulates are in Los Angeles, Salt Lake City, San Francisco, and Seattle.

The embassy of the United Kingdom is at 3100 Massachusetts Ave. NW, Washington, DC 20008 (☎ 202-588-6500; http://ukinusa.fco.gov.uk). A British consulate is in New York.

Emergencies

For police, fire, and ambulance, call ☎ 911. For the Poison Control Center, call ☎ 800-222-1222 or 212-340-4494.

Holidays

Banks, government offices, post offices, and many stores, restaurants, and museums are closed on the following legal national holidays: January 1 (New Year's Day), the third Monday in January (Martin Luther King, Jr., Day), the third Monday in February (Presidents' Day), the last Monday in May (Memorial Day), July 4 (Independence Day), the first Monday in September (Labor Day), the second Monday in October (Columbus Day), November 11 (Veterans Day), the fourth Thursday in November (Thanksgiving), and December 25 (Christmas). The Tuesday after the first Monday in November is Election Day, a federal government holiday in presidential-election years (held every 4 years, and next in 2012).

Hospitals

From south to north, here are the numbers of specific Manhattan hospitals: New York

Downtown Hospital, 170 William St. (at Beekman Street, near City Hall; ☎ 212-312-5000); Beth Israel Medical Center, First Avenue at 16th Street (☎ 212-420-2000); Bellevue Hospital Center, First Avenue at 27th Street (☎ 212-562-1000); New York University Medical Center, First Avenue at 33rd Street (☎ 212-263-7300); Roosevelt Hospital Center, Tenth Avenue at 58th Street (☎ 212-523-4000); Lenox Hill Hospital, 77th Street between Park and Lexington avenues (☎ 212-434-2000); St. Luke's Hospital Center, Amsterdam Avenue at 113th Street (☎ 212-523-4000). In the downtown Brooklyn area, there's Long Island College Hospital, 339 Hicks St. (between Atlantic Avenue and Pacific Street; ☎ 718-780-1000).

Hot Lines

The 24-hour crime-victim hot line is ☎ 212-577-7777; the sex-crime report line is ☎ 212-267-7273; the suicide-prevention line is ☎ 212-673-3000. For Alcoholics Anonymous, call ☎ 212-647-1680. For local police precinct numbers, call ☎ 646-610-5000. You can file a consumer complaint by calling ☎ 311.

Internet Access

Free wireless access is available in various locations around town, including Union Square Park, Bryant Park, City Hall Park, and South Street Seaport, and all branches of the New York Public Library (www.nypl.org). If you find yourself in need of an old-fashioned Internet cafe, go to **CyberCafe**, 250 W. 49th St. (between Broadway and Eighth Avenue; ☎ 212-333-4109; www.cyber-cafe.com), open Monday through Friday 8 a.m. to 11 p.m., Saturday and Sunday 11 a.m. to 11 p.m.

Legal Aid

If you're pulled over for a minor infraction (such as speeding), never attempt to pay the fine directly to a police officer; this could be construed as attempted bribery, a much more serious crime. Pay fines by mail, or directly into the hands of the clerk of the court. If accused of a more serious offense, say and do nothing before consulting a lawyer. The burden is on the state to prove a person's guilt beyond a reasonable doubt, and everyone has the right to remain silent, whether he or she is suspected of a crime or actually arrested. Once arrested, a person can make one telephone call to a party of his or her choice. International visitors should call their embassy or consulate.

Mail

At press time, domestic postage rates were 28¢ for a postcard and 44¢ for a letter. For international mail, a first-class letter of up to 1 ounce costs 98¢ (75¢ to Canada and 79¢ to Mexico); a first-class postcard costs the same as a letter. For more information, go to www.usps.com.

If you aren't sure what your address will be in the United States, mail can be sent to you, in your name, c/o General Delivery at the main post office of the city or region where you expect to be. (Call ☎ 800-275-8777 for information on the nearest post office.) The addressee must pick up mail in person and must produce proof of identity (for example, a driver's license or passport). Most post offices will hold mail for up to one month and are open Monday through Friday 8 a.m. to 6 p.m., and Saturday 9 a.m. to 3 p.m.

Always include zip codes when mailing items in the U.S. If you don't know the zip code, visit www.usps.com/zip4.

Maps

Transit maps for the subways and buses are available free at token booths inside subway stations and public libraries; bus maps are also available on the buses. Free city maps are available at hotels inside the free city guides. To buy maps of all kinds, go to Hagstrom Map and Travel Center, 51 W. 43rd St. (between Fifth and Sixth avenues; ☎ 212-398-1222), open Monday through Friday 8:30 a.m. to 6 p.m., Saturday 10:30 a.m. to 4:30 p.m. For simple New York City street maps, go to any of the bookstores in town.

Passports

See "Embassies and Consulates," earlier in this section, for whom to contact if you lose your passport while traveling in the U.S. For other information, contact the following agencies:

In Australia, contact the Australian Passport Information Service at ☎ 131-232, or visit www.passports.gov.au.

In Canada, contact the central Passport Office, Department of Foreign Affairs and International Trade, Ottawa, ON K1A 0G3 (☎ 800-567-6868; www.ppt.gc.ca).

In Ireland, contact the Passport Office, Setanta Centre, Molesworth Street, Dublin 2 (☎ 01-671-1633; www.foreign affairs.gov.ie).

In New Zealand, contact the Passports Office, Department of Internal Affairs, 47 Boulcott St., Wellington, 6011 (☎ 0800-225-050 in New Zealand or 04-474-8100; www.passports.govt.nz).

In the United Kingdom, visit your nearest passport office, major post office, or travel agency or contact the Identity and Passport Service (IPS), 89 Eccleston Sq., London, SW1V 1PN (☎ 0300-222-0000; www.ips.gov.uk).

Pharmacies

Duane Reade (www.duanereade.com) has multiple 24-hour locations around

town, including in SoHo at 598 Broadway (between Houston and Prince; ☎ 212-343-2567); in Midtown at Broadway and 57th Street (☎ 212-541-9708); and on the Upper East Side at Third Avenue and 74th Street (☎ 212-744-2668). In addition, CVS (www.cvs.com) and Rite Aid (www.riteaid.com) have branches throughout the city. For homeopathic cures and other natural medicines, try C. O. Bigelow Chemists, 414 Sixth Ave. (between 8th and 9th streets; ☎ 212-533-2700; www.bigelow chemists.com).

Police

Dial ☎ 911 for emergencies and ☎ 646-610-5000 for the phone number of the nearest police precinct.

Restrooms

Public restroom facilities are located in all transportation terminals (Grand Central Terminal, Penn Station, and the Port Authority Bus Terminal), in Central Park and Bryant Park, and in the New York Public Library and some other branch libraries — but in some of these places, cleanliness may leave much to be desired. Department stores, museums, and large hotels have wonderful restrooms (such as the one in Saks Fifth Avenue), as does Trump Tower at 56th Street and Fifth Avenue. Some large coffee shops, such as Dean & Deluca, Au Bon Pain, and larger Starbucks, as well as some chains such as McDonald's, also have decent restrooms. If you see a restrooms for customers only sign, you may have to buy a snack or beverage to use the facilities. The Web site and mobile app **Diaroogle** (www.diaroogle.com) provides thoughtful reviews of public toilets for discerning tastes.

Safety

New York has been *the* safest large city in the United States for several years. Still, it's a good idea to trust your instincts: If it feels unsafe, it probably is, so go else-where. Don't flash money or look in your wallet in public; pickpockets sometimes loiter near ATMs to fleece unsuspecting customers. Keep valuables (especially iPods and iPhones) out of sight. Don't leave a purse or jacket with a wallet inside hanging on your chair in a restaurant; someone could brush by and snag it while you're enjoying your meal. Although most hotel-room doors lock automatically, double-check when you're coming and going. Subway stations have off-hours waiting areas, usually near the entrances, with camera surveillance; look for the signs overhead. And in the unlikely and unfortunate event that you're mugged, don't be foolish enough to resist. Give the mugger what he wants, get to a safe place, and call the police.

Smoking

City regulations forbid smoking in all places of employment and commerce, including offices, bars, restaurants, public transportation, taxis, and indoor arenas. A city tax added to the cost of cigarettes makes them quite expensive. If you're a smoker, bring enough to last your trip, and expect to duck out to the sidewalk if you'd like a smoke when you're at a restaurant, bar, or club. You have plenty of company in what's sometimes called the "Bloomberg Lounge," after Mayor Bloomberg, who pushed the antismoking regulations through.

Taxes

The United States has no value-added tax (VAT) or other indirect tax at the national level. Every state, county, and city may levy its own local tax on all purchases, including hotel and restaurant checks and airline tickets. These taxes will not appear on price tags.

New York City sales tax is 8.875 percent on meals, most goods, and some services. Hotel tax is 5.875 percent plus $3.50 per room per night plus sales tax. Parking-garage tax is 18.375 percent.

Taxis

Authorized, legal taxis in Manhattan are yellow. Yellow cabs have city medallions posted inside the vehicles that have the driver's name and identification number, in case you need to lodge a complaint (or, heaven forbid, if you leave something in the cab and need to track down the driver — call ☎ 311 or 212-639-9675 to do so). A taxi will cost you $2.50 just for stepping in the door, plus 40¢ per ⅕ mile and a 50¢ New York State tax surcharge per ride. A sur-charge of $1 is applied to all rides Monday through Friday from 4 to 8 p.m., and a 50¢ surcharge applies nightly from 8 p.m. to 6 a.m. The flat rate from JFK Airport is $45. Taxis are required to accept American Express, MasterCard, Visa, and Discover in addition to cash.

Time Zone

The continental United States is divided into **four time zones:** Eastern Standard Time (EST), Central Standard Time (CST), Mountain Standard Time (MST), and Pacific Standard Time (PST). Alaska and Hawaii have their own zones. For example, when it's 9 a.m. in Los Angeles (PST), it's 7 a.m. in Honolulu (HST),10 a.m. in Denver (MST), 11 a.m. in Chicago (CST), noon in New York City (EST), 5 p.m. in London (GMT), and 2 a.m. the next day in Sydney.

Daylight saving time is in effect from 2 a.m. on the second Sunday in March to 2 a.m. on the first Sunday in November, except in Arizona, Hawaii, the U.S. Virgin Islands, and Puerto Rico. Daylight saving time moves the clock one hour ahead of stan-dard time.

Tipping

In restaurants in New York City, you can double the 8.875 percent tax to figure the appropriate tip. Other tipping guidelines: 15 percent to 20 percent of the fare to taxi drivers; 10 percent to 15 percent of the tab to bartenders; $1 to $2 per bag to bellhops; at least $1 per day to hotel maids; $1 per item to checkroom attendants. Tipping theater ushers isn't expected.

Transit Info

For ground transportation to and from all the area airports, call Air-Ride (☎ 800-247-7433). For all transit information, call the Metropolitan Transit Authority (MTA) Travel Information Center (☎ 718-330-1234; operators available daily 6 a.m.–10 p.m.).

Where to Get More Information

I packed this book with information, but if you still haven't had enough, you can consult the following resources for additional info.

Tourist-information offices

NYC & Company offers a 24-hour telephone hot line (☎ **800-692-8474** or 212-397-8222; www.nycgo.com) that you can call to order an *Official Visitor Guide* and an *Official NYC Visitor Map;* you pay only shipping, and you should receive them in seven days. The guide contains tons of information about hotels, restaurants, theaters, and events, and is updated quarterly. NYC & Company also maintains a sleek, updated **Visitor Information Center** at 810 Seventh Ave. (between 52nd and 53rd streets; ☎ **212-484-1222**), open Monday through Friday 8:30 a.m. to 6 p.m., weekends 9 a.m. to 5 p.m., and holidays 9 a.m. to 3 p.m.

You can get information about current **theater** productions from **NYC/On Stage** (www.nyconstage.org) and the **Broadway League** (www.ilovenytheater.com). For all **transit** information, call the **MTA Travel Information Center** (☎ **718-330-1234**).

Air-Ride (☎ **800-247-7433**) is a service that provides recorded information about ground transportation from all area airports.

Newspapers, magazines, and wireless apps

New York City has four daily newspapers: *The New York Times* (www.nytimes.com), the *Daily News* (www.nydailynews.com), the *New York Post* (www.nypost.com), and *Newsday* (www.newsday.com). Each paper offers daily calendars of events and usually runs full sections of weekend listings on Fridays.

The best weekly magazines for information and listings about upcoming events are *Time Out New York* (www.timeoutny.com), *New York* magazine (www.newyorkmag.com), and *The New Yorker* (www.newyorker.com). The weekly free newspaper *The Village Voice* (www.villagevoice.com) has extensive listings with staff picks and recommendations.

Here are some of the more useful online sources:

- ✔ The **Metropolitan Transit Authority** (MTA) site (www.mta.info) provides easy access to bus and subway maps and information.

- ✔ **NYC & Company,** New York City's official tourism site (www.nycgo.com), provides a wealth of information and links, and you can book hotels online with a few clicks of your mouse.

- ✔ The **Frommer's** site (www.frommers.com) offers much of the content from Frommer's guidebooks, as well as online updates of changes in the area since the guidebook was published. You can also subscribe to an Internet newsletter that spotlights travel deals and offers articles and service information on destinations worldwide. Message boards are available for travelers to ask for and share traveling tips.

If you're looking for additional guidebooks on New York City, I recommend *Frommer's New York City, Frommer's New York City Day by Day, NYC Free & Dirt Cheap,* and *Frommer's New York City with Kids* (all published by Wiley). Also check out Suzy Gershman's *Born to Shop New York City, Pauline Frommer's New York City,* and *Frommer's Memorable Walks in New York City* (all published by Wiley, as well).

As a New York City resident, I also highly recommend the following practical and informative mobile applications:

- ✔ **CabSense** (www.cabsense.com) is a handy free download that uses GPS data to help you locate the best corner from which to hail a taxi.

- ✔ **Ride the City** (www.ridethecity.com) is useful if you want to take advantage of the relatively new system of bike lanes to tour on two wheels. The $2 app shows you the shortest and safest routes.

- ✔ **StreetEats** (www.ilovestreeteats.com/nyc) is a free app that leads you to the gourmet mobile trucks around town, including Van Leeuwen Artisan Ice Cream and Schnitzel & Things.

- ✔ **Trees Near You** (www.treesnearyou.com) is a sweet freebie that identifies the trees all around you in the concrete jungle.

Index

See also separate Accommodations and Restaurant indexes at the end of this index.

General Index

• A •

Abyssinian Baptist Church, 200
Academy Records, 236
accommodations. *See also*
        Accommodations Index
    best of, 16–17
    budget planning, 38, 92–95
    cost-cutting tips, 41–42
    family travel, 54
    gratuities, 40–41
    Internet access, 65
    maps, 96, 98–100
    neighborhood listing, 119–120
    pricing information, 95, 120–121
    travelers with disabilities, 56
    types of, 91–92
Acela, 50
Adventures on a Shoestring, 210
African Burial Ground National
        Monument, 195–196
air travel. *See also specific airports*
    airports, 46–47
    discounts, 48
    getting to hotel from airport,
        69, 71–75
    major airlines, 47–48
    online booking, 49
    security, 65–66
alcohol, 298
Alice Tully Hall, 258
Allen Room, 258
Almondine Bakery, 162
ambulances, 297

American Ballet Theater, 263
American Folk Art Museum, 192
American Museum of Natural
        History, 19, 172, 262–263
Amore Opera, 261
Amtrak, 50
Angel's Share, 275
antiques shopping, 215, 222–223
apartment rentals, 92
Apollo Theater, 82, 260
Apple Store, 234
APT, 278
aquariums, 201–202
architecture, 25–26, 198–199,
        210–211
Arlene's Grocery, 272
art museums. *See specific museums*
Asia Society and Museum, 196
Atlantic Theater Company, 254
ATM (cash machine), 43, 297
attractions. *See also specific
        attractions*
    best of, 18–19
    budget planning, 39, 42
    family travel, 54–55, 201–204
    maps, 174–179
    overview, 171
    recommended, 172–173, 180–206
auto shows, 31
Avery Fisher Hall, 32, 258

• B •

baby sitters, 54, 297
bagels, 155–156, 288–289
bakeries, 161–162

ballet, 263
B&H Photo & Video, 234
bargain hunting, 79, 224
Bargemusic, 261
Barneys, 20, 214, 224
Barracuda, 277
bars. *See* club/bars
baseball, 206–207
basketball, 207
Bateaux New York, 209
B.B. King Blues Club & Grill, 273
Beacon's Closet, 230
beauty goods, 231–232
bed-and-breakfasts, 92
Bemelmans Bar, 17, 102, 275
Bergdorf Goodman, 214, 225
Big Apple Circus, 33
Big Apple Greeter, 211, 283
Big Apple Jazz Tours, 211
biking, 211, 286
Birdland, 265
Bloomingdale's, 214, 225
blues music, 260, 265, 273
Bluestockings, 229
boating, 40, 180–181, 209
Boiler Room, 277
book
  conventions, 2–3
  icons, 5
  organization, 3–5
books about New York City, 26–27
Books of Wonder, 232
bookstores, 20, 59, 229, 232–233
Bouchon Bakery, 226
Bowery Ballroom, 272
breakfast, 154–155
Broadway (Street), 19
Broadway League, 302
Broadway show. *See* theater
Broadway Ticket Center, 83, 256
Bronx, 173, 191, 206, 286
Brooklyn, 120, 132, 164, 174–175,
  230, 284
Brooklyn Academy of Music,
  259–260, 261
Brooklyn Bowl, 273
Brooklyn Bridge, 19, 173

Brooklyn Cyclones, 207
Brooklyn Flea, 20, 222–223, 230
Brooklyn Museum of Art, 192–193,
  263
brunch, 154–155
Bryant Park, 65
budget planning. *See* money
Burger Joint, 157
bus travel
  cost-cutting tips, 87–88
  guided tours, 208, 239
  in/to New York City, 50–51, 86–87
  travelers with disabilities, 56–57
  typical costs, 38, 42

• C •

cab rides
  general information, 88–90
  safety, 301
  travelers with disabilities, 56–57
  typical costs, 38
cabaret, 39, 273–274
Café Carlyle, 102, 274
Café Sabarsky, 154–155
calendar of events, 30–34
candy, 21, 161, 226, 233
car service, 69, 71–72
car travel
  to New York City, 76–77
  overview, 49–50
  parking, 38, 49, 61
  rental cars, 61
  towed car, 295
Carnegie Hall, 20, 259, 261
Caroline's on Broadway, 274
carriage rides, 208, 295
cash, 43
Cathedral Church of St. John the
  Divine, 200
cellphones, 64
Central Park, 19, 180, 181, 240–241,
  253
Central Park Conservancy, 212
chain hotels, 92
cheesecake, 290
Chelsea, 12–13, 80, 203, 227

chicken and waffles, 289
children. *See* family travel
Children's Museum of Manhattan, 201
Chinatown, 228–229
Chinese food, 141, 165, 167
Chinese New Year, 30
Chino-Latino food, 141, 289
Christmas, 34
Chrysler Building, 18, 26, 180, 182
Cielo, 278
Circle Line, 209
circuses, 31, 33
Citi Field, 206
City Center, 263
City Hall, 77, 79
City Sonnet, 92
CityPass, 39, 171
classical music, 257–261
The Cloisters, 182
Cloth, 230
clothing stores, 40, 213–215, 224. *See also specific stores*
club/bars. *See also specific types*
  best of, 20–21, 273
  cultural venues, 276–277
  pubs, 275–276
  venues with views, 277
  world music venues, 276
C.O. Bigelow, 231
Colonia Transportation, 75
Colony Music Center, 236
Comedy Cellar, 274–275
comedy clubs, 274–275
commuter rail, 49
concerts, 31, 32, 260, 272. *See also specific events*
consulates, 298
Cooper-Hewitt National Design Museum, 193
credit cards, 43
The Creek Bar, 276
cruises, 209–210
Cuban food, 135, 141
cupcakes, 161–162

• D •

The Daily Show with Jon Stewart (TV show), 205
Damrosch Park, 259
dance clubs, 278–279
dance performances, 263
DanceAfrica, 259
Dangerfield's, 275
Dean & DeLuca, 233
Delacorte theater, 32
delis, 159
Diamond District, 231
diners, 289–290
dinner cruises, 209
disability, travelers with, 55–57
dive bars, 277
Dizzy's Club Coca-Cola, 258, 265
doctors, 62–64, 297
dog shows, 30
Don Hill's, 278
Downtown
  maps, 96, 126–127, 174–175, 266–267
  overview, 10–11, 77
  shopping, 216–217, 227–230
Drama Book Shop, 232
Dublin House, 276
Duplex, 277
Dylan's Candy Bar, 233

• E •

Ear Inn, 21, 276
East River State Park, 262
East Village, 10–11, 79–80
Easter Parade, 31
Economy Candy, 233
electricity, 298
electronics, 234, 294, 297
Ellis Island, 182, 184
e-mail, 64–65
embassies, 298
emergencies, 298
Empire State Building, 18, 26, 184–185

escorted tours, 51–52
ethnic cuisine, 17–18, 164–166,
    215, 222–223, 283–284
  best cheap entertainment,
    283–284
  best restaurants, 17–18
  markets, 215, 222–223
  restaurants listing, 164–166
events, 9, 16, 30–34
express train, 50, 85
EZ-Pass program, 71–72, 76–77

• F •

Fairway, 233
fall visit, 30
family travel
  accommodations, 54
  baby-sitters, 54, 297
  children's attractions, 31, 33,
    54–55, 201–204
  cost-cutting tips, 41
  kid-friendly restaurants, 152
  overview, 53–55
  sample itineraries, 254–256
  theater picks, 254
FAO Schwarz, 236–237
fashion shopping hot spots,
    81, 226–227
fast-food chains, 124
Feast of San Gennaro, 296
Federal Hall National Memorial, 26
Feinstein's at the Regency, 274
festivals, 31, 32, 33, 161
Fifth Avenue shopping, 225–226
The Fillmore New York at Irving
    Plaza, 272
film festivals, 33
Financial District. *See* Wall Street/
    Financial District
Fisher Landau Center for Art, 284
Flatiron Building, 26, 198
Flatiron District/Union Square,
    12–13, 80
flea markets, 20, 215, 222–223
Fleet Week, 31
folk art, 192

food. *See also* Restaurant Index
  budgeting for, 38–39
  festival, 31
  markets, 124
  shopping for, 233–234
Forbidden Planet, 232
Fourth of July fireworks, 32
frequent fliers, 48
The Frick Collection, 193
full fare, 48
Fun Pass, 48

• G •

Garment District, 81, 226–227
gay/lesbian travelers, 32, 58–59,
    277–278
gelato, 160
gift stores, 235
Gotham Comedy Club, 21, 275
gourmet food stores, 185, 215,
    227, 234
Gramercy Park, 12–13, 80
Grand Central Terminal, 19, 26, 185
gratuities, 40–41, 301
Gray Line, 56–57, 208
The Great Saunter, 31
GreenFlea, 222
Greenlight Bookstore, 230
Greenwich Village, 10–11, 19, 79–80
Ground Zero (World Trade Center
    site), 77, 191
Guggenheim Museum, 172, 188, 263
guided tours, 207–212

• H •

Halloween Parade, 33
hamburgers, 157–159
Hampton Jitney, 75
H&H Bagels, 156
Harlem
  attractions map, 183
  guided tours, 210–211
  museums, 195, 197, 244–245
  music venues, 260
  overview, 82

Harlem Week, 32
helicopter tours, 208
Hell's Kitchen, 81–82, 215
Henri Bendel, 214
Henrietta Hudson, 278
Herald Square, 81, 226–227
Hester Street Fair, 222
High Line, 19, 185–186, 286
Highline Ballroom, 273
Highway, 228
Historic Orchard Street Shopping
    District, 229
history of New York City, 22–25,
    246–248
hockey, 207
Holocaust Museum, 196
hospitals, 298–299
Hot Chocolate Festival, 161
hot dogs, 157–159, 290
hotels. *See* accommodations
House of Oldies, 236
Hudson River Park, 286

• *I* •

ice cream, 160–161
ice hockey, 207
icons, explained, 5
illness, 63–64
inns, 92
insurance, 62–63
Internet access, 64–65, 299
Intrepid Sea-Air-Space Museum, 186
Isaac Stern Auditorium, 259
itinerary samples, 238–248

• *J* •

J&R Music & Computer World, 229,
    234
jazz music, 211, 236, 258, 264–265,
    272
jewelry, 215, 222–229, 231, 235
Jimmy's Corner, 277
Joe's Pub, 274
John F. Kennedy International
    Airport (JFK), 46–47, 71–72

Joyce Gold History Tours of New
    York, 210
Joyce Theater, 263
Julliard School, 258

• *K* •

Kayak, 49
Kee's Chocolates, 233–234
Keyspan Park, 207
Kid Robot, 227–228
Kiehl's, 231
Kiki de Montparnasse, 227
Kiosk, 235
Knitting Factory, 273

• *L* •

LaGuardia Airport, 46, 72–73
Late Night with Jimmy Fallon
    (TV show), 205
The Late Show with David Letterman
    (TV show), 205
Lenox Lounge, 265
Leonard Nimoy Thalia Theater, 260
lesbian/gay travelers, 32, 58–59,
    277–278
LGBT Pride Week and March, 32
libraries, 193–194, 239
limo service, 141
Lincoln Center, 32–33, 257–259
Little Italy, 10–11, 79, 174, 286
Live with Regis and Kelly (TV
    show), 205–206
lodgings. *See* accommodations
Loeb Boathouse, 180
Long Island City (Queens), 284–285
Long Island Rail Road, 72, 75
Lopate, Leonard (podcaster), 28
Lord & Taylor, 214–215, 226
lost/stolen wallets, 44–45
Lower East Side
    best accommodations, 16–17
    maps, 10–11, 126–127, 174–175,
        266–267
    overview, 79
    shopping, 228–229

Lower East Side Tenement
    Museum, 247
luggage, 66, 75
Lush, 231–232

• M •

MacArthur Airport, 75
Macy's, 215, 226
Macy's Thanksgiving Day
    Parade, 34
Madame Tussaud's New York, 189
Madison Avenue shopping, 224–225
Madison Square Garden, 207, 260
mail, 299
malls, 226
Manhattan Rickshaw Company, 295
maps
    accommodations, 96, 98–100
    attractions, 174–179, 181
    city overview, 10–15
    Harlem and Upper Manhattan, 183
    neighborhoods, 78
    New York metropolitan area, 70
    nightlife, 266–271
    restaurants, 126–132
    shopping, 216–221
    sources for, 299–300
    Williamsburg, 222
marathons, 28, 33
markets, 215, 222–223
McCartney, Stella (designer), 227
McNally Jackson, 20, 232
McQueen, Alexander (designer),
    227
Meatpacking District, 227
medical insurance, 62–63
Mercury Lounge, 21, 272
MetroCard, 87–88
Metropolitan Museum of Art,
    19, 186, 235, 263
Metropolitan Opera House,
    257–258, 261, 262
Metropolitan Transportation
    Authority (MTA), 49, 57,
    72, 303
Mexican food, 148

Midsummer Night's Swing, 32
Midtown
    maps, 12–13, 98–99, 128–129,
        176–177, 268–269
    overview, 80–81
    shopping, 218–219, 225–227
Midtown Shuttle, 74
Mitzi E. Newhouse Theater, 258
MoMA (Museum of Modern Art),
    187, 235
Momofuku Milk Bar, 162
money
    access to, 297
    cutting costs, 41–42
    handling, 42–45
    overview, 37–41
Morgan Library & Museum,
    193–194
Mostly Mozart, 32
Motorino, 157
movies, 27–28, 33
MTA (Metropolitan Transportation
    Authority), 49, 57, 72, 303
Municipal Art Society, 210
Murray Hill, 12–13, 81, 93
Museum Mile Festival, 32
Museum of American Finance, 190
Museum of Jewish Heritage–A
    Living Memorial to the
    Holocaust, 196
Museum of Modern Art
    (MoMA), 187
Museum of Television & Radio, 194
Museum of the City of
    New York, 196
Museum of the Moving Image, 204
museums. *See also specific*
    museums
    best picks, 19
    calendar of events, 30–34
    cost-cutting tips, 42
    monthly parties, 284
    sample itineraries, 244–245
    stores, 235–236
music. *See also specific types*
    alfresco venues, 262
    best cheap entertainment, 285

music *(continued)*
  best venues, 257–263
  club listings, 264–265, 272
  electronics shopping, 294
  record/CD shopping, 236
  schools, 258
Music Hall of Williamsburg, 272

• *N* •

NBA Store, 226
NBC Studios, 187
neighborhoods. *See also specific
    neighborhoods*
  accommodations, 96, 98–100,
      119–120
  attractions, 174–179
  hotel rates, 95
  overview, 10–15, 77, 79–82
  restaurants, 126–132, 162–164
  shopping hot spots, 224–231
  walking tours, 211–212
New Jersey Transit train, 75
New Victory Theater, 254
New Year's Eve, 34, 292
New York Airport Service, 71–72, 73
New York Aquarium, 201–202
New York City Ballet, 263
New York City Fire Museum, 202
New York City Marathon, 33
New York City Opera, 261
New York City Transit, 49, 57
New York City Vacation
    Packages, 52
New York CityPASS, 172
New York Film Festival, 33
New York Habitat, 92
New York International Auto
    Show, 31
New York Knicks, 207
New York Liberty, 207
New York Mets, 206
New York National Boat Show, 30
New York Philharmonic, 28, 261,
    262
New York Public Library, 26, 198

New York Rangers, 207
New York State Theater, 263
New York Stock Exchange, 23, 190
New York Transit Museum, 202,
    235–236
New York Waterways, 209
New York Yankees, 206
Newark International Airport, 47,
    73–75
Newark Liberty Airport Express, 74
newspapers, 302–303
The New Museum, 194
New-York Historical Society, 197
Next Wave Festival, 33
nightlife. *See also specific venues*
  best of, 20–21
  budget planning, 39
  cover charges, 279
  gay/lesbian travelers, 277–278
  listings and reviews, 251–252
  maps, 266–271
  smoking, 25, 276
Ninth Avenue International Food
    Festival, 31
No. 7 Sub, 159–160
NoHo, 10–11, 20, 79–80, 96, 228
Noisette, 230
Nolita, 10–11, 20, 228
NoshWalks, 211
NYC & Company, 52, 83, 302, 303
NYC Discovery Tours, 20
NYC/On Stage, 302

• *O* •

Oak, 228, 230
Oak Room Supper Club, 274
Off-Broadway show. *See* theater
off-peak travel, 41
The Old Town Bar & Grill, 276
Open Table, 122
open-air markets, 215, 222–223
opera, 257–258, 261
Opodo, 49
Orchard Street, 79, 229
oysters, 290–291

• P •

Pacha, 28, 278
package tours, 41, 52
Paley Center for Media, 194
The Paper Bag Players, 20, 254
parades, 9, 31–34, 294
parking, 294–295
Partners & Crime, 232–233
passports, 45, 66, 300
PATH train, 75
Paul Smith Sale Shop, 230
Pearl River, 229
pedicabs, 208
Pegu Club, 21, 275–276
performing arts, 20–21, 42, 257–260
Peter Jay Sharp Theater, 260
Peter Pan Bus Lines, 51
Pete's Tavern, 276
pharmacies, 300
pizza, 156–157
places of worship, 199–201
Playbill Online Theater club, 94
podcasts, 28
police, 300
Port Authority of New York &
    New Jersey, 49
Pravda, 276
Public Theater, 32
Puerto Rican Day Parade, 32

• Q •

Queens, 284–285

• R •

rack rate, 92
Radio City Music Hall, 26, 260, 263
rental cars, 61
reservations, 94–95, 122–123
Restaurant Week, 32, 124
restaurants. *See also* Restaurant
    Index
  bagels, 155–156
  best of, 17–18

breakfast and brunch, 154–155
budget planning, 41–42, 124–125
cuisine listing, 164–166
delicatessens, 159
family-friendly, 152
hamburgers and hot dogs,
    157–159
maps, 126–132
national chains, 292–293
neighborhood listing, 162–164
Ninth Avenue International Food
    Festival, 31
pizza, 156–157
pre-/post-theater dining, 256, 262
price listing, 166–168
reservations, 122–123
resources, 123
Restaurant Week, 32
sandwiches and snacks, 159–160
sweet treats, 160–162
takeout, 125
uniquely New York, 288–291
Winter Restaurant Week, 30
restrooms, 300
Richmond County Bank Ballpark,
    207
rickshaws, 208, 295
Ricky's, 232
Ride the City, 303
Ringling Brothers and Barnum &
    Bailey Circus, 31
River to River Festival, 31
rock music, 272
Rockefeller Center, 26, 34, 125, 187,
    188
Rockettes, 187
roller-skating, 285
Rose Hall, 258

• S •

safety
  air travel, 65–66
  ATM machine, 297
  cabs, 301
  general information, 300–301
  hotlines, 299

safety *(continued)*
  police information, 300
  street scams, 293
  on subways, 85–86
  walking in the city, 90
Sakagura, 276–277
Saks Fifth Avenue, 20, 215, 225
sales tax, 40, 213
sample sales, 224
sandwiches, 159–160
Santos Party House, 279
Saturday Night Live (TV show), 206
Scholastic Store, 237
Schomburg Center for Research in
  Black Culture, 197
Screaming Mimi's, 228
seasons
  best time to travel, 16
  calendar of events, 30–34
  cost-cutting tips, 93
  overview, 29–30
Seize sur Vingt, 228
Selima Optique, 228
senior travelers, 55
Serendipity 3, 161
Shakespeare in the Park, 20, 32, 253
Shea Stadium, 206
shopping
  antiques, 215, 222–223
  beauty shops, 231–232
  best of, 20
  big-name stores, 214–215
  books, 232–233
  budget planning, 39–40
  edibles, 233–234
  electronics, 234
  fashion industry locale, 226–227
  gifts, 235
  maps, 216–221
  museum stores, 235–236
  music, 236
  national chains, 292–293
  neighborhood hot spots, 224–231
  open-air markets, 215, 222–223
  overview, 213
  sample sales, 224

scams, 293
specialty items, 294
street fairs, 30, 215, 222
toys, 236–237
Shops at Columbus Circle, 226
Sigerson Morrison, 228
Skyscraper Museum, 199
Smalls, 265
Smoke, 265
smoking, 25, 123, 301
snacking, 159–160
SNL (Saturday Night Live), 194, 206
S.O.B.'s, 273
Socrates Sculpture Park, 285
SoHo, 10–11, 20, 79–80, 227–228,
  240, 294
Solomon R. Guggenheim
  Museum, 188
Sony Building, 26
Sony Wonder Technology Lab, 204
South Street Seaport, 202–203, 230
Southwest, 47
Space Kiddets, 237
Spanish Harlem, 82
specialty tours, 210–211
Spirit Cruises, 210
Spoonbill & Sugartown
  Booksellers, 230
sports. *See specific sports*
spring visit, 9–10, 29
St. Nick's Jazz Pub, 265
St. Patrick's Cathedral, 200
St. Patrick's Day Parade, 31, 294
St. Paul's Chapel, 26
Staten Island Ferry, 19, 188–189
Staten Island Yankees, 207
Statue of Liberty, 18, 189
steakhouses, 291
Steven Alan, 230
Stock Exchange, 190–191
stolen/lost wallets, 44–45
Strand, 233
street fairs, 30, 215, 222
street vendors, 223, 227
StreetEats, 303
Studio Museum in Harlem, 195

subway. *See also* train travel
  best cheap entertainment,
      283–284
  family travel, 54
  International Express train,
      283–284
  MetroCard tips, 38
  overview, 84–86
  safety, 85–86
  senior discounts, 55
  travelers with disabilities, 57
  typical costs, 38, 42
  weekend delays, 293
summer visit, 29
SummerStage, 31, 262
SuperShuttle, 72, 73, 74
Swedish Cottage Marionette
      Theater, 254
sweet treats, 160–162
Swing 46 Jazz & Supper Club, 279
Symphony Space, 260

• *T* •

TADA! Youth Theater, 254
Taschen, 228
taxes, 40, 301
taxi rides
  general information, 88–90
  safety, 301
  travelers with disabilities, 56–57
  typical costs, 38
teen attractions, 203–204, 231
television taping, 204–206
Tenement Museum, 197
tennis, 33
Terminal 5, 272
Thanksgiving Day, 34
theater. *See also specific venues*
  Broadway basics, 252–253
  listings and reviews, 251–252
  overview, 252
  pre-/post-show dining, 256, 262
  Shakespeare in the Park, 20, 32
  ticket information, 253–257
Theatermania, 252
Ticketmaster, 206

Tiffany & Co., 215, 225
time zone, 301
Times Square/Theater District,
      12–13, 81, 125, 189–190, 292
tips (gratuities), 40–41, 301
TKTS booth, 42
tolls, 71–73, 76–77
Top of the Rock, 188
Topshop, 228
tourist information, 83, 301
tours. *See specific types*
Town Hall, 260
toy stores, 236–237
Toys "R" Us, 237
traffic, 49–50
train travel, 50, 75–76. *See also*
      subway
transportation. *See specific types*
travel agencies, 56
travel insurance, 51, 62–63
traveler's checks, 43–44
Trees New York, 303
TriBeCa, 10–11, 79
Trinity Church, 26, 201
trip-cancellation insurance, 62

• *U* •

Union Square, 12–13, 80
Union Square Greenmarket, 223
UNIQLO, 228
United Nations, 190
Uptown (East/West Side)
  maps, 14–15, 100, 130–131,
      178–179, 220–221, 270–271
  overview, 82
  shopping hot spots, 224–225
U.S. Customs House, 26, 199
U.S. Open Tennis
      Championships, 33

• *V* •

Varvatos, John (designer), 228
Village Vanguard, 20, 272
The Village, 10–11, 19, 79–80

Vivian Beaumont Theater, 258
Voice over Internet Protocol
   (VoIP), 64
Von Furstenberg, Diane (designer),
   227

• *W* •

walking, 90, 211–212, 283–287
Wall Street/Financial District
   overview, 77, 190–191
   shopping hot spots, 229–230
   shopping map, 216–217
   walking tours, 211–212
wallets, lost or stolen, 44–45
Walter Reade Theater, 258
warehouse sales, 214
Washington Heights, 82
wax museums, 189
weather, 29–30
weddings, 59–60
weekend visits, 93–94
West 25th Street Market, 215
West Indian-American Day Carnival
   and Parade, 9, 33
West Village, 10–11, 19, 79–80
Westchester Airport, 47
Westminster Kennel Club, 30
White Horse Tavern, 276
Whitney Museum of American
   Art, 195
Williamsburg, 222
Winter Restaurant Week, 30
winter visit, 29
wireless apps, 302–303
wireless networks, 64–65
Woolworth Building, 26, 199
World Trade Center site (Ground
   Zero), 77, 191

• *Y* •

Yankee Stadium, 191, 206

• *Z* •

Zabar's, 234
Zagat Survey, 123
Zitomer, 232
zoos, 173, 180
Zum Schneider, 277

Accommodations Index

The Ace Hotel, 16, 97
Affinia Dumont, 97
The Algonquin, 97, 101
Bemelmans Bar, 17
The Benjamin, 101
The Bowery Hotel, 16, 101–102
The Carlton Hotel, 102
The Carlyle, A Rosewood Hotel,
   102–103
Casablanca Hotel, 103
Chambers Hotel, 103
Chelsea Lodge, 104
Colonial House Inn, 112
Cosmopolitan Hotel–Tribeca, 104
Country Inn the City, 112
Crosby Street Hotel, 17, 104–105
Doubletree Guest Suites Times
   Square, 105
Gershwin Hotel, 105
Hotel 41, 118
Hotel Beacon, 17, 106
Hotel Elysée, 106
Hotel Gansevoort, 106–107
Hotel Giraffe, 107
Hotel Le Jolie, 118
Hotel Metro, 107–108
Hotel Newton, 108
Hôtel Plaza Athénée, 16, 109
Hotel Thirty Thirty, 109
The Hotel on Rivington, 108
Inn at Irving Place, 112
Inn on 23rd, 112
The Iroquois New York, 119

The Kitano New York, 109–110
Larchmont Hotel, 110
Le Parker Meridien, 110
The Library Hotel, 111
Loews Regency Hotel, 119
The London NYC, 111
The Lowell, 112–113
The Lucerne, 16, 113
The Mercer, 16, 113
New York Marriott at the Brooklyn
    Bridge, 119
Novotel New York Times
    Square, 119
The Peninsula New York, 114
Pod Hotel, 16, 114
Red Roof Inn Manhattan, 115
Ritz-Carlton New York, Battery
    Park, 115
Ritz-Carlton New York, Central
    Park, 16, 115–116
The Roger, 116
Sofitel New York, 116
Travel Inn, 117
Trump International Hotel &
    Tower, 117
The Waldorf-Astoria and the
    Waldorf Towers, 117–118
Wall Street Inn, 118
Washington Square Hotel, 119

Restaurant Index

Absolute Bagels, 156
Alice's Tea Cup, 154
Amy Ruth's, 289
Antique Garage, 125, 132
àpizz, 133
Aquavit, 133
Artie's Delicatessen, 159
Babbo, 137
Barney Greengrass, 289
Beard Papa, 162
Big Nick's Burger Joint, 157
Billy's Bakery, 161–162
BLT Fish, 133–134
BLT Steak, 134
Blue Ribbon, 134–135, 152, 154

Brooklyn Ice Cream Factory, 18,
    160, 291
Bubby's Pie Co., 135, 152
Burger Joint, 18, 157
Buttercup Bake Shop, 161
Cafe des Artistes, 137
Calle Ocho, 135–136
Carmine's, 136, 152
Carnegie Deli, 159
'Cesca, 136
Chanterelle, 137
Charles' Country Pan-Fried
    Chicken, 137–138
ChikaLicious Dessert Bar, 162
Chinatown Ice Cream Factory, 160
Chocolate Bar, 161
Churrascaria Plataforma, 138
City Bakery, 161
Clinton St. Baking Company, 155
Cowgirl, 152
Craftbar, 138
Daniel, 17, 138–139
db Bistro Moderne, 139, 256
Dressler, 139–140
Eileen's Special Cheesecake, 290
Eisenberg's Sandwich Shop, 159,
    289–290
El Faro, 140
Eleven Madison Park, 140
Empanada Mama, 159
Ess-A-Bagel, 18, 156, 288–289
Famous Joe's Pizza, 157, 288
Five Points, 155
Flor de Mayo, 141, 289
Frankie & Johnnie's, 17, 141, 291
Good Enough to Eat, 18, 152, 155
Gramercy Tavern, 17, 141–142
Grand Central Oyster Bar &
    Restaurant, 290–291
Gray's Papaya, 158
Grimaldi's Pizza, 156
Haveli, 18, 142
Il Laboratorio del Gelato, 160
'inoteca, 142–143
Island Burgers and Shakes, 158
Jacques Torres Chocolate, 161
Jean Georges, 17, 143

John's Pizzeria, 156
Junior's, 290
Katz's Delicatessen, 159
Keens Steakhouse, 143–144, 291
La Bonne Soupe, 256
La Caridad 78, 289
Landmarc, 144
Lombardi's, 156–157
Lupa, 17, 144
Lure, 17, 144–145
Mandoo Bar, 145
Marea, 145–146
Mas, 146
Mermaid Inn, 146
Minetta Tavern, 137
Molyvos, 147, 256
Murray's Bagels, 156
Nathan's Famous, 290
New York Burger Co., 158
Noche Mexicana, 147
Norma's, 155
The Odeon, 147–148
Ouest, 148
P. J. Clarke's, 158
Pampano, 148
Paola's, 149
Papaya, 290
Patsy's Pizzeria, 157

Per Se, 137
Peter Luger Steakhouse, 149, 291
Pho Viet Huong, 149–150
Pinkberry, 160
Rainbow Room, 137
Russ & Daughters, 289
Scarpetta, 150
Schiller's Liquor Bar, 155
2nd Avenue Deli, 18, 159
Serendipity 3, 152
79th Street Boat Basin Cafe, 277
Shade, 160
Shake Shack, 158
Smörgås Chef, 150–151
Soul Fixins, 151
Spice Market, 151
Strip House, 152–153
Sugar Sweet Sunshine, 161
Tamarind, 153
Tavern on the Green, 137
Two Boots, 157
Veneiro's, 162
Veselka, 155
Virgil's Real Barbecue, 18, 152,
    153–154, 256
Waverly Restaurant, 290
'wichcraft, 160

Apple & Macs

iPad For Dummies
978-0-470-58027-1

iPhone For Dummies,
4th Edition
978-0-470-87870-5

MacBook For
Dummies, 3rd Edition
978-0-470-76918-8

Mac OS X Snow
Leopard For
Dummies
978-0-470-43543-4

Business

Bookkeeping For
Dummies
978-0-7645-9848-7

Job Interviews
For Dummies,
3rd Edition
978-0-470-17748-8

Resumes For
Dummies,
5th Edition
978-0-470-08037-5

Starting an
Online Business
For Dummies,
6th Edition
978-0-470-60210-2

Stock Investing
For Dummies,
3rd Edition
978-0-470-40114-9

Successful
Time Management
For Dummies
978-0-470-29034-7

Computer Hardware

BlackBerry
For Dummies,
4th Edition
978-0-470-60700-8

Computers For
Seniors
For Dummies,
2nd Edition
978-0-470-53483-0

PCs For Dummies,
Windows 7 Edition
978-0-470-46542-4

Laptops For
Dummies,
4th Edition
978-0-470-57829-2

Cooking & Entertaining

Cooking Basics
For Dummies,
3rd Edition
978-0-7645-7206-7

Wine For Dummies,
4th Edition
978-0-470-04579-4

Diet & Nutrition

Dieting For Dummies,
2nd Edition
978-0-7645-4149-0

Nutrition For
Dummies,
4th Edition
978-0-471-79868-2

Weight Training
For Dummies,
3rd Edition
978-0-471-76845-6

Digital Photography

Digital SLR Cameras
& Photography For
Dummies, 3rd Edition
978-0-470-46606-3

Photoshop Elements 8
For Dummies
978-0-470-52967-6

Gardening

Gardening Basics
For Dummies
978-0-470-03749-2

Organic Gardening
For Dummies,
2nd Edition
978-0-470-43067-5

Green/Sustainable

Raising Chickens
For Dummies
978-0-470-46544-8

Green Cleaning
For Dummies
978-0-470-39106-8

Health

Diabetes For
Dummies,
3rd Edition
978-0-470-27086-8

Food Allergies
For Dummies
978-0-470-09584-3

Living Gluten-Free
For Dummies,
2nd Edition
978-0-470-58589-4

Hobbies/General

Chess For Dummies,
2nd Edition
978-0-7645-8404-6

Drawing
Cartoons & Comics
For Dummies
978-0-470-42683-8

Knitting For Dummies,
2nd Edition
978-0-470-28747-7

Organizing
For Dummies
978-0-7645-5300-4

Su Doku For
Dummies
978-0-470-01892-7

Home Improvement

Home Maintenance
For Dummies,
2nd Edition
978-0-470-43063-7

Home Theater
For Dummies,
3rd Edition
978-0-470-41189-6

Living the
Country Lifestyle
All-in-One
For Dummies
978-0-470-43061-3

Solar Power Your
Home
For Dummies,
2nd Edition
978-0-470-59678-4

Available wherever books are sold. For more information or to order direct: U.S. customers visit www.dummies.com or call 1-877-762-2974. U.K. customers visit www.wileyeurope.com or call (0) 1243 843291. Canadian customers visit www.wiley.ca or call 1-800-567-4797.

Internet

Blogging For
Dummies,
3rd Edition
978-0-470-61996-4

eBay For Dummies,
6th Edition
978-0-470-49741-8

Facebook For
Dummies, 3rd Edition
978-0-470-87804-0

Web Marketing
For Dummies,
2nd Edition
978-0-470-37181-7

WordPress
For Dummies,
3rd Edition
978-0-470-59274-8

Language & Foreign Language

French For Dummies
978-0-7645-5193-2

Italian Phrases
For Dummies
978-0-7645-7203-6

Spanish For
Dummies, 2nd Edition
978-0-470-87855-2

Spanish For
Dummies, Audio Set
978-0-470-09585-0

Math & Science

Algebra I
For Dummies,
2nd Edition
978-0-470-55964-2

Biology
For Dummies,
2nd Edition
978-0-470-59875-7

Calculus For
Dummies
978-0-7645-2498-1

Chemistry For
Dummies
978-0-7645-5430-8

Microsoft Office

Excel 2010 For
Dummies
978-0-470-48953-6

Office 2010 All-in-One
For Dummies
978-0-470-49748-7

Office 2010 For
Dummies,
Book + DVD Bundle
978-0-470-62698-6

Word 2010 For
Dummies
978-0-470-48772-3

Music

Guitar For Dummies,
2nd Edition
978-0-7645-9904-0

iPod & iTunes
For Dummies,
8th Edition
978-0-470-87871-2

Piano Exercises
For Dummies
978-0-470-38765-8

Parenting & Education

Parenting For
Dummies,
2nd Edition
978-0-7645-5418-6

Type 1 Diabetes
For Dummies
978-0-470-17811-9

Pets

Cats For Dummies,
2nd Edition
978-0-7645-5275-5

Dog Training
For Dummies,
3rd Edition
978-0-470-60029-0

Puppies For
Dummies,
2nd Edition
978-0-470-03717-1

Religion & Inspiration

The Bible For
Dummies
978-0-7645-5296-0

Catholicism For
Dummies
978-0-7645-5391-2

Women in the Bible
For Dummies
978-0-7645-8475-6

Self-Help & Relationship

Anger Management
For Dummies
978-0-470-03715-7

Overcoming Anxiety
For Dummies,
2nd Edition
978-0-470-57441-6

Sports

Baseball
For Dummies,
3rd Edition
978-0-7645-7537-2

Basketball
For Dummies,
2nd Edition
978-0-7645-5248-9

Golf For Dummies,
3rd Edition
978-0-471-76871-5

Web Development

Web Design
All-in-One
For Dummies
978-0-470-41796-6

Web Sites
Do-It-Yourself
For Dummies,
2nd Edition
978-0-470-56520-9

Windows 7

Windows 7
For Dummies
978-0-470-49743-2

Windows 7
For Dummies,
Book + DVD Bundle
978-0-470-52398-8

Windows 7 All-in-One
For Dummies
978-0-470-48763-1

Available wherever books are sold. For more information or to order direct: U.S. customers visit www.dummies.com or call 1-877-762-2974. U.K. customers visit www.wileyeurope.com or call (0) 1243 843291. Canadian customers visit www.wiley.ca or call 1-800-567-4797.